Family Violence

2nd Edition

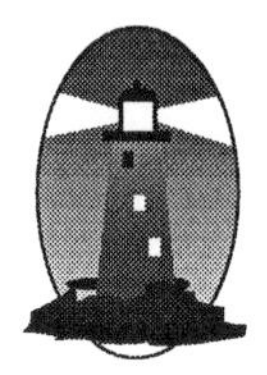

Issues in Children's and Families' Lives

AN ANNUAL BOOK SERIES

Senior Series Editor

Thomas P. Gullotta, *Child and Family Agency of Southeastern Connecticut*

Editors

Gerald R. Adams, *University of Guelph, Ontario, Canada*
Bruce A. Ryan, *University of Guelph, Ontario, Canada*
Robert L. Hampton, *University of Maryland, College Park*
Roger P. Weissberg, *University of Illinois at Chicago, Illinois*

Drawing upon the resources of the Child and Family Agency of Southeastern Connecticut, one of this nation's leading family service agencies, **Issues in Children's and Families' Lives** is designed to focus attention on the pressing social problems facing children and their families today. Each volume in this series will analyze, integrate, and critique the clinical and research literature on children and their families as it relates to a particular theme. Believing that integrated multidisciplinary approaches offer greater opportunities for program success, volume contributors will reflect the research and clinical knowledge base of the many different disciplines that are committed to enhancing the physical, social, and emotional health of children and their families. Intended for graduate and professional audiences, chapters will be written by scholars and practitioners who will encourage readers to apply their practice skills and intellect to reducing the suffering of children and their families in the society in which those families live and work.

Volume 1: **Family Violence: Prevention and Treatment (2nd Edition)**
LEAD EDITOR: Robert L. Hampton
CONSULTANTS: Vincent Senatore, *Child and Family Agency, Connecticut*; Ann Quinn, *Connecticut Department of Children, Youth, and Family Services, Connecticut*

Volume 2: **The Family-School Connection**
EDITORS: Bruce A. Ryan and Gerald R. Adams

Volume 3: **Adolescent Dysfunctional Behavior**
EDITORS: Gary M. Blau and Thomas P. Gullotta

Volume 4: **Preventing Violence in America**
EDITORS: Robert L. Hampton, Pamela Jenkins, and Thomas P. Gullotta

Volume 5: **Primary Prevention Practices**
AUTHOR: Martin Bloom

Volume 6: **Primary Prevention Works**
EDITORS: George W. Albee and Thomas P. Gullotta

Volume 7: **Children and Youth: Interdisciplinary Perspectives**
EDITORS: Herbert J. Walberg, Olga Reyes, and Roger P. Weissberg

Volume 8: **Healthy Children 2010: Enhancing Children's Wellness**
EDITORS: Roger P. Weissberg, Thomas P. Gullotta, Robert L. Hampton, Bruce A. Ryan, and Gerald R. Adams

Volume 9: **Healthy Children 2010: Establishing Preventive Services**
EDITORS: Roger P. Weissberg, Thomas P. Gullotta, Robert L. Hampton, Bruce A. Ryan, and Gerald R. Adams

Volume 10: **Substance Abuse, Family Violence & Child Welfare: Bridging Perspectives**
EDITORS: Robert L. Hampton, Vincent Senatore, and Thomas P. Gullotta

Prevention and Treatment

Editor
Robert L. Hampton

For information:

SAGE Publications, Inc.
2455 Teller Road
Thousand Oaks, California 91320
E-mail: order@sagepub.com

SAGE Publications Ltd.
6 Bonhill Street
London EC2A 4PU
United Kingdom

SAGE Publications India Pvt. Ltd.
M-32 Market
Greater Kailash I
New Delhi 110 048 India

Printed in the United States of America

Library of Congress Cataloging-in-Publication Data

Main entry under title:

Family violence: Prevention and treatment / edited by Robert L. Hampton. — 2nd ed.
p. cm. — (Issues in children's and families' lives; v. 1)
Includes bibliographical references and index.
ISBN 0-7619-0664-9 (cloth)
ISBN 0-7619-0665-7 (pbk.)
1. Family violence—United States—Prevention. 2. Family violence—Treatment—United States. I. Hampton, Robert L. II. Series.
HV6626.2.F38 1999
362.82′92—dc21 98-40175

This book is printed on acid-free paper.

01 02 03 10 9 8 7 6 5 4 3 2

Acquiring Editor: C. Deborah Laughton
Editorial Assistant: Eileen Carr
Production Editor: Astrid Virding
Editorial Assistant: Nevair Kabakian
Designer/Typesetter: Janelle LeMaster

For his leadership, advocacy, scholarship, friendship, mentorship, and tireless efforts to improve the quality of life for children and families, this work is dedicated to

• *Thomas P. Gullotta* •

and all the lives he has touched.

Contents

Preface

There are many forms of family and intimate violence in the United States. Some capture our attention because of the sheer magnitude of the event, as in multiple murders or murder suicides, because of the celebrity status of either the victim or perpetrator, or because they are exceptionally horrific in other respects. Despite more than three decades of research, acknowledged public concern, advocacy, and intervention services, interpersonal violence remains one of our most pressing national social problems. Recent studies have indicated that the incidence of intimate violence in the United States remains extremely high and shows no indication of a significant decrease.

The first edition of this book was also the first volume in the *Issues in Children's and Families' Lives* book series. Like the others in the series, this volume is devoted to issues affecting children and their families. When we decided to devote the first volume to family violence, it was because we recognized that violence remains one of the major factors undermining the quality of family life, especially for women and children. Although we can acknowledge some progress in the areas of social policy and clinical practice, the number of individuals and families affected by violence is still at an alarming level.

The chapters in this volume testify to the ongoing expansion of knowledge in the field of family and intimate violence. They attempt to summarize some of the best of current scholarship conducted by family violence researchers. The contributors are all leaders in the field and reflect a variety of disciplines and different approaches. Several chapters address issues of prevention, treatment, and intervention services. The diverse perspectives brought to bear on the subject by professionals from a range of disciplines add to the richness of this volume.

Richard J. Gelles provides an overview of research, theory, and several controversies in the study of family violence. He also provides insightful comments about steps that could prevent family and intimate violence. Joel S. Milner and Julie L. Crouch build on the more general theoretical overview presented in Chapter 1 by reviewing research on child physical abuse theory and research. They also discuss the physical sequelae across the life span of child maltreatment. Brenda Jones Harden and Sally Koblinsky explore an often ignored subject, children who have been exposed to community violence, family violence, or both. They conclude their chapter about this often ignored subject by examining interventions for violence-exposed children. Theodore J. Stein addresses legal perspectives on violence against children. In the final chapter devoted exclusively to child maltreatment, Donna Harrington and Howard Dubowitz challenge us to answer the question, "Can we prevent child maltreatment?" They cite both promising work in this field and some social policies that potentially could allow many children to remain at high risk for maltreatment.

People of color are often ignored in mainstream scholarship and practice in the field of family violence. Jo-Ellen Asbury explores how ethnic or cultural groups affect cultural expressions, how those expressions may affect the nature of violence in the family, and the potential effectiveness of intervention strategies across cultural groups. Although we are encouraged by the growth of scholarship in this field, there are still many unanswered questions.

The next three chapters address partner violence. The chapter by Robert L. Hampton, Pamela Jenkins, and Maria Vandergriff-Avery focuses on physical and sexual violence in marriage. The authors include a discussion of institutional responses to violence and some potential implications of recent legislation. Christopher M. Murphy and Michele Cascardi expand the discussion by exploring psychological violence between spouses and in dating relationships. Although most researchers acknowledge that psychological abuse often accompanies physical and sexual violence, they often do not focus on psychological abuse as a separate area of inquiry. One of the main points raised by Larry W. Bennett and Oliver J. Williams is that for many years, the field has permitted the batterer to remain in relative obscurity. In the past decade, there has been increased interest in research on men who abuse their female partners and ex-partners. Much of this work focuses on batterer invention programs.

Three areas of growing concern are also addressed in this volume; abuse of the elderly, substance abuse, and treatment programs. Linner Ward Griffin provides an overview of elder maltreatment, addressing both the growth in this segment of our population and its implications for social policy and practice. Many studies report that many victims of domestic violence live in families in which alcohol and others drugs are abused. H. David Banks and Suzanne M. Randolph remind us that the association between substance abuse and family abuse is complex, nonlinear, and influenced by a variety of other social factors. Finally, Gary M. Blau and Dorian Long explore assessment and treatment. They conclude that much remains to be learned about the relationship between risk factors and family violence. Better understanding of this relationship could possibly affect treatment outcomes.

I hope that students will again find this volume an essential introduction to a complex set of issues related to family violence research, treatment, and interventions. I also hope that experienced practitioners will find the volume helpful in updating their knowledge base and expanding their repertoire of approaches to intimate violence.

—Robert L. Hampton
The University of Maryland

Acknowledgments

Many people contributed to this volume. The authors of the 12 outstanding chapters are the key contributors. These individuals come from different academic disciplines; however, they share a commitment to research and practice in the field of family violence. This book would not have been possible without them.

I want to thank Tom Gullotta, chief executive officer of the Child and Family Agency of Southeastern Connecticut and series editor for **Issues in Children's and Families' Lives**. Moreover, I want to thank him for encouraging me to do a second edition of *Family Violence* and for encouraging all of us to contribute to this series. I would like to thank Joan Kim and Maria Vandergriff Avery, who assisted me throughout this project and assisted with the painstaking details that are associated with an edited volume. Next, I want to thank Sondra Alexis, Sara Dillier, Marianne Eismann, Diane Gaboury, Tawanna Gaines, Mary Lou Gayda, Meagan Noyes, Noreen O'Hare, and Mary Wesley for their assistance with this project. I also want to thank my colleagues in the Department of Family Studies and in the Division of Undergraduate Studies who understand the role of scholar/teacher/dean in higher education. Finally, I want to thank our colleagues at Sage Publications, C. Deborah Laughton and Eileen Carr, who have always made our work easier.

• *CHAPTER 1* •

Family Violence

RICHARD J. GELLES

Over the last three decades, family and intimate violence has been transformed from an issue obscured by selective inattention to a problem that receives increasing professional, public, and policy attention. The explosive growth in our knowledge and understanding of the various aspects and facets of family violence has produced a wealth of empirical data as well as deep and intensive controversies about those data and their meaning. This chapter is titled "Family Violence," but there really is no unified field of study or practice that falls neatly under that term. Family violence is only rarely viewed as a holistic problem.

Despite the segmentation or balkanization of the field, there is one consensus that may have been reached. There is evidence that virtually every type and form of family and intimate relationship has the potential of being violent. Researchers and clinicians have found violence and abuse in every type of intimate relationship.

The rapid increase in public awareness of child abuse, sexual abuse, violence against women, and other forms of family violence has led some professionals and many lay people to conclude that family violence is a new phenomenon that has increased to epidemic proportions in the last decade or so. Although family violence receives considerably more attention today, it has been part of the family throughout its history, not only in the United States but in England, Western Europe, and many other countries and societies around the globe. In the history of Western society, women and children have been subjected to unspeakable cruelties. In ancient times, infants had no rights until the right to live was bestowed on them by their fathers, typically as part of some formal cultural ritual (Radbill, 1980). When the right to live was withheld, infants were abandoned or left to die. Although we do not know how often children were killed or abandoned, we do know that infanticide was widely accepted among ancient and prehistoric cultures. Infants could be put to death because they cried too much, because they were sickly or deformed, or because they had some perceived imperfection. Girls, twins, and children of unmarried women, for example, were special targets (Robin, 1982). Infanticide continued through the eighteenth and nineteenth centuries; children born out of wedlock continue to run the greatest risk of infanticide, even today. In November 1996, two college freshman from well-to-do families in New Jersey fractured the skull of their newborn child, killing the child, who was born out of wedlock.

Killing children was not the only harm inflicted by generations of parents. Since prehistoric times, children have been mutilated, beaten, and maltreated. Such treatment was not only condoned, it was often mandated as the most appropriate child-rearing method. Children were hit with rods, canes, and switches. Our forefathers in colonial America were implored to "beat the devil" out of their children (Greven, 1990; Straus, 1994).

The subordinate status of women in the United States and most of the world's societies is well documented. Because physical force and violence are the last resort to keep subordinate groups in their place, the history of women in European and American societies has been one in which women have been victims of physical assault (Dobash & Dobash, 1979; Gordon, 1988; Peterson del Mar, 1996; Pleck, 1987). A Roman husband could chastise, divorce, or kill his wife.

Although legend has it that Blackstone's codification of English common law in 1768 asserted that a husband had the right to "physically chastise" an errant wife provided that the stick was no thicker than his thumb (and thus the "rule of thumb" was born), such a passage cannot be found in Blackstone (Sommers, 1994). Actually, there have been laws prohibiting wife beating in the United States since the time of the Revolution (Pleck, 1987). However, although the laws existed, they were often indifferently enforced. Furthermore, although the laws outlawed assault and battery and prescribed punishments such as fines and whippings as punishment, courts often allowed a certain amount of chastisement or correction of so-called errant wives "within legal bounds." In 1824, a Mississippi Court allowed corporal punishment of wives by husbands. The right to chastise wives was finally overturned by courts in Alabama and Massachusetts in 1871.

Siblings have also been the victims of family violence. The first case of family violence described in the Bible is Cain killing Abel. There has been less historical and current interest in sibling violence, violence toward men, violence toward parents, and violence toward the elderly compared to violence toward children and women. In part, this is because social concern for victims of family violence is tied to the perceived powerlessness and helplessness of victims. Thus, there is greater social concern for violence toward infants and young children than violence toward adolescents and men.

Discovering Family Violence

The historical treatment of children is not entirely bleak. Six thousand years ago, children in Mesopotamia were protected by a patron goddess. The Greeks and Romans established orphan homes, and some historical accounts also mention the existence of foster care for children. Child protection laws were legislated as long ago as 450 B.C. (Radbill, 1980). The Renaissance was the beginning of a new morality regarding children, who were seen as a dependent class in need of protection by society. The Enlightenment of the eighteenth century brought children increased attention and services. For example, the London Foundling Hospital, established during this time, not only provided pediatric care but also was the center of the moral reform movement on behalf of children (Robin, 1982). The hospital was the center of a campaign to control consumption of gin, which was seen as the root cause of many problems that affected families and children.

In the United States, the case of Mary Ellen Wilson is almost always singled out as the turning point in concern for children's welfare. In 1874, the then 8-year-old Mary Ellen lived in the home of Francis and Mary Connolly but was not the blood relative of either. Mary Ellen was the illegitimate daughter of Mary Connolly's first husband. A neighbor noticed the plight of Mary Ellen, who was beaten with a leather thong and allowed to go ill-clothed in bad weather. The neighbor reported the case to Etta Wheeler—a "friendly visitor" who worked for a St. Luke's Methodist Mission. In the mid-1800s, child welfare was church-based rather than government-based. Wheeler turned to the police and the

New York City Department of Charities for help for Mary Ellen Wilson and was turned down—first by the police, who said there was no proof of a crime, and second by the charity agency, which said it did not have custody of Mary Ellen. The legend goes on to note that Henry Berge, founder of the Society for the Prevention of Cruelty to Animals, intervened on behalf of Mary Ellen, and the courts accepted the case because Mary Ellen was a member of the animal kingdom. In reality, the court reviewed the case because the child needed protection. The case was argued, not by Henry Berge, but by his colleague, Elbridge Gerry. Mary Ellen Wilson was removed from her foster home and initially placed in an orphanage. Her foster mother was imprisoned for a year, and the case received detailed press coverage for months. In December 1874, the New York Society for the Prevention of Cruelty to Children was founded.

Protective societies rose and fell during the next 80 years. The political scientist Barbara Nelson (1984) notes that by the 1950s, public interest in abuse and neglect was practically nonexistent. Technology helped to pave the way for the rediscovery of child abuse. In 1946, the radiologist John Caffey reported on a number of cases of children who had multiple long bone fractures and subdural hematomas. Caffey used the X-ray to identify the fractures, although he did not speculate about the causes. In 1955, P. V. Wooley and W. A. Evans speculated that the injuries might be inflicted by the children's parents. Caffey (1957) looked again at his X-ray data and speculated that such injuries could have been inflicted by parents or caretakers. By 1962, the physician C. Henry Kempe and his colleagues at the University of Colorado Medical Center (Kempe, Silverman, Steele, Droegemueller, & Silver, 1962) were quite certain that many of the injuries they were seeing and the healed fractures that appeared on X-rays were intentionally inflicted by parents.

Kempe et al.'s (1962) article became the benchmark of the public and professional rediscovery of child abuse. Kempe's article and a strong editorial that accompanied it created considerable public and professional concern. *Time, Newsweek, The Saturday Evening Post,* and *Life* followed up the Kempe article with news or feature stories. Barbara Nelson (1984) has traced the record of professional and mass media articles on child abuse and neglect. Prior to 1962, it was unusual that a single mass media article on abuse would be published in a year. After Kempe's article, there was a 10-fold increase in popular articles that discussed child abuse.

There was no Mary Ellen for battered women, and there were no technological breakthroughs like the one in pediatric radiology to uncover years of broken jaws and broken bones. No medical champion would capture public and professional attention for battered women in the way that Henry Kempe had for battered children. There was no "Women's Bureau" in the federal government. And initially, there was no powerful senator who used a congressional committee chairmanship as a bully pulpit to bring attention to the plight of battered women.

The discovery of wife abuse was a traditional grassroots effort. Attention to the problem of woman battering came from women themselves. A women's center in the Chiswick section of London, founded by Erin Pizzey, became a refuge for victims of battering. Pizzey (1974) wrote the first book on wife abuse, *Scream Quietly or the Neighbors Will Hear*, and produced a documentary movie of the same name. Both captured the attention of women in Europe and the United States. Women's groups began to organize safe houses or battered woman shelters as early as 1972 in the United States. The National Organization for Women created a task force to examine wife battering in 1975.

The results of research on violence against women in the United States began to be published in 1973. The data on the extent of the problem, the patterns of violence, factors associated with violence and abuse, and other analyses were quickly seized on by those who believed that the abuse of women deserved the same place on the public agenda that child abuse had attained. As with child abuse, the scholarly publications fed media articles, and the media articles fed public interest, which led to more research and professional attention.

Still, by the early 1980s, public and professional interest in violence against women had lagged far behind interest in child abuse. There were some congressional hearings on wife abuse, and then-Congresswoman Barbara Milkulski introduced legislation for a National Domestic Violence Prevention and Treatment Act. A Federal Office of Domestic Violence was established in 1979, only to be closed in 1981.

Some progress was made in the mid 1980s. The National Domestic Violence Prevention and Treatment Act was passed into law, although spending from this legislation was but a trickle. The U.S. Attorney General's Task Force on Family Violence held hearings across the country in 1984 and published the final report in September of that year.

The year 1994 was a watershed for the issue of violence against women. Perhaps not coincidentally, this was the year that Nicole Brown

Simpson and Ron Goldman were slain and Brown Simpson's ex-husband, O. J. Simpson, was charged with the murder. At about the same time that the murders took place, Congress was completing the 1994 crime bill, which included the Violence Against Women Act (VAWA). The crime bill, with the VAWA, was passed by Congress in August 1994 and was signed into law by President Clinton on September 13, 1994. The VAWA appropriated $1.5 billion to fight violence against women, including $3 million over 3 years to re-establish a national hot line to help victims and survivors of domestic violence. An additional $26 million was appropriated for state grants that would encourage states to take more creative, innovative, and effective approaches in law enforcement and prosecutor training; development and expansion of law enforcement and prosecution, such as special domestic violence units; improved data collection and communication strategies, improved victim service programs, and improved programs concerning stalking. The VAWA also included various provisions to increase protection of battered women, including a civil rights title that declared "all persons in the United States shall have the right to be free from crimes of violence motivated by gender." Last, an office on domestic violence was established within the U.S. Department of Justice.

At about the same time the VAWA was passed, the Family Violence Prevention Fund, along with the Advertising Council, began a national public awareness campaign titled, "No Excuse for Domestic Violence." Public service announcements designed to educate the public about domestic violence and promote prevention and intervention appeared on television and in newspapers.

Legal reforms also occurred at the state level. States enacted legislation designed to establish domestic violence prosecution units, to criminalize sexual assault of wives by their husbands or ex-husbands, to improve protection for victims of stalking, and to develop more effective legal sanctions for domestic violence offenders.

The Development of Family Violence Research

As noted at the beginning of this chapter, family violence was not initially defined as a holistic problem; rather, like an onion's layers of skin, specific violent relationships were uncovered one at a time. In time, the term *family violence* was applied to a broader concept of maltreatment that included harmful, but not necessarily physically violent acts.

Family violence also refers to maltreatment between individuals who may not actually be members of a family—for example, violence in dating relationships.

Physical child abuse (or violence toward children) received much of the clinical and research attention in the early 1960s. Gradually, the study of child maltreatment broadened beyond the early narrow conceptualization of the battered child syndrome (Kempe et al., 1962) to include other forms of maltreatment, including neglect and sexual abuse. The expansion to the examination of the extent, causes, and consequences of sexual abuse was primarily the result of efforts by feminists to focus attention on the broad spectrum of victimization of women. In the early 1970s, feminists and women's advocates were also responsible for identifying the problem of violence toward women. Finally, abuse and maltreatment of the elderly were identified as a social problem in the late 1970s and early 1980s, primarily by advocates for the elderly.

The substantive focus of research on family violence broadened as the field developed. Research in the early 1960s, and especially the 1970s, focused mainly on three major topics: (a) the extent of family violence, (b) factors associated with family violence, and (c) causal explanations. Research in the 1980s and 1990s was less heavily weighted toward measuring the extent of family violence and was more concerned with assessing the changing rates of family violence, the consequences of victimization, and the effectiveness of prevention and intervention efforts.

Issues of Research Methodology

There are three main sources of data on family violence: (a) clinical data, (b) official report data, and (c) social surveys. Clinical studies carried out by psychiatrists, psychologists, and counselors continue to be a frequent source of data on family violence. This is primarily due to the fact that these investigators have the most direct access to cases of family violence. The clinical or agency setting (including hospital emergency rooms and battered woman shelters) provides access to extensive in-depth information about particular cases of violence. Studies of violence toward women have relied heavily on samples of women who seek help at battered woman shelters (Dobash & Dobash, 1979; Giles-Sims, 1983; Pagelow, 1981). Such samples are important because they are often the only way of obtaining detailed data on the most severely battered women. Such data are also necessary to study the impact of intervention programs. However, because they are based on small, nonrepresentative samples, such data cannot be used to estimate the incidence and prevalence of intimate violence.

The most common data source for research on child maltreatment is official reports. The establishment of mandatory reporting laws for suspected cases of child abuse and neglect made case-level and aggregate-level data on maltreatment available to researchers. Official report data, however, are limited to cases that fall under the investigation mandate of state agencies. In most states, such reports are limited to abuse by family or quasi-family (e.g., teachers) members. Between 1976 and 1987, the American Humane Association and the American Association for Protecting Children (a division of the American Humane Association) collected data from each state on officially reported child abuse and neglect (see American Association for Protecting Children, 1988, 1989). Following the termination of the grant to the American Association for Protecting Children, the National Committee to Prevent Child Abuse collected data on official reports of child maltreatment in the 50 states. Beginning in 1990, the National Center on Child Abuse and Neglect developed the National Child Abuse and Neglect Data System, which collects data on officially reported child abuse maltreatment (U.S. Department of Health and Human Services, 1996). The federal government sponsored three national surveys of officially reported child maltreatment (Burgdorf, 1980; National Center on Child Abuse and Neglect, 1988, 1996).

There has not been a tradition of officially reporting spouse abuse, with the exception of a handful of states that collect data on spouse abuse. The *Uniform Crime Reports* provide data on criminal family violence and family homicide, but these are limited to instances of family violence that are reported to the police.

The use of *social surveys* to study family violence has been constrained by the low base rate of most forms of abuse and family violence and the sensitive and taboo nature of the topic. Some investigators cope with the problem of the low base rate by employing purposive or nonrepresentative sampling techniques to identify cases. A second approach has been to use available large groups of subjects. Students of courtship violence have made extensive use of survey research techniques using college students as subjects (Cate, Henton, Christopher, & Lloyd, 1982; Henton, Cate, Koval, Lloyd, & Christopher, 1983; Laner, 1983;

Makepeace, 1981, 1983). Straus and Gelles carried out two national surveys of family violence in 1976 and 1986 (Straus, Gelles, & Steinmetz, 1980; Gelles & Straus, 1988). They conducted in-person interviews with a nationally representative sample of 2,145 family members in 1976 and telephone interviews with a nationally representative sample of 6,002 respondents in 1985 (Gelles & Straus, 1988; Straus & Gelles, 1986). Pillemer and Finkelhor (1988) interviewed a representative sample of 2,020 community-dwelling elderly people in the Boston metropolitan area for their study on the prevalence of elder abuse. Russell (1984) examined sexual victimization by surveying 930 San Francisco women, whereas Kilpatrick and his associates examined rape in marriage and other forms of sexual assault with a telephone sample of 391 women (Kilpatrick, Best, Saunders, & Veronen, 1988).

Another source of survey data on violence between intimates is the victimization data collected in the annual National Crime Victimization Survey (NCVS). The U.S. Bureau of Justice Statistics published a number of reports on violence against women prior to 1994 (Bachman, 1994; U.S. Department of Justice, 1980, 1984, 1994), but these studies were based on National Crime Victimization Surveys, which did not specifically ask or cue respondents to the issue of violence between intimates. The Bureau of Justice Statistics redesigned the study and began administering the new survey in 1992. According to data from the redesigned survey, 9 women in 1,000, or 1 million women each year, experience violence at the hands of an intimate (Bachman & Saltzman, 1995). The rate of violent victimization at the hands of a stranger was 7.4 per 1,000.

Each of the major data sources has its own validity problems. Clinical data cannot be used to generalize information on incidence or the frequency and strength of factors associated with violence. Such samples are never representative, and few investigators gathering data from clinical samples employ comparison groups. Official records suffer from variations in definitions, differing reporting and recording practices, and biased samples of violent and abusive behaviors and people (Finkelhor & Hotaling, 1984; Weis, 1989; Widom, 1988). In addition, official report records tend to be limited to a small set of variables. Data needed to answer key research, practice, or policy questions are often not included in official data sets. Self-report surveys have a number of significant limitations. The low base rate of intimate violence requires large samples, which in turn limits the amount of data that can be collected. The biases of social survey data on intimate violence include inaccurate recall, differential interpretation of questions, and intended and unintended response error (Weis, 1989). Some social surveys are limited by extremely low response rates (e.g. Russell, 1984). The NCVS data are limited because the minimum age for respondents is 14; thus, the NCVS data allow no estimates of violence toward young children. The reported rates of intimate violence in the NCVS are smaller than other self-report surveys. This could be because the NCVS measures "criminal" violence, and respondents may fail to report intimate violence that they do not view as criminal.

The most common research design for the study of family violence has been the cross-sectional nonexperimental design. Longitudinal and experimental studies of family violence are rare.[1]

Theoretical Approaches to Family Violence

The first people to identify a problem often shape how others will perceive it (Nelson, 1984, p. 13). The initial conceptualizations of family violence were developed in the study of battered children in the early 1960s. Descriptions of battered children portrayed abuse and violence between intimates as a rare event, typically caused by the psychopathology of the offender. The perception of the abuser as suffering from some form of psychopathology has persisted, in part because the first conceptualization of family violence was the guiding framework for the work that followed. The psychopathological or psychiatric conceptualization has also persisted because the tragic picture of a defenseless child, woman, or grandparent subjected to abuse and neglect arouses the strongest emotions in clinicians and others who see and/or treat the problem of intimate violence. There frequently seems to be no rational explanation for harming a loved one, especially one who appears to be helpless and defenseless.

Family violence has been approached from three general theoretical levels of analysis: (a) the intra-individual level of analysis, or the psychiatric model; (b) the social-psychological level of analysis; and (c) the sociological or sociocultural level of analysis.

The *psychiatric model* focuses on the offender's personality characteristics as the chief determinants of violence and abuse of intimates, although some applications focus on the individual personality characteristics of the victims (see, for example, Shainess, 1979; Snell, Rosenwald, & Robey, 1964). The psychiatric model includes theoretical approaches that link personality disorders, character disorders, mental illness, alcohol and substance abuse, and other intra-individual processes to acts of family violence.

The *social-psychological model* assumes that violence and abuse can best be understood by careful examination of the external environmental factors that affect the family, family organization and structure, and the everyday interactions between intimates that are precursors to acts of violence. Theoretical approaches that examine family structure, stress, the transmission of violence from one generation to the next, and family interaction patterns fit the social psychological model. Such general theories as learning theory, frustration aggression, exchange theory, and attribution theory approach family violence from the social psychological level.

The *sociocultural model* provides a macro level of analysis. Violence is examined in light of socially structured variables such as inequality, patriarchy, or cultural norms and attitudes about violence and family relations.

Theories

A number of sociological and psychological theories have been developed to explain family violence. They include the following:

Social Learning Theory

Social learning theory proposes that individuals who experience violence are more likely to use violence in the home than those who have experienced little or no violence. The theory's central proposition is that children who either experience violence themselves or who witness violence between their parents are more likely to use violence when they grow up. The family is the institution and social group where people learn the roles of husband and wife, parent and child. The home is the prime location where people learn how to deal with various stresses, crises, and frustrations. In many instances, the home is also the site where a person first experiences violence. Not only do people learn violent behavior, but they learn how to justify being violent. For example, hearing a father say, "This will hurt me more than it will hurt you," or a mother say, "You have been bad, so you deserve to be spanked," contribute to how children learn to justify violent behavior.

Social Situation/Stress and Coping Theory

Social situation/stress and coping theory explains why violence is used in some situations and not others. The theory proposes that abuse and violence occur because of two main factors. The first is structural stress and the lack of coping resources in a family. For instance, the association between low income and family violence indicates that an important factor in violence is inadequate financial resources. The second factor is the cultural norm concerning the use of force and violence. In contemporary American society, and many other societies, violence in general, and violence toward children in particular, is normative (Straus, 1994; Straus et al., 1980). Thus individuals learn to use violence both expressively and instrumentally as a means of coping with a pile-up of stressor events.

Resource Theory

Resource theory assumes that all social systems (including the family) rest to some degree on force or the threat of force. The more resources—social, personal, and economic—a person can command, the more force he or she can muster. However, the fewer resources a person has, the more he or she will actually use force in an open manner. Thus, a husband who wants to be the dominant person in the family but has little education, holds a job low in prestige and income, and lacks interpersonal skills may choose to use violence to maintain the dominant position. In addition, family members (including children) may use violence to redress a grievance when they have few alternative resources available. Thus, wives who have few social resources or social contacts may use violence toward their husbands to protect themselves.

Exchange Theory

Exchange theory proposes that child abuse and violence against women are governed by the principle of costs and benefits. Violence is used when the rewards are greater than the costs (Gelles, 1983). The private nature of the family, the reluctance of social institutions and agencies to intervene—in spite of mandatory child abuse reporting laws or mandatory arrest laws for domestic violence—and the low risk of other interventions reduce the costs of abuse and violence. The cultural approval of violence as both expressive and instrumental behavior raises the potential rewards for violence. The most significant reward is social control, or power.

Sociobiological Theory

A sociobiological or evolutionary perspective of family violence suggests that violence toward human or nonhuman primate offspring is the result of the reproductive success potential of children and parental investment. The theory's central assumption is that natural selection is the process of differential reproduction and reproductive success (Daly & Wilson, 1980). Males can be expected to invest in offspring when there is some degree of parental certainty (how confident the parent is that the child is his own genetic offspring), and females are also inclined to invest under conditions of parental certainty. Parents recognize their offspring and avoid squandering valuable reproductive effort on someone else's offspring. Children not genetically related to the parent (e.g., step-, adopted, or foster children) or children with low reproductive potential (e.g., handicapped or retarded children) are at the highest risk for infanticide and abuse (Burgess & Garbarino, 1983; Daly & Wilson, 1980; Hrdy, 1979). Large families can dilute parental energy and lower attachment to children, thus increasing the risk of child abuse and neglect (Burgess, 1979).

Smuts (1992) applied an evolutionary perspective to male aggression against females. Smuts (1992), Daly and Wilson (1988), and Burgess and Draper (1989) argue that male aggression against females often reflects male reproductive striving. Both human and nonhuman male primates are postulated to use aggression against females to intimidate females so that they will not resist future male efforts to mate with them and to reduce the likelihood that females will mate with other males. Thus, males use aggression to control female sexuality to males' reproductive advantage. The frequency of male aggression varies across societies and situations depending on the strength of female alliances, the support women can receive from their families, the strength and importance of male alliances, the degree of equality in male-female relationships, and the degree to which males control the economic resources within a society. Male aggression toward females, both physical violence and rape, is high when female alliances are weak, when females lack kin support, when male alliances are strong, when male-female relationships are unbalanced, and when males control societal resources.

Feminist Theory

Feminist theorists (e.g., Dobash & Dobash, 1979; Pagelow, 1984; Yllö, 1983, 1988, 1993) see violence against women as a unique phenomenon that has been obscured and overshadowed by what they refer to as a "narrow" focus on domestic violence. The central thesis of this theory is that economic and social processes operate directly and indirectly to support a patriarchal (male-dominated) social order and family structure. Patriarchy is seen as leading to the subordination of women and causing the historical pattern of systematic violence directed against women.

An Ecological Perspective

The ecological perspective is an attempt to integrate the three levels of theoretical analysis (individual, social psychological, and sociocultural) into a single theoretical model. James Garbarino (1977) and Jay Belsky (1980, 1993) have proposed an ecological model to explain the complex nature of child maltreatment. The model rests on three levels of analysis: the relationship between the organism and environment, the interacting and overlapping systems in which human development occurs, and environmental quality. The ecological model proposes that violence and abuse arise out of a mismatch of parent to child and family to neighborhood and community. The risk of abuse and violence is greatest when the functioning of the children and parents is limited and constrained by developmental problems. Children with learning disabilities and social or emotional handicaps are at increased risk for abuse. Parents under considerable stress, or who have personality problems, are at increased risk for abusing their children. These conditions are worsened when social interaction between the spouses or the parents and children heighten the stress or make the personal problems worse. Finally, if there are few institutions and agencies in the community to support troubled families, then the risk of abuse is further raised. Garbarino (1977) identifies two necessary conditions for child maltreatment. First, there must be cultural justification for the use of force against children. Second, the maltreating family is isolated from potent family or community support systems. The ecological model has served as a perspective to examine other forms of family violence. However, the model has mostly served as a heuristic device to organize thinking and research about family violence. There has not yet been an actual empirical test of the integrated model, other than the research conducted by Garbarino in the 1970s.

Controversies in the Study of Family Violence

Thirty-five years after the publication of Kempe and his colleagues' (1962) ground-breaking article on the battered child syndrome, considerable research and theory development has occurred in the study of family violence. There are now more than a half-dozen scholarly journals devoted to one or more aspects of family and intimate violence. The growth in the volume of articles and books published on the various facets of family violence is perhaps unprecedented in the social sciences (Straus, 1992). We now have data on almost every aspect of the extent, correlates, consequences, treatment, and prevention of family violence, including three summary reports prepared by the National Academy of Sciences (National Research Council, 1993, 1996, 1998).

Despite the enormous growth of professional and public interest in child maltreatment, violence against women, sexual abuse, elder abuse, emotional abuse, and other forms of intimate and family violence, the field is far from unified, and there is no single dominant theory or body of knowledge that guides the investigation of efforts to prevent and treat family violence. In fact, a number of significant controversies have emerged in the study of family violence. This section reviews some of the more significant controversies and differences of opinion and interpretation of data and theory (see Gelles & Loseke, 1993, for a more detailed examination of these and other controversies).

Abused Husbands: Fact or Myth?

Data from the earliest studies of spousal or conjugal violence detected violence by women toward their husbands or partners (see, for example, Gelles, 1974). These early data were often dismissed, however, by those whose main goal was to use incidence and prevalence data to prove that the problem of abuse and battering was a significant public health problem for women in our society. With the publication of the results of the First National Family Violence Survey (Steinmetz, 1977-1978; Straus, 1977-1978; Straus et al., 1980), however, the question of whether males were victims as well as offenders became a major controversy that continues to this day. Murray Straus, Suzanne Steinmetz, and I found that women reported high levels of violence toward their husbands and partners. In fact, the data indicated that the rate of violence was the same or even higher than that reported for male-to-female violence. We initially qualified our findings by noting that much of the female violence appeared to be in self-defense and that females, because of their size and strength, appeared to inflict less injury than their male attackers. Later analyses (Gelles, 1994; Straus, 1993) found that women were not more likely to use violence in self-defense than were men, but that women were in fact much more likely to be injured than were men. We also posited that the apparently similar results were probably the result of a methodological artifact whereby females were more likely to report offenses and males more likely to report victimization than vice versa. However, later analyses (Straus, 1993) found that the similar rates of female-to-male and male-to-female violence were reported when the respondents were only women.

The reaction against the data on female-to-male violence was swift and emotional. Straus and Steinmetz were, and continue to be, subjects of vitriolic and personal attacks, including bomb scares and death threats (Straus, 1990, 1993). More reasonable critics of the data have focused on the deficits of the main measure of violence, the Conflict Tactics Scales, and the limitations of positivist, quantitative social science for studying the victimization of women (Berk, Berk, Loseke, & Rauma, 1983; Dobash & Dobash, 1979; Dobash, Dobash, Wilson, & Daly, 1992; Okun, 1986; Pleck, Pleck, Grossman, & Bart, 1977-1978; Stark & Flitcraft, 1985; Yllö, 1988). Straus (see, for example, Stets & Straus, 1990; Straus, 1993) continues to maintain that women are frequent users of violence in their relationships with men, that women initiate acts of violence, and that women often cause injury.

Is Violence Transmitted Intergenerationally?

One of the most consistent and persistent findings from research on physical child abuse is the so-called intergenerational transmission of violence. The intergenerational transmission of violence proposition, simply stated, is that children who have been physically abused tend to grow up to be abusive adults. Researchers generally recognize that intergenerational transmission is probabilistic, and not all abused children grow up to be abusive.

Joan Kaufman and Edward Zigler (1987, 1993) have argued that the intergenerational transmission hypothesis is overstated. They have analyzed the available research on physical child abuse and found that the best empirical data available suggest that only 30% of abused children will go on to be abusive adults. Kaufman and Zigler conclude that it is time for researchers to set aside the intergenerational myth and cease asking, "Do abused children become abusive parents?" and ask, instead, "Under what conditions is the transmission of abuse likely to occur?"

Although a 30% transmission rate is not even the majority of abused children, the rate of abuse among formerly abused children is considerably higher than the overall societal rate of between 2% and 3%. Nevertheless, the intergenerational transmission theory is often simplistically presented and viewed as a single-cause, deterministic explanation for abuse. A more sophisticated model of abuse is still needed to explain child maltreatment.

Is Child Abuse Overreported?

After the publication of Kempe and his colleagues' (1962) article on the battered child syndrome 35 years ago, considerable effort was put into establishing mandatory child abuse reporting laws. The assumption behind those laws was that child abuse was often detected but not reported to child welfare agencies by physicians, psychologists, teachers, and others in routine contact with children. If maltreatment was detected, those who suspected maltreatment were thought to be reluctant to report cases for fear of legal problems arising out of possible false reports. Mandatory reporting laws provided legal protection for those making good faith reports of suspected child maltreatment. Such laws were assumed to motivate professionals and the public alike to report child maltreatment to child protection agencies.

Those who framed the early reporting laws assumed that child abuse could be accurately detected and that children would be better served if their abuse was reported to appropriate and well-trained professionals. At the time mandatory reporting laws were proposed, most professionals were focusing on physical abuse and assumed that physicians and others could be properly trained to differentiate intentional injuries to children from medical problems or accidents. They did not foresee the difficulties of accurately assessing neglect, emotional maltreatment, or sexual abuse of children.

Over the last 35 years, the definition of maltreatment in mandatory reporting laws has been broadened, more groups and individuals (including the general public in some states) have been mandated as reporters, and the laws have been strengthened by implementing penalties for failure to report. In addition, the laws continue to protect those who report suspected maltreatment from legal action if the report turns out to be unsubstantiated or even false. Reporters who *deliberately* make false reports are no longer protected from prosecution.

Not surprisingly, the number of reports received by child welfare agencies has increased dramatically (see, for example, National Center on Child Abuse and Neglect, 1996). Douglas Besharov (1985, 1990, 1993) argues that child abuse is now overreported. Too many false or inaccurate reports are received. These reports consume considerable time and resources of child protection agencies and reduce the time and attention that could be provided to valid, serious, and dangerous cases of abuse.

David Finkelhor (1990, 1993) believes that there is no reliable empirical evidence to support the claim that abuse is overreported. Not only is there a question about whether there are too many reports of child abuse, but there is also the question that such reports are biased. Thus, a third point of view in this controversy is offered by pediatrician Eli Newberger (1985), who notes that poor and minority individuals are more likely to be accurately and inaccurately reported for child maltreatment, whereas more affluent families who abuse their children often escape detection. Newberger sidesteps the debate about overreporting and argues that the entire child protection system is biased against lower class and minority families and thus fails to meet its overall objectives of providing protection for all maltreated children.

Are Child Sexual Abuse Prevention Programs Effective?

With the discovery of the extent of sexual abuse, there was considerable effort put into developing sexual abuse prevention programs. Many programs were developed and implemented in schools and aimed at school-age populations. Program developers felt that school-age children were the most vulnerable to sexual exploitation and sexual abuse and that abuse could be prevented if children knew how to identify and thwart attempts to sexually victimize them. Although a massive number of publications have extolled the effectiveness of school-based prevention programs (see Plummer, 1993, for a review), some critics argue that the available evidence indicates only limited support for the efficacy of sexual abuse prevention programs (Reppucci & Haugaard, 1993). Although there is evidence for some statistically significant improvements as a result of the programs, such as more assertive actions by children when approached by strangers, critics argue that the increases are slight.

Are Intensive Family Preservation Services Effective?

Family preservation programs are not new. They go back at least to the settlement house movement created at Hull House in Chicago by Jane Addams in 1910. Family preservation programs are designed to help children and families (including extended and adoptive families) that are at risk or in crisis.

Although family preservation programs have been a key component of the child welfare system for nearly a century, the rediscovery of child abuse and neglect in the early 1960s and the conceptualization of the problem as one arising out of the psychopathology of the parents or caretakers changed the child welfare emphasis from one of preserving families to one of protecting children. With the implementation of mandatory reporting laws and the resulting dramatic increase in child abuse and neglect reports, child welfare agencies turned more to removal of children from homes deemed at risk. Maltreated children were placed in temporary placements, typically foster homes. By 1978, it was estimated that some 500,000 children were in foster care in the United States (Pelton, 1989; Tatara, 1993).

By the end of the 1970s, there was increasing concern about the number of children in foster care and the cost. In addition, the model of child abuse that explained abuse as a result of individual personality disorder or mental illness had been replaced by explanations of maltreatment that emphasized social factors, such as poverty, stress, social isolation, and lack of understanding of proper parenting skills (see, for example, Gelles, 1973).

Thus, there was widespread questioning of both the need to remove so many children from their biological homes and the effectiveness of foster care as a means of dealing with child maltreatment. Researchers and practitioners assumed that the funds spent on foster care could be more effectively used supporting and preserving families.

Intensive Family Preservation Programs were developed as a means of protecting children and preserving families. The essential feature of such programs is that they are intensive, short-term, and oriented toward crisis intervention. Services are provided in the client's home. The length of session is variable—it is not confined to the 50-minute clinical hour. Services are available 7 days a week, 24 hours a day, not just during business hours Monday through Friday. Caseloads are small—two or three families per worker. Services are both soft and hard.

The initial evaluations of intensive family preservation programs were uniformly enthusiastic. The programs were claimed to have reduced the placement of children while at the same time assuring the safety of those children. Foundation program officers and program administrators claimed that the families involved in intensive family preservation programs had low rates of placement and "100 percent safety records" (Barthel, 1991; Forsythe, 1992).

There were, however, major methodological problems with the early evaluations of intensive family preservation programs, including the fact that most of the evaluations did not use control groups and those that did failed to use appropriately matched control groups (the control groups were not similar in terms of type of maltreatment and social characteristics to the groups receiving intensive family preservation services). In his 1992 review, sociologist Peter Rossi concluded that evaluation studies he reviewed did not demonstrate that intensive family preservation programs reduced placement or reduced child welfare program costs.

To date, no evaluation study that uses a randomly assigned control group has found that intensive family preservation programs reduce placement, costs, or the risk of maltreatment (Gelles, 1996; Heneghan, Horwitz, & Leventhal, 1996; Lindsey, 1994; Schuerman, Rzepnicki, & Littell, 1994). Thus, the empirical case for intensive family preservation has not been made.

Moreover, many critics of family preservation, such as myself (Gelles, 1996), argue that the belief that intensive family preservation programs are effective and the emphasis on keeping children with abusive parents or reuniting children with parents after the parents have had intensive services, actually places many children at risk of re-abuse or even fatal abuse.

The Battered Woman Syndrome: Are Battered Women Helpless?

A cornerstone of early research on wife abuse and violence toward women was Lenore Walker's (1979) conceptualization of the battered woman syndrome and the notion that women who are battered suffer from "learned helplessness." Both conceptualizations are significant elements of the battered woman defense, offered to explain why some women kill their husbands in self-defense rather than flee to safety. In addition, the notion of the battered woman syndrome and learned helplessness has been used to explain why battered women choose to remain with abusive husbands, partners, and/or boyfriends, even after being subjected to long-term and severe physical, emotional, and sexual abuse.

There are some questions about whether the syndrome exists, whether battered women do indeed suffer from learned helplessness, and whether these conceptualizations paint an inaccurate picture of helpless women (Bowker, 1993). Gelles and Straus (1988), for example, found that the vast majority of women who were assaulted by their husbands had left their homes for some period of time. The typical battered woman is hardly passive; she actively seeks to prevent further victimization and is handicapped, not by her own psychological limitations, but by constraints posed by social institutions and social structures and the lack of effective remedies available from social agencies and agencies of social control. Walker (1993) herself has abandoned her earlier conceptualization of learned helplessness and a battered woman syndrome and now talks about the battered women suffering from a form of post-traumatic stress disorder.

Does Mandatory Arrest Deter Violence Against Women?

Twenty-five years ago, the typical police response to a domestic assault was either indifference or attempts to calm the situation down, either by removing the offender or by counseling the couple. A field experiment conducted by Lawrence Sherman and Richard Berk (1984) helped to change the way police departments handled domestic assault. Sherman and Berk (1984) found that when police randomly assigned one of three interventions—arrest, separation, or mediation—in cases of misdemeanor domestic violence, the arrest intervention resulted in the lowest recidivism rate. Arrested men were least likely to be violent again, compared to men who were separated or men with whom the police mediated. The results of the Sherman and Berk study, along with a number of class action suits against police departments and a costly lawsuit by a battered woman against the Torrington, Connecticut, Police Department (*Thurman v. City of Torrington,* 1985), resulted in the adoption of mandatory arrest or presumptive arrest policies for misdemeanor assault by hundreds of police departments. Mandatory arrest policies require police to arrest the offender for misdemeanor assault, whereas presumptive policies allow the police to make an arrest without a complaint by the victim (felony assault cases allow the police to make arrests without complainants).

It seemed for the moment that an effective broad-based prevention policy had been found that would reduce the toll of violence against women. Subsequent to the Sherman and Berk study, the National Institute of Justice funded six replications of the original study. In none of the five replications that reported data were the original findings replicated. Arrest, in and of itself, did not reduce violence against women.

Although arrest, in and of itself, did not appear to put victims at greater or less danger of continued violence compared to separation or mediation, results from the studies indicated under what circumstances arrest might be effective or might create danger for women. Sherman (1992) found that men who were married to the women they assaulted and who were employed were less likely to be violent again after being arrested. However, men who were not married to their victims and who were unemployed reduced their use of violence for a short period of time and then actually were more violent than they had been prior to their arrest. Sherman explains that "stake in conformity" explained the deterrent effect of arrest for married and employed men. The more men had to lose, the more they were deterred by arrest. For men who had little to lose, an arrest actually enraged them and caused them to retaliate against their partners.

A second finding from the series of arrest studies supported the deterrent effect of the threat of legal sanctions. If the offender was not present when the police arrived and an arrest warrant was issued, these men were deterred from engaging in future violence (Dunford, Huizinga, & Elliott, 1990). This result supports the efficacy of the threat of legal sanctions, even though actual arrest seems to do little to reduce subsequent domestic violence.

Although arrest may have a deterrent effect only for certain types of offenders, this does not mean that control interventions are of no use in treating and preventing violence against women. Most of the offenders who are arrested are not prosecuted. Second, the studies of the deterrent effects of arrest only examined cases of misdemeanor violence. Thus, it is possible that arrest combined with sanctions and arrest of felony offenders may reduce the occurrence of domestic assault.

Are Memories of Sexual Abuse Lost and Recovered?

Perhaps the most volatile controversy in the field of family violence has been the debate over the recall of childhood trauma or what some call "recovered memories." The controversy arose in the wake of a number of high profile cases of sexual abuse in which children, adolescents, young adults, and even adults recalled instances of sexual abuse that they had previously not reported and for which they apparently had no conscious memory. The most widely discussed were the McMartin Preschool case in Los Angeles; a series of accusations of sexual abuse in Bakersfield, California; allegations of sexual abuse at the Fells Acre Day Care Center, outside of Boston; the Kelly Michaels/Wee Care Day Care case in New Jersey; allegations of sexual abuse in Wenatchee, Washington; and the case of Jennifer Freyd, a psychology professor at the University of Oregon, who alleged that she was molested by her father when she was young. Jennifer Freyd's mother, Pamela, founded the False Memory Foundation, which coined the term *false memory syndrome* (Nathan & Snedeker, 1995).

On one side of the controversy are those, including the False Memory Foundation, who argue that recovered memories are fabricated by disturbed or vindictive adults or fostered by overzealous or poorly trained therapists (Dawes, 1992; Nash, 1992; Nathan, 1992; Tavris, 1993; Wakefield & Underwager, 1992). A more moderate argument, based on laboratory research on memory, is that adults are susceptible to acquiring memories of child sexual abuse that did not actually occur (Loftus, 1993).

On the other side of the controversy are those, mostly advocates for victims of sexual abuse, who argue that children do not lie about sexual abuse and that adolescents and adults can repress memories of sexual abuse and then recover the memories. Some advocates go so far as to state that children "never lie."

Researchers have documented the fact that people do, in fact, forget traumatic events. Williams (1994) found that 38% of a sample of women for whom there were documented reports of sexual abuse did not recall the abuse that had been reported 17 years earlier. Other researchers (Briere & Conte, 1993; Herman & Schatzow, 1987) also report that a large portion of women sexually abused in childhood have no recall of the abuse.

In some respects, the scientific examinations of repressed and recovered memories talk past one another. Even though adults can be susceptible to acquiring memories of child sexual abuse that did not occur, some, or even many, recovered memories may be accurate. On the other hand, given that individuals can accurately recover memories of abuse and trauma accurately, it is also likely that some recovered memories can be distorted or inaccurate and that poorly trained and overzealous therapists can facilitate the recovery of distorted or inaccurate memories.

Summary

One overriding factor that influences the study and consideration of family and intimate violence is the emotional nature of research, practice, and public policy. Few other areas of inquiry and practice generate the strong feelings and reactions that child abuse, child sexual abuse, violence against women, and elder abuse generate. Even the most grotesque case examples fail to adequately capture the devastating physical and psychological consequences of family violence. Clinicians must not only face difficult and complex cases, but they are often frustrated by the inadequate conceptual, clinical, and service resources they can bring to bear on behalf of victims, offenders, and/or families. Amid the emotional and frustrating nature of research and clinical work with violent families, there is the tendency to look for and latch onto simple explanations and solutions.

There are no simple answers or "cheap fixes." The relative recency of family and intimate violence as an area of study, and the fact that the first decade of research was dominated by the psychopathology model of causation, has resulted in the limited level of theoretical development of the field. Yet, despite the rather primitive level of theory building and testing, one conclusion is inescapable: No one factor can explain the presence or absence of family and intimate violence. Characteristics of the child, parent, family, social situation, and community are related to which children are abused and neglected and under what conditions. Individual emotional states of caretakers, psychological characteristics, and community factors, such as cultural attitudes regarding violence, are moderated and influenced by family structure and family situations. Although there are indeed multiple factors related to abuse of children and women, most operate through the structure and function of the family group. In addition, power and control are common features of nearly all forms of family and intimate violence, especially violence and abuse of women. Thus, interventions and prevention efforts need to address both the importance of control and power and the functions of the family system, if family and intimate violence is to be treated and prevented.

Currently, the vast majority of programs aimed at dealing with family and intimate violence, such as shelters, crisis day care centers, police intervention programs, and parent support groups, are treatment programs that are implemented *after* the abusive incident. What are needed, and what have not been attempted on any large scale, are services that would prevent violence and abuse before they begin. But such programs require sweeping changes in both the society and the family. Among the steps that could prevent family and intimate violence are the following:

1. *Eliminate the norms that legitimize and glorify violence in the society and the family.* The elimination of spanking as a child-rearing technique and corporal punishment in school; gun control to get deadly weapons out of the home; elimination of the death penalty; and elimination of media violence that glorifies and legitimizes violence—these are all necessary steps. In short, we need to cancel the hitting license in society.

2. *Reduce violence-provoking stress created by society.* Reducing poverty, inequality, and unemployment and providing for adequate housing, food, medical and dental care, and educational opportunities are steps that could reduce stress in families.

3. *Integrate families into a network of kin and community.* Reducing social isolation would be a significant step that would help reduce stress and increase the abilities of families to manage stress.

4. *Change the sexist character of society.* Sexual inequality makes violence possible in homes. The elimination of men's work and women's work would be a major step toward equality in and out of the home.

5. *Break the cycle of violence in the family.* This step repeats the message of Step 1—violence cannot be prevented as long as we are taught that it is appropriate to hit the people we love. Physical punishment of children is perhaps the most effective means of teaching violence, and eliminating it would be an important step in violence prevention.

Such steps require long-term changes in the fabric of society. These proposals call for such fundamental change in families and family life that many people resist the proposals and argue that they could not work or would ruin the family. The alternative, of course, is that not making such changes continues the harmful and deadly tradition of family and intimate violence.

Note

1. For a complete review of the methodological and design issues in the study of family violence, see Gelles, 1989; Weis, 1989.

References

American Association for Protecting Children. (1988). *Highlights of official child neglect and abuse reporting, 1986*. Denver: American Humane Association.

American Association for Protecting Children. (1989). *Highlights of official child neglect and abuse reporting, 1987*. Denver: American Humane Association.

Bachman, R. (1994). *Violence against women: A National Crime Victimization Survey report*. Washington, DC: U.S. Department of Justice, Bureau of Justice Statistics.

Bachman, R., & Saltzman, L. (1995). *Violence against women: Estimates from the redesigned survey*. Washington, DC: U.S. Department of Justice, Bureau of Justice Statistics.

Barthel, J. (1991). *For children's sake: The promise of family preservation*. New York: Edna McConnell Clark Foundation.

Belsky, J. (1980). Child maltreatment: An ecological integration. *American Psychologist, 35*, 320-335.

Belsky, J. (1993). Etiology of child maltreatment: A developmental-ecological approach. *Psychological Bulletin, 114,* 413-434.

Berk, R., Berk, S. F., Loseke, D., & Rauma, D. (1983). Mutual combat and other family violence myths. In D. Finkelhor, R. Gelles, M. Straus, & G. Hotaling (Eds.), *The dark side of families: Current family violence research* (pp. 197-212). Beverly Hills, CA: Sage.

Besharov, D. J. (1985). Right versus rights: The dilemma of child protection. *Public Welfare, 43,* 19-46.

Besharov, D. J. (1990). *Recognizing child abuse: A guide for the concerned.* New York: Free Press.

Besharov, D. J. (1993). Overreporting and underreporting are twin problems. In R. J. Gelles & D. Loseke (Eds.), *Current controversies on family violence* (pp. 257-272). Newbury Park, CA: Sage.

Bowker, L. H. (1993). A battered woman's problems are social, not psychological. In R. J. Gelles & D. Loseke (Eds.), *Current controversies on family violence* (pp. 154-165). Newbury Park, CA: Sage.

Briere, J., & Conte, J. (1993). Self-reported amnesia for abuse in adults molested as children. *Journal of Traumatic Stress, 6,* 21-31.

Burgdorf, K. (1980). *Recognition and reporting of child maltreatment.* Rockville, MD: Westat.

Burgess, R. L. (1979, November). *Family violence: Some implications from evolutionary biology.* Paper presented at the Annual Meeting of the American Society of Criminology, Philadelphia.

Burgess, R. L., & Draper, P. (1989). The explanation of family violence: The role of biological, behavioral, and cultural selection. In L. Ohlin & M. Tonry (Eds.), *Family violence: Crime and justice: A review of research* (Vol. 11, pp. 59-116). Chicago: University of Chicago Press.

Burgess, R. L., & Garbarino, J. (1983). Doing what comes naturally? An evolutionary perspective on child abuse. In D. Finkelhor, R. Gelles, M. Straus, & G. Hotaling (Eds.), *The dark side of families: Current family violence research* (pp. 88-101). Beverly Hills, CA.: Sage.

Caffey, J. (1946). Multiple fractures in the long bones of infants suffering from chronic subdural hematoma. *American Journal of Roentgenology, Radium Therapy, and Nuclear Medicine, 58,* 163-173.

Caffey, J. (1957). Some traumatic lesions in growing bones other than fractures and dislocations. *British Journal of Radiology, 23,* 225-238.

Cate, R. M., Henton, J. M., Christopher, F. S., & Lloyd, S. (1982). Premarital abuse: A social psychological perspective. *Journal of Family Issues, 3,* 79-90.

Daly, M., & Wilson, M. (1980). Discriminative parental solicitude: A biosocial perspective. *Journal of Marriage and the Family, 42,* 277-288.

Daly, M., & Wilson, M. (1988). *Homicide.* New York: Aldine DeGruyter.

Dawes, R. (1992, July). *Why believe that for which there is no good evidence?* Paper presented at the Convention of the American Psychological Society, San Diego, CA.

Dobash, R., Dobash, R. E., Wilson, M., & Daly, M. (1992). The myth of sexual symmetry in marital violence. *Social Problems, 39*(1), 71-91.

Dobash, R. E., & Dobash, R. (1979). *Violence against wives: A case against the patriarchy.* New York: Free Press.

Dunford, F. W., Huizinga, D., & Elliott, D. (1990). The role of arrest in domestic assault: The Omaha Police Experiment. *Criminology, 28,* 183-206.

Finkelhor, D. (1990). Is child abuse overreported? The data rebut arguments for less intervention. *Public Welfare, 48,* 23-29.

Finkelhor, D. (1993). The main problem is still underreporting, not overreporting. In R. J. Gelles & D. Loseke (Eds.), *Current controversies on family violence* (pp. 273-287). Newbury Park, CA: Sage.

Finkelhor, D., & Hotaling, G. (1984). Sexual abuse in the national incidence study of child abuse and neglect: An appraisal. *Child Abuse & Neglect: The International Journal, 8,* 23-33.

Forsythe, P. (1992). Homebuilders and family preservation. *Children and Youth Services Review, 14,* 37-47.

Garbarino, J. (1977). The human ecology of child maltreatment. *Journal of Marriage and the Family, 39,* 721-735.

Gelles, R. (1973). Child abuse as psychopathology: A sociological critique and reformulation. *American Journal of Orthopsychiatry, 43,* 611-621.

Gelles, R. J. (1974). *The violent home.* Beverly Hills, CA: Sage.

Gelles, R. J. (1983). An exchange/social control theory. In D. Finkelhor, R. Gelles, M. Straus, & G. Hotaling (Eds.), *The dark side of families: Current family violence research* (pp. 151-165). Beverly Hills, CA: Sage.

Gelles, R. J. (1989). Methodological issues in the study of family violence. In G. R. Patterson (Ed.), *Depression and aggression in family interaction* (pp. 49-74). Hillsdale, NJ: Lawrence Erlbaum.

Gelles, R. J. (1994, April). *Violence toward men: Fact or fiction?* Paper prepared for the American Medical Association Council on Scientific Affairs.

Gelles, R. J. (1996). *The book of David: How preserving families can cost children's lives.* New York: Basic Books.

Gelles, R. J., & Loseke, D. (Eds.). (1993). *Current controversies on family violence.* Newbury Park, CA: Sage.

Gelles, R. J., & Straus, M. A. (1988). *Intimate violence.* New York: Simon & Schuster.

Giles-Sims, J. (1983). *Wife-beating: A systems theory approach.* New York: Guilford.

Gordon, L. (1988). *Heroes of their own lives: The politics and history of family violence.* New York: Viking Penguin Books.

Greven, P. (1990). *Spare the child: The religious roots of punishment and the psychological impact of physical abuse.* New York: Knopf.

Heneghan, A. M., Horwitz, S. M., & Leventhal, J. M. (1996). Evaluating intensive family preservation programs: A methodological review. *Pediatrics, 97,* 535-542.

Henton, J., Cate, R., Koval, J., Lloyd, S., & Christopher, S. (1983). Romance and violence in dating relationships. *Journal of Family Issues, 4,* 467-482.

Herman, J. L., & Schatzow, E. (1987). Recovery and verification of memories of childhood sexual trauma. *Psychoanalytic Psychology, 4,* 1-18.

Hrdy, S. B. (1979). Infanticide among animals: A review classification and examination of the implications for reproductive strategies of females. *Ethology and Sociobiology, 1,* 13-40.

Kaufman, J., & Zigler, E. (1987). Do abused children become abusive parents? *American Journal of Orthopsychiatry, 57,* 186-192.

Kaufman, J., & Zigler, E. (1993). The intergenerational transmission of abuse is overstated. In R. J. Gelles & D. Loseke (Eds.), *Current controversies on family violence* (pp. 209-221). Newbury Park, CA: Sage.

Kempe, C. H., Silverman, F. N., Steele, B. F., Droegemueller, W., & Silver, H. K. (1962). The battered child syndrome. *Journal of the American Medical Association, 181,* 107-112.

Kilpatrick, D., Best, C. L., Saunders, B. E., & Veronen, L. J. (1988). Rape in marriage and dating relationships: How bad is it for mental health? *Annals of the New York Academy of Sciences, 528,* 335-344.

Laner, M. (1983). Courtship abuse and aggression: Contextual aspects. *Sociological Spectrum, 3,* 69-83.

Lindsey, D. (1994). *The welfare of children.* New York: Oxford University Press.

Loftus, E. (1993). The reality of repressed memories. *American Psychologist, 48,* 518-537.

Makepeace, J. (1981). Courtship violence among college students. *Family Relations, 30,* 97-102.

Makepeace, J. (1983). Life events stress and courtship violence. *Family Relations, 32,* 101-109.

Nash, M. R. (1992, August). *Retrieval of childhood memories in psychotherapy: Clinical utility and historical verifiability are not the same.* Paper presented at the 100th Annual Conference of the American Psychological Association, Washington, DC.

Nathan, D. (1992, October). Cry incest. *Playboy,* p. 84.

Nathan, D., & Snedeker, M. (1995). *Satan's silence: Ritual abuse and the making of a modern American witch hunt.* New York: Basic Books.

National Center on Child Abuse and Neglect. (1988). *Study findings: Study of national incidence and prevalence of child abuse and neglect: 1988.* Washington, DC: U.S. Department of Health and Human Services.

National Center on Child Abuse and Neglect. (1996). *Study findings: Study of national incidence and prevalence of child abuse and neglect: 1993.* Washington, DC: U.S. Department of Health and Human Services.

National Research Council. (1993). *Understanding child abuse and neglect.* Washington, DC: National Academy Press.

National Research Council. (1996). *Understanding violence against women.* Washington, DC: National Academy Press.

National Research Council. (1998). *Violence in families: Assessing prevention and treatment programs.* Washington, DC: National Academy Press.

Nelson, B. J. (1984). *Making an issue of child abuse: Political agenda setting for social problems.* Chicago: University of Chicago Press.

Newberger, E. H. (1985). The helping hand strikes again: Unintended consequences of child abuse reporting. In E. H. Newberger & R. Bourne (Eds.), *Unhappy families* (pp. 171-178). Littleton, MA: PSG Publications.

Okun, L. (1986). *Women abuse: Facts replacing myths.* Albany: State University of New York Press.

Pagelow, M. (1981). *Woman-battering: Victims and their experiences.* Beverly Hills, CA: Sage.

Pagelow, M. (1984). *Family violence.* New York: Praeger.

Pelton, L. (1989). *For reasons of poverty: A critical analysis of the public child welfare system in the United States.* New York: Praeger.

Peterson del Mar, D. (1996). *What trouble I have seen: A history of violence against wives.* Cambridge, MA: Harvard University Press.

Pillemer, K., & Finkelhor, D. (1988). The prevalence of elder abuse: A random sample survey. *The Gerontologist, 28,* 51-57.

Pizzey, E. (1974). *Scream quietly or the neighbors will hear.* Harmondsworth, UK: Penguin.

Pleck, E. (1987). *Domestic tyranny: The making of American social policy against family violence from colonial times to the present.* New York: Oxford University Press.

Pleck, E., Pleck, J. H., Grossman, M., & Bart, P. (1977-78). The battered data syndrome: A comment on Steinmetz' article. *Victimology, 2,* 680-684.

Plummer, C. (1993). Prevention is appropriate, prevention is successful. In R. J. Gelles & D. Loseke (Eds.), *Current controversies on family violence* (pp. 288-305). Newbury Park, CA: Sage.

Radbill, S. (1980). Children in a world of violence: A history of child abuse. In R. Helfer & R. Kempe (Eds.), *The battered child* (3rd ed., pp. 3-20). Chicago: University of Chicago Press.

Reppucci, N. D., & Haugaard, J. (1993). Problems with child sexual abuse prevention programs. In R. J. Gelles & D. Loseke (Eds.), *Current controversies on family violence* (pp. 306-322). Newbury Park, CA: Sage.

Robin, M. (1982). Historical introduction: Sheltering arms: The roots of child protection. In E. H. Newberger (Ed.), *Child abuse* (pp. 1-41). Boston: Little, Brown.

Rossi, P. (1992). Assessing family preservation program. *Child and Youth Services Review, 14,* 77-97.

Russell, D. (1984). *Sexual exploitation: Rape, child sexual abuse, and workplace harassment.* Beverly Hills, CA: Sage.

Schuerman, J., Rzepnicki, T. L., & Littell, J. H. (1994). *Putting families first: An experiment in family preservation.* New York: Aldine de Gruyter.

Shainess, N. (1979). Vulnerability to violence: Masochism as process. *American Journal of Psychotherapy, 33,* 174-189.

Sherman, L. (1992). *Policing domestic violence: Experiments and dilemmas.* New York: Free Press.

Sherman, L., & Berk, R. (1984). The specific deterrent effects of arrest for domestic assault. *American Sociological Review, 49,* 261-272.

Smuts, B. (1992). Male aggression against women: An evolutionary perspective. *Human Nature, 3,* 1-44.

Snell, J. E., Rosenwald, R. J., & Robey, A. (1964). The wifebeater's wife: A study of family interaction. *Archives of General Psychiatry, 11,* 107-113.

Sommers, C. H. (1994). *Who stole feminism? How women have betrayed women.* New York: Simon & Schuster.

Stark, E., & Flitcraft, A. (1985). Woman battering, child abuse, and social heredity: What is the relationship? In N. Johnson (Ed.), *Marital violence* (pp. 147-171). London: Routledge & Kegan Paul.

Steinmetz, S. (1977-78). The battered husband syndrome. *Victimology, 2,* 499-509.

Stets, J. E., & Straus, M. A. (1990). Gender differences in reporting marital violence and its medical and psychological consequences. In M. A. Straus & R. J. Gelles (Eds.), *Physical violence in American families* (pp. 151-166). New Brunswick, NJ: Transaction Publishers.

Straus, M. A. (1977-1978). Wife beating: How common and why. *Victimology, 2,* 443-458.

Straus, M. A. (1990). The Conflict Tactics Scales and its critics: An evaluation and new data on validity and reliability. In M. A. Straus & R. J. Gelles, (Eds.), *Physical violence in American families: Risk factors and adaptations to violence in 8,145 families* (pp. 133-148). New Brunswick, NJ: Transaction Publishers.

Straus, M. A. (1992). Sociological research and social policy: The case of family violence. *Sociological Forum, 7,* 211-237.

Straus, M. A. (1993). Physical assaults by wives: A major social problem. In R. J. Gelles & D. Loseke (Eds.), *Current controversies on family violence* (pp. 67-87). Newbury Park, CA: Sage.

Straus, M. A. (1994). *Beating the devil out of them: Corporal punishment in American families.* New York: Lexington Books.

Straus, M. A., & Gelles, R. J. (1986). Societal change and family violence from 1975 to 1985 as revealed by two national surveys. *Journal of Marriage and the Family, 48,* 465-479.

Straus, M. A., Gelles, R. J., & Steinmetz, S. K. (1980). *Behind closed doors: Violence in the American family.* Garden City, NY: Anchor Press.

Tatara, T. (1993). *Characteristics of children in substitute and adoptive care.* Washington, DC: Voluntary Cooperative Information System, American Public Welfare Association.

Tavris, C. (1993, January). Beware the incest-survivor machine. *New York Times Book Review,* p. 1

Thurman v. City of Torrington, 595 F. Supp. 1521 (1985).

U.S. Department of Health and Human Services. (1996). *Child maltreatment 1994: Reports from the states to the National Center on Child Abuse and Neglect.* Washington, DC: Government Printing Office.

U.S. Department of Justice. (1980). *Intimate victims: A study of violence among friends and relatives.* Washington, DC: Government Printing Office.

U.S. Department of Justice. (1984, September). *Attorney General's Task Force on Family Violence: Final report.* Washington, DC: Author.

U.S. Department of Justice. (1994). *Domestic violence: Violence between intimates.* Washington, DC: U.S. Department of Justice, Bureau of Justice Statistics.

Wakefield, H., & Underwager, R. (1992). Recovered memories of alleged sexual abuse: Lawsuits against parents. *Behavioral Sciences and the Law, 10,* 483-507.

Walker, L. (1979). *The battered woman.* New York: Harper & Row.

Walker, L. (1993). The battered woman syndrome is a psychological consequence of abuse. In R. J. Gelles & D. Loseke (Eds.), *Current controversies on family violence* (pp. 133-153). Newbury Park, CA: Sage.

Weis, J. G. (1989). Family violence research methodology and design. In L. Ohlin & M. Tonry (Eds.), *Family violence* (pp. 117-162). Chicago: University of Chicago Press.

Widom, C. S. (1988). Sampling biases and implications for child abuse research. *American Journal of Orthopsychiatry, 58,* 260-270.

Williams, L. M. (1994). Recall of childhood trauma: A prospective study of women's memories of child sexual abuse. *Journal of Consulting and Clinical Psychology, 62,* 1167-1176.

Wooley, P., & Evans, W. (1955). Significance of skeletal lesions resembling those of traumatic origin. *Journal of the American Medical Association, 158,* 539-543.

Yllö, K. (1983). Using a feminist approach in quantitative research. In D. Finkelhor, R. Gelles, M. Straus, & G. Hotaling (Eds.), *The dark side of families: Current family violence research* (pp. 277-288). Beverly Hills, CA: Sage.

Yllö, K. (1988). Political and methodological debates in wife abuse research. In K. Yllö & M. Bograd (Eds.), *Feminist perspectives on wife abuse* (pp. 28-50). Newbury Park, CA: Sage.

Yllö, K. (1993). Through a feminist lens: Gender, power, and violence. In R. Gelles & D. Loseke (Eds.), *Current controversies on family violence* (pp. 47-62). Newbury Park, CA: Sage.

• *CHAPTER 2* •

Child Physical Abuse: Theory and Research

JOEL S. MILNER
JULIE L. CROUCH

This chapter, which provides an introduction to the topic of child physical abuse, begins with a description of explanatory models and theories. The discussion of models builds on the more general theoretical overview of family violence presented in Chapter 1 by Richard J. Gelles. We will then summarize two organizational models and several explanatory models specific to child physical abuse, emphasizing child abuse models because of their importance as conceptual frameworks for understanding research and treatment. Following the discussion of models, we will provide a review of risk factors associated with child physical abuse that represent different ecological levels (e.g., offender, family, and society). Although the review reveals varying levels of support for the factors in the different child abuse models, the review does indicate that, in contrast to a single cause, multiple factors from different ecological levels contribute to the occurrence of child abuse. The last major section of the chapter describes the effects of child physical abuse. In describing victim effects, we attempt to place the reported consequences of child abuse in a developmental context. This orientation emphasizes the view that child abuse may have

---

AUTHORS' NOTE: Preparation of this chapter was supported in part by National Institute of Mental Health Grant MH 34252 to Joel S. Milner.

different short- and long-term consequences as a function of the child's developmental level at the time of the abuse.

Theoretical Considerations

Numerous models have been developed to describe factors that are believed to contribute to child physical abuse. Examples of different models are presented in Table 2.1, and additional discussions of child physical abuse models are available elsewhere (Azar, 1991; Tzeng, Jackson, & Karlson, 1991). One of the earliest models had its beginnings in a now classic article by Kempe, Silverman, Steele, Droegemueller, and Silver (1962), which described clinical problems related to the battered child syndrome. As part of this description, Kempe et al. listed psychiatric disturbances believed to occur in abusive parents. This description formed the basis for what today is referred to as the psychiatric model of child physical abuse.

Although research has supported the view that perpetrators vary on a variety of psychological dimensions, less than 10% of all child physical abusers have psychiatric disturbances. An early competing perspective is found in the sociological model promulgated by Gil (1970). This model was radically different from the psychiatric approach because it focused on sociological factors (e.g., economic conditions, societal values), instead of perpetrator factors, as causing child physical abuse.

A major limitation of these early models is that they only included factors from single domains or ecological levels (i.e., individual, society). In addition, the psychiatric and sociological models are unidirectional and hence do not allow for the possibility of interactions between putative causal factors. In response to these model limitations, a number of multidomain, multifactor interactional models were proposed.

Early interactional models were organizational models that designated the domains or factors thought to be important in describing and explaining child physical abuse. Two of the best known and most useful organizational models, the ecological model and the transactional model, are described in the next section. Following the description of these organizational models, we describe several current models that attempt to provide additional specification of variables that contribute to child physical abuse. Although much progress has been made, it is critical to recognize that the field still lacks adequately validated models of child physical abuse.

Table 2.1 Examples of Child Physical Abuse Models

Early single-factor models	
Psychiatric model	(Kempe et al., 1962)
Sociological model	(Gil, 1970)
Early multifactor organizational models	
Three-component theory	(Schneider, Pollock, & Helfner, 1972)
Social-psychological theory	(Gelles, 1973)
Social-situational model	(Parke & Collmer, 1975)
Symbiosis theory	(Justice & Justice, 1976)
Social interaction theory	(Burgess, 1979)
Ecological model	(Belsky, 1980, 1993)
Transactional model	(Cicchetti & Rizley, 1981)
Biological models	
Sociobiological theory	(Burgess & Garbarino, 1983; Daly & Wilson, 1981)
Neuropsychological theory	(Elliott, 1988)
Learning models	
Two-factor theory	(Vasta, 1982)
Social learning theory	(Tzeng et al., 1991)
Social/cultural models	
Resource theory	(Goode, 1971)
Culture theory	(Gelles & Straus, 1979)
Social systems theory	(Gil, 1987)
Interactional models	
Family systems theory	(Straus, 1973)
Choice theory	(Nye & McDonald, 1979)
General stress theory	(Farrington, 1980, 1986)
Three-factor theory	(Lesnik-Oberstein, Cohen, & Koers, 1982)
Situational theory	(Wiggins, 1983)
Cognitive developmental model	(Newberger & Cook, 1983)
Encounter theory	(Zimrin, 1984)
Cognitive behavioral model	(Twentyman et al., 1984)
Coercion theory	(Stringer & LaGreca, 1985)
Social cognitive model	(Azar, 1986, 1989; Azar & Siegal, 1990)
Attachment theory	(Aber & Allen, 1987; George, 1996)
Transitional model	(Wolfe, 1987)
Social information-processing model	(Milner, 1993)
Stress and coping model	(Hillson & Kupier, 1994)

Organizational Models

Ecological Model

Belsky (1980, 1993) has provided a comprehensive ecological model of child physical abuse that describes the ecological levels thought to be important in understanding physical child abuse. Belsky's model contains four domains or categories of factors, including individual factors (ontogenic level), family factors (microsystem level), community factors (exosystem level), and cultural factors (macrosystem level). Although this model does not describe which specific factors cause child physical abuse, the model is important because it organizes the different domains of contributing factors and expands the focus of previous models.

Transactional Model

Building on an awareness that factors from different ecological levels contribute to child abuse, Cicchetti and Rizley (1981) provided an organizational model that included both contributing and protective factors at different ecological levels. In the transactional model, factors are classified along two dimensions. The first dimension describes two major types of influence on the likelihood of child abuse: potentiating or compensatory. The second dimension describes the temporal nature of the influence: transient or enduring.

Potentiating and compensatory conditions are combined with transient and enduring conditions so that four types of factors are defined. Potentiating factors that are transient are called *challengers,* whereas potentiating factors that are enduring are referred to as *vulnerability* factors. Compensatory factors that are transient are called *buffers,* whereas compensatory factors that are enduring are referred to as *protective* factors.

According to Cicchetti and Rizley (1981), the four types of factors are thought to exist at the individual, family, and societal levels. Similarly, they could be said to exist at each of Belsky's (1980) four ecological levels. Factors from each ecological level are believed to be bidirectional and interactive. In the simplest application of this model, child physical abuse is expected to occur when potentiating conditions override compensatory conditions.

Etiological Models

This section summarizes three models of child physical abuse. The first model, the transitional model, describes the development of parent-child conflict through three stages and includes potentiating and compensatory factors from several ecological levels. The second model, a cognitive-behavioral model, describes with greater specificity perpetrator and child-related factors that are thought to cause child physical abuse. The third model, a social information-processing model, provides a greater focus on factors within the abusive parent and presents a framework for developing even more specificity in explaining perpetrator-related cognitive factors that contribute to child physical abuse.

Transitional Model

Wolfe (1987) has proposed a transitional model that describes how severe parent-child conflict, including child physical abuse, develops. Within this model, stress is viewed as a key element that serves to increase the likelihood of conflict within the family system. The transitional model, which includes multiple destabilizing and compensatory factors, is composed of three stages. The stages are not discrete but overlap and represent an ongoing development of parent-child conflict.

Stage 1 describes factors that help to reduce the parent's stress tolerance and ability to inhibit aggression. Destabilizing factors include the presence of stressful life events and inadequate preparation for parenting. Parental behaviors at this stage represent marginal attempts to cope with life's stressors and to manage his or her child's noncompliant behaviors. Compensatory factors include economic stability and social supports, which can moderate the impact of stress.

Stage 2 begins when the parent significantly fails to manage life stress and his or her child's behavior. During this stage, the parent becomes increasingly reactive to stressful events, attributes responsibility for negative behavior to the child, views the child as deliberately defiant, and perceives a loss of control. Stage 2 occurs when stressful life events and limited coping skills result in abusive parenting. Compensatory factors at this stage include parental acquisition of new coping skills and improvements in the child's behavior.

Stage 3 describes a situation in which the parent develops patterns of continuous arousal and child physical abuse. During this period, the parent is confronted with multiple stressful stimuli and is ineffective in coping with these stressful events. The pattern of arousal and blaming the child is more frequent. Feelings of hopelessness may appear. The parent increases the intensity and frequency of his or her aggressive behavior in an attempt to regain control. Compensatory factors at this stage include the parent developing dissatisfaction with the increasingly severe physical punishment, with child compliance following nonaversive discipline, and with community intervention. At Stage 3, however, compensatory factors are viewed as having a minimal impact on the habitual pattern of child abuse that has developed.

Cognitive-Behavioral Model

Twentyman and his associates (Morton, Twentyman, & Azar, 1988; Twentyman, Rohrbeck, & Amish, 1984) have proposed a four-stage cognitive-behavioral model of child physical abuse. Key elements of this model are unrealistic parental expectations and misattributions of negative intent, which are viewed as mediators of abusive behavior. In Stage 1, the parent develops and maintains unrealistic expectations of the child. In Stage 2, the child behaves in a manner inconsistent with the parent's expectations. In Stage 3, the parent misattributes the child's behavior to negative intent (e.g., desire to annoy the parent) on the part of the child. In Stage 4, the parent overreacts and engages in excessive and severe punishment of the child.

Azar (1986, 1989) has expanded the original conceptualization of Twentyman's cognitive-behavioral model by suggesting additional deficits in three core areas: parental cognitions, parental impulse control, and parent-child interactions. The levels of family stress and social support are also seen as important factors. Furthermore, Azar and Siegal (1990) have recently argued that child physical abuse, which occurs at different stages in the child's development, may not always be associated with the same parental deficits. For example, unrealistic expectations may be a significant perpetrator deficit during any developmental period, whereas a lack of certain parenting skills (e.g., reasoning and explaining) may be more detrimental at specific developmental stages (e.g., adolescence).

Social Information-Processing Model

Milner (1993) has proposed a social information-processing model of child physical abuse, which was designed to increase our understanding of child physical abuse perpetrator cognitions and their relationship to parental behavior. He describes three cognitive stages of social information processing, which lead to a fourth cognitive/behavioral stage of response execution. The three cognitive stages include perceptions of social behavior; interpretations, evaluations, and expectations that give meaning to social behavior; and the response selection process. The fourth stage involves response implementation and monitoring. Each stage of this social information-processing model is believed to be affected by preexisting cognitive schema, involving beliefs and values held by the parent.

Stage 1 (perceptions) of this social information-processing model states that abusers, compared to nonabusers, have perceptual distortions and biases in the representation of the child and the child's behavior. According to this model, child physical abusers tend to be less attentive and/or are less aware of social events (e.g., child behaviors) in their environment. Accordingly, with respect to situational factors, abusers experience more distress, which negatively affects their perceptions.

Stage 2 (interpretations, evaluations, and expectations) of the model states that abusers, compared to nonabusers, display differences in their interpretations and evaluations of children's behavior and expectations of children's compliance. Abusers interpret noncompliant child behavior as having more hostile intent and evaluate the behavior as being more wrong or blameworthy. Abusers also make inaccurate predictions of child compliance following different types of transgressions and disciplinary techniques. As predicted for perceptions at Stage 1, interpretations, evaluations, and expectations are believed to become more distorted and biased as distress levels increase.

Stage 3 (response selection) of the model states that abusers process information differently than nonabusers, which affects their response choice. This processing difference contributes to the response selection decision, which is separate from the contributions of distorted and biased cognitions. It is proposed that abusers are less likely to use situational information in their evaluation of children's behavior. Thus, even if social information is perceived and interpreted correctly, the abuser tends to ignore important information during this processing stage. For example, an abusive parent may be aware of mitigating events related to a child's transgression, but, because of his or her processing style, the mitigating information (e.g., big brother bumped little Johnny and caused Johnny to spill the milk) has little impact on the parent's belief that a transgression (Johnny's spilling of the milk) has occurred.

This processing style allows the abuser to maintain explanations of the child's behavior that are consistent with the parent's rigidly held cognitive distortions and biases (e.g., Johnny is a "bad" child with hostile intent), which justify the more frequent use of power-assertive discipline. Finally, but most important, the response selection process is limited by the number and types of response choices that are available. Parental skill deficits obviously set limits on the response choice outcome.

Stage 4 (response implementation and monitoring) describes the parent's ability to adequately implement parenting skills and the associated ability to monitor and modify his or her behavior as needed. Numerous factors may affect the parent's ability to implement and monitor his or her behavior. For example, cognitive factors (e.g., expectations of child noncompliance) may reduce the likelihood that a parent will carefully implement or monitor a disciplinary technique. Furthermore, higher levels of parental distress may negatively affect the parent's ability to implement or continue a disciplinary strategy (such as explaining consequences to a child). Failure to achieve child compliance as a result of the parental behavior used at this stage serves to confirm the parent's biases and distortions, increasing the likelihood that power-assertive (verbal and physical) discipline will be used in the future.

The question remains as to where this social information-processing style originates. Although data are generally lacking, this style may originate as a consequence of early social learning. Chilamkurti and Milner (1993) demonstrated that several of the cognitive biases and distortions described in the social information-processing model exist prior to abuse in high-risk parents, compared to low-risk parents. Furthermore, children in each risk group displayed cognitive styles similar to their respective parents. These data are consistent with the view that parental cognitions may be passed on to the children and may mediate the intergenerational transmission of abuse. Finally, to explain child physical abuse adequately, the social information-processing model must be embedded in a comprehensive model that includes contributing and compensatory factors from other ecological levels.

Risk Factors Associated With Child Physical Abuse

As previously noted, models of child physical abuse tend to be either broad organizational models or relatively specific explanatory models limited to a few constructs. The following review uses the broader perspective of the organizational models to provide a multi-domain focus for the summary of the child physical abuse literature. As outlined in Table 2.2, this review describes perpetrator, family, and sociological characteristics believed to be associated with the physical abuse of children.

Perpetrator Characteristics

Biological Factors. The role of perpetrator neurological and neuropsychological factors in child physical abuse remains unclear. To date, there has been little research on the topic, and extant research has not demonstrated a causal relationship between neurological and neuropsychological factors and child physical abuse. Elliott (1988), nevertheless, has indicated that abusers' neurological handicaps have been overlooked. Elliott believes that "patchy" cognitive deficits (e.g., limited vocabulary and slowness of thought), related to minimal brain dysfunction, decrease the parents' ability to cope adequately with family and child-related problems, increasing the likelihood of child physical abuse. In addition, Milner and McCanne (1991) have speculated that in some cases, a childhood history of physical assault may produce neurological and neuropsychological deficits that contribute to the intergenerational transmission of child physical abuse. Additional discussions of the possible role of neurological and neuropsychological factors in child physical abuse are provided elsewhere (Elliott, 1988; Milner & McCanne, 1991).

The only known controlled study on neuropsychological factors and child physical abuse was conducted by Nayak and Milner (1998), who gave neuropsychological measures to a group of high-risk and demographically matched low-risk mothers. As expected, the high-risk mothers showed inferior performance on measures that assessed conceptual ability, cognitive flexibility, and problem-solving ability. Although some of the impairments remained in an analysis that controlled for group differences in intelligence, no neuropsychological differences were evident after group differences in intelligence, depression, and anxiety were statistically controlled. This analysis, however, does not tell us if the differences in affect caused the inferior neuropsychological performance or if the neuropsychological problems produced the nega-

Table 2.2 Examples of Perpetrator, Family, and Sociological Characteristics Believed to Be Associated With Child Physical Abuse

Perpetrator characteristics
Biological factors
neurological and neuropsychological problems
physiological hyperreactivity
physical health problems
Cognitive/affective factors
low self-esteem and ego-strength
negative perceptions, attributions, and evaluations of child behavior
inappropriate expectations of child behavior
numerous stressors/distress
depression
other psychological factors
Behavioral factors
alcohol and drug use
social isolation
problems in parent-child interactions
frequent use of harsh disciplinary techniques
inadequate coping skills
Family characteristics
conflict, little support in family of origin
marital discord
poor communication skills
verbal and physical conflict
value the use of force
lack of cohesion
child factors
Sociological characteristics
Perpetrator demographics
nonbiological parent
single parent
age
education level
childhood history of abuse
Family demographic factors
lack of resources
large number of children
Social isolation
Multiple environmental stressors
Culturally sanctioned use of force
Violent community

tive affect or if some other (third) variable was related to each of these variables.

Compared to the information available on neurological and neuropsychological characteristics, more theory and data are available on psychophysiological differences between abusers and nonabusers. On a theoretical level, Knutson (1978) has suggested that abusers have a hyperreactive trait. Supporting this view, Wolfe, Fairbank, Kelly, and Bradlyn (1983) found that abusers had large increases in skin conductance and respiration rates in response to both stressful and nonstressful mother-child interactional scenes. Frodi and Lamb (1980) found that abusers, relative to nonabusers, were more physiologically reactive to a crying child. Furthermore, abusers showed physiological reactivity to a smiling child, whereas nonabusers did not, leading Frodi and Lamb to conclude that the abusers found both the crying and the smiling child aversive. Similar increases in physiological reactivity to infants who are crying (Crowe & Zeskind, 1992; Pruitt & Erickson, 1985) and smiling (Pruitt & Erickson, 1985) have been reported in high-risk childless adults, which suggests that some adults may enter the parent-child relationship with increased autonomic reactivity to child stimuli. One recent study supports the view that high-risk parents also show increased reactivity to nonchild-related stimuli. Casanova, Domanic, McCanne, and Milner (1992) found greater and more prolonged physiological reactivity in high-risk parents, compared to low-risk parents, following the presentation of two different stressful non-child-related stimuli.

Despite study limitations and inconsistent results, most investigators have concluded that abusers show increased physiological reactivity to child-related stimuli (McCanne & Milner, 1991). Even if these conclusions are valid, it still must be demonstrated that the autonomic changes are causally related to child physical abuse. Furthermore, if autonomic changes are causally related to abuse, the manner in which they interact with other variables must be determined.

Although this topic is infrequently studied, several researchers indicate that perpetrators, compared to nonabusers, have more physical handicaps and health problems (Conger, Burgess, & Barrett, 1979; Lahey, Conger, Atkeson, & Treiber, 1984). Abusers also report more physical handicaps and health problems on the Child Abuse Potential Inventory (Milner, 1986). The extent to which these physical concerns are real or perceived, however, needs further investigation. Steele and Pollock (1974) report that abusers suffer from more psychosomatic illnesses; thus, reported health complaints may be associated with other psychological conditions.

Cognitive/Affective Factors. As a group, child physical abusers have low self-esteem and poor ego-strength (Friedrich & Wheeler, 1982; Milner, 1988). Low self-esteem is important because it has been linked to negative parental perceptions of child behavior (Mash, Johnston, & Kovitz, 1983) and to an inability to cope with stress (McCubbin, Cauble, & Patterson, 1982). Other research indicates that physically abusive parents have negative perceptions of their children, including the perception that their children are intentionally disruptive, disobedient (Helfer, McKinney, & Kempe, 1976; Wood-Shuman & Cone, 1986), and annoying (Bauer & Twentyman, 1985). Two studies, using independent observers, found that abusers rated their children as more problematic (Mash et al., 1983), as being more aggressive, as having more conduct disorders, as being more active, and as having less intellectual ability (Reid, Kavanagh, & Baldwin, 1987) than did parents of comparison children. In these two studies, however, independent raters did not observe the differences reported by the abusive parents, suggesting an abuser evaluation bias.

Although the data are mixed (see Milner & Foody, 1994), differences in attributions have been reported for abusive parents. Physically abusive parents have reportedly perceived their children's negative behavior as due to internal and stable factors and their children's positive behavior as due to external and unstable factors (Larrance & Twentyman, 1983). Comparison parents displayed the opposite attributional style. With respect to the evaluation of wrongness, high-risk parents, relative to low-risk parents, have been reported to assign a greater degree of wrongness to child transgressions overall and to minor transgressions in particular (Chilamkurti & Milner, 1993).

Abusive and high-risk parents have been observed to have more unrealistic expectations of their children. The literature suggests that in some cases, child expectations are too high and in other cases, expectations are too low (Kravitz & Driscoll, 1983; Perry, Wells, & Doran, 1983; Twentyman & Plotkin, 1982). Research suggests that some reported differences may be due to the type of measure used and the type of expectation evaluated (Azar, Robinson, Hekimian, & Twentyman, 1984). Research also indicates that differences in parental expectations may occur because of contextual factors. For example, Chilamkurti and Milner (1993) found that high-risk parents, compared to low-risk parents, had higher expectations for child compliance following discipline for minor child transgressions and lower expectations for child compliance following discipline for serious transgressions.

In most physical abuse models, stress is seen as a central etiological factor. Stress is viewed as increasing the likelihood that the parent with limited resources will react in an aggressive manner toward his or her children. Supporting this contention, Schellenbach, Monroe, and Merluzzi (1991) found that high-risk parents are more aroused, controlling, punishing, and rejecting of their children, and stress increases the magnitude of these behaviors. Furthermore, Holden and Banez (1996) reported that parenting stress moderates the relationship between child-related stress and abuse potential, so that the combination of parenting and child-related stress produced the greatest child abuse risk.

It is unclear, however, if abusers experience more environmental stressors, as some researchers have reported (Straus, 1980), or if they merely perceive more events as stressful and experience more distress. In a study where abusers and matched comparison parents were used, the amount of environmental stress did not differ between the two groups (Gaines, Sandgrund, Green, & Power, 1978). The presence of high levels of distress in abusers is supported, however, by studies indicating that abusers show more physiological reactivity to child and non-child related stimuli (Casanova et al., 1992; Frodi & Lamb, 1980). It is also important to note that high levels of distress are related to reports of health-related problems and to depression.

Since an early report by Gil (1970), numerous studies have indicated that parental depression is associated with child physical abuse. As with other factors, it is unclear if depression is a marker variable or if it is causally related to child abuse. It has been reported, however, that depressed mothers are unaffectionate, distant, irritable, and punitive with their children, which may result in a lower threshold for perceived child misbehavior and more punitive reactions to child behavior (Lahey et al., 1984).

In addition to depression, abusers and high-risk parents have been reported to have higher levels of state and trait anxiety (Aragona, 1983), to exhibit more anger and less assertiveness (Mee, 1983), and to indicate more loneliness (Milner, 1986). High-risk and abusive parents have an external locus of control (Stringer & LaGreca, 1985), which may be associated with the clinical observation that some abusers blame their children for the abuse. Abusers also have been reported to be defensive (Milner, 1986), to deny knowledge of child injury (Rivara, Kamitsuka,

& Quan, 1988), and to have less empathy (Milner, Halsey, & Fultz, 1995) for their children. Although these personality characteristics are descriptive of the abuser, again it is unclear which factors are marker factors and which are causal factors in child physical abuse.

Behavioral Characteristics. Although alcohol use has been related to the likelihood and severity of assault in the general aggression literature (Taylor & Leonard, 1983), reviews of the child abuse literature suggest that alcohol consumption is only modestly related to child physical abuse (Black & Mayer, 1980; Leonard & Jacob, 1988). Nevertheless, alcohol use still may be an important factor under some conditions. For example, alcohol use may be associated with the more severe types of child physical abuse. Because alcohol has been reported to negatively affect cognitive processing abilities in normal individuals, it may exacerbate any cognitive deficits that exist in abusers. Furthermore, in individuals for whom alcohol use and depression coexist, the level of dysfunction has been observed to increase (Bland & Orn, 1986). Finally, apart from a proximal contribution, a study that used a community sample and controlled for demographic and other potentially confounding variables found the expected relationship between the lifetime occurrence of alcohol and drug disorders and child physical abuse (Kelleher, Chaffin, Hollenberg, & Fischer, 1994). This finding may result from both substance disorders and a relationship between child abuse and some common (third) personality variable.

Child physical abusers report social isolation, although some research indicates that the actual number of social contacts may not be significantly different (Coohey, 1996). Abusers therefore may simply perceive more social isolation and experience more loneliness. These characteristics may be related to their perceptions that others cannot be trusted or depended on, perceptions that have been shown to discriminate between physically abusive and demographically matched nonabusive parents (Milner, 1986).

Studies support the contention that abusive parents exhibit highly aversive parent-child interactional patterns. For example, abusive mothers engage in more negative interactions and are less supportive of their children (Burgess & Conger, 1978). They display more verbal and nonverbal aggression and provide less positive verbal and nonverbal support (Bousha & Twentyman, 1984). Not only do abusers spend less time in positive interactions with their children (e.g., praising, playing), they respond less often to children's initiations of interactions (Kavanagh, Youngblade, Reid, & Fagot, 1988). Abusers display less emotional responsiveness (Egeland, Breitenbucher, & Rosenberg, 1980), use less age-appropriate stimulation (Dietrich, Starr, & Kaplan, 1980), and fail to modify their behavior in response to their children's behavior (Crittenden, 1981). Physically abusive (Cerezo, D'Ocon, & Dolz, 1996) and at-risk parents (Dolz, Cerezo, & Milner, 1997) also make more indiscriminant (noncontingent) responses to their children's prosocial behaviors.

Most studies support the conclusion that abusive parents use more physical punishment to control their children than comparison parents. Abusers use assaultive behavior (e.g., hitting, grabbing, pushing; Lahey et al., 1984) and punitive strategies more often and use reasoning strategies less frequently (Chilamkurti & Milner, 1993; Kelley, Grace, & Elliott, 1990; Oldershaw, Walters, & Hall, 1986). Abusers may use punishment more often because they view punishment as more effective than reasoning techniques (Trickett & Susman, 1988).

Familial Characteristics

Abusers report more deprivation, hostility, and abuse in their families of origin. Perpetrators also report less social support from parents, adults, siblings, and peers during childhood. Several authors have reported that parents who have experienced childhood physical abuse but who do not continue the cycle of violence have received social support during childhood or adulthood (Caliso & Milner, 1994; Egeland, Jacobvitz, & Sroufe, 1988; Hunter & Kilstrom, 1979). Congruent with these findings, higher levels of childhood social support have been reported to be associated with lower scores on the Child Abuse Potential Inventory (Crouch, Milner, & Caliso, 1995; Milner, Robertson, & Rogers, 1990).

Families in which child physical abuse occurs have more family and marital distress. The family members have poor or distorted communication patterns and suffer from role confusions, power imbalances, distrust, and a greater likelihood of spouse abuse and multiple forms of child maltreatment. Not surprisingly, abusive families report more conflict and less cohesion and expressiveness (Milner & Chilamkurti, 1991). With respect to child discipline, the family in which abuse occurs tends to value physical punishment (Trickett & Susman, 1988).

Historically, certain child characteristics were viewed as increasing the likelihood of child physical abuse by contributing to negative parent-child interactions (Friedrich & Boriskin, 1976). Child-related characteristics include prematurity, low birthweight, physical handicaps, and a difficult temperament. Furthermore, most social-interactional models of child abuse include the child as a significant component in the model. At the least, child characteristics appear to contribute to the level of stress in the parents' environment, thus increasing the likelihood of physical abuse. Although, historically, the child victim has been viewed as playing a major role in the abuse event, more recent critical reviews of the literature have questioned the degree to which the child contributes to the abuse (e.g., Ammerman, 1991).

Sociological Characteristics

Since Gil's (1970) initial development of the sociological model, a broad array of social factors related both to the perpetrator and to social systems have been associated with child physical abuse. As with factors at other ecological levels, it remains unclear which of the sociological factors are marker variables and which are causal variables.

With respect to perpetrator demographic characteristics, abusers tend to be single, young, and poorly educated; they report a history of observing and/or receiving abuse. They suffer from multiple environmental stressors, which are often related to family demographic factors (e.g., crowded living environment, large number of children, occupational difficulties; Milner & Chilamkurti, 1991). Some investigators view the lack of economic resources as a central factor in child abuse. Research indicates that important correlates of lower income include lower parental intelligence, lower educational status, single-parent status, lower levels of health, and higher levels of personal distress and psychopathology (Herrenkohl, Herrenkohl, Toedter, & Yanushefski, 1984).

Although the lack of resources appears to contribute to the problem, the presence of resources may act as a compensatory factor. For example, higher family income has been related to higher levels of affectionate behavior, communication skills, and positive parent-child interactions (Herrenkohl et al., 1984). Thus, income level appears to be associated with both contributing and compensatory factors that affect parent-child interactions. In a general sense, it seems that negative demographic conditions set the stage for the intergenerational transmission of child abuse because these conditions make it difficult for the parent to teach the child how to function adequately (Gabinet, 1983).

Developmental Effects of Child Physical Abuse

Consistent with the organizational models discussed above (Belsky, 1980, 1993; Cicchetti & Rizley, 1981), the life-span perspective emphasizes that the developing individual is embedded in, and dynamically interactive with, a social context (Lerner, 1988). According to this view, the course of development remains relatively plastic throughout life, and changes in either the individual or the context may alter the developmental course of the individual-context system (Lerner, 1988).

With respect to understanding the development of the physically abused child, the life-span perspective does not suggest that simple, direct relationships exist between the receipt of abuse and particular sequelae (Starr, MacLean, & Keating, 1991). Rather, the developmental perspective assumes that the receipt of physical abuse is only one of many factors from various ecological levels (ontogenic, microsystem, exosystem, and macrosystem) that simultaneously influence the development of the abused child. Each influencing factor may be viewed as increasing (potentiating factors) or reducing (compensatory factors) the risk of developmental difficulties in the physically abused child (Cicchetti, 1989). According to a life-span perspective, the developmental impact of physical abuse depends not only on the chronicity and severity of the abuse but also on the developmental level of the child at the time of the assault and the balance of current and future potentiating and compensatory factors.

The following is a summary of empirical findings related to the effects of physical abuse across the life span. Although the information has been organized according to broad developmental stages, it is important to note that, currently, insufficiencies in data make it impossible to link directly the emergence and persistence of particular sequelae to specific life stages. The developmental framework used here is intended only to suggest the importance of considering the impacts of abuse from a life-span perspective.

Physical Sequelae: Risk Across the Life Span

At any point in development, a potential sequelae of physical abuse is bodily damage to the victim. In their description of the battered child syndrome, Kempe et al. (1962) suggested a relationship between the receipt of physical abuse and certain physical symptoms in the child, such as subdural hematoma, fracture of long bones, multiple soft tissue injuries, poor skin hygiene, malnutrition, and poor general health. In a recent telephone survey of a nationally representative sample of youth, Finkelhor and Dziuba-Leatherman (1994) reported that 22% of youth who experienced a physical assault by a family member in the past year reported that they had been physically injured as a result of that event. The most severe outcome of physical abuse is death. Although national registry data are incomplete, an estimated 1,261 children in the United States died as a result of child maltreatment in 1992 (McCurdy & Daro, 1994). From 1990 to 1994, national registry data suggest that the total number of child fatalities attributed to child maltreatment "has not varied by more than 100 victims, or 10 percent, between any two years" (U.S. Department of Health & Human Services, 1996, pp. 3-9). Nevertheless, these annual rates probably underestimate the problem due to inadequate investigation procedures in many child fatality cases.

Victims of physical abuse are also at risk for neurological and neuropsychological impairments that may result in detrimental effects across the life span. With the exception of accidental trauma (e.g., car accidents), the most frequent cause of infant head trauma is physical abuse (Rivara et al., 1988). Elliott (1988) noted that damage or disorder in the nervous system may impair cognition, perception, and behavior and hence may play a role in determining the developmental effects of physical abuse. Lewis, Shanok, Pincus, and Glaser (1980) proposed that damage to the central nervous system as a result of physical abuse may contribute to the cognitive and behavioral difficulties (e.g., impulsivity, attention disorders, learning disabilities) often exhibited by abused children. Although they noted that additional evidence is needed, Milner and McCanne (1991) suggested that the neuropsychological consequences of child physical abuse may extend into adulthood.

Early Childhood

One of the first observable differences between physically abused children and their nonabused counterparts is the manner in which they respond to their caretaker when stressed. Researchers suggest that physically abused infants, compared to nonabused infants, demonstrate higher frequencies of less secure attachments to their primary caretakers (Browne & Saqi, 1988; Carlson, Cicchetti, Barnett, & Braunwald, 1989; Crittenden & Ainsworth, 1989; Egeland & Sroufe, 1981). At 12 months of age, physically abused children, after being left alone in a strange situation and then reunited with their parent, tended to avoid contact and maintain distance from their parent. In contrast, securely attached children directly approached and sought proximity with their caretaker after exposure to a strange situation (Egeland & Sroufe, 1981). Investigators in the area of early social development suggest that patterns of infant-mother interaction may be related to the child's subsequent development in a number of areas. For example, the quality of infant-mother interaction has been reported to be significantly related to the child's later intellectual and linguistic abilities (Bee et al., 1982).

Middle and Late Childhood

Intellectual Deficits. Compared to their nonabused counterparts, physically abused children reportedly earn lower scores on tests of general intellectual abilities during childhood (Barahal, Waterman, & Martin, 1981; Hoffman-Plotkin & Twentyman, 1984; Vondra, Barnett, & Cicchetti, 1990). It should be noted, however, that environmental variables that often coexist with child physical abuse (e.g., impoverished environment, neglect) may also contribute to the intellectual deficits observed in physically abused children (Bee et al., 1982; Vondra et al., 1990).

Affective and Behavioral Problems. During middle childhood, physically abused children reportedly exhibit a number of affective and behavioral difficulties, including anxiety, depression, sleep disturbance, self-destructive behavior, low self-esteem, social detachment, hyperactivity, excessive aggression, and noncompliance (Egeland & Sroufe, 1981; Kaufman & Cicchetti, 1989; Kazdin, Moser, Colbus, & Bell, 1985; Straker & Jacobson, 1981). There is also evidence that a direct relationship exists between the severity of abuse to which the child is exposed (i.e., received and/or observed) and the degree of child maladjustment. That is, increasing severity of received or observed abuse appears to be related to higher levels of emotional and behavioral dysfunction (Fantuzzo et al., 1991; Kaufman & Cicchetti, 1989; Kazdin et al., 1985).

Perhaps the most frequently cited behavioral sequela of child physical abuse is the prevalence of externalizing behavior problems, such as excessive aggressiveness, hyperactivity, and conduct problems (Hoffman-Plotkin & Twentyman, 1984; Widom, 1989; Wolfe & Mosk, 1983). Kaufman and Cicchetti (1989) reported that children who were physically abused, as compared to children who received other forms of maltreatment, were rated by their peers as significantly more aggressive. Boney-McCoy and Finkelhor (1995) reported that for girls, but not for boys, physical abuse by a parent was significantly associated with having trouble with a teacher in the past year. Interestingly, Wolfe and Mosk (1983) reported significant differences in behavior problems and social competencies between abused children and nonabused children from high-distress families. These authors concluded that the abused child's social and behavioral development may be more a function of general family interaction patterns than isolated abusive episodes.

Although externalizing behavior problems have received a great deal of attention in the literature on physically abused children, these children also have been reported to demonstrate higher levels of internalizing behavior (e.g., withdrawal, self-destructiveness) than nonabused children (Kaufman & Cicchetti, 1989; Swenson, Crouch, Saunders, & Kilpatrick, 1995). However, Kaufman and Cicchetti noted that the relationship between physically abused children's use of aggression and withdrawal as coping strategies is unclear; some children demonstrate both behavioral tendencies, and other children display a preference for one versus the other response strategy.

The complex clinical presentation noted among physically abused children may possibly result from post-traumatic stress disorder (PTSD), including symptoms of reexperiencing, avoidance/numbing, and increased arousal. Indeed, a physical assault during childhood may serve as a PTSD criterion event to the extent that it results in physical injury or perceived life threat and produces an intense sense of fear and/or helplessness for the child (McNally, 1991). Recent work suggests that parental physical violence has a moderate to large effect in causing PTSD-related symptomatology (Boney-McCoy & Finkelhor, 1995). In a telephone survey of a nationally representative sample of youth, Swenson et al. (1995) found that victims of physically abusive punishment were more likely to meet diagnostic criteria for PTSD than youth who did not receive physical abuse.

Social Development. Physically abused children have been reported to be significantly less empathic than nonabused children (Main & George, 1985; Straker & Jacobson, 1981). For example, abused children have reacted to distressed peers with physical attacks, fear, or anger, whereas their nonabused counterparts predominantly responded with expressions of concern (Main & George, 1985). Differences between physically abused and nonabused children in empathic ability have been reported to disappear, however, when levels of intellectual ability are controlled (Frodi & Smetana, 1984).

Physically abused children also appear to differ from their nonabused counterparts in the area of social cognition. Specifically, abused children have been reported to have less confidence in their ability to affect events (i.e., more external locus of control), a decreased understanding of social roles (Barahal et al., 1981), hostile attributional styles, and aggressive approaches to problem solving (Dodge, Bates, & Pettit, 1990).

A study of the relationship between children's and their mothers' social cognitions found that children of high-risk mothers evaluated conventional (e.g., disobeying family rules) and personal transgressions (e.g., wearing wrinkled clothes) as more wrong compared to evaluations made by children of low-risk mothers (Chilamkurti & Milner, 1993). Although the two groups differed in their relative evaluations, both groups of children adopted patterns of evaluation that paralleled their mother's style of evaluating transgressions. This finding suggests that children may internalize certain parental social cognitions, and such cognitions may affect the child's assessment of the appropriateness of responding with aggression.

Adolescence

It is important to note that some cases of adolescent physical abuse are simply the continuation of abuse that began in childhood, whereas others represent a deterioration of parent-child interactions as the child becomes an adolescent (Lourie, 1979). Families in which physical abuse emerges only as the child becomes an adolescent appear to be different from families in which preadolescent children are abused (Garbarino, 1989). For example, Garbarino noted that research on adolescent abuse indicates that lower social economic class appears to play a smaller role as a risk factor in adolescent maltreatment than preadolescent abuse (i.e., adolescent abuse is more equally distributed across socioeconomic classes). Also, parents who physically abuse their adolescents, as compared to parents who abuse their preadolescent children, are less likely to have been abused themselves as children (Garbarino, 1989). As these data suggest, physical abuse that emerges only in adolescence presents a number of features that differentiate it from preadolescent victimization, and research specifically focused on each phenomenon is needed.

Substance Use. A history of violent assault during childhood appears to increase risk of substance use, abuse, and/or dependency problems in adolescence and adulthood (see Stewart, 1996, for a review). Dembo et al. (1989) reported that both physical and sexual abuse had direct effects on illicit drug use within a sample of adolescents being held in a detention center. Within a nationally representative sample of youth, adolescents who reported having received physically abusive punishment had higher rates of past-year heavy alcohol use (26.9% vs. 14.0%), and drug use (22.1% vs. 7.5%) than those who did not report physical abuse (Swenson et al., 1995).

In addition to the direct effects of childhood physical abuse on subsequent risk of problems with alcohol and drugs, psychological processes (i.e., depression, PTSD) may mediate the relationship between childhood physical abuse and substance use (see Stewart, 1996, for a review). For example, using data from a large national probability sample of adult women, Duncan, Crouch, Saunders, Kilpatrick, and Resnick (1997) assessed the relationships between childhood physical and/or sexual abuse, major depressive episodes (MDE) and/or PTSD, and problems related to substance use. Duncan et al. found that women who experienced childhood physical and/or sexual assault and developed MDE or PTSD were at greater risk of substance use problems than individuals exposed to childhood assaults who did not develop MDE or PTSD.

Delinquency. The experience of child abuse appears to be a risk factor for involvement with delinquent peers and the development of delinquent behavior in adolescence. With regard to physical abuse, Swenson et al. (1995) found that within a nationally representative sample of adolescents, 31.6% of youth who had been victims of physically abusive punishment reported having committed a delinquent act at some point in their lifetime, and 25.0% of physically abused youth reported having committed a delinquent act within the past year. These rates were significantly higher than rates of delinquent activity (10.4% lifetime and 7.9% past year) found among youth who had not received physically abusive punishment. Although research provides initial support for the expected relationships, additional research is needed to explore more adequately the complex relationships between childhood physical abuse, psychological status, substance use, and involvement in delinquent activity.

Adulthood

A comprehensive review of the long-term consequences of childhood physical abuse has been presented elsewhere (i.e., Malinosky-Rummell & Hansen, 1993). After reviewing the relevant literature, these authors suggest that the long-term sequelae of childhood physical abuse may be variable, and appear to be influenced by a number of moderating variables, including characteristics of the abuse (e.g., perpetrator's relationship to victim) and factors related to the victims (e.g., gender), their families (e.g., presence of other forms of violence, parental substance abuse), and their environment (e.g., lower socioeconomic status).

General Adaptation. In a 23-year follow-up of individuals who were severely physically abused as children, Martin and Elmer (1992) reported a broad range of adaptation among their adult sample. According to these authors, some individuals appeared to be functioning adequately (i.e., raising families, remaining employed, and maintaining social relationships), whereas others exhibited exceptional difficulties in coping (i.e., depression, feelings of isolation, substance abuse). Although a general measure of aggressiveness did not appear elevated for the group of adults who had experienced physical abuse as children, Martin and Elmer noted that the abused individuals did exhibit more suspiciousness and resentment compared to the control group. In contrast, other studies have noted a relationship between the receipt of child physical abuse and adult levels of anger and aggression (Briere & Runtz, 1990).

It should be noted that, in the Martin and Elmer (1992) study, many participants from the original 1963 sample were unavailable at the time of the 23-year follow-up. Furthermore, the unavailable participants had been rated (at the outset of the study in 1963) as having more difficulties than those participants who were available at the time of the follow-up. Due to the unavailability of some of the more disturbed participants at follow-up, Martin and Elmer noted that their study may underestimate the deleterious impact of child physical abuse on later adult functioning. Such a conclusion is congruent with a longitudinal study by Silverman,

Reinherz, and Giaconia (1996) that reported that a majority of males and females physically abused during childhood had clinical disorders when evaluated at 21 years of age.

Increased Criminal Behavior. Research exploring the relationship between childhood physical abuse and later violent criminal activity has produced contradictory reports (Widom, 1989). One prospective study that supports a relationship between receipt of childhood physical abuse and later adult risk of criminality was conducted by McCord (1983). McCord assessed the quality of interaction between 232 males and their respective parents (classifying each child as loved, rejected, abused, or neglected) and then followed this group over a 40-year period. According to this study, men who had been physically abused, neglected, and/or rejected as children were at a higher risk of becoming alcoholic, mentally ill, or involved in criminal activity than those who were loved. Because the experiences of abuse, neglect, and rejection are not mutually exclusive, it is difficult to discern any distinct contribution of physical abuse to the increased risk of antisocial behavior reported in the McCord study.

Intergenerational Transmission of Physical Abuse. In its general form, the intergenerational transmission of aggression hypothesis states that patterns of violent behavior are passed from one generation to the next. With reference to child physical abuse, this hypothesis suggests that victims of childhood physical abuse are more likely to abuse their own children.

Although the idea is intuitively appealing, the intergenerational transmission of physical abuse has been received critically by many researchers. When Kaufman and Zigler (1987) integrated the findings of a number of studies related to the intergenerational transmission of abuse, they estimated that only 30% of parents with a childhood history of abuse go on to abuse their own children. This estimate has been criticized, however, due to the limited follow-up period in many of the studies (Belsky, 1993). Regardless of the actual rates, research does suggest a higher likelihood of abuse by parents if the parents themselves were abused as children. Research also indicates, however, that the majority of adults who abuse their children may not have been abused in their own childhood (Widom, 1989).

Investigators have suggested that concurrent or subsequent social support for the victim of childhood abuse may buffer the intergenerational transmission of physical abuse (Caliso & Milner, 1994; Crouch et al., 1995; Egeland et al., 1988; Hunter & Kilstrom, 1979; Milner et al., 1990). In a review of the literature on offender characteristics, Milner and Chilamkurti (1991) suggested that in cases of intergenerational transmission of abuse, a childhood experience of abuse may be a marker variable for other factors (e.g., family dysfunction, lack of support) that may more directly affect the probability of subsequent perpetration of child physical abuse.

Conclusion

The breadth of understanding added by multidomain, bidirectional organizational models and the specificity provided by more recent explanatory models demonstrate conceptual advances in the child physical abuse field. Research efforts have generated data on child physical abuse risk factors and on the effects of physical abuse on the child. However, additional research is needed to inform prevention and treatment efforts more adequately. Substantial limitations are evident in the research base. For example, few controlled studies have examined the role of gender (physically abusive fathers are rarely studied) or the possible role of ethnic differences in child physical abuse. Furthermore, when studies have identified risk or victim variables they often lack evidence on whether the variables actually have a causal relationship, or simply mark a correlation with child physical abuse because of some common third variable.

References

Aber, J. L., & Allen, J. P. (1987). Effects of maltreatment on young children's socioemotional development: An attachment theory perspective. *Developmental Psychology, 23,* 406-414.

Ammerman, R. T. (1991). The role of the child in physical abuse: A reappraisal. *Violence and Victims, 6,* 87-101.

Aragona, J. A. (1983). Physical child abuse: An interactional analysis (Doctoral dissertation, University of South Florida, 1983). *Dissertation Abstracts International, 44,* 1225B.

Azar, S. T. (1986). A framework for understanding child maltreatment: An integration of cognitive behavioural and developmental perspectives. *Canadian Journal of Behavioural Science, 18,* 340-355.

Azar, S. T. (1989). Training parents of abused children. In C. E. Schaefer & J. M. Briesmeister (Eds.), *Handbook of parent training* (pp. 414-441). New York: John Wiley.

Azar, S. T. (1991). Models of child abuse: A metatheoretical analysis. *Criminal Justice and Behavior, 18,* 30-46.

Azar, S. T., Robinson, D. R., Hekimian, E., & Twentyman, C. T. (1984). Unrealistic expectations and problem-solving ability in maltreating and comparison mothers. *Journal of Consulting and Clinical Psychology, 52,* 687-691.

Azar, S. T., & Siegal, B. R. (1990). Behavioral treatment of child abuse: A developmental perspective. *Behavior Modification, 14,* 279-300.

Barahal, R. M., Waterman, J., & Martin, H. P. (1981). The social cognitive development of abused children. *Journal of Consulting and Clinical Psychology, 49,* 508-516.

Bauer, W. D., & Twentyman, C. T. (1985). Abusing, neglectful, and comparison mothers' responses to child-related and non-child-related stressors. *Journal of Consulting and Clinical Psychology, 53,* 335-343.

Bee, H. L., Barnard, K. E., Eyres, S. J., Gray, C. A., Hammond, M. A., Spietz, A. L., Synder, C., & Clark, B. (1982). Prediction of IQ and language skill from perinatal status, child performance, family characteristics, and mother-infant interaction. *Child Development, 53,* 1134-1156.

Belsky, J. (1980). Child maltreatment: An ecological integration. *American Psychologist, 35,* 320-335.

Belsky, J. (1993). Etiology of child maltreatment: A developmental-ecological analysis. *Psychological Bulletin, 114,* 413-434.

Black, R., & Mayer, J. (1980). Parents with special problems: Alcoholism and opiate addiction. *Child Abuse & Neglect, 4,* 45-54.

Bland, R. C., & Orn, H. (1986). Psychiatric disorders, spouse abuse, and child abuse. *Acta Psychiatrica Belgica, 86,* 444-449.

Boney-McCoy, S., & Finkelhor, D. (1995). Psychosocial sequelae of violent victimization in a national youth sample. *Journal of Consulting and Clinical Psychology, 63,* 726-736.

Bousha, D. M., & Twentyman, C. T. (1984). Mother-child interactional style in abuse, neglect, and control groups: Naturalistic observations in the home. *Journal of Abnormal Psychology, 93,* 106-114.

Briere, J., & Runtz, M. (1990). Differential adult symptomatology associated with three types of child abuse histories. *Child Abuse & Neglect, 14,* 357-364.

Browne, K., & Saqi, S. (1988). Mother-infant interaction and attachment in physically abusing families. *Journal of Reproductive and Infant Psychology, 6,* 163-182.

Burgess, R. L. (1979). Project interact: A study of patterns of interaction in abusive, neglectful, and normal families. *Child Abuse & Neglect, 3,* 781-791.

Burgess, R. L., & Conger, R. D. (1978). Family interaction in abusive, neglectful, and normal families. *Child Development, 49,* 1163-1173.

Burgess, R. L., & Garbarino, J. (1983). Doing what comes naturally? An evolutionary perspective on child abuse. In D. Finkelhor, R. J. Gelles, G. T. Hotaling, & M. A. Straus (Eds.), *The dark side of families: Current family violence research* (pp. 88-101). Beverley Hills, CA: Sage.

Caliso, J. A., & Milner, J. S. (1994). Childhood physical abuse, childhood social support, and child abuse potential. *Child Abuse & Neglect, 16,* 647-659.

Carlson, V., Cicchetti, D., Barnett, D., & Braunwald, K. (1989). Disorganized/disoriented attachment relationships in maltreated infants. *Developmental Psychology, 25,* 525-531.

Casanova, G. M., Domanic, J., McCanne, T., & Milner, J. S. (1992). Physiological responses to non-child-related stressors in mothers at risk for child abuse. *Child Abuse & Neglect, 16,* 31-44.

Cerezo, M. A., D'Ocon, A., & Dolz, L. (1996). Mother-child interactive patterns in abusive families: An observational study. *Child Abuse & Neglect, 20,* 573-587.

Chilamkurti, C., & Milner, J. S. (1993). Perceptions and evaluations of child transgressions and disciplinary techniques in high- and low-risk mothers and their children. *Child Development, 64,* 1801-1814.

Cicchetti, D. (1989). How research on child maltreatment has informed the study of child development: Perspectives from developmental psychopathology. In D. Cicchetti & V. Carlson (Eds.), *Child maltreatment: Theory and research on the causes and consequences of child abuse and neglect* (pp. 377-431). New York: Cambridge University Press.

Cicchetti, D., & Rizley, R. (1981). Developmental perspectives on the etiology, intergenerational transmission, and sequelae of child maltreatment. *New Directions for Child Development, 11,* 31-55.

Conger, R. D., Burgess, R. L., & Barrett, C. (1979). Child abuse related to life change and perceptions of illness: Some preliminary findings. *Family Coordinator, 28,* 73-78.

Coohey, C. (1996). Child maltreatment: Testing the social isolation hypothesis. *Child Abuse & Neglect, 20,* 241-254.

Crittenden, P. M. (1981). Abusing, neglecting, problematic, and adequate dyads: Differentiating by patterns of interaction. *Merrill-Palmer Quarterly, 27,* 201-218.

Crittenden, P. M., & Ainsworth, M. D. (1989). Child maltreatment and attachment theory. In D. Cicchetti & V. Carlson (Eds.), *Child maltreatment: Theory and research on the causes and consequences of child abuse and neglect* (pp. 432-463). New York: Cambridge University Press.

Crouch, J. L., Milner, J. S., & Caliso, J. A. (1995). Childhood physical abuse, perceived social support, and socioemotional status in adult women. *Violence and Victims, 10,* 273-283.

Crowe, H. P., & Zeskind, P. S. (1992). Psychophysiological and perceptual responses to infant cries varying in pitch: Comparisons of adults with low and high scores on the Child Abuse Potential Inventory. *Child Abuse & Neglect, 16,* 19-29.

Daly, M., & Wilson, M. I. (1981). Child maltreatment from a sociobiological perspective. *New Directions for Child Development, 11,* 93-112.

Dembo, R., Williams, L., La Voie, L., Berry, E., Gerteu, A., Wish, E. D., Schimeidler, J., & Washburn, M. (1989). Physical abuse, sexual victimization, and illicit drug use: Replication of a structural analysis among a new sample of high-risk youths. *Violence and Victims, 4,* 121-138.

Dietrich, K. N., Starr, R. H., Jr., & Kaplan, M. G. (1980). Maternal stimulation and care of abused infants. In T. M. Field, S. Goldberg, D. Stern, & A. M. Sostek (Eds.), *High-risk infants and children* (pp. 25-41). New York: Academic Press.

Dodge, K. A., Bates, J. E., & Pettit, G. S. (1990). Prospective study of the significance of life stress in the etiology of child abuse. *Science, 250,* 1678-1683.

Dolz, L., Cerezo, M. M., & Milner, J. S. (1997). Mother-child interactive patterns in high- and low-risk mothers. *Child Abuse & Neglect, 21,* 1149-1158.

Duncan, R., Crouch, J. L., Saunders, B. E., & Kilpatrick, D. (1997, January). *Substance abuse and related problems in adult survivors of childhood rape and serious physical assaults.* Paper presented at the San Diego Conference on Responding to Child Maltreatment, San Diego, CA.

Egeland, B., Breitenbucher, M., & Rosenberg, D. (1980). Prospective study of the significance of life stress in the etiology of child abuse. *Journal of Consulting and Clinical Psychology, 48,* 194-205.

Egeland, B., Jacobvitz, D., & Sroufe, L. A. (1988). Breaking the cycle of abuse. *Child Development, 59,* 1080-1088.

Egeland, B., & Sroufe, L. A. (1981). Developmental sequelae of maltreatment in infancy. *New Directions for Child Development, 11,* 77-92.

Elliott, F. A. (1988). Neurological factors. In V. B. Van Hasselt, R. L. Morrison, A. S. Bellack, & M. Hersen (Eds.), *Handbook of family violence* (pp. 359-382). New York: Plenum.

Fantuzzo, J. W., DePaola, L. M., Lambert, L., Martino, T., Anderson, G., & Sutton, S. (1991). Effects of interparental violence on the psychological adjustment and competencies of young children. *Journal of Consulting and Clinical Psychology, 59,* 258-265.

Farrington, K. (1980). Stress and family violence. In M. Straus & G. Hotaling (Eds.), *Social causes of husband-wife violence.* Minneapolis: University of Minnesota Press.

Farrington, K. (1986). The application of stress theory to the study of family violence: Principles, problems, and prospects. *Journal of Family Violence, 1,* 131-147.

Finkelhor, D., & Dziuba-Leatherman, J. (1994). Children as victims of violence: A national survey. *Pediatrics, 94,* 413-420.

Friedrich, W. N., & Boriskin, J. A. (1976). The role of the child in abuse: A review of the literature. *American Journal of Orthopsychiatry, 46,* 580-590.

Friedrich, W. N., & Wheeler, K. K. (1982). The abusing parent revisited: A decade of psychological research. *Journal of Nervous and Mental Disease, 170,* 577-587.

Frodi, A. M., & Lamb, M. E. (1980). Child abusers' responses to infant smiles and cries. *Child Development, 51,* 238-241.

Frodi, A. M., & Smetana, J. (1984). Abused, neglected, and nonmaltreated preschoolers' ability to discriminate emotions in others: The effects of IQ. *Child Abuse & Neglect, 8,* 459-465.

Gabinet, L. (1983). Child abuse treatment failures reveal need for redefinition of the problem. *Child Abuse & Neglect, 7,* 395-402.

Gaines, R., Sandgrund, A., Green, A. H., & Power, E. (1978). Etiological factors in child maltreatment: A multivariate study of abusing, neglecting, and normal mothers. *Journal of Abnormal Psychology, 87,* 531-540.

Garbarino, J. (1989). Troubled youth, troubled families: The dynamics of adolescent maltreatment. In D. Cicchetti & V. Carlson (Eds.), *Child maltreatment: Theory and research on the causes and consequences of child abuse and neglect* (pp. 685-706). New York: Cambridge University Press.

Gelles, R. (1973). Child abuse as psychopathology: A sociological critique and reformulation. *American Journal of Orthopsychiatry, 43,* 611-621.

Gelles, R. J., & Straus, M. A. (1979). Determinants of violence in the family: Toward a theoretical integration. In W. R. Burr, R. Hill, F. I. Nye, & I. L. Reiss (Eds.), *Contemporary theories about the family* (pp. 549-581). New York: Free Press.

George, C. (1996). A representational perspective of child abuse and prevention: Internal working models of attachment and caregiving. *Child Abuse & Neglect, 20,* 411-424.

Gil, D. G. (1970). *Violence against children.* Cambridge, MA: Harvard University Press.

Gil, D. G. (1987). Maltreatment as a function of the structure of social systems. In M. R. Brassard, R. Germain, & S. N. Hart (Eds.), *Psychological maltreatment of children and youth.* New York: Pergamon.

Goode, W. J. (1971). Force and violence in the family. *Journal of Marriage and the Family, 33,* 624-636.

Helfer, R. E., McKinney, J., & Kempe, R. (1976). Arresting or freezing the developmental process. In R. E. Helfer & C. H. Kempe (Eds.), *Child abuse and neglect: The family and the community* (pp. 134-163). Cambridge, MA: Balinger.

Herrenkohl, E. C., Herrenkohl, R. C., Toedter, L. J., & Yanushefski, A. M. (1984). Parent-child interactions in abusive and non-abusive families. *Journal of the American Academy of Child Psychiatry, 23,* 641-648.

Hillson, J. M. C., & Kupier, N. A. (1994). A stress and coping model of child maltreatment. *Clinical Psychology Review, 14,* 261-285.

Hoffman-Plotkin, D., & Twentyman, C. T. (1984). A multimodal assessment of behavioral and cognitive deficits in abused and neglected preschoolers. *Child Development, 55,* 794-802.

Holden, E. W., & Banez, G. A. (1996). Child abuse potential and parenting stress within maltreating families. *Journal of Family Violence, 11,* 1-12.

Hunter, R. S., & Kilstrom, N. (1979). Breaking the cycle in abusive families. *American Journal of Psychiatry, 136,* 1320-1322.

Justice, B., & Justice, R. (1976). *The abusing family.* New York: Human Sciences Press.

Kaufman, J., & Cicchetti, D. (1989). Effects of maltreatment on school-age children's socioemotional development: Assessments in a day-camp setting. *Developmental Psychology, 25,* 516-524.

Kaufman, J., & Zigler, E. (1987). Do abused children become abusive parents? *American Journal of Orthopsychiatry, 57,* 186-192.

Kavanagh, K. A., Youngblade, L., Reid, J. B., & Fagot, B. I. (1988). Interactions between children and abusive versus control parents. *Journal of Clinical Child Psychology, 17,* 137-142.

Kazdin, A. E., Moser, J., Colbus, D., & Bell, R. (1985). Depressive symptoms among physically abused and psychiatrically disturbed children. *Journal of Abnormal Psychology, 94,* 298-307.

Kelleher, K., Chaffin, M., Hollenberg, J., & Fischer, E. (1994). Alcohol and drug disorders among physically abusive and neglectful parents in a community-based sample. *American Journal of Public Health, 84,* 1586-1590.

Kelley, M. L., Grace, N., & Elliott, S. N. (1990). Acceptability of positive and punitive discipline methods: Comparisons among abusive, potentially abusive, and nonabusive parents. *Child Abuse & Neglect, 14,* 219-226.

Kempe, C. H., Silverman, F. N., Steele, B. F., Droegemueller, W., & Silver, H. K. (1962). The battered child syndrome. *Journal of the American Medical Association, 181,* 105-112.

Knutson, J. F. (1978). Child abuse as an area of aggression research. *Journal of Pediatric Psychology, 3,* 20-27.

Kravitz, R. I., & Driscoll, J. M. (1983). Expectations for childhood development among child-abusing and nonabusing parents. *American Journal of Orthopsychiatry, 53,* 336-344.

Lahey, B. B., Conger, R. D., Atkeson, B. M., & Treiber, F. A. (1984). Parenting behavior and emotional status of physically abusive mothers. *Journal of Consulting and Clinical Psychology, 52,* 1062-1071.

Larrance, D. T., & Twentyman, C. T. (1983). Maternal attributions and child abuse. *Journal of Abnormal Psychology, 92,* 449-457.

Leonard, K. E., & Jacob, T. (1988). Alcohol, alcoholism, & family violence. In V. B. Van Hasselt, R. L. Morrison, A. S. Bellack, & M. Hersen (Eds.), *Handbook of family violence* (pp. 383-406). New York: Plenum.

Lerner, R. M. (1988). Personality development: A life-span perspective. In E. M. Hetherington, R. M. Lerner, & E. M. Perlmutter (Eds.), *Child development in life-span perspective* (pp. 21-46). Hillsdale, NJ: Lawrence Erlbaum.

Lesnik-Oberstein, M., Cohen, L., & Koers, A. J. (1982). Research in the Netherlands on a theory of child abuse: A preliminary report. *Child Abuse & Neglect, 6,* 199-206.

Lewis, D. O., Shanok, S. S., Pincus, J. H., & Glaser, G. H. (1980). Violent juvenile delinquents: Psychiatric, neurological, psychological, and abuse factors. *Annual Progress in Child Psychiatry & Child Development,* 591-603.

Lourie, I. S. (1979). Family dynamics and the abuse of adolescents: A case for a developmental phase specific model of child abuse. *Child Abuse & Neglect, 3,* 967-974.

Main, M., & George, C. (1985). Responses of abused and disadvantaged toddlers to distress in agemates: A study in the day care setting. *Developmental Psychology, 21,* 407-412.

Malinosky-Rummell, R., & Hansen, D. J. (1993). Long-term consequences of childhood physical abuse. *Psychological Bulletin, 114,* 68-79.

Martin, J. A., & Elmer, E. (1992). Battered children grown up: A follow-up study of individuals severely maltreated as children. *Child Abuse & Neglect, 16,* 75-87.

Mash, E. J., Johnston, C., & Kovitz, K. (1983). A comparison of the mother-child interactions of physically abused and non-abused children during play and task situations. *Journal of Clinical Child Psychology, 12,* 337-346.

McCanne, T. R., & Milner, J. S. (1991). Physiological reactivity of physically abusive and at-risk subjects to child-related stimuli. In J. S. Milner (Ed.), *Neuropsychology of aggression* (pp. 147-166). Boston: Kluwer Academic.

McCord, J. (1983). A forty-year perspective on effects of child abuse and neglect. *Child Abuse & Neglect, 7,* 265-270.

McCubbin, H. I., Cauble, A. E., & Patterson, J. M. (1982). *Family stress, coping, and social support.* Springfield, IL: Charles C Thomas.

McCurdy, K., & Daro, D. (1994). Child maltreatment: A national survey of reports and fatalities. *Journal of Interpersonal Violence, 9,* 75-94.

McNally, R. J. (1991). Assessment of posttraumatic stress disorder in children. *Psychological Assessment, 3,* 531-537.

Mee, J. (1983). *The relationship between stress and the potential for child abuse.* Unpublished thesis, Macquarie University, Australia.

Milner, J. S. (1986). *The Child Abuse Potential Inventory: Manual* (2nd ed.). Webster, NC: Psytec.

Milner, J. S. (1988). An ego-strength scale for the Child Abuse Potential Inventory. *Journal of Family Violence, 3,* 151-162.

Milner, J. S. (1993). Social information processing and physical child abuse. *Clinical Psychology Review, 13,* 275-294.

Milner, J. S., & Chilamkurti, C. (1991). Physical child abuse perpetrator characteristics: A review of the literature. *Journal of Interpersonal Violence, 6,* 346-367.

Milner, J. S., & Foody, R. (1994). The impact of mitigating information on attributions for positive and negative child behavior by adults at low- and high-risk for child abusive behavior. *Journal of Social and Clinical Psychology, 13,* 335-351.

Milner, J. S., Halsey, L. B., & Fultz, J. (1995). Empathic responsiveness and affective reactivity in infant stimuli in high- and low-risk for physical child abuse mothers. *Child Abuse & Neglect, 19,* 767-780.

Milner, J. S., & McCanne, T. (1991). Neuropsychological correlates of physical child abuse. In J. S. Milner (Ed.), *Neuropsychology of aggression* (pp. 131-145). Norwell, MA: Kluwer Academic.

Milner, J. S., Robertson, K. R., & Rogers, D. L. (1990). Childhood history of abuse and adult abuse potential. *Journal of Family Violence, 5,* 15-34.

Morton, T. L., Twentyman, C. T., & Azar, S. T. (1988). Cognitive-behavioral assessment and treatment of child abuse. In N. Epstein, S. E. Schlesinger, & W. Dryden (Eds.), *Cognitive-behavioral therapy with families* (pp. 87-117). New York: Brunner/Mazel.

Nayak, M. B., & Milner, J. S. (1998). Neuropsychological functioning: Comparison of mothers at high- and low-risk for child physical abuse. *Child Abuse & Neglect, 22,* 687-703.

Newberger, C. M., & Cook, S. J. (1983). Parental awareness and child abuse: A cognitive-developmental analysis of urban and rural samples. *American Journal of Orthopsychiatry, 53,* 512-524.

Nye, F. I., & McDonald, G. W. (1979). Family policy research: Emergent models and some theoretical issues. *Journal of Marriage and the Family, 41,* 473-485.

Oldershaw, L., Walters, G. C., & Hall, D. K. (1986). Control strategies and noncompliance in abusive mother-child dyads: An observational study. *Child Development, 57,* 722-732.

Parke, R. D., & Collmer, C. W. (1975). Child abuse: An interdisciplinary analysis. In E. M. Hetherington (Ed.), *Review of child development research* (Vol. 5, pp. 509-590). Chicago: University of Chicago Press.

Perry, M. A., Wells, E. A., & Doran, L. D. (1983). Parent characteristics in abusing and nonabusing families. *Journal of Clinical Child Psychology, 12,* 329-336.

Pruitt, D. L., & Erickson, M. R. (1985). The Child Abuse Potential Inventory: A study of concurrent validity. *Journal of Clinical Psychology, 41,* 104-111.

Reid, J. B., Kavanagh, K., & Baldwin, D. V. (1987). Abusive parents' perceptions of child problem behaviors: An example of parental bias. *Journal of Abnormal Child Psychology, 15,* 457-466.

Rivara, F. P., Kamitsuka, M. D., & Quan, L. (1988). Injuries to children younger than 1 year of age. *Pediatrics, 81,* 93-97.

Schellenbach, C. J., Monroe, L. D., & Merluzzi, T. V. (1991). The impact of stress on cognitive components of child abuse potential. *Journal of Family Violence, 6,* 61-80.

Schneider, G., Pollock, C., & Helfner, H. C. (1972). The predictive questionnaire: A preliminary report. In R. E. Helfner & C. H. Kempe (Eds.), *Helping the battered child and his family* (pp. 271-282). Philadelphia: Lippincott.

Silverman, A. B., Reinherz, H. Z., & Giaconia, R. (1996). The long-term sequelae of child and adolescent abuse: A longitudinal community study. *Child Abuse & Neglect, 20,* 709-723.

Starr, R. H., Jr., MacLean, D. J., & Keating, D. P. (1991). Life-span developmental outcomes of child maltreatment. In R. H. Starr, Jr. & D. A. Wolfe (Eds.), *The effects of child abuse and neglect* (pp. 1-32). New York: Guilford.

Steele, B. F., & Pollock, C. B. (1974). A psychiatric study of parents who abuse infants and small children. In R. E. Helfer & C. H. Kempe (Eds.), *The battered child* (2nd ed., pp. 103-147). Chicago: University of Chicago Press.

Stewart, S. H. (1996). Alcohol abuse in individuals exposed to trauma: A critical review. *Psychological Bulletin, 120,* 83-112.

Straker, G., & Jacobson, R. S. (1981). Aggression, emotional maladjustment, and empathy in the abused child. *Developmental Psychology, 17,* 762-765.

Straus, M. A. (1973). A general systems theory approach to a theory of violence between family members. *Social Science Information, 12,* 105-125.

Straus, M. A. (1980). Stress and child abuse. In R. E. Helfer & C. H. Kempe (Eds.), *The battered child* (3rd ed., pp. 86-103). Chicago: University of Chicago Press.

Stringer, S. A., & LaGreca, A. M. (1985). Correlates of child abuse potential. *Journal of Abnormal Child Psychology, 13,* 217-226.

Swenson, C., Crouch, J., Saunders, B., & Kilpatrick, D. (1995, January). *Physical assault of adolescents: Prevalence, case characteristics, and mental health consequences.* Paper presented at the San Diego Conference on Responding to Child Maltreatment, San Diego.

Taylor, S., & Leonard, K. (1983). Alcohol and human physical aggression. In R. Geen & D. Donnerstein (Eds.), *Aggression: Theoretical and empirical reviews* (pp. 77-101). New York: Academic Press.

Trickett, P. K., & Susman, E. J. (1988). Parental perceptions of child-rearing practices in physically abusive and nonabusive families. *Developmental Psychology, 24,* 270-276.

Twentyman, C. T., & Plotkin, R. (1982). Unrealistic expectations of parents who maltreat their children: An educational deficit that pertains to child maltreatment. *Journal of Clinical Psychology, 38,* 497-503.

Twentyman, C. T., Rohrbeck, C. A., & Amish, P. L. (1984). A cognitive-behavioral model of child abuse. In S. Saunders, A. M. Anderson, C. A. Hart, & G. M. Rubenstein (Eds.), *Violent individuals and families: A handbook for practitioners* (pp. 87-111). Springfield, IL: Charles C Thomas.

Tzeng, O. C., Jackson, J. W., & Karlson, H. C. (1991). *Theories of child abuse and neglect.* New York: Praeger.

U.S. Department of Health and Human Services. (1996). *Child maltreatment 1994: Reports from the states to the National Center on Child Abuse and Neglect.* Washington, DC: Government Printing Office.

Vasta, R. (1982). Physical child abuse: A dual-component analyses. *Developmental Review, 2,* 125-149.

Vondra, J. I., Barnett, D., & Cicchetti, D. (1990). Self-concept, motivation, and competence among preschoolers from maltreating and comparison families. *Child Abuse & Neglect, 14,* 525-540.

Widom, C. S. (1989). Does violence beget violence? A critical examination of the literature. *Psychological Bulletin, 106,* 3-28.

Wiggins, J. A. (1983). Family violence as a case on interpersonal aggression: A situational analysis. *Social Forces, 62,* 102-123.

Wolfe, D. A. (1987). *Child abuse: Implications for child development and psychopathology.* Newbury Park, CA: Sage.

Wolfe, D. A., Fairbank, J. A., Kelly, J. A., & Bradlyn, A. S. (1983). Child abusive parents' physiological responses to stressful and non-stressful behavior in children. *Behavioral Assessment, 5,* 363-371.

Wolfe, D. A., & Mosk, M. D. (1983). Behavioral comparisons of children from abusive and distressed families. *Journal of Consulting and Clinical Psychology, 51,* 702-708.

Wood-Shuman, S., & Cone, J. D. (1986). Differences in abusive, at-risk for abuse, and control mothers' descriptions of normal child behavior. *Child Abuse & Neglect, 10,* 397-405.

Zimrin, H. (1984). Child abuse: A dynamic process of encounter between needs and personality traits within the family. *American Journal of Family Therapy, 12,* 37-47.

• *CHAPTER 3* •

Double Exposure: Children Affected by Family and Community Violence

BRENDA JONES HARDEN
SALLY A. KOBLINSKY

Fourteen-year-old Tony is expelled from school for hiding a knife in his locker and threatening his peers with it after school. Tony, a boy of slight build, has been bullied by larger youth and is frightened by the gang activity on the street. He once witnessed two male teenagers gunned down in a drive-by shooting. When the school social worker visited Tony's home to discuss the school's action, his angry father declared that Tony must fight to gain "respect." Tony's mother attempted to ask the social worker if her son could return to school, but his father demanded that she "shut up" and pushed her out of the living room.

Angie and Tomika are 6-year-old twin sisters who have recently moved to a battered women's shelter with their mother, Sharon. Sharon entered the shelter after experiencing 2 years of battering by her boyfriend. Sharon believes her boyfriend felt remorse about his behavior, but she decided to move after he began striking her in front of the children. As a result of moving to the shelter, the family experienced new fears of the street muggings and drug activity that plague the neighborhood. Sharon restricted her daughters' play to their shelter room, and the family never ventures out of the shelter after dark. Sharon also taught the girls to lie quickly on the floor whenever they hear the sound of gunshots.

Tony, Angie, and Tomika are among the growing number of children who daily confront violence in their homes and communities. Violence has become epidemic in the United States, placing children of all ages at risk for victimization (Children's Defense Fund, 1998). Each year, millions of children suffer maltreatment at the hands of adult caregivers. Children also endure a more hidden and less researched form of victimization: witnessing family and community violence. Garbarino (1995) has compared the violent environments in which these children live to a war zone. Although children may not be direct targets of aggressive behavior, they are often caught in the crossfire of violence between loved ones and neighbors. The sense of security that should pervade their homes and communities is absent, leaving them vulnerable to physical and psychological harm (Osofsky & Fenichel, 1994). Moreover, a disturbing number of children exposed to violence early in their lives are becoming perpetrators of violence themselves (Farrington, 1991; Office of Juvenile Justice and Delinquency Prevention, 1993). Research indicates that early and continuous exposure to this environmental toxin will produce adverse outcomes in children (Lorion, Brodsky, & Cooley-Quille, in press).

Chapter Scope

Disciplines such as criminology, sociology, and psychology have rich traditions of family and community violence research. However, investigations of children's exposure to marital and family violence lag behind most other areas of domestic violence research (Barnett, Miller-Perrin, & Perrin, 1997). Similarly, until recently, there has been little research examining the impact of children's exposure to community violence (Osofsky, 1995). Even fewer studies have explored the interrelationships among different forms of violence witnessed by children.

Clearly, there is a need to examine the separate and interactive effects of children's increasing exposure to family and community violence. Determining how parents and communities attempt to protect children and help them cope with violence-related stress is another important area of inquiry. Such research provides valuable direction for intervention efforts designed to mitigate the negative effects of violence exposure.

This chapter examines current literature on children's experiences of family and community violence, with a focus on the linkages between these violent experiences. The chapter does not address the direct victimization of children, although clearly there is a correlation between violence exposure and victimization (Holden & Ritchie, 1991).

The first section presents prevalence data on children's exposure to intrafamilial and extrafamilial violence. Then, a conceptual framework for considering the impact of children's exposure to family and community violence is discussed, followed by a section addressing the consequences of experiencing these two forms of violence. Next, the chapter considers ecological factors that may influence children's responses to violence exposure. The chapter concludes with a summary of prevention and intervention strategies for children who are exposed to violence in their homes and communities.

Prevalence of Exposure to Violence

Contemporary research on children's exposure to violence has established that children are witnessing violence at alarming rates. Increasing poverty and its concomitant stressors on community and family life have escalated levels of violence across the United States (Children's Defense Fund, 1998).

Exposure to Family Violence. Current evidence suggests that most of the violence that children witness occurs in and/or near their homes. Violence emanating from intrafamial conflict, such as spousal violence, accounts for a considerable proportion of this exposure. Estimates regarding the percentages of families affected by intrafamilial violence vary widely, ranging from 16% (Gelles & Straus, 1988) to 60% (O'Leary, Curley, Rosenbaum, & Clarke, 1985). Likewise, there is a major disparity in reports of the number of children who have observed marital violence, with estimates ranging from 3.3 million (Carlson, 1984) to 10 million (Straus, 1991). The existing research on the incidence and prevalence of children exposed to marital violence is extremely limited. Much of the data emanates from retrospective studies of victims of marital violence (Fantuzzo, Boruch, Beriama, Atkins, & Marcus, 1997), raising questions about the reliability of information.

Exposure to Community Violence. Community violence has reached epidemic proportions in urban areas across the country, primarily due to the illicit drug trade and the availability of handguns (Children's Defense Fund, 1998). Pioneering research conducted by the National Institute of Mental Health (Martinez & Richters, 1993; Richters & Martinez, 1993a, 1993b) established a methodology for the study of children's exposure to community violence and led to a spate of prevalence studies. Although there are no national investigations of children's exposure to community violence, researchers have examined urban exposure within specific geographic regions of the country.

Current empirical studies, summarized in Table 3.1, reveal unprecedented levels of community violence exposure for children from the preschool through adolescent years. Although child and parent reports of community violence exposure are often discrepant, both groups consistently report high rates of child exposure in urban neighborhoods (Osofsky, 1995; Richters & Martinez, 1993a). This research further reveals that male and older children are more likely to be exposed to community violence than female and younger children (Richters & Martinez, 1993a, 1993b).

Exposure to Family and Community Violence. Although family and community violence are generally examined separately, evidence suggests that a large number of children are exposed to both forms of aggression (DuRant, Cadenhead, Pendergrast, Slavens, & Linder, 1994). Disproportionately high levels of family and community violence have been reported in low-income, urban neighborhoods (Garbarino, Dubrow, Kostelny, & Pardo, 1992; Garbarino, Kostelny, & Dubrow, 1991b). In their study of children exposed to community violence, Richters and Martinez (1993a) found that 50% of the elementary school children sampled were exposed to minor within-family violence and 32% were exposed to severe within-family violence. Osofsky, Wewers, Hann, and Fick (1993) found significant associations between children's exposure to community violence and their experience of family conflict. In a related study of adolescents, it was documented that 86% had witnessed peer violence, 74% had witnessed stranger violence, and 50% had witnessed family violence (Langhinrichsen-Rohling & Neidig, 1995).

Consequences of Exposure to Violence

Conceptual Framework

A multilevel ecological model can be used to examine the impact of children's exposure to family and community violence on various developmental and mental health outcomes. This model suggests there are four major levels that influence children's response to violence: the individual, the family, the community, and the culture. When factors

Table 3.1 Prevalence of Children's Exposure to Community Violence

Study	*Sample Age Ranges*	*Prevalence Rates*
Bell & Jenkins (1991)	elementary school-age children and adolescents	one third witnessed shooting/ stabbing; one quarter adolescents witnessed homicide
Berman, Kurtines, Silverman, & Serafini (1996)	adolescents	93% witnessed some form of violence; 44% were victims
Burton, Foy, Bwanausa, Johnson, & Moore (1994)	adolescents (delinquents only)	71% witnessed gang violence; 56% experienced death of friend; 75% victim of weapon
Campbell & Schwarz (1996)	young adolescents	89% suburban and 96% urban knew victim of violence; 67% urban victims
Dubrow & Garbarino (1989)	preschoolers	100% exposed to shooting
DuRant, Cadenhead, Pendergrast, Slavens, & Linder (1994)	adolescents	85% witnessed and 70% were victims of violent incident; 40% witnessed homicide
Harden (1997)	elementary school-age children	75% witnessed violence
Hausman, Spivak, & Prothrow-Stith (1992)	adolescents	69% witnessed violence; 37% experienced threat
Horowitz, Weine, & Jekel (1995)	adolescents (females only)	65% witnessed shooting; 58% witnessed stabbing; 41% witnessed friend's murder
Marans & Cohen (1993)	elementary school-age children	40% witnessed violence
Osofsky, Wewers, Hann, & Fick (1993)	older elementary school-age children	91% witnessed violence
Richters & Martinez (1993a, 1993b)	elementary school-age children	97% older children & 84% younger children witnessed violence
Saltzman (1992)	elementary school-age children	85% witnessed moderate/ severe violence
Schwab-Stone, Ayers, & Weissberg (1995)	adolescents	40% witnessed shooting/ stabbing
Shahinfar (1997)	preschool-age children	74% (by child's report) and 60% (by parent's report) witnessed violence
Shakoor & Chalmers (1991)	adolescents	75% boys and 70% girls witnessed severe violence
Taylor, Zuckerman, Harik, & McAlister Groves (1994)	preschool-age children	47% exposed to violence

within these levels are stressful, they place children at physical, cognitive, and socioemotional risk. When they are supportive and protective, they facilitate effective coping and positive developmental outcomes. Both risk and protective factors may occur at different levels of the child's ecology (Belsky, 1980; Cicchetti & Lynch, 1993).

Risk factors can be defined as events or characteristics that increase the likelihood of children experiencing adverse life outcomes. At the individual level, examples of risk factors include insecure attachment relationships, low self-esteem, problematic peer relationships, developmental disabilities, and poor school performance (e.g., Wurtele & Miller-Perrin, 1992). At the family level, factors such as marital discord, spousal violence, substance abuse, and parental use of corporal punishment may increase children's vulnerability to violence exposure and subsequent maladaptive behavior (e.g., Rosenbaum & O'Leary, 1981). Among the community level factors thought to place children at risk for violence exposure are poverty, poor housing, unemployment, and the prevalence of drugs and illegal neighborhood activities. Finally, a number of cultural factors may also serve as risk factors for children, including societal acceptance of guns and violence, patriarchal beliefs, male and female socialization practices, violence in the media, and forms of child exploitation such as child pornography (e.g., Straus, Gelles, & Steinmetz, 1980).

Ecological theorists note that risk factors within one level of this system may also influence outcomes at other levels. For example, the combined stress of poverty, crowded housing, and unemployment in urban inner-city neighborhoods may enhance the likelihood of violence in both the family and community. On the basis of cumulative risk research (e.g., Sameroff & Chandler, 1975; Sameroff, Seifer, Barocas, Zax, & Greenspan, 1987), one can speculate that children who are exposed to more risk factors and experience stress at more than one level of the system will be at greatest risk for adverse outcomes in their cognitive, academic, and socioemotional development.

An ecological model also accounts for the protective factors that may mediate some of the negative effects of violence exposure. These protective factors may explain why some children exhibit resilient behavior despite witnessing significant violence within their homes and communities (Cicchetti & Lynch, 1993; Garbarino et al., 1992). Researchers have identified protective factors at various ecological levels that may help to buffer children from maladaptive outcomes associated with violence exposure. These factors include positive parenting behaviors, social support for families, personal and neighborhood safety programs, and developmentally appropriate educational programs that build children's coping skills (e.g., Garbarino et al., 1992; Hendrix & Malloy, 1990). Currently, researchers are exploring both the risk and protective factors associated with various ecological levels and assessing their power in predicting violence exposure and targeted child outcomes.

Linkages in Outcomes of Violence Exposure

The effects of community and family violence exposure are often parallel and synergistic. Both types of violence place children in positions of vulnerability and insecurity. Witnessing familiar adults engaging in aggressive, sometimes fatal confrontations is traumatic for children (Terr, 1991). Research reveals that children may exhibit generalized effects of trauma that are not specific to a specific type of violence exposure (McCloskey, Figueredo, & Koss, 1995; Terr, 1979, 1991).

A number of factors have been found to influence the nature and intensity of children's responses to violence exposure. For example, direct victimization has a more severe impact than witnessing violence (Davis & Carlson, 1987; Hughes, 1988). Gender- and age-related effects have also been noted. Boys exposed to violence are more likely than girls to exhibit violent behaviors (Jenkins, 1996). Children at different ages display different outcomes based on their current stage of development. In addition, children's perception of violence exposure is more predictive of their adjustment than their parents' perception (Grych, Seid, & Fincham, 1992; Richters & Martinez, 1993b). Finally, witnessing intrafamilial violence may be more deleterious than witnessing extrafamilial violence, particularly in the case of younger children (Hughes, 1988).

Contemporary research suggests that the effects of family and community violence are significantly intertwined. There is some evidence that one may beget the other; for example, children exposed to family violence are more likely to engage in extrafamilial assault (Hotaling, Straus, & Lincoln, 1989). Exposure to both forms of violence may exacerbate negative outcomes associated with exposure to only one type. In the landmark study by Richters and Martinez (1993b), children exposed to community violence had lower rates of academic and behavioral adaptation if they also experienced family violence.

Domain-Specific Outcomes

A solid evidentiary base illustrates the myriad ways in which children suffer as a consequence of family and community violence exposure. Every facet of children's development is affected; negative outcomes have been documented in the physical, cognitive/academic, and socioemotional domains. Table 3.2 summarizes the results of many of these outcome studies.

Physical Development. Although less information has been collected about the impact of violence exposure on physical development than on other domains, clinical evidence reveals that some exposed children experience problems with eating, sleeping, and toileting behavior (Drell, Siegel, & Gaensbauer, 1993; Osofsky, 1995). Researchers suggest that infants and toddlers, who face the developmental challenge of physiologic regulation, are particularly vulnerable to the physical effects of violence exposure (Drell et al., 1993). Violence-exposed children have been found to have a higher than average rate of psychosomatic illnesses as well (Stagg, Wills, & Howell, 1989). They may also be the recipients of unintentional injuries during violent confrontations (Christoffel, 1990).

Cognitive/Academic Development. Several studies suggest that cognitive and academic functioning may be compromised in children exposed to family violence (e.g., Moore & Pepler, 1991). There is substantial evidence that adolescents exposed to school and community violence display cognitive and academic deficits (e.g., Gorski & Pilotto, 1993). Preschool and elementary school children exposed to community violence have not been found to exhibit cognitive/academic deficits (e.g., Harden, 1997; Shahinfar, 1997). Developmental delays, which have implications for later cognitive/academic competence, have been found in children exposed to family violence (Westra & Martin, 1981) and community violence (Drell et al., 1993).

Socioemotional Functioning. The bulk of the literature on children's violence exposure addresses this domain of development. The data consistently suggest that exposure to family and community violence produces stress that adversely affects children's mental health. Various psychosocial effects have been documented, including internalizing disorders (i.e., difficulties in the individual's internal state, such as

Table 3.2 Domain-Specific Effects of Exposure to Violence

Effects	*Family Violence Research*	*Community Violence Research*
Physical development		
psychosomatic illnesses	Keronac, Taggart, Lescop, & Fortin, 1986 Moore, Galcius, & Pettican, 1981 Stagg, Wills, & Howell, 1989	
bedwetting/toileting problems		Drell, Siegel, & Gaensbauer, 1993
sleeping disruption		Drell et al., 1993 Pynoos et al., 1987
eating problems; failure to thrive	Moore et al., 1981	Drell et al., 1993 Pynoos et al., 1987
compromised motor skills		Holland, Koblinsky, & Anderson, 1995
Cognitive/academic development		
cognitive difficulties	Westra & Martin, 1981 Hart & Brassard, 1987 Shakoor & Chalmers, 1991	Nuttal & Kalesnik, 1987
verbal/language deficits	Westra & Martin, 1981	Drell et al., 1993
poor achievement	Moore & Pepler, 1991 Pfouts, Schopler, & Henry 1982 Pynoos & Nader, 1988 Carlson, 1984 Richters & Martinez, 1993b Keronac et al., 1986	Bell & Jenkins, 1991
memory/concentration problems		Gorski & Pilotto, 1993 Shakoor & Chalmers, 1991 Nuttal & Kalesnik, 1987

developmental delay	Westra & Martin, 1981 Garbarino, Kostelny, & Dubrow, 1991a, 1991b Drell et al., 1993	Osofsky, 1995
Socioemotional functioning		
traumatic stress symptoms (PTSD)	Silvern, Karyl, & Landis, 1995 Hilton, 1992 Pynoos & Nader, 1990 Pynoos & Eth, 1985	Berton & Stabb, 1996 Campbell & Schwarz, 1996 Singer, Anglin, Song, & Lunghofer, 1995 Burton, Foy, Bwanausa, Johnson, & Moore, 1994 Martinez & Richters, 1993 Fitzpatrick & Boldizar, 1993 Jensen & Shaw, 1993 Pynoos & Nader, 1988
depression	O'Keefe, 1994 Fantuzzo et al., 1991 Christopoulos et al., 1987 Davis & Carlson, 1987 Keronac et al., 1986 Hershorn & Rosenbaum, 1985	Singer et al., 1995 Freeman, Mokros, & Poznanski, 1993 Saltzman, 1992 Fitzpatrick, 1993
anxiety	Fantuzzo et al., 1991 McKay, 1994 Randolf & Conkle, 1993 Hughes, 1988 Davis & Carlson, 1987	Singer et al., 1995 Jensen & Shaw, 1993 Dubrow & Garbarino, 1989 Pynoos et al., 1987
feelings of loss, sadness, guilt	Jaffe, Hurley, & Wolfe, 1990	Pynoos & Nader, 1988
low self-esteem	Hughes, 1988 McKay, 1987, 1994 Elbow, 1982	Rubinetti, 1996

(continued)

Table 3.2 Continued

Effects	*Family Violence Research*	*Community Violence Research*
low empathy	Rosenberg, 1987 Hinchey & Gavelek, 1982	Rubinetti, 1996
emotional intensity	Holden & Ritchie, 1991	Lorion, Brodsky, & Cooley-Quille, in press
withdrawal	Hughes, 1986 Pynoos et al., 1987	Jensen & Shaw, 1993
aggression	Kolbo, Blakely, & Engleman, 1996 O'Keefe, 1994 Sternberg et al., 1994 Randolf & Conkle, 1993 Osofsky, Wewers, Hann, & Fick, 1993 Holden & Ritchie, 1991 Jaffe et al., 1990 Jouriles, Barling, & O'Leary, 1987	Shahinfar, 1997 Hill & Madhere, 1996 Saltzman, 1995 DuRant, Cadenhead, Pendergrast, Slavens, & Linder, 1994 Jensen & Shaw, 1993 Bell & Jenkins, 1991, 1993 Fantuzzo et al., 1991

anxiety), externalizing disorders (i.e., negative behaviors directed toward the environment, such as aggression), and social competence difficulties (i.e., interpersonal problems).

Following the groundbreaking work of Pynoos and colleagues (Pynoos, Fredrick, Nader, Arroyo, et al., 1987; Pynoos & Nader, 1988), researchers have extensively investigated one internalizing problem in violence-exposed children: post-traumatic stress disorder (PTSD). Several studies document that some children exposed to severe family and community violence display symptoms of traumatic stress, such as: re-experiencing of the traumatic event; avoidance of and psychic numbing against potentially traumatic events; and increased arousal including hypervigilance, anxiety, and disrupted physiologic processes (e.g., Drell et al., 1993; Scheeringa, Zeanah, Drell, & Larrieu, 1995; Terr, 1991).

Younger children, as well as female children of all ages, tend to report more PTSD symptomatology than their respective counterparts. Higher levels of traumatic stress in children have been associated with higher academic functioning in children (Harden, 1997), increased parental stress (Martinez & Richters, 1993), severe family conflict (Osofsky et al., 1993), and greater familiarity with the direct victim (Nader, 1989).

Depression and anxiety are internalizing disorders that have been documented disproportionally among children exposed to family violence (e.g., Fantuzzo et al., 1991) and community violence (Osofsky et al., 1993). Negative emotions, such as guilt, shame, anger, and grief, are also more prevalent among violence-exposed children (Osofsky, 1995). Higher rates of these internalizing problems have been associated with female children, older children, and directly victimized children (Sternberg et al., 1994).

Externalizing disorders, such as aggression, are child outcomes reported in studies of family (e.g., Jaffe, Hurley, & Wolfe, 1990) and community violence (e.g., DuRant et al., 1994). Children exposed to violence witness aggression as a chief style of human relatedness and conflict resolution and may imitate the aggressive models they see. Other externalizing disorders that are found among violence-exposed children and adolescents are: (a) conduct disorder (Hershorn & Rosenbaum, 1985), (b) poor impulse control (Lorion et al., in press), and (c) increased activity and restlessness (Cooley-Quille et al., 1995b). Higher rates of externalizing problems have been found among boys and among children who were direct victims of violence (Jouriles, Barling, & O'Leary, 1987).

There is a dearth of data regarding the social relationships of children exposed to family and community violence. The limited evidence available is equivocal and focuses mainly on peer relationships. The peer conflicts experienced by violence-exposed children seem related to their overuse of interpersonal aggression and violence (DuRant et al., 1994).

The Social Ecologies of Violence-Exposed Children

Literature examining the effects of children's exposure to familial and community violence reveals many common patterns of harmful consequences. Such investigations also point to the multiple risk and protective factors that may mediate the effects of violence exposure and contribute to maladaptive or resilient outcomes. Children's responses to violence exposure are influenced both by their individual characteristics and the characteristics of the larger ecologies in which they live, including the family, community, and culture.

Individual Characteristics

There is a paucity of research examining individual attributes of children that mediate the harmful effects of witnessing violence. However, in the family violence arena, one study found that difficult temperamental characteristics, such as emotional intensity and poor adaptability, placed children at risk for negative outcomes (Holden & Ritchie, 1991). Among the protective factors that buffered children from some of the adverse consequences of marital violence exposure were their feelings of self-worth, high sociability, low emotionality, and school competence (O'Keefe, 1994).

Investigations of community violence have also documented mediating factors at the individual level. In a study of preschool children, difficult child temperament was associated with negative outcomes (Shahinfar, 1997). Academic competence was associated with higher levels of stress symptoms in a study of elementary school children (Harden, 1997). As emphasized in the previous section, gender and age are additional individual factors found to influence children's vulnerability to positive or negative effects of violence exposure.

Family Characteristics

The family is the ecological level with the most profound impact on children's development (Bronfenbrenner, 1979). The first and major developmental milestone of childhood is to have a trusting relationship with a parent or adult caregiver who serves as role model, cognitive interpreter of the world, and emotional scaffold (Garbarino, 1995). For children exposed to violence, parents play a pivotal role in children's adjustment. Parents who exhibit positive coping and parenting behaviors may buffer children from the deleterious effects of violence exposure, whereas parents who are themselves traumatized by violence may be unable to help their children manage violence-related stress.

Risk Factors. Several risk factors further compromise the family environments of children exposed to violence. Intrafamilial violence is more likely to occur among impoverished minority families who are coping with the pressures of low socioeconomic status (Gelles & Straus, 1988). Families characterized by interpersonal violence demonstrate less cohesion, adaptability, expressiveness, recreational orientation, organization, control, and independence than their nonviolent counterparts (Christopoulos et al., 1987; Resik & Reese, 1986). Victimized parents may also experience low self-worth, feelings of guilt, and fears for their personal safety (Aguilar & Nightingale, 1994). Such parents may lack the physical or psychological resources to provide protection and nurturance for their children (Elbow, 1982; Hart & Brassard, 1987).

Research on both battered women and their abusive husbands reveals problematic parenting practices, which predict negative outcomes for children. In one study (Holden & Ritchie, 1991), battered women displayed more conflictual interactions, were less attentive, and were less consistent with their children than women free from partner abuse. When compared to nonabusing fathers, abusive fathers were less likely to be involved in parenting, less physically affectionate, and more likely to use physical punishment with their children. Other research reveals a strong association between wife battering and child maltreatment, with child abuse 18 times more likely to occur in homes where there is interparental violence (Straus & Smith, 1990).

The effect of maternal mental health on child functioning is a relatively recent line of inquiry in the family violence field. One survey found that battered women had four times the rate of clinical depression and 5.5 times the number of suicide attempts of nonbattered women

(Straus & Gelles, 1990). Although there is a rich literature on the adverse effects of maternal depression on children (Downey & Coyne, 1990), there is an absence of relevant data in the family violence field. One study addressing this issue did not find a relationship between abused women's mental health and their children's psychological well-being (McCloskey et al., 1995).

Little is known about the family lives of children exposed to community violence. The limited evidence suggests that they are more likely to be poor (Hill & Madhere, 1996) and to exhibit high levels of family conflict (Cooley-Quille et al., 1995b; Osofsky et al., 1993). Anecdotal reports, however, indicate that some parents experience depression, anxiety, denial, and reduced feelings of self-efficacy as a result of their inability to provide safe conditions for their children (e.g., Garbarino et al., 1991a; Lorion & Saltzman, 1993; Osofsky et al., 1993). Such feelings of fear and helplessness may compromise parents' ability to protect children and help them cope with negative life events (Cicchetti & Rizley, 1987).

Protective Factors. In spite of their residence in violent homes and neighborhoods, many parents possess positive parenting and coping skills that can buffer the negative child outcomes generally associated with chronic violence exposure. Although the family violence literature is limited in this area, one study found that parental warmth, nurturance, and support within the family failed to buffer children from the immediate negative effects of marital violence exposure (McCloskey et al., 1995). In interpreting this outcome, the authors noted that previous research illustrating protective effects of positive parenting and close parent-child relationships (e.g., Garmezy, 1981) addressed stress emanating from outside the family, rather than within the family itself.

Parents living in dangerous neighborhoods have adopted a variety of parenting strategies to protect their children from witnessing violence and to reduce the deleterious effects of violence exposure. For example, in one study of elementary school-age children, safe, violence-free, and stable home environments were more predictive of adaptational success (i.e., teacher-rated academic achievement and lack of behavior problems) than exposure to community violence (Richters & Martinez, 1993b). In another investigation of elementary school children exposed to community violence, family social support was found to reduce children's violence-related anxiety (Hill & Madhere, 1996).

A qualitative study of preschool children living in a violent housing project revealed that mothers used active parenting practices to shield their children from community violence (Garbarino et al., 1991a, 1991b). Mothers frequently restricted children's play to their apartments and developed special rules to keep children safe, such as not sitting by windows, staying together at all times, and going to specific locations (e.g., closets) when there was gunfire. Another study of violence-exposed preschool children documented the following strategies used by mothers to increase their children's safety: restricting neighborhood contact with other children and adults, providing close physical supervision, developing a structured home environment, teaching practical safety skills, and prayer (Holland, Koblinsky, & Anderson, 1995).

Community Characteristics

The immediate neighborhood or community is a level of the social ecology from which stress, coping, and support processes emerge (Hill & Madhere, 1996). Neighborhoods with high levels of disorganization, as evidenced by unemployment, crime, and poor housing, affect all residents, including children (Wilson, 1987, 1996). The availability of community supports plays a critical role in facilitating the positive functioning of children living under these circumstances (Garbarino et al., 1992).

Risk Factors. Both family and community violence are more prevalent among families who must also cope with the stressors of poor neighborhoods (Burgess & Draper, 1989; Pfouts, Schopler, & Henley, 1982; Richters & Martinez, 1993b). In a large-scale study of Chicago neighborhoods, concentrated disadvantage was the largest predictor of community violence (Sampson, Raudenbush, & Earls, 1997). Poor communities are often without the personal, financial, and institutional resources that mitigate the deleterious outcomes of violence exposure.

Ethnographic research highlights parents' perceptions of factors contributing to the growth of community violence in low-income neighborhoods. In one study (Kaljee, Stanton, Ricardo, & Whitehead, 1995), respondents reported an increase in male-female relationship violence, group violence, gang activity, the drug trade, the use of firearms, and the victimization of innocent bystanders, as well as a decrease in parental authority and supervision. A qualitative study of resilient mothers in poor neighborhoods found that mothers often distanced themselves from their communities as a defense against violence and other stressors, which seemed to lead to better outcomes for parents and children (Brodsky, 1996). Similarly, Hill and Jones (1997) and Hill and Madhere (1996) found that mothers became more isolated in their communities and refrained from trying to change neighborhood conditions, particularly if they had been personally victimized or had witnessed severe violence.

Research examining community influences on the incidence and outcomes of family violence is conspicuously absent from the literature. There is some evidence that family violence is more likely to occur in communities where families are isolated (Ohlin & Tonry, 1989). Thus, families living in areas characterized by physical or psychological distance between people are more susceptible to interpersonal violence. In addition, batterers are more likely to persist in their violent behavior if they are surrounded by social networks that support this behavior (Fagan, 1990).

Protective Factors. Community involvement can buffer children and families against the negative influences of exposure to family and neighborhood violence. For example, Hill and her colleagues (Hill & Jones, 1997; Hill & Madhere, 1996) found that mothers with some college education used community activism as a strategy for coping with neighborhood violence. In another study, Hill and Madhere (1996) found that contact with supportive people in the community, such as teachers and peers, was associated with social competence among violence-exposed children. Social support has also been found to mediate PTSD symptomatology in violence-exposed children (Berman, Kurtines, Silverman, & Serafini, 1996).

Community institutions, such as schools, Head Start programs, child care centers, and recreational centers provide children a daily respite from the trials of violence exposure (Garbarino et al., 1992; Jones & Better, 1997; Osofsky & Fenichel, 1994). These institutions offer children relationships with adults who are nurturing and limit-setting, as well as enriching, protective environments (Gamache & Snapp, 1995). In one study (Brodsky, 1996), mothers who generally distanced themselves from their violent communities did selectively participate in neighborhood programs that might enhance family protection and development, such as tenant councils, Head Start, or children's program. Such findings suggest that community support networks and secure facilities within the neighborhood can provide a safe haven for children and families who live with violence in their homes and communities (Osofsky & Fenichel, 1994).

Cultural Characteristics

Both culture of violence (Burgess & Draper, 1989) and social learning (Bandura, 1977; Fagan & Wexler, 1987) theories suggest that violence stems from socialization experiences that promote violence as an acceptable behavior. Many scholars have pointed to the overt and insidious ways in which violence is promulgated in American culture. Widespread support for the use of handguns is one such cultural phenomena that is associated with the increase in violence in American homes and neighborhoods (Children's Defense Fund, 1998). The legal support of violence (e.g., capital punishment, unpunished revenge killings) is also perceived to influence Americans' views about the acceptability of violence. Glorification of violence in the media, including the motion picture, television, and music industries, transmits powerful messages sanctioning the use of violence (Huston et al., 1992). Although research on these macro-level issues is difficult to implement, there is a compelling need for information about how children's responses to family and community violence exposure are influenced by these cultural messages.

Interventions for Violence-Exposed Children

As with any service delivery system, interventions for violence-exposed children span a continuum from universal preventive to treatment programs. Universal preventive interventions, which target all children, would naturally benefit violence-exposed children. Treatment interventions address the specific consequences of violence exposure, whether intra- or extrafamilial. Such programs show promise for meeting the needs of this vulnerable population of children. Using ecological theory as a framework, these prevention and intervention approaches can be examined at the individual, family, community, and cultural levels.

Individual-Level Approaches

Although interventions at the individual level are premised on the need for children to adjust to their environment, most scholars and practitioners emphasize that providing physical safety is the primary goal of any intervention for children (Osofsky & Fenichel, 1994). Clearly, this is difficult to accomplish with children exposed to violence, particularly when moving the child is impossible or may be traumatic in its own right. Nevertheless, the goal of maintaining or obtaining physical safety for children should remain paramount.

Mental Health Programs. Many clinicians have used individual psychological treatment, play therapy for young children, and verbal therapies for older children and adolescents to address the aftermath of exposure to family and community violence (e.g., Elbow, 1982; Pynoos & Nader, 1987; Terr, 1991). Silvern and colleagues (Silvern & Kaersvang, 1989; Silvern, Karyl, & Landis, 1995) have proposed a framework for individual treatment of children who witness violence. The treatment goal is to help the child symbolically act out the trauma and then explicitly discuss the child's cognitive and affective experience of the actual event. Strategies employed with this therapeutic model include: assessment and treatment of post-trauma symptomatology, facilitating disclosure about the event, desensitization to and cognitive restructuring of the traumatic event, and interpretation of the meaning of symbolic play.

Pynoos and colleagues (1987) have conducted a psychological "first-aid" program to treat children and adolescents who have been exposed to family and community violence. Guided by a developmental framework, this approach aims to restore a sense of security and to facilitate psychological "working through" of the traumatic experience for children. The child is provided with immediate respite from the trauma and with support from a nurturing, protective adult. Treatment helps children affectively label their reactions, verbalize their feelings, hold on to positive memories, talk and act out their experiences of the trauma, and refrain from impulsive acts. The therapist provides explanations for the violent event, tolerates the child's regression, and helps the child cope with the trauma by doing something constructive for the victims.

School-Based Interventions. School programs have shown promise for ameliorating the consequences of violence exposure among preschool and school-age youngsters. Hendrix and Malloy (1990) grouped school-based interventions in the following categories: cognitive mediation, self-esteem enhancement, anger management, conflict resolution and communication skill building, and prevention of bullying. Some programs incorporate objectives and draw activities from several of these categories. An example is Choosing Non-Violence, a program for young children used in Chicago's Head Start and child care programs (Parry, 1993). Teachers and parents work with young children to help them understand violence and its consequences, empower them to determine how they will treat others and be treated by others, and facilitate their use of language to express feelings and protect themselves nonviolently.

Some early intervention programs specifically focus on the prevention of children's later use of violence against others. The FAST Track program (Conduct Problems Prevention Research Group, 1992) targets kindergarten children with behavioral problems. A comprehensive intervention model is employed that includes social skills training, academic tutoring, teacher-based classroom intervention, and family supports. Early childhood programs, such as Head Start, have been found to prevent the later emergence of conduct problems (Zigler, Taussig, & Black, 1992). By putting emphasis on developing children's socioemotional competence and involving parents in children's educational experiences, these programs are viewed as major contributors to such positive behavioral outcomes in children.

For school-age children and adolescents, universal prevention programs have been conducted at the classroom level. One example is an elementary-school interdisciplinary program that is a component of a comprehensive health education effort (Weiler & Dorman, 1995). Lessons regarding violence are incorporated in each subject area, and children are encouraged to discuss their perceptions of and experiences with violence. Another example is a violence prevention curriculum designed for adolescents that includes sessions on anger, violence, and conflict resolution (Prothrow-Stith, 1991). This curriculum has been found to reduce conflicts between adolescent participants.

Other programs for adolescents are comprehensive, with a goal of reducing several risky behaviors, such as premature sexuality, substance abuse, school failure, delinquency, and interpersonal violence (Kazdin, 1993). Such programs often provide an array of services, including social skills training, mediation and conflict resolution, behavior management, peer group activities, tutoring, and counseling (Guerra, Tolan, & Hammond, 1994; Mendel, 1995; Weist & Warner, in press).

Psychoeducational Programs. Psychoeducational groups for the children of battered spouses have been implemented and evaluated. Jaffe and colleagues (Jaffe, Wilson, & Wolfe, 1986) designed a direct instruction group intervention with three major goals: changing children's use of violence as a strategy to cope with anger and resolve conflict, promoting children's use of personal safety skills and community resources, and teaching children to attribute responsibility for violence to the appropriate party. An evaluation of this approach revealed an increase in children's safety skills and positive perceptions of their parents (Jaffe, Wilson, & Wolfe, 1986). An evaluation of the same intervention conducted by another group of scholars (Wagar & Rodway, 1995) found that children adopted more appropriate anger strategies and did not shoulder responsibility for violence they did not perpetrate.

Many violence prevention programs for adolescents employ a group model. For example, Wolfe, Wekerle, Reitzel, and Gough (1995) conducted a 16-week psychoeducational intervention focused on intrafamilial violence with the goals of: increasing awareness of attitudes about women and violence; promoting noncontrolling, nonviolent communication skills; and increasing interpersonal competency through community involvement and social action. This intervention had a positive influence on adolescents' attitudes about violence and communication skills.

Psychoeducational programs for adolescents have targeted community violence as well. Greene (1993) advocates that interventions for adolescents exposed to pervasive community violence should be comprehensive and entail eight components: street outreach, assessment of needs and interests, facilitation of supportive relationships with adults, accessibility of role models, peer group discussions, family-level interventions, neighborhood projects, and education and employment training.

Family-Level Approaches

Family-focused interventions addressing children's violence exposure are designed to support caregivers in their roles as protectors of children. Caregivers are helped to create a violence-free home environment for children and to serve as buffers when children do experience violence. Sometimes, this means relocating the family to a shelter or other safehouse away from the perpetrators of violence (Saunders & Azar, 1989). For both family and community violence, family-based interventions entail providing psychological support to families as they attempt to cope with their violent experiences.

Family therapy and family systems intervention may benefit children and parents exposed to intrafamilial and extrafamilial violence (Bell & Jenkins, 1993; Greene, 1993; Saunders & Azar, 1989). Ameliorating violence within the family system may be accomplished by reducing parental stress and anger through counseling, support, and education regarding stress/anger management skills and parenting (Hendrix & Malloy, 1990; Mendel, 1995). Providing parents of children exposed to community violence with instruction in the areas of personal mastery and safety education may lead to more positive outcomes for these families (Osofsky & Fenichel, 1996). Similarly, therapeutic services for adults may enhance personal well-being, coping with daily living and trauma, and the capacity to parent children effectively (Osofsky & Fenichel, 1996). Individual therapy for battering spouses may help them refrain from using violence in their interactions with their families (Ohlin & Tonry, 1989).

Parent education is another family-centered approach with direct implications for children exposed to violence. Parenting interventions can increase parents' knowledge about their children's development, including the effects of family and community violence on children's functioning (Holland et al., 1995). Parent education can also instruct parents on how to protect their children and help them cope with violence-related stress. Educating parents about conflict resolution and appropriate disciplinary practices has also been found to improve parenting skills and facilitate positive parent-child interaction (Patterson, 1982).

Bilinkoff (1995) offers a unique approach to intervening with parents who are battered women. Based on a feminist empowerment philosophy, this model encourages mothers to: balance the nurturing and work roles of parenting, avoid power-control strategies in parenting, create new family rituals, overcome financial challenges, and seek extended family support. Parenting groups for men who batter have also been conducted (Mathews, 1995). Such interventions foster fathers' understanding of child development, awareness of how their violent behavior affects their children, and development of parenting/discipline strategies that are less reliant on power-control techniques.

Grassroots organizations have sprouted in several communities across the country to support parents of children exposed to community violence. These organizations adopt Anonymous Group models to enable victims of violence to provide peer support to other victims of violence. The Save Our Sons and Daughters (SOSAD) group provides support and crisis intervention not only for parents whose children have been injured or killed by community violence, but also for parents of children exposed to violence (Osofsky & Fenichel, 1994).

Parent-child therapy is another approach that may be effective in ameliorating the consequences of violence exposure (Davies, 1991; Osofsky & Fenichel, 1994, 1996). This relationship-based approach capitalizes on the attachment experience between parent and child. The therapist supports the parent (usually the mother) in understanding the child's behavior as an outgrowth of his/her violence exposure and in facilitating the child's "working through" the trauma through symbolic play. Mothers are encouraged to observe their young children and to talk about how their perception of their children may be based on past relationships (e.g., son looks/acts like father who battered mother). Evaluations of this approach with general high-risk populations have shown promise (Pawl & Lieberman, 1993).

Family support programs represent still another preventive intervention that may benefit violence-affected families. Such programs serving populations affected by family violence have incorporated services such as groups for battered women and perpetrators of violence (Schorr, 1989). Comprehensive family support programs, which often include parent education, mentoring, and mental health services, strengthen the parents of young children so they will be more self-sufficient and emotionally available to their children. Such interventions have been found to reduce later conduct difficulties in children (Yoshikawa, 1994).

Community-Level Approaches

Interventions targeted at the community are crucial for the eradication of community violence and its negative effects on children. Given scholars' and practitioners' contentions that the roots of family violence are in the larger society, efforts to eradicate it should emanate from and be targeted toward the community (Walker, 1993). Escalating crime rates have precipitated a move toward community empowerment focused on preserving safety in the street and within the home (Whitman, 1988).

Community intervention is an integral component of the "psychological first-aid" treatment advocated by Pynoos and Nader (1988) to address the aftermath of acute violent incidents (e.g., sniper attacks).

Such intervention includes screening for adverse outcomes across the community, collaboration with community leaders, provision of psychological services near or at the site of the violence, and efforts to restore the community's sense of safety, organization, and connectedness.

Community-based policing is another important strategy for addressing the consequences of both family and community violence for children (Manning, 1989). A program in New Haven, Connecticut, has revealed how collaboration between a local police department and a mental health entity can result in more effective approaches to working with children traumatized by violence (Marans & Cohen, 1993). The Yale Child Study Center provides weekly educational, interactive sessions for a 10-week period to teach new police officers about child development and mental health. Child development fellowships are also available for supervising officers, who participate in more advanced child development and mental health courses. Case conferences and a 24-hour consultation service enable police officers to obtain assistance on particularly challenging cases.

Community programs have also been developed to prevent adolescent violence and peer conflict, as well as to help adolescents cope with these experiences (Guerra et al., 1994). Community supports that foster positive outcomes for youth, such as peer activities, educational and employment experiences, conflict-resolution training, and increased adult involvement with adolescents exist in many urban areas (Mendel, 1995).

Sports and recreation programs in the community not only provide a safe haven for participating children but also offer the structure many adolescents need to avoid and/or cope with violence (National Recreation and Parks Association, 1994). More directly, mentorship and rites of passage programs provide the role models and adult nurturing relationships that help adolescents overcome the negative effects of violence exposure. In work with adolescents exposed to violence, Greene (1993) employs street outreach, referrals to other services, and neighborhood projects to connect with and enhance the functioning of this population.

Collaborations between community-based institutions have great potential for enhancing outcomes for violence-exposed children. As noted earlier, there has been wide support for the use of various community institutions as safe havens for children exposed to intra- and extrafamilial violence. Advocacy for children of battered women (Hughes & Marshall, 1995) and for children exposed to community violence (Osofsky & Fenichel, 1994) may likewise be provided by community agencies and volunteer groups to access a wide range of community resources for affected children and families.

The inevitable linkage between child welfare and family violence services has been met with some controversy (Echlin & Marshall, 1995), given the tendency to remove children from their homes, rather than the violent perpetrator. More child- and family-sensitive approaches within the child welfare system have been advocated by practitioners, such as family preservation programs, safe houses for children and the battered spouse, and visitation centers (Peled & Edleson, 1995).

Cultural-Level Approaches

On the cultural level, large-scale awareness campaigns can be mounted in an effort to eradicate the effects of family and community violence. The power of the media can be harnessed to modify children's views about the power and effectiveness of violence. Friedlander (1993) discusses the use of television, music, movies, and other mass media to provide nonviolent images to children and adolescents. Public events that focus on violence and are held in high schools have been found to reshape how adolescents think about violence in their lives (Sudermann, Jaffe, & Hastings, 1995).

Another important cultural intervention concerns raising public awareness about the impact of laws supporting violence on children's well-being. Public pressure in many states and localities has led to more stringent laws protecting victims of intrafamilial violence and punishing perpetrators (Maguigan, 1991). The Children's Defense Fund and similar groups attempt to educate citizens about the human costs accompanying the decline in gun control and persistently advocate for legislation that safeguards children's physical and mental health.

Characteristics of Effective Interventions

Whether interventions are offered at the child, family, community, or cultural level, children need intensive support as they traverse the violent contexts in which they live. Exposure to family and community violence represents trauma for children and should be treated as such. Intervention programs should be designed to target children exposed to both forms of violence and to address the general psychological aftermath of the violent experience. They should be immediate, individualized to meet the unique needs of the children, and focused on creating and maintaining child safety. Interventions for children should facilitate their access to adult caregivers who can nurture and support them, as they try to overcome the consequences of the violence they have experienced.

Another key characteristic of effective interventions for violence-exposed children is comprehensiveness. Comprehensive interventions employ a multilevel, multipronged approach to address the needs of the child, family, and community affected by violence. Such programs include psychological treatment, enhancement of informal and formal group relationships, advocacy, and family and community empowerment services. They are based on the premise that collaborative efforts increase the likelihood of success in reducing violent behavior. Collaborative partners may come from the police department, recreation programs, legal services, mental health programs, community advocacy groups, health facilities, schools, churches, and other community institutions.

High-quality interventions for violence-exposed children are also developmentally appropriate. They are consistent with the cognitive capability of the target children and designed with the understanding that violence affects children differently at different developmental stages. As in other areas of child development, it has been suggested that interventions introduced early in children's lives and in their experience of violence exposure will result in more persistently positive outcomes (Lorion et al., in press).

Concluding Remarks

This chapter has argued for a more integrated approach to children's violence exposure due to the complexity of family and community violence and their effects on children. Just as there are multiple pathways to development, there are multiple contributors to how children ultimately cope with violent experiences. Risk and protective factors unrelated to the violence can influence the outcomes of children who have been exposed to violence.

Poverty is one such risk factor that has an adverse effect on children across domains. Not only does poverty increase the likelihood that children will experience violent events, it also exacerbates the consequences of violence exposure (Wilson, 1987, 1996). Thus, poor children exposed to violence are the most vulnerable to negative outcomes. They often live with the constant threat of violence in their homes and communities and have few options for safety and support.

In contrast, a strong protective factor for children in violent environments is the child's intimate relationship with a caring adult. Parents and other caregivers have a significant influence on how children perceive and cope with violent experiences. Thus, it is crucial that the family environment serve as a safe haven for children. Stressors outside the family, such as community violence, appear more amenable to parental buffering than interior stressors such as interparental violence (e.g., McCloskey et al., 1995).

Clearly, all children who witness family and community violence are vulnerable to deleterious outcomes, even if they are not the direct targets of aggression. Our society, which promulgates violence in so many overt and insidious ways, must assume greater responsibility for the innocent victims of family and community violence. Resources from the public and private sectors should be marshaled for interventions that protect children and help them overcome the trauma emanating from violence exposure. Equally important, a national campaign should be launched to reduce the acceptance and prevalence of violence in our culture so that children may grow up in the safe, secure environments that are essential for their optimal development.

References

Aguilar, R., & Nightingale, N. (1994). The impact of specific battering experiences on the self-esteem of abused women. *Journal of Family Violence, 9*(1), 35-45.

Arroyo, W., & Eth, S. (1995). Assessment following violence-witnessing trauma. In E. Peled, P. G. Jaffe, & J. Edleson (Eds.), *Ending the cycle of violence: Community responses to children of battered women.* Thousand Oaks, CA: Sage.

Bandura, A. (1977). *Social learning theory.* Englewood Cliffs, NJ: Prentice Hall.

Bell, C., & Jenkins, E. (1991). Traumatic stress and children. *Journal of Health Care for the Poor and Underserved, 2*(1), 175-188.

Bell, C., & Jenkins, E. (1993). Community violence and children on Chicago's southside. *Psychiatry, 56,* 46-54.

Belsky, J. (1980). Child maltreatment: An ecological integration. *American Psychologist, 35,* 320-335.

Berman, S., Kurtines, W., Silverman, W., & Serafini, L. (1996). The impact of crime and violence on urban youth. *American Journal of Orthopsychiatry, 66*(3), 329-336.

Berton, M., & Stabb, S. (1996). Exposure to violence and post-traumatic stress disorder in urban adolescents. *Adolescence, 31*(122), 489-498.

Bilinkoff, J. (1995). Empowering battered women as mothers. In E. Peled, P. Jaffe, & J. Edleson (Eds.), *Ending the cycle of violence: Community responses to children of battered women.* Thousand Oaks, CA: Sage.

Brodsky, A. (1996). Resilient mothers in risky neighborhoods: Negative psychological sense of community. *Journal of Community Psychology, 24*(4), 346-347.

Bronfenbrenner, U. (1979). *The ecology of human development: Experiments by nature and design.* Cambridge, MA: Harvard University Press.

Burgess, R., & Draper, P. (1989). The explanation of family violence: The role of biological, behavioral, and cultural selection. In L. Ohlin & M. Tonry (Eds.), *Family violence.* Chicago: University of Chicago.

Burman, S., & Allen-Meares, P. (1994). Neglected victims of murder: Children's witness to parental homicide. *Social Work, 39*(1), 28-34.

Burton, D., Foy, D., Bwanausa, C., Johnson, J., & Moore, L. (1994). The relationship between traumatic exposure to family dysfunctions and posttraumatic stress symptoms in male juvenile offenders. *Journal of Traumatic Stress, 7*(1), 83-93.

Campbell, C., & Schwarz, D. (1996). Prevalence and impact of exposure to interpersonal violence among suburban and urban middle school students. *Pediatrics, 98*(3), 396-402.

Carlson, B. (1984). Children's observations of interparental violence. In A. Roberts (Ed.), *Battered women and their families: Intervention strategies and treatment programs* (pp. 147-167). New York: Springer.

Children's Defense Fund. (1998). *The state of America's children yearbook, 1997.* Washington, DC: Author.

Christoffel, K. (1990). Violent death and injury in U.S. children and adolescents. *American Journal of Disease Control, 144,* 697-706.

Christopoulos, C., Cohn, D., Shaw, D., Joyce, S., Sullivan-Hanson, J., Kraft, S., & Emery, R. (1987). Children of abused women: I. Adjustment at time of shelter residence. *Journal of Marriage and the Family, 49,* 611-619.

Cicchetti, D., & Lynch, M. (1993). Toward an ecological/transactional model of community violence and child maltreatment: Consequences for children's development [Special Issue: Children and violence]. *Psychiatry, 56*(1), 96-118.

Cicchetti, D., & Rizley, R. (1987). Developmental perspectives on the etiology, intergenerational transmission, and sequelae of child maltreatment. In R. Rizley & D. Cicchetti (Eds.), *Developmental perspectives on child maltreatment.* San Francisco: Jossey-Bass.

Cicchetti, D., & Toth, S. (Eds.). (1993). *Child abuse, child development, and social policy.* Norwood, NJ: Ablex.

Cooley-Quille, M., Turner, S., & Beidel, D. (1995a). Assessing community violence: The children's report of exposure to violence. *American Academy of Child and Adolescent Psychiatry, 34*(2), 201-208.

Cooley-Quille, M., Turner, S., & Beidel, D. (1995b). Emotional impact of children's exposure to community violence: A preliminary study. *Journal of the American Academy of Child and Adolescent Psychiatry, 34*(10), 1362-1368.

Davies, D. (1991). Intervention with male toddlers who have witnessed parental violence. *Families in Society, 72*(9), 515-524.

Davis, L., & Carlson, B. (1987). Observation of spouse abuse: What happens to the children? *Journal of Interpersonal Violence, 2*(3), 278-291.

Downey, G., & Coyne, J. (1990). Children of depressed parents: An integrative review. *Psychological Bulletin, 108*(1), 50-76.

Drell, M., Siegel, C., & Gaensbauer, T. (1993). Post-traumatic stress disorder. In C. Zeanah (Ed.), *Handbook of infant mental health.* New York: Guilford.

Dubrow, N., & Garbarino, J. (1989). Living in the war zone: Mothers and young children in a public housing development. *Child Welfare, 89*(1), 3-18.

DuRant, R., Cadenhead, C., Pendergrast, R., Slavens, G., & Linder, C. (1994). Factors associated with the use of violence among black adolescents. *American Journal of Public Health, 84*(4), 612-617.

Echlin, C., & Marshall, L. (1995). Child protection services for children of battered women: Practice and controversy. In E. Peled, P. Jaffe, & J. Edleson (Eds.), *Ending the cycle of violence: Community responses to children of battered women.* Thousand Oaks, CA: Sage.

Elbow, M. (1982). Children of violent marriages: The forgotten victims. *Social Casework, 63*(8), 465-417.

Emde, R. (1993). The horror! The horror! Reflections on our culture of violence and its implications for early development and morality [Special Issue: Children and Violence]. *Psychiatry, 56*(1).

Fagan, J. (1990). Contributions of research to criminal justice policy on wife assault. In D. Besharov (Ed.), *Family violence: Research and public policy issues.* New York: American Enterprise.

Fagan, J., & Wexler, S. (1987). Crime at home and in the streets: The relationship between family and stranger violence. *Violence and victims, 2,* 5-23.

Fantuzzo, J., Boruch, R., Beriama, A., Atkins, M., & Marcus, S. (1997). Domestic violence and children: Prevalence and risk in five major U.S. cities. *Journal of the American Academy of Child and Adolescent Psychiatry, 36*(1), 116-122.

Fantuzzo, J., DePaola, L., Lambert, L., Martino, T., Anderson, G., & Sutton, S. (1991). Effects of interparental violence on the psychological adjustment and competencies of young children. *Journal of Consulting and Clinical Psychology, 59*(2), 258-265.

Farrington, D. (1991). Childhood aggression and adult violence: Early precursors and later life outcomes. In D. Pepler & K. Rubin (Eds.), *The development and treatment of childhood aggression.* Hillsdale, NJ: Lawrence Erlbaum.

Fitzpatrick, K. (1993). Exposure to violence and presence of depression among low-income African-American youth. *Journal of Consulting and Clinical Psychology, 61*(3), 528-531.

Fitzpatrick, K., & Boldizar, J. (1993). The prevalence and consequences of exposure to violence among African-American youth. *Journal of the American Academy of Child and Adolescent Psychiatry, 32*(2), 424-430.

Freeman, L., Mokros, H., & Poznanski, E. (1993). Violent events reported by urban school-aged children: Characteristics and depression correlates. *Journal of the American Academy of Child and Adolescent Psychiatry, 32,* 419-423.

Friedlander, B. (1993). Community violence, children's development, and mass media: In pursuit of new insights, new goals, and new strategies [Special Issue: Children and Violence]. *Psychiatry: Interpersonal and Biological Processes, 56*(1), 66-87.

Furlong, M., & Smith, D. (1994). *Anger, hostility, and aggression: Assessment, prevention, and intervention strategies for youth.* Brandon, VT: Clinical Psychology.

Gamache, D., & Snapp, S. (1995). Teach your children well: Elementary schools and violence prevention. In E. Peled, P. Jaffe, & J. Edleson (Eds.), *Ending the cycle of violence: Community responses to children of battered women.* Thousand Oaks, CA: Sage.

Garbarino, J. (1995). The American war zone: What children can tell us about living with violence. *Developmental and Behavioral Pediatrics, 16*(6), 431-435.

Garbarino, J., Dubrow, N., Kostelny, K., & Pardo, C. (1992). *Children in danger.* San Francisco, CA: Jossey-Bass.

Garbarino, J., Kostelny, K., & Dubrow, N. (1991a). *No place to be a child.* Lexington, MA: Lexington Press.

Garbarino, J., Kostelny, K., & Dubrow, N. (1991b). What children can tell us about living in danger. *American Psychologist, 46*(4), 376-383.

Garmezy, N. (1981). Children under stress: Perspectives on antecedents and correlates of vulnerability and resistance to psychopathology. In A. Rabin, J. Aronoff, A. Barclay, & R. Zucker (Eds.), *Further explorations in personality.* New York: Wiley-Interscience.

Gelles, R. (1987). *Family violence.* Newbury Park, CA: Sage.

Gelles, R., & Straus, M. (1988). *Intimate violence.* New York: Simon & Schuster.

Gerbner, G. (1994). *Violence and drugs on television: The cultural environment approach to prevention.* Philadelphia: Annenberg School for Communication.

Gorski, J., & Pilotto, L. (1993) Interpersonal violence among youth: A challenge for school personnel [Special Issue: School related health and safety]. *Educational Psychology Review, 5*(1), 35-61.

Greenberg, M., Kusche, C., Cook, E., & Quamma, J. (1995). Promoting emotional competence in school-aged children: The effects of PATHS curriculum. *Development and Psychopathology, 7,* 117-136.

Greene, M. (1993). Chronic exposure to violence and poverty: Interventions that work for youth. *Crime and Delinquency, 39*(1), 106-124.

Grych, J., Seid, M., & Fincham, F. (1992). Assessing marital conflict from the child's perspective: The Children's Perception of Interpersonal Conflict Scale. *Child Development, 63,* 558-572.

Guerra, N., Tolan, P., & Hammond, R. (1994). Prevention and treatment of adolescent violence. In L. Eron, J. Gentry, & P. Schlegal (Eds.), *Reason to hope: A psychosocial perspective on violence and youth.* Washington, DC: American Psychological Association.

Harden, B. (1997). *The role of the educational context in children's experience of community violence.* Manuscript submitted for publication.

Hart, S., & Brassard, M. (1987). A major threat to children's mental health: Psychological maltreatment. *American Psychologist, 42,* 160-165.

Hausman, A., Spivak, H., & Prothrow-Stith, D. (1992). Patterns of teen exposure to a community-based violence prevention project. *Journal of Adolescent Health, 13*(8), 668.

Hendrix, K., & Malloy, P. (1990). *Interventions in early childhood.* Atlanta, GA: Centers for Disease Control.

Hershorn, M., & Rosenbaum, A. (1985). Children of marital violence: A closer look at the unintended victims. *American Journal of Orthopsychiatry, 55*(2), 260-266.

Hill, H., & Jones, L. (1997). Children's and parents' perceptions of children's exposure to violence in urban neighborhoods. *Journal of the National Medical Association, 89*(4), 270-276.

Hill, H., & Madhere, S. (1996). Exposure to community violence and African-American children: A multidimensional model of risks and resources. *Journal of Community Psychology, 24,* 26-43.

Hilton, N. (1992). Battered women's concerns about their children witnessing wife assault. *Journal of Interpersonal Violence, 7,* 77-86.

Hinchey, F., & Gavelek, J. (1982). Empathic responding in children of battered mothers. *Child Abuse & Neglect, 6,* 395-401.

Holden, G., & Ritchie, K. (1991). Linking extreme marital discord, child rearing, and child behavior problems: Evidence from battered women. *Child Development, 62,* 311-327.

Holland, C., Koblinsky, S., & Anderson, E. (1995). *Maternal strategies for protecting Head Start children from community violence: Implications for family-focused violence education programs.* Paper presented at the National Head Start Association Annual Meeting, Washington, DC.

Horowitz, K., Weine, S., & Jekel, J. (1995). PTSD symptoms in urban adolescent girls: Compounded community trauma. *Journal of the American Academy of Child and Adolescent Psychiatry, 34*(10), 1353-1361.

Hotaling, G., Straus, M., & Lincoln, A. (1989). Intrafamily violence and crime and violence outside the family. In L. Ohlin & M. Tonry (Eds.), *Family violence.* Chicago: University of Chicago Press.

Hughes, H. (1986). Research with children in shelters: Implications for clinical services. *Children Today,* 21-25.

Hughes, H. (1988). Psychological and behavioral correlates of family violence in child witnesses and victims. *American Journal of Orthopsychiatry, 58*(1), 77-88.

Hughes, H., & Barad, S. (1983). Psychological functioning of children in a battered women's shelter: A preliminary investigation. *American Journal of Orthopsychiatry, 53*(3), 525-531.

Hughes, H., & Marshall, M. (1995). Advocacy for children of battered women. In E. Peled, P. Jaffe, & J. Edleson (Eds.), *Ending the cycle of violence: Community responses to children of battered women.* Thousand Oaks, CA: Sage.

Hughes, H., Parkinson, D., & Vargo, M. (1989). Witnessing spouse abuse and experiencing physical abuse: A "Double Whammy"? *Journal of Family Violence, 4*(2), 197-208.

Huston, A., Donnerstein, E., Fairchild, H., Fesbach, N., Katz, P., Murray, J., Rubinstein, B., Wilcox, B., & Zuckerman, D. (1992). *Big world, small screen: The role of television in American society.* Lincoln: University of Nebraska Press.

Jaffe, P., Hurley, D., & Wolfe, D. (1990). Children's observations of violence: I. Critical issues in child development and intervention planning [Special Issue: Child psychiatry]. *Canadian Journal of Psychiatry, 35*(6), 466-470.

Jaffe, P., Wilson, S., & Wolfe, D. A. (1986). Promoting changes in attitudes and understanding of conflict resolution among child victims and witnesses of family violence. *Canadian Journal of Behavioral Science, 18*(4), 356-366.

Jaffe, P., Wolfe, D., Wilson, S., & Zak, L. (1986). Similarities in behavioral and social maladjustment among child victims and witnesses to family violence. *American Journal of Orthopsychiatry, 56*(1), 142-146.

Jenkins, P. (1996). Threads that link community and family violence. In R. Hampton, P. Jenkins, & T. Gullotta (Eds.), *Preventing violence in America.* Thousand Oaks, CA: Sage.

Jensen, P., & Shaw, J. (1993). Children as victims of war: Current knowledge and future research needs. *Journal of the American Academy of Child and Adolescent Psychiatry, 32*(4), 697-708.

Jones, B., & Better, M. (1997). *The implementation and evaluation of a preschool violence prevention project.* Paper presented at the Biennial Meeting of the Society for Research in Child Development, Washington, DC.

Jouriles, E., Barling, J., & O'Leary, K. (1987). Predicting child behavior problems in maritally violent families. *Journal of Abnormal Child Psychology, 15*(2), 165-173.

Kaljee, L., Stanton, B., Ricardo, L., & Whitehead, T. (1995). Urban African American adolescents and their parents: Perceptions of violence within and against their communities. *Human Organization, 54*(4), 373-382.

Kashani, J. et al., (1992). Family violence: Impact on children. *Journal of the American Academy of Child and Adolescent Psychiatry, 31*(2), 181-189.

Kazdin, A. (1993). Adolescent mental health: Prevention and treatment programs. *American Psychologist, 48*(2), 127-141.

Keronac, S., Taggart, M., Lescop, J., & Fortin, M. (1986). Dimensions of health in violent families. *Health Care for Women International, 7,* 413-426.

Kolbo, J., Blakely, E., & Engleman, D. (1996). Children who witness domestic violence: A review of empirical literature. *Journal of Interpersonal Violence, 11*(2), 281-293.

Langhinrichsen-Rohlin, J., & Neidig, P. (1995). Violent backgrounds of economically disadvantaged youth: Risk factors for perpetrating violence? *Journal of Family Violence, 10*(4), 379-397.

Leavitt, L., & Fox, N. (Eds.). (1993). *The psychological effects of war and violence on children.* Hillsdale, NJ: Lawrence Erlbaum.

Loeber, R. (1982). The stability of antisocial and delinquent child behavior: A review. *Child Development, 53,* 1431-1446.

Lorion, R., Brodsky, A., & Cooley-Quille, M. (in press). Exposure to pervasive community violence: Resisting the contaminating effects of risky settings. In D. Biegel & A. Blum (Eds.), *Innovations in practice and service delivery across the lifespan.* New York: Oxford University Press.

Lorion, R., & Saltzman, W. (1993). Children's exposure to community violence: Following a path from concern to research to action [Special Issue: Children and Violence]. *Psychiatry, 56,* 55-65.

Maguigan, H. (1991). Battered women and self-defense: Myths and misconceptions in current reform proposals. *University of Pennsylvania Law Review, 140,* 379-486.

Manning, P. (1989). Community policing. In R. Dunham & G. Alpert (Eds.), *Critical issues in policing.* Prospect Heights, IL: Waveland.

Marans, S., & Cohen, D. (1993). Children and inner-city violence: Strategies for intervention. In L. Leavitt & N. Fox (Eds.), *The psychological effects of war and violence on children.* Hillsdale, NJ: Lawrence Erlbaum.

Martinez, P., & Richters, J. (1993). The NIMH community violence project: II. Children's distress symptoms associated with violence exposure. [Special issue: Children and Violence]. *Psychiatry, 56*(1), 782-788.

Mathews, D. (1995). Parenting groups for men who batter. In E. Peled, P. Jaffe, & J. Edleson (Eds.), *Ending the cycle of violence: Community responses to children of battered women.* Thousand Oaks, CA: Sage.

McCloskey, L., Figueredo, A., & Koss, M. (1995). The effects of systemic family violence on children's mental health. *Child Development, 66,* 1239-1261.

McKay, E. (1987). *Children of battered women.* Paper presented at the Third National Family Violence Conference, Durham, NH.

McKay, M. (1994). The link between domestic violence and child abuse: Assessment and treatment considerations. *Child Welfare, 73,* 29-39.

Mendel, R. (1995). *Prevention or pork? A hard-headed look at youth-oriented anti-crime programs.* American Youth Policy Forum.

Moore, J., Galcius, A., & Pettican, K. (1981). Emotional risk to children caught in violent marital conflict: The Basildon treatment project. *Child Abuse and Neglect, 5,* 147-152.

Moore, T., & Pepler, D. (1991). *Children at risk within violent and transient families.* Paper presented at the Biennial Meeting of the Society for Research in Child Development, Seattle, WA.

Nader, K. (1989). Childhood post-traumatic stress reaction: A response to violence. *Dissertation Abstracts International, 51,* 4272B.

National Recreation and Parks Association. (1994). *Beyond fun and games: Emerging roles of public recreation.* Arlington, VA: Author.

Nuttal, E., & Kalesnik, J. (1987). Personal violence in the schools: The role of the counselor. *Journal of Counseling and Development, 65,* 372-375.

Office of Juvenile Justice and Delinquency Prevention. (1993). *Juveniles taken into custody, 1992.* Washington, DC: U.S. Department of Justice.

Ohlin, L., & Tonry, M. (1989). Family violence in perspective. In L. Ohlin & M. Tonry (Eds.). *Family violence.* Chicago, IL: University of Chicago Press.

O'Keefe, M. (1994). Racial/ethnic differences among battered women and their children. *Journal of Child and Family Studies, 3*(3), 283.

O'Leary, K., Curley, A., Rosenbaum, A., & Clarke, C. (1985). Asserting training for abused wives: A potentially hazardous treatment. *Journal of Marital and Family Therapy, 11*(3), 319-322.

Osofsky, J. (1995). The effects of exposure to violence on young children. *American Psychologist, 50*(9), 782-788.

Osofsky, J., & Fenichel, E. (Eds.) (1994). *Caring for infants and toddlers in violent environments: Hurt, healing, and hope.* Arlington, VA: Zero to Three/National Center for Clinical Infant Programs.

Osofsky, J., & Fenichel, E. (Eds.). (1996). *Islands of safety: Assessing and treating young victims of violence.* Arlington, VA: Zero to Three/National Center for Clinical Infant Programs.

Osofsky, J., Wewers, S., Hann, D., & Fick, A .(1993). Chronic community violence: What is happening to our children? [Special Issue: Children and violence]. *Psychiatry, 56*, 36-45.

Parry, A. (1993). Children surviving in a violent world—"Choosing Non-Violence." *Young Children*, 13-15.

Patterson, G. (1982). *Coercive family process*. Eugene, OR: Castalia Publishing.

Pawl, J., & Lieberman, A. (1993). Parent-infant psychotherapy. In C. Zeanah (Ed.), *Handbook of infant mental health*. New York: Guildford.

Peled, E., & Edleson, J. (1992). Multiple perspectives on group work with children of battered women. *Violence and Victims*, *7*(4), 327-346.

Peled, E., & Edleson, J. (1995). Process and outcome in small groups for children of battered women. In E. Peled, P. Jaffe, & J. Edleson (Eds.), *Ending the cycle of violence: Community responses to children of battered women*. Thousand Oaks, CA: Sage.

Peled, E., Jaffe, P., & Edleson, J. (Eds.) (1995). *Ending the cycle of violence: Community responses to children of battered women*. Thousand Oaks, CA: Sage.

Pfouts, J., Schopler, J., & Henley, C. (1982). Forgotten victims of family violence. *Social Work, 27*, 367-368.

Porter, B., & O'Leary, K. (1980). Marital discord and childhood behavior problems. *Journal of Abnormal Child Psychology, 8*(3), 287-295.

Prothrow-Stith, D. (1991). *Deadly consequences: How violence is destroying our teenage population and a plan to begin solving the problem*. New York: HarperCollins.

Pynoos, R., & Eth, S. (1985). The child as witness to homicide. *Journal of Social Issues, 40*(2), 87-100.

Pynoos, R., Fredrick, C., Nader, K., Arroyo, W., et al. (1987). Life threat and posttraumatic stress in school age children (Annual meeting of the American Psychiatric Association). *Archives of General Psychiatry, 44*(12), 1057-1063.

Pynoos, R., & Nader, K. (1988). Psychological first-aid treatment approach to children exposed to community violence: Research implications. *Journal of Traumatic Stress, 1*(4), 445-473.

Pynoos, R., & Nader, K. (1990). Children's exposure to violence and traumatic death. *Psychiatric Annals, 20*, 334-344.

Randolf, M., & Conkle, L. (1993). Behavioral and emotional characteristics of children who witness parental violence. *Family Violence and Sexual Assault Bulletin, 9*(2), 23-27.

Reiss, A., & Roth, J. (Eds.). (1993). *Understanding and preventing violence*. Washington, DC: National Academy Press.

Resick, P., & Reese, D. (1986). Perception of family social climate and physical aggression in the home. *Journal of Family Violence, 1*(1), 71-83.

Richters, J., & Martinez, P. (1993a). The NIMH Community Violence Project: 1. Children as victims of and witnesses to violence [Special issue: Children and Violence]. *Psychiatry, 56*, 7-21.

Richters, J., & Martinez, P. (1993b). Violent communities, family choices, and children's chances: An algorithm for improving the odds. *Development and Psychopathology, 5*, 609-627.

Rosenbaum, A., & O'Leary, K. (1981). Children: The unintended victims of marital violence. *American Journal of Orthopsychiatry, 51*(4), 692-699.

Rosenberg, M. (1987). New directions for research on the psychological maltreatment of children. *American Psychologist, 42,* 166-171.

Rubinetti, F. (1996). *Empathy, self-esteem, hopelessness, and belief in the legitimacy of aggression in adolescents exposed to pervasive community violence.* Unpublished doctoral dissertation, University of Maryland, College Park.

Saltzman, W. (1992). *The effect of children's exposure to community violence.* Unpublished master's thesis, University of Maryland, College Park.

Saltzman, W. (1995). *Exposure to community violence and the prediction of violent antisocial behavior in a multi-ethnic sample of adolescents.* Unpublished doctoral dissertation, University of Maryland, College Park.

Sameroff, A., & Chandler, M. (1975). Reproductive risk and the continuum of caretaking casualty. In F. Horowitz, M. Hetherington, S. Scarr-Salaptek, & G. Siegel (Eds.), *Review of Child Development Research, 4,* 187-244.

Sameroff, A., Seifer, R., Barocas, R., Zax, M., & Greenspan, S. (1987). Intelligence quotient scores of 4-year-old children: Social environment risk factors. *Pediatrics, 79,* 343-350.

Sampson, R., Raudenbush, S., & Earls, F. (1997, August 15). Neighborhoods and violent crime: A multilevel study of collective efficacy. *Science, 277.*

Saunders, D., & Azar, S. (1989). Treatment programs for family violence. In L. Ohlin & M. Tonry (Eds.), *Family violence.* Chicago: University of Chicago.

Scheeringa, M., Zeanah, C., Drell, M., & Larrieu, J. (1995). Two approaches to the diagnosis of post-traumatic stress disorder during infancy and early childhood. *Journal of the American Academy of Child and Adolescent Psychiatry, 34,* 191-200.

Schorr, L. (1989). *Within our reach: Breaking the cycle of disadvantage.* New York: Anchor.

Schwab-Stone, M., Ayers, T., & Weissberg, R. (1995). No safe haven: A study of violence exposure in an urban community. *Journal of the American Academy of Children and Adolescents, 34*(10), 1343.

Shahinfar, A. (1997). *Preschool children's exposure to community violence: Prevalence, correlates, and moderating factors.* Unpublished doctoral dissertation, University of Maryland, College Park.

Shakoor, B., & Chalmers, D. (1991). Co-victimization of African-American children who witness violence: Effects on cognitive, emotional, and behavioral development. *Journal of the National Medical Association, 83*(3), 233-238.

Sheline, J., Skipper, B., & Broadhead, E. (1994). Risk factors for violent behavior in elementary school boys: Have you hugged your child today? *American Journal of Public Health, 84*(4), 661-663.

Silvern, L., & Kaersvang, L. (1989). The traumatized children of violent marriages. *Child Welfare, 68*(4).

Silvern, L., Karyl, J., & Landis, T. Y. (1995). Individual psychotherapy for the traumatized children of abused women. In E. Peled, P. G. Jaffe, & J. Edleson (Eds.), *Ending the cycle of violence: Community responses to children of battered women.* Thousand Oaks, CA: Sage.

Singer, M., Anglin, T., Song, L., & Lunghofer, L. (1995). Adolescents: Exposure to violence and associated symptoms of psychological trauma. *Journal of the American Medical Association, 273*(6), 477-482.

Stagg, V., Wills, G., & Howell, M. (1989). Psychopathology in early childhood witnesses of family violence. *Topics in Early Childhood Special Education, 9*(2), 73-87.

Sternberg, K., Lamb, M., Greenbaum, C., Dawud, S., Manela Cortes, R., & Lorey, F. (1994). The effects of domestic violence on children's perceptions of their perpetrating and non-perpetrating parents. *International Journal of Behavioral Development, 17*(4), 770-795.

Straus, M. (1991). Family violence in American families: Incidence rates, causes, and trends. In D. Knudsen & J. Miller (Eds.), *Abused and battered: Social and legal responses of family violence.* Hawthorne, NY: Aldine de Gruyter.

Straus, M., & Gelles, R.(1990). *Physical violence in American families.* New Brunswick, NJ: Transaction Publishing.

Straus, M., Gelles, R., & Steinmetz, S. (1980). *Behind closed doors: Violence in the American family.* Garden City, NY: Doubleday.

Straus, M., & Smith, T. (1990). Family patterns and child abuse. In M. Straus & R. Gelles (Eds.), *Physical violence in American families.* New Brunswick, NJ: Transaction Publishing.

Sudermann, M., Jaffe, P., & Hastings, E. (1995). Violence prevention programs in secondary (high) schools. In E. Peled, P. Jaffe, & J. Edleson (Eds.), *Ending the cycle of violence: Community responses to children of battered women.* Thousand Oaks, CA: Sage.

Taylor, L., Zuckerman, B., Harik, V., & McAlister Groves, B. (1994). Witnessing violence by young children and their mothers. *Developmental and Behavioral Pediatrics, 15*(2), 120-123.

Terr, L. (1979) Children of Chowchilla: A study of psychic trauma. *Psychoanalytic Study of the Child, 34,* 547-623.

Terr, L. (1991). Childhood traumas: An outline and overview. *American Journal of Psychiatry, 148*(1), 10-20.

Thormaehlen, D., & Bass-Feld, E. (1994, April). Children: The secondary victims of domestic violence. *Maryland Medical Journal,* pp. 355-359.

Wagar, J., & Rodway, M. (1995). An evaluation of a group treatment approach for children who have witnessed wife abuse. *Journal of Family Violence, 10*(3), 295-307.

Walker, L. (1993). The battered woman syndrome is a psychological consequence of abuse. In R. Gelles & D. Loseke (Eds.), *Current controversies on family violence.* Newbury Park, CA: Sage.

Weiler, R., & Dorman, S. (1995). The role of school health instruction in preventing interpersonal violence. *Educational Psychology Review, 7*(1), 69-91.

Weist, M., & Warner, B. (in press). School-based violence interventions. *Annals of Adolescent Psychiatry.*

Westra, B., & Martin, H. (1981). Children of battered women. *Maternal-Child Nursing Journal, 10,* 41-55.

Whitman, S. (1988). Ideology and violence prevention. *Journal of the National Medical Association, 80*(7), 737-743.

Widom, C. (1989). Violence begets violence? A critical examination of the literature. *Psychological Bulletin, 106,* 3-28.

Wilson, W. (1987). *The truly disadvantaged.* Chicago: University of Chicago Press.

Wilson, W. (1996). *When work disappears.* New York: Knopf.

Wolfe, D., Wekerle, C., Reitzel, D., & Gough, R. (1995). Strategies to address violence in the lives of high-risk youth. In E. Peled, P. G. Jaffe, & J. Edleson (Eds.), *Ending the cycle of violence: Community responses to children of battered women*. Thousand Oaks, CA: Sage.

Wurtele, S., & Miller-Perrin, C. (1992). *Preventing child sexual abuse: Sharing the responsibility*. Lincoln: University of Nebraska Press.

Yoshikawa, H. (1994). Prevention as cumulative protection: Effects of early family support and education on chronic delinquency and its risks. *Psychological Bulletin, 115*(1), 28-54.

Zigler, E., Taussig, C., & Black, K. (1992). Early childhood intervention: A promising preventative for juvenile delinquency. *American Psychologist, 47*(8), 997-1006.

Zuravin, S. (1989). The ecology of child abuse and neglect: Review of the literature and presentation of data. *Violence and Victims, 4*(2), 101-120.

• *CHAPTER 4* •

Legal Perspectives on Family Violence Against Children

THEODORE J. STEIN

This chapter will acquaint the reader with the legal framework for state intervention to protect children from harm and with issues pertaining to court intervention on behalf of abused and neglected children. The foundation for child protection is found in federal law and in the laws of the states, the District of Columbia, and the territories (hereafter, the states) that require the reporting of and investigation into known or suspected instances of child abuse and neglect. The first part of this chapter contains a brief overview of the common elements of state laws that sanction action to protect children from intrafamilial violence[1] and violence committed by foster caretakers, including institutional caretakers and staff of day-care centers.[2] Next, statutory requirements that provide for services to protect children in their own homes and that provide for placement of children in out-of-home care are discussed.

The material in the remainder of this chapter focuses on safeguarding children who are at risk for abuse or neglect and those who have been abused or neglected through court intervention. Issues pertaining to court intervention that are covered include: standard of proof, evidence, juvenile court jurisdiction, representation for children in juvenile court proceedings, child testimony, and expert testimony.

Child Abuse and Neglect Reporting Laws

The elements of reporting laws differ state by state (see Davidson, 1996; Stein, 1998a). In general, they define as mandated reporters all professionals who come into contact with children, such as social service, medical, psychiatric, psychological, educational, day-care, and law enforcement personnel. All citizens are required to report in about 20 states, and all states accept reports from any member of the public. Reporting is required whenever a mandated reporter has knowledge of, or reasonable cause to believe, a child is being neglected or physically or sexually abused.

Most states define abuse and neglect in their statutes, but definitions vary in their specificity. Federal law requires that the states, at a minimum, define child abuse as "any recent act or failure to act on the part of a parent or caretaker, which results in death, serious physical or emotional harm, sexual abuse or exploitation, or an act or failure to act which presents an imminent risk of serious harm" (U.S. Senate, 1995). Definitions found at the state level refer generally to physical injuries as injuries that are caused by other than accidental means and that cause or create a substantial risk of death, disfigurement, impairment of physical health, or loss or impairment of function of any bodily organ. Sexual abuse provisions may cover specific acts, such as vaginal intercourse and obscene or pornographic photographing of a child engaged in sexual acts and may include vague and undefined provisions, such as permitting or encouraging a child to engage in offenses against public morality. The neglect clauses of state statutes are often ambiguous. They typically define as neglected a child who does not receive proper care (including the provision of necessary medical care), supervision, or discipline from his or her parent or who lives in an environment injurious to his or her health. Some state laws also include emotional neglect or abuse, which may be defined as the infliction of physical, mental, or emotional injury or the causing of the physical or emotional deterioration of a child. In a number of states, mandatory reporting laws are triggered if a newborn tests positive for drugs or is born with the signs or symptoms of maternal alcohol use during pregnancy (Stein, 1998b).

Other elements commonly found in the reporting laws of a majority of states specify that: (a) reports are to be made only to a state department of social services or to the police;[3] (b) social service, law enforcement, and/or hospital personnel may take children into protective custody if there is reason to believe that a child will be endangered if left in or returned to their home; (c) X-rays and photographs may be taken and medical treatment authorized under emergency circumstances; (d) criminal and/or civil penalties may be levied for failure to make a report (criminal penalties may allow for filing of misdemeanor charges and the levying of a fine, whereas civil penalties create liability for damages caused to a child); (e) those reporting in good faith are immune from liability in all states, but both civil and criminal charges may be lodged against people who knowingly make a false report; (f) privileged communication between husbands and wives or between professionals and their clients is waived in most states.

All states provide time frames, stating when investigations must begin (from 24 to 48 hours following receipt of a report) and when they must be concluded (from 30 days to 6 months following their commencement). In more than 40 states, legislation has been enacted requiring child protective agencies to report to the police or to a prosecutor's office serious cases of abuse or neglect or cases that might result in criminal prosecution. In most states, police conduct an investigation of reported cases (Martin & Besharov, 1991).

Protecting Children From Harm in Their Own Homes and Placement in Foster Care

Federal and state laws provide two approaches to protecting from harm children at risk of abuse or neglect and those who have been maltreated. On either a voluntary or an involuntary basis, children may be served in their own homes or placed in out-of-home care.

Federal law requires that states have programs to prevent family breakup when desirable and possible. Through the Title IV-B Child Welfare Services Program, the federal government provides funds to the states to encourage and enable them to "develop and establish, or expand, and to operate a program of family preservation services and community-based family support services" so that placement of children in foster care can be avoided (Social Security Act, 1996, Section 625(a)(1)). To emphasize its commitment to family preservation, Congress amended the Title IV-B program in 1992 with the enactment of the Family Preservation Act, which made funds available to the states, beginning in fiscal year 1994, to develop and implement or expand programs to preserve families (Social Security Act, 1996, Section 629).

Prevention programs provide for services to children in their own homes to reduce the likelihood of abuse or neglect or a recurrence thereof. To ensure that states provide preventive services before placing a child in foster care, the law requires that a judicial determination be made, in writing, on a case-by-case basis,

> that the continuation in the home would be contrary to the welfare of the child, and also to the effect that reasonable efforts were made to prevent or eliminate the need for removal. . . . and to make it possible for the child to return home. (Social Security Act, 1996, Section 671 (a)(15))

The judicial determination must be made for states to claim federal funds to defray the cost of maintaining children in out-of-home care.

All states have laws that permit placement in out-of-home care to protect children. When children are removed under emergency circumstances, eligibility for receipt of federal funds is contingent on the court's finding that the lack of preventive efforts was reasonable. Failure to provide services is not necessarily reasonable in all emergency situations. If the emergency arose because services were not provided to a family whose case was open to the agency, the court may make a determination of no reasonable efforts (Stein & Comstock, 1987). Moreover, there are crisis intervention services designed specifically to be used to alleviate immediate danger to a child. When a child is removed from her or his home and retained in custody, most states require that a petition be filed with the juvenile court to initiate a custody hearing, often within 24 to 48 hours.

Protecting Children Through the Courts

Social workers are involved mainly with juvenile or family courts (hereafter, juvenile courts) whose procedures are governed by civil law. Civil law involves disputes between individuals and organizations and is distinct from criminal law, which involves violations against the state.

When a child has been abused or neglected, it must be decided whether or not to bring the case to court. State law or agency policy may require workers to petition the juvenile court under certain circumstances or to refer a case to a prosecutor who will decide whether or not criminal charges will be filed. In the absence of statutory or policy requirements, the decision to file a court petition may be made following consultation with agency counsel or may be left to worker and supervisory discretion. A decision to petition the court may be made if: (a) parents will not cooperate with protective or preventive services; (b) there is reason to question whether parents who agree to work cooperatively will do so (for example, if agency records show that the parents have not been cooperative in the past); or (c) if clients withdraw from services and there is reason to think that withdrawal creates risk for a child.

Social workers may testify in court as fact or expert witnesses. As fact witnesses, social workers will testify as to what they heard, saw, said, or did. Testifying in this capacity, their testimony may be used to support a petition that a child be declared abused or neglected or to support a parent's request that her or his child be returned to her or his care. Experts, once qualified in an area, may testify as to their opinion. Thus, qualified social workers may testify that it is their opinion a child will suffer emotional harm if left in the custody of a certain parent (*Interest of D.S.P.,* 1992) or that inconsistent statements are typical reactions of victims of sex abuse (*Oregon v. Munro,* 1984). Regardless of whether social workers testify in court, their case records may contribute evidence to the case that an attorney presents in court.

Standard of proof refers to the burden of proof required in a particular case: for example, the requirement that the prosecution in a criminal case prove beyond a reasonable doubt that the defendant committed a crime. This standard of proof means that the judge or jury must be fully satisfied or convinced that the evidence shows that the accused committed a crime in order to render a guilty verdict.

The standard of proof that is required in civil proceedings (a petition to sustain an allegation of child abuse or neglect, for example) is less stringent than that required in a criminal proceeding. Most states require that the "preponderance of the evidence" offered in support of an allegation be greater or more convincing than the evidence that is offered in opposition to it.

"Clear and convincing evidence" is a standard intermediate between "preponderance of the evidence" and "beyond a reasonable doubt." Clear and convincing evidence exists when there is a "high probability" that the facts that are asserted are true (Black, 1990, p. 251).

Evidence refers to the different kinds of proof that are admitted in court to convince a judge or jury of the truth of the matter being heard. *Direct evidence* comes from firsthand knowledge. It consists of facts describing what a person heard, saw, said, and did. If someone observed a parent strike a child, the statement, "I observed Mr. Kennedy hit his son with a belt," would be admissible in court as direct evidence.

Real evidence consists of documents and photographs. A copy of school attendance records showing a high rate of absenteeism and certified by school authorities is one type of real evidence that may be presented to the court to support an allegation of educational neglect. X-rays and photographs may be important evidence in substantiating allegations of abuse.

Circumstantial evidence consists of deductions that are drawn from other kinds of evidence. For example, real evidence may consist of photographs showing burns on an infant's buttocks. A physician may testify that the burns, in light of the child's age and their location, could not have been sustained accidentally. We might infer, from knowledge of who was taking care of the child at the time the injury was sustained, that the caretaker caused the child's injury.

Hearsay evidence is secondhand information whose truth cannot be ascertained through cross-examination. The person whose observation is being reported is either unable, unwilling, or unavailable to testify. If you were to testify that a neighbor of a family under investigation for physical abuse told you that he saw the child being beaten, this statement would be considered hearsay and would not be admissible in court. The statement may or may not be true. While true, it may exaggerate the situation and not accurately reflect the events that it purports to describe. There are exceptions to the hearsay rule permitting testimony that would otherwise be excluded.

Excited utterances are statements made while the declarant is under stress caused by a startling event or condition. An excited utterance is presumed to be reliable since it is spontaneous and uncalculated and may be reported in court by the person to whom it was made.

Medical exceptions permit the introduction of evidence given to a medical person for the purpose of receiving treatment. This form of hearsay, which may be entered through the testimony of a physician or nurse, is allowed because it is assumed that a person would not lie to a medical person if they needed treatment.

Prior recollections recorded permit you (or another witness) to enter into evidence information found in notes that were made at the time an incident occurred. These may be used in court if you cannot recall an event. Notes may be read aloud if you testify that: (a) at one time, you had firsthand knowledge of the event; (b) you do not now remember the event; (c) the notes were made when your memory of the event was fresh; (d) the notes were accurate when they were made.

Admissions are statements made by a party to a legal action. A party is a person whose interests are at risk in the legal proceedings. If a parent tells you that he abused his son, you may repeat this statement in court. This admission is allowed as evidence to prove that the parent committed the act.

If a neighbor told you that she abused the child, her statement cannot be repeated in court if she is not a party to the proceeding. An admission cannot be self-serving. The statement, "I did not abuse my son," would not be permitted under this exception.

Admissions by silence consist of statements made in the presence of an alleged perpetrator who chooses not to deny the allegation made. For example, if, in an interview with the parents of an allegedly abused child, the mother tells you that the father "always uses his belt to discipline their son," you could testify to this in court if: (a) the statement was made in the father's presence, and (b) it can be shown that he heard the statement, understood it, and did not object to it. His silence is construed as agreement with what was said by his wife. This testimony would not be admissible if: (a) the father was not present, (b) did not hear the statement made, or (c) had consulted with an attorney and was acting on his attorney's advice not to talk about the incident.

Official records, such as birth and death certificates, information from a child abuse registry, and school or hospital records are allowed into evidence. It is assumed that a public official has no motive to create a false record, because they have no personal connection to the people or events about which they create records.

Catch-all or residual exceptions permit a judge the discretion to allow the introduction of evidence that would otherwise be deemed inadmissable hearsay, if the nature and circumstances under which a statement was made offer strong assurances of its accuracy. For example, in *State v. Sorenson* (1988), where a father and an uncle were charged with the sexual abuse of a 7-year-old, the court determined that a child's hearsay statements made to a social worker regarding the abuse were reliable. In determining whether the statements were reliable, the court considered five factors: (a) attributes of the child, such as age, ability to communicate, and ability to know the difference between truth and falsehood; (b) the relationship of the victim to the person told and the motivation of that person to "fabricate or distort" (p. 77) contents; (c) the circumstances of the disclosure; (d) the content of the statement (e.g., does it allude to knowledge of sexual matters not ordinarily known by children of the victim's age); and (e) other corroborative evidence (e.g., physical evidence).

Juvenile Court Jurisdiction

The jurisdiction of the juvenile court is specified in state statutes. In general, juvenile courts have jurisdiction over juvenile delinquents, status offenders, and children who are dependent, neglected, or abused. Whereas juvenile delinquents and status offenders come before the court because of their own conduct, dependent, neglected, and abused children come before the court because of the behavior of their parents. Dependent children are those whose parents cannot afford to provide for them; neglected children are youngsters whose parents have engaged in acts of omission (such as failing to send a child to school or failing to provide medical care); and abused children are those who are said to suffer from parental acts of commission that cause children to suffer injuries.

Juvenile court hearings are divided into fact-finding stages (adjudicational or jurisdictional hearings) and decision-making stages (dispositional hearings). Prior to adjudication, a petition is filed. The petition states the facts of the case and requests a particular finding from the court. For example, a social worker, subsequent to investigating a report of child abuse, will describe in writing what he or she observed during the investigation (for example, bruises on a child's body or a child who was found unsupervised) and what he or she was told by the child and/or parent. Corroborating evidence may be presented by physicians, mental health experts who have examined the youngster, and school officials. At the adjudicatory hearing, the central question that a judge must answer is whether or not the facts of the case allow him or her to draw the conclusion that the court has jurisdiction over a young person.

Our system of jurisprudence assumes that a child's best interests are served by vesting custody with the child's biological parents (*Meyer v. Nebraska,* 1923; *Pierce v. Society of Sisters,* 1925; *Prince v. Massachusetts,* 1944). Thus, the burden of proof is on the state to show, by a preponderance of the evidence, that a parent is unfit, before the court may assume jurisdiction over a child.

If the facts do not support the request for jurisdiction, the case will be dismissed. If the child had been removed from her or his home, she or he will then be returned home. If the court assumes jurisdiction, a dispositional hearing will occur at which social facts describing the circumstances in which the child was living will be presented. Recommendations for services and living arrangements will then be made. Dispositional alternatives may differ state by state but generally include: (a) leaving the child in her or his own home, but granting the department of social services the right to supervise the child's care; or (b) placing the child in a substitute care setting, such as a foster home, group home, or institution.

Dispositional alternatives are limited by the requirement in federal law that, consistent with the best interests and special needs of the child, children's placement be in the least restrictive and most family-like setting in close proximity to the parent's home (Social Security Act, 1996, Section 675(5)(A). This requirement places a responsibility on the courts to review whether the dispositional alternative under consideration meets this requirement and to overrule an agency's placement choice if it does not.

Representation to Protect Children's Interests. For most of its history, a central premise of the juvenile court was that all parties were concerned with and able to act in the best interests of the child. There was no purpose to be served by appointing separate counsel for children.

In 1967, the U.S. Supreme Court ruled that juveniles have a right to counsel at the adjudicatory stage of delinquency proceedings (*In re Gault,* 1967). This ruling did not protect children in civil proceedings. However, provisions in the federal Child Abuse Prevention and Treatment Act require that a Guardian ad Litem or Court Appointed Special Advocate (CASA) be assigned to represent a child's interests in all judicial proceedings (U.S. Senate, 1995), thus extending a right to representation to all youth.

A Guardian ad Litem or CASA may be an attorney or a layperson. People acting in the role of guardian or CASA conduct an investigation of the child's situation and make a recommendation to the court as to what, in their opinion, is in the child's best interests. Unlike the guardian, who offers his or her own opinion to the court, an attorney, in the traditional role of counsel, represents the expressed wishes of the client.

Child as Witness. Because available evidence may not be sufficient to sustain an allegation of child abuse, children may be called on to testify in court, especially when criminal charges are lodged against an alleged perpetrator. In recent years, federal and state legislators, social workers, and attorneys have struggled with the question of how to use a child's testimony without further victimizing the child by subjecting her or him to the rigors of providing testimony and being cross-examined while also maintaining the presumption of innocence for the person who is charged with committing an abusive act.

Issues that arise about child testimony include: (a) competency to testify; (b) use of corroborating evidence, including evidence presented by experts; (c) protection of children from the effects of giving testimony about events assumed to be traumatic; and (d) protection from the effects of being cross-examined about evidence that is given.

Competency. Whether a person is competent to testify is determined by a two-part test that asks whether the witness: (a) is intelligent enough to make his or her testimony worthwhile, and (b) recognizes the need to testify truthfully (Horowitz & Davidson, 1984).

Most states assume that a child is competent to testify unless otherwise established (Henry, 1986). Competency may be established by a judge after questioning a child if the judge determines that the child: (a) is capable of observing and recalling facts, (b) is able to relate facts to the judge or jury, and (c) has a moral sense of obligation to tell the truth (*Griffin v. State,* 1988). In *Griffin,* the Florida Court of Appeals overturned a conviction of sexual abuse, ruling that the trial court had erred by not personally questioning the child to determine her competency to testify.

Concern with competency directs attention to a child's testimony and asks whether a child's testimony has been influenced by pretrial events, notably repetitive and suggestive questioning that results in creating false memories (Ceci & Bruck, 1993). The credibility of testimony given by children has been called into question, due, in part, to the failure to obtain convictions in well-publicized cases alleging sex abuse in day care settings (e.g., the McMartin Pre-School case). Another factor is the overturning of convictions in cases like that of Margaret Kelly Michaels in the Wee Care Day School case (Besharov, 1990; *State v. Michaels*, 1994).

The suggestion that the testimony of children has been unduly influenced by pretrial interrogations where interviewers "suggest" to children the answers they wish to hear is not a new one. In 1985, parents accused of sexually abusing their children filed suit against various government officials, alleging, in part, that their children were "worn-down and brainwashed" into making accusations against them (*In re Scott County Master Docket,* 1985, p. 1544). Defendants, including county attorneys, sheriffs, therapists, and social workers, were said to have coerced the children to give the responses that defendants desired by differentially reinforcing children through verbal and nonverbal cues for providing "correct" answers.

Recognizing the various problems child-victims face during child abuse investigations and in court, a number of states have enacted statutes governing the questioning of child witnesses, requiring, for example, (a) that investigators receive special training, (b) that limits be set as to the number of times a child can be interviewed, (c) that limits be set as to the amount of time a child spends on the witness stand, and (d) that safeguards be put in place to protect children from harassment (Walker & Nguyen, 1996).

Corroborating evidence supplements other evidence and is offered to strengthen other evidence. Corroborating evidence may take different forms. Examples are: The subsequent pregnancy and abortion of a minor were sufficient to corroborate an 11-year-old's out-of-court statements to her social worker in which she named her father as the abuser (*In the Matter of Joli M.,* 1986). There was no requirement of independent proof that her father was the perpetrator, said the court.

A child's out-of-court statement, coupled with *in camera* testimony (testimony given in the privacy of a judge's chambers or in the courtroom with witnesses excluded) and expert opinion that the child was sexually abused, when there was virtually no likelihood that the child was lying, was sufficient evidence (*In the Matter of Melissa M.,* 1987).

New York State's Family Court Act establishes a standard for corroborating testimony that is defined as "any other evidence tending to support the reliability of the [child's] statements. . . . " (New York State, Family Court Act, Section 1046). The testimony of the child is not necessary to make a factual finding of abuse or neglect. Applying this standard, the court ruled that expert validation, standing alone, may be sufficient corroboration of a child's out-of-court statement to a social worker (*In the Matter of E.M. et al.,* 1987).

Referring to the corroboration requirement of the Family Court Act, the court said that the "validator" must (a) be highly qualified (in the E.M. case, the validators were a clinical psychologist and a psychiatrist), (b) use a reliable methodology or system of analysis (play therapy and the use of anatomically correct dolls and carefully phrased questions), and (c) be able to articulate precisely how the conclusions were a product of the methodology (the expert said that the child had a good capacity for accurate recall, her story was clear and coherent, she behaved in an age appropriate manner, her emotional reactions to the interview included manifestations of anxiety and shame consistent with post-traumatic stress). Other courts have ruled that expert testimony can suffice to corroborate a child's out-of-court testimony in making a prima facie case for maltreatment (*In the Matter of Dutchess County Department of Social Services,* 1987; *In the Matter of Linda K.,* 1987; *In the Matter of Meggan C.,* 1987).

Protective Devices. Concern with protecting from harm child-victims of physical and sexual abuse who testify in court in criminal cases has led to the use of protective devices, such as closed-circuit television and videotaped testimony. The statutes of 31 states allow the use of closed-circuit televised testimony. Videotaped testimony is permitted in 33 states (Montoya, 1993).

The use of protective devices for child witnesses raises the question: Is a defendant's Sixth Amendment right to confront and cross-examine witnesses in a criminal trial violated? Sixth amendment protections are not generally applicable in civil procedures. The purpose of the *confrontation clause* of the Sixth Amendment is threefold: (a) to allow for effective cross-examination, (b) to allow the trier of fact to observe the demeanor of the witness, and (c) to impress upon the witness the requirement that the truth be told (*State v. Thomas,* 1988).

The courts have struggled with the need to create a balance between protecting children and upholding the constitutional rights of criminal defendants. A New York State court ruled that the confrontation clause was not violated by the use of closed-circuit testimony when: (a) a prosecuting attorney and one defense attorney were in the room with the child, (b) another defense attorney was in the courtroom with the defendant, (c) the image and voice of the child and attorneys were transmitted live to the court room, (d) the voice of the judge and the images of the jury and defendant were transmitted to the testimonial room, and (e) a two-way private communication system was set up between the defense table and the defense lawyer in the testimonial room that allowed the defendant to participate in his defense (*People v. Algarin,* 1986).

In *Coy v. Iowa* (1988), a screen was placed between the defendant and two complaining child witnesses, which blocked the defendant from the view of the witnesses. The use of this protective device was permitted by Iowa statute. Coy objected to the use of the screen on two grounds. First, it prevented the witnesses from seeing him during their testimony, which he argued violated his Sixth Amendment right to face-to-face confrontation. Second, he claimed that use of the screen made him appear guilty to a jury. The judge had instructed the jury to draw no inference from use of screen. Coy was found guilty.

Attorneys for the State of Iowa argued that the purpose of the statute was to protect children from trauma during courtroom testimony. The U.S. Supreme Court rejected this argument, ruling that the presumption of trauma was too generalized. Use of the screen violated Coy's rights under the confrontation clause.

Justice Sandra Day O'Connor, concurring with the majority, wrote a separate opinion in which she left open the door for use of other procedural devices to protect children. She recognized the "disturbing proportions of (child abuse) in today's society" (p. 2804) and acknowledged the difficulty of detecting and prosecuting abuse because there are often no witnesses available. According to O'Connor, the right to face-to-face confrontation is not absolute. The confrontation clause reflects a preference that may be overcome if "close examination of competing interests warrants" (*Coy v. Iowa,* 1988) Thus, while agreeing that the assumption in the Iowa law that a child witness will suffer trauma from testifying was too general, she suggested that case-by-case determinations of the necessity for protective devices may suffice.[4] The Victims of Child Abuse Act of 1990 codified the Supreme Court's decision in *Coy,* amending the federal criminal code to provide for videotaping of a child's testimony for cases that are prosecuted under federal law based on a particularized finding that the child will likely suffer trauma from testifying in open court.

Expert testimony may be offered to (a) rehabilitate a child's testimony (when, for example, the child's behavior is at variance with adult expectations of how a sexually abused person would behave), and (b) to assist a judge or jury in understanding the general characteristics of those who suffer abuse.

Those whose testimony is offered as expert opinion must be qualified by the court, and the theories to which experts refer, or the methods used to elicit information, must be reliable. A judge has a great deal of latitude in determining who is an expert, and social workers have qualified as experts in a variety of cases and circumstances. (See, for example, *Newkirk v. Commonwealth,* 1996; *People v. White,* 1996; *Shippen v. Parrott,* 1996; *State v. Perkins,* 1996). Experience with the subject matter and/or educational requirements are likely to be considered. "Usual education and experience" were sufficient for one court to qualify as an expert a social worker who testified that a child was deprived (*In re RMB,* 1987). The credentials of expert witness trained in nursing, psychology, and social work were sufficient despite the fact that the witnesses had only been in practice 1 year (*Westbrook v. State,* 1988).

A mental health expert may describe the behavior patterns of sexually abused children to help a judge or jury understand that certain behaviors may be characteristic of children who have been sexually abused (*Flanagan v. State,* 1991; *State v. Spigardo,* 1984). Without this explanation, behaviors such as recanting testimony and presenting conflicting versions of events may be interpreted by the jury as reflecting inaccurate recall or prevarication (*State v. Bailey,* 1988; *State v. Lindsey,* 1985; *Ward v. State,* 1988). But expert opinion may not be used to conclude that the victim was telling the truth. Thus, an expert may say that children who are abused tend to act in certain ways but may not conclude that the actions of the alleged victim should be interpreted as being truthful. The determination of truthfulness lies solely within the province of the judge or jury (*Commonwealth v. Ianello,* 1987; *Dunnington v. State,* 1987; *State v. Lindsey,* 1985).

A variety of syndromes have been postulated to explain the behavior of children who have been maltreated, or the condition of a child that leads an expert to conclude that she or he has been physically or sexually abused. The battered child syndrome, defined as a "clinical condition in young children who receive serious physical abuse" (Kempe, 1974, p. 174), is perhaps the best known of these and one that the courts accept as a basis for expert testimony because it has been extensively studied by medical science and is accepted within the medical profession (*Commonwealth v. Rogers,* 1987; *People v. Jackson,* 1971).

Until the summer of 1993, whether or not to admit testimony that rests on scientific studies was determined by use of a test established in 1923 by the Circuit Court for the District of Columbia (*Frye v. United States,* 1923). Under the Frye Test, evidence culled from scientific studies was admissible if there was a reliable body of scientific opinion supporting a particular theory. The theory need only have general acceptance in the field in which it belonged, not the unanimous endorsement of the scientific community. Evidence that a method is acceptable by a professional community was offered by introducing scientific or legal articles, by evaluating the reliability of the methodology used to arrive at the conclusions, or by presenting expert witness testimony concerning the reliability and general acceptance of the methodology.

In the summer of 1993, the U.S. Supreme Court liberalized the standard for admissibility of scientific evidence. The Court's decision paved the way for the introduction of expert testimony based on scientific studies not generally accepted in the scientific community, while at the same time delineating a series of guidelines for lower courts to consider in determining admissibility that could severely restrict admission of novel scientific evidence (*Daubert v. Dow Pharmaceuticals,* 1993). However, state courts are not bound to follow the 1993 Supreme Court decision when they decide cases under state law. Some states have chosen to continue their reliance on the Frye standard of general acceptability within the scientific community. (See, generally, *People v. Leahy,* 1994; *People v. Watson,* 1994, 1995; *State v. Cissne,* 1994; *State v. Merritt,* 1994). Because state law is decisive in almost all matters involving child abuse and neglect, the Frye Test for admissibility of scientific evidence will continue to be applied in many cases.

Syndrome evidence offered in cases involving alleged child sex abuse has presented a great deal of difficulty for courts, and offers of proof that rest on "profiles" of alleged victims and alleged perpetrators have been judged vague and unreliable (*Flanagan v. State,* 1991; *State v. Rimmasch,* 1989). On the issue of syndrome evidence, an appellate court in California ruled that testimony based on the child molester syndrome was inadmissible because the syndrome lacked acceptance in the professional community (*In re Sara M.,* 1987). For the same reason, courts have rejected testimony based on the use of anatomically correct dolls (*In re Amber B.,* 1987; *United States v. Gillespie,* 1988). Testimony based on post-traumatic stress disorder has been deemed admissible (*Acuna v. State,* 1992; *State v. Allewalt,* 1986), whereas expert testimony that children were sexually abused, based on the experts' observations of the children's behavior, was deemed inadmissible because the testimony was not based on reliable and scientifically accepted measures and was thus considered prejudicial (*State v. Lawrence,* 1988).

Conclusion

Child abuse reporting laws provide the basic legal framework sanctioning state action to protect children from abuse and neglect. These laws are broad and far-reaching, providing a great deal of latitude to state agents to accept and to investigate reports. Most states: (a) require investigations whenever known or suspected maltreatment is reported, (b) accept reports from professional and lay persons, (c) limit or preclude screening out of reports, (d) cover a wide range of physical and emotional conditions, and (e) do not define clearly the conditions covered.

Whether child abuse reporting laws adequately protect children is a question that has been raised a number of times over the years (Merriweather, 1986; Stein, 1984; Wald, 1978). In 1993, about 3 million reports of suspected abuse or neglect were made to the states, but only one third of these were substantiated as valid incidents of child maltreatment (U.S. Senate, 1995). Rates of substantiation have changed little since 1987, when they ranged from a low of 37% of cases substantiated to a high of 40% of cases substantiated (American Association for Protecting Children, 1988).

The discrepancy between reported and substantiated cases may be the result of: (a) ambiguously worded statutes that encourage overreporting (reporting all observations of injured children because what is to be reported is not clear) and underreporting (failing to report incidents because of uncertainty as to whether they are covered by the law), (b) weak investigatory practices due to lack of worker training and/or the inability of workers to conduct thorough investigations due to the volume of reports, (c) insufficient information to commence an investigation (e.g., family cannot be found), and (d) an unwillingness of workers to substantiate cases because services to assist families are in short supply. Ambiguously worded statutes may be self-defeating. Rather than resulting in the protection of children, poorly conceived laws and regulations may increase the likelihood of danger because overworked and undertrained child protective staff cannot conduct thorough investigations.

Suggestions that have been made to deal with the difficulties that child protection agencies confront include: (a) defining more clearly reportable conditions, (b) restricting the focus of the law to child abuse only, (c) accepting reports from professionals only, and (d) improving training of protective service staff. (See, generally: Merriweather, 1986; Stein, 1984; Wald, 1978.)

Children may be called on to testify in court, especially when criminal charges are filed. Children are presumed competent to testify if they are able to observe, recall, and truthfully communicate their observations. Children may testify via closed-circuit television if it is determined on a case-by-case basis that a child will experience trauma from testifying in the presence of the accused. The decision to allow a child to testify via closed-circuit television does not violate a defendant's Sixth Amendment right to confront and cross-examine witnesses as long as the decision is made according to rules laid down by the U.S. Supreme Court.

Notes

1. Actions of a parent, guardian, or caretaker that cause harm or failure of a parent, guardian, or caretaker to protect a child from known harm.

2. Child abuse reporting laws were not intended to protect children from violence committed by nonfamily members, absent a showing that a parent's negligence contributed to a child's injuries. Violence against children by nonfamily members may be prosecuted under a state's penal code.

3. New York State requires that reports be made to the Central Registry.

4. In *Maryland v. Craig* (1990), the U.S. Supreme Court reaffirmed its ruling in *Coy v. Iowa,* limiting constitutional protections to those enumerated in Coy. The Court vacated a decision of the Maryland Court of Appeals (*Craig v. State*, 1988), which, while correctly requiring an individual determination of necessity for the use of closed-circuit television, had added two requirements for the use of this protective device: first, that an attempt be made to question a child in the presence of the defendant; and second, that alternatives to the use of one-way closed-circuit television be considered to better protect the defendant's right to confront witnesses. The Court ruled that the Constitution did not require either of these protections.

References

Acuna v. State, 629 A.2d 1233 (Md. App. 1992).

American Association for Protecting Children. (1988). *Highlights of official child neglect and abuse reporting laws 1986*. Denver, CO: The American Humane Association.

Besharov, D. J. (1990, July). Protecting the innocent: The McMartin preschool case. *National Review,* pp. 44-46.

Black, H. C. (1990). *Black's law dictionary.* St. Paul, MN: West Publishing.

Ceci, S. J., & Bruck, M. (1993). Suggestibility of the child witness: A historical review and synthesis. *Psychological Bulletin, 113,* 403-439.

Child Abuse Prevention and Treatment Act, 42 U.S.C. 5103(b)(2)(G).

Commonwealth v. Ianello, 515 N.E.2d 1181 (Mass. 1987).

Commonwealth v. Rogers, 528 A.2d 610 (1987), appeal denied 542 A.2d 1368 (1988).

Coy v. Iowa, 108 S. Ct. 2798 (1988).

Craig v. State, 544 A.2d 784 (Md. App. 1988).

Daubert v. Dow Pharmaceuticals, 113 S. Ct. 2786 (1993).

Davidson, S. A. (1996). When is parental discipline child abuse? The vagueness of child abuse. *University of Louisville Journal of Family Law, 34,* 403-419.

Dunnington v. State, 740 S.W.2d 896 (Tex. App. 1987), review refused 1988.
Flanagan v. State, 586 So.2d 1085 (Fla. App. 1991).
Frye v. United States, 293 F. 1013, 1014 (D.C. Cir. 1923).
Griffin v. State, 526 So.2d 752 (Fla. App. 1988).
Henry, M. (1986). States act to protect child victim/witnesses. *Youth Law News, 7,* 1-4.
Horowitz, R. M., & Davidson, H. A. (1994). *Legal rights of children.* New York: Sheppard's McGraw Hill.
In re Amber B., 191 Cal. App.3d 682 (Cal. App. 1 Dist. 1987)
In re Gault, 387 U.S. 1 (1967).
In re RMB, 402 N.W.2d 912 (N.D. 1987).
In re Sara M., 239 Cal. Rptr. 605 (Cal. App. 3 Dist. 1987).
In re Scott County Master Docket, 618 F. Supp. 1534 (D.C. Minn. 1985), *aff'd in part rev'd in part*, 810 F.2d 1437 (1987), *cert. denied* by Myers v. Morris (484 U.S. 828), cert. denied by Lallak v. Morris, 484 U.S. 828 (1987), *aff'd by* Myers v. Scott County, 868 F.2d 1017 (8th Cir. 1989).
Interest of D.S.P., 480 N.W.2d 234 (Wisc. 1992).
In the Matter of Dutchess County Department of Social Services, 522 N.Y.S.2d 210 (N.Y.A.D. 2nd Dept. 1987), *appeal denied*, 532 N.Y.S.2d 368 (1988).
In the Matter of E.M., 137 Misc.2d 197 (N.Y. Fam. Ct. 1987).
In the Matter of Joli, 131 Misc.2d 1088 (N.Y. Fam. Ct. 1986).
In the Matter of Linda K., 521 N.Y.S.2d 705 (N.Y.A.D. 2nd Dept. 1987), *appeal denied*, 526 N.Y.S.2d 437 (1988).
In the Matter of Meggan C., N.Y.L.J., December 17, 1987, at 27. col. 4 (N.Y. Fam. Ct.).
In the Matter of Melissa M., 136 Misc.2d 773 (N.Y. Fam. Ct. 1987).
Kempe, C. H. (1974). Child abuse and neglect. In N. B. Talbot (Ed.), *Raising children in modern America.* Boston: Little, Brown.
Martin, S. E., & Besharov, D. J. (1991). *Police and child abuse: New policies for expanded responsibilities.* Washington, DC: U.S. Department of Justice, Office of Justice Programs, National Institute of Justice.
Maryland v. Craig, 110 S. Ct. 3157 (1990).
Merriweather, M. H. (1986). Child abuse reporting laws: Time for a change. *Family Law Quarterly, 20,* 141-171.
Meyer v. Nebraska, 262 U.S. 390 (1923).
Montoya, J. (1993). Something not so funny happened on the way to conviction: The pretrial interrogation of child witnesses. *Arizona Law Review, 35,* 927-987.
Newkirk v. Commonwealth, 1996 WL 492715 (Ky. 1996).
Oregon v. Munro, 680 P.2d 708 (Or. 1984).
People v. Algarin, 498 N.Y.S.2d 977 (Sup. Ct. 1986).
People v. Jackson, 18 Cal. App.3d 504 (1971).
People v. Leahy, 34 Cal. Rptr.2d 663 (1994)
People v. Watson, 629 N.E.2d 634 (Ill. App. 1994).
People v. Watson, 634 N.Y.S.2d 935 (Sup. Ct. 1995).
People v. White, 645 N.Y.S.2d 562 (A.D. 1996).
Pierce v. Society of Sisters, 268 U.S. 510 (1925).
Prince v. Massachusetts, 321 U.S. 158 (1944).
Shippen v. Parrott, 1996 WL 490133 (S.D. 1996)
Social Security Act, 42 U.S.C. (1996).
State v. Allewalt, 517 A.2d 741 (Md. App. 1986).

State v. Bailey, 365 S.E.2d 651 (N.C. App. 1988).
State v. Cissne, 865 P.2d 564 (Wash. App. 1994), *review denied*, 877 P.2d 1288 (Wash. 1994).
State v. Lawrence, 541 A.2d 1291 (Me. 1988).
State v. Lindsey, 720 P.2d 94 (Ariz. App. 1985), *aff'd in part, vacated in part*, 720 P.2d 73 (Ariz. 1986).
State v. Merritt, 647 A.2d 1021 (Ct. App. 1994).
State v. Michaels, 642 A.2d 1372 (N.J. App. 1994).
State v. Perkins, 1996 WL 442085 (Wis. App. 1996).
State v. Rimmasch, 755 P.2d 388 (1989).
State v. Sorenson, 421 N.W.2d 77 (Wis. 1988).
State v. Spigardo, 556 A.2d 112 (Conn. 1984).
State v. Thomas, 425 N.W.2d 641 (Wis. 1988), *cert denied*, 110 S. Ct. 188 (1989).
Stein, T. J. (1984). The Child Abuse Prevention and Treatment Act. *Social Service Review, 58*, 302-314.
Stein, T. J. (1998a). *Child welfare and the law* (2nd ed.). Washington, DC: Child Welfare League of America.
Stein, T. J. (1998b). *The social welfare of women and children with HIV and AIDS: Legal protections, policy and programs.* New York: Oxford University Press.
Stein, T. J., & Comstock, G. D. (1987). *Reasonable efforts: A report on implementation by child welfare agencies in five states.* Washington, DC: American Bar Association, National Legal Resource Center for Child Advocacy and Protection.
U.S. Senate, Child Abuse Prevention and Treatment Act Amendments of 1995, Committee Report, 104-117, 104th Congress; 1st Session (July 20, 1995), Pub. L. No. 104-235, codified at 110 Stat. 3063 (1996).
United States v. Gillespie, 852 F.2d 475 (9th Cir. 1988).
Wald, M. (1978). State intervention on behalf of "neglected" children: Standards for removal of children from their homes, monitoring the status of children in foster care, and termination of parental rights. *Stanford Law Review, 28*, 628-706.
Walker, N. E., & Nguyen, M. (1996). Interviewing the child witness: The do's and the dont's, the how's and the why's. *Creighton Law Review, 29*, 1587-1606.
Ward v. State, 519 So.2d 1082 (Fla. Dist. Ct. 1988).
Westbrook v. State, 368 S.E.2d 131 (Ga. App. 1988).

• *CHAPTER 5* •

Preventing Child Maltreatment

DONNA HARRINGTON
HOWARD DUBOWITZ

Can we prevent child maltreatment? Yes, in many instances, if we are willing to commit the resources needed to provide necessary preventive services to families (Garbarino, 1994; Leventhal, 1996). Although preventing child maltreatment will be expensive, in the long run, it is likely to be cost-effective (Daro, 1988; Werner, 1994). Historically, as the amount of federal money spent to support families has decreased, the costs associated with foster care and other child protective services have increased (Weisz, 1994). Finally, humanitarian reasons should compel us to try to prevent the suffering associated with child maltreatment (Schorr, 1988).

The prevention of child maltreatment has been difficult for at least four reasons. First, the political will to prioritize the needs of children and families has been lacking (National Commission on Children, 1991; Rodwell & Chambers, 1994). Many of the programs that have been found to help high-risk families, such as Head Start and the Special Supplemental Food Program for Women, Infants, and Children (WIC), do not have sufficient funding to serve more than about half of eligible families (National Commission on Children, 1991). Second, it has been difficult to develop prevention programs because of limited information about the causes of maltreatment. Even with the advances that have been made in understanding the etiology of child maltreatment, it remains difficult to predict which families are at highest risk (Rodwell & Chambers, 1994). The relatively low base rates of abuse and neglect mean that many families need to be served for each occurrence of maltreatment that is successfully prevented; consequently, prevention efforts need to target many families. The possibility of stigmatizing families receiving prevention services needs to be minimized. Third, there has been relatively little evaluation research on prevention programs (Dubowitz, 1987; Helfer, 1982), although this has been changing, with more attention being paid to evaluation. Fourth, a fundamental right to privacy and the belief in the sanctity of the family leads to the view that intervention by the state in family matters (including child maltreatment) should only occur when absolutely necessary (e.g., to protect a child from serious harm) (Beatty, 1996). As a result, many resources are only available after abuse or neglect has occurred, has been identified, and is substantiated.

In this chapter, we will provide an overview of the ecological model of child maltreatment, summarize the three levels of prevention efforts, and discuss primary and secondary prevention efforts directed toward the four levels of the ecological model. Because an exhaustive review of current prevention efforts is beyond the scope of this chapter, we will provide examples of programs that have been developed and evaluated recently.

The Ecological Model of Child Maltreatment

To understand and prevent child maltreatment, the entire context in which it occurs must be considered. Child maltreatment is not committed by a parent in isolation, independent of the parent's past experiences and current circumstances. Rather, child maltreatment is the product of factors within the individual parent, the family (including the child), the community, and the culture or society (Belsky, 1980, 1993), which exist at differing levels of proximity to the child (Belsky & Vondra, 1989). All four of these levels may contribute to the abuse and neglect of children.

Parent Level

Factors influencing the occurrence of maltreatment at the individual level include a person's past experience and characteristics. When people become parents, their personal histories influence their parenting behavior. The type of parenting they themselves received provides a model for their new role as parents. There is a widely held belief that many abusive parents were themselves abused as children (Egeland, Jacobvitz, & Sroufe, 1988; Kaufman & Zigler, 1989; Main & Goldwyn, 1984); however, not all abused children necessarily become abusive parents. In her prospective study, Widom (1989a) found that adults who had been maltreated as children were no more likely to abuse their own children than adults who had not been previously maltreated. Although the research findings are inconsistent, having been maltreated as a child is thought to be a risk factor for becoming a parent who maltreats one's own children (Kaufman & Zigler, 1989).

Parenting can be difficult and often requires support. Several recent studies have examined programs offering support for parents, including small group meetings and extensive psychotherapy. Egeland et al. (1988) studied mothers who reported being maltreated as children. These mothers were divided into two groups: those who had abused their children and those who had not. The mothers who did not abuse their own children were more likely than the others to report having had a "supportive relationship with some adult in their own childhood and having undergone extensive therapy" (p. 1085). These findings suggest that therapeutic services for maltreated children and the availability of a supportive parent or adult may prevent future maltreatment.

Compared with their nonabusive counterparts, abusive parents tend to be more depressed and have more health problems (Wolfe, 1984); however, empirical evidence for this association is limited (Culbertson & Schellenbach, 1992). Although it is unclear whether the health problems are a cause or result of the occurrence of child maltreatment, it is likely that severe mental or physical health problems, such as depression, could have a negative effect on parenting ability.

Parenting may also be adversely affected by the abuse of alcohol and other drugs. An estimated 11% of all pregnant women were found to use illicit drugs (Reddick & Goodwin, 1991), and 3% to 4% drank excessive amounts of alcohol during pregnancy (Gomby & Shiono, 1991). Drug use during pregnancy may be associated with low birthweight, impaired fetal growth, microcephaly, lethargy, poor response, irritability, abnormal reflexes, poor muscle tone (Deren, 1986; Zuckerman, 1991), prematurity, developmental delay, and child maltreatment (Deren, 1986; Merrick, 1985). It is estimated that 30% to 90% of all substantiated child maltreatment reports involve families with some degree of adult alcohol or drug abuse (McCullough, 1991). In a study of 78 families with an alcohol- or drug-addicted parent, Mayer and Black (1977) found 13% had physically abused a child; 31% reported angry, impulsive behavior indicative of a high potential for abuse; and 63% were identified as high risk for parenting problems.

Drug treatment is needed for about 105,000 pregnant women each year; of these, only about 30,000 receive any treatment (Kumpfer, 1991). The special needs of pregnant women, and women with children, are very seldom addressed by treatment programs (Kumpfer, 1991). In the child welfare system, the fastest-growing foster care population is that of drug-exposed infants and children of alcohol- or drug-addicted parents; these children are further overwhelming an already stressed system (McCullough, 1991).

In addition to parents' histories of maltreatment, the ecological theory suggests that current parenting knowledge, substance use, and other factors such as social support influence how people will parent their children.

Family Level

Parents function within a family that includes parents, children, grandparents, and other extended family members. The relationship between parents and children has been thought to be influenced by the traits of the parent (e.g., impulsiveness) and child (e.g., difficult temperament) that may contribute to the occurrence of maltreatment (Belsky, 1980, 1993). Two studies did not find a relationship between child characteristics and physical abuse (Dodge, Bates, & Pettit, 1990; Whipple & Webster-Stratton, 1991), suggesting that child characteristics do not contribute significantly toward child physical abuse. Other studies suggest that children who are perceived as having difficult temperaments are more likely to be neglected (Goodman-Campbell, 1979; Houldin, 1987; Mangelsdorf, Gunnar, Kestenbaum, Lang, & Andreas, 1990; Milliones, 1978). Regardless of whether child characteristics have a direct effect, the ecological model suggests that they interact with parent characteristics; for example, the combination of a child with a difficult temperament and a parent with high levels of stress and little patience may lead to maltreatment. Furthermore, child characteristics may indirectly influence the parent-child relationship and parenting, which in turn leads to child maltreatment.

The relationship between parents and children may also be influenced by other family members (Belsky, 1980, 1993). For example, the mother-child interaction may be influenced by the mother-father relationship. Because it may be easier to lash out at a child, parents may redirect their anger with each other toward the child. In contrast, a supportive grandparent can be a valuable buffer against the stresses a family is experiencing.

Families may also be stressed by several factors that make it difficult for many parents to maintain jobs. For example, child care is needed by all families with young children without a stay-at-home parent. High-quality child care is often unavailable for several reasons. First, the quality of child care is often poor or variable. Second, child care providers are greatly undervalued in this society; potentially good providers may not enter or stay in the field because of limited recognition and compensation for their work. Third, good child care is relatively expensive. If good and affordable child care is not available, parents may be unable to work or may leave their children in marginal or inadequate arrangements; child neglect and abuse are concerns.

Community Level

The family functions within the larger context of the community, which influences maltreatment through work conditions, community resources, formal and informal social supports, and role models for parents (Belsky, 1980, 1993). Community resources include the availability of job training, jobs, housing, and education, which are all linked to income levels and poverty, which in turn are related to child maltreatment (Sedlak & Broadhurst, 1996).

Poverty and unemployment have been associated with maltreatment (Dodge et al., 1990; Gelles, 1989; Halpern, 1990; Pelton, 1994; Sedlak & Broadhurst, 1996; Trickett, Aber, Carlson, & Cicchetti, 1991; Volpe, 1989). Currently, one in five children in the United States lives in poverty (Children's Defense Fund, 1996a; National Commission on Children, 1991); half of black children under 6 years old live in poverty (Children's Defense Fund, 1996a; National Center for Children in Poverty, 1991). Not all families living in poverty have an unemployed or single head of household; a mother working full-time at a minimum wage job may not earn enough to keep herself and a single child above the poverty line (National Commission on Children, 1991). Neglect is also strongly associated with living in poverty and its associated stresses, such as unemployment, lower educational achievement, household crowding, and limited access to needed services (Garbarino & Crouter; 1978; Martin & Walters, 1982; Nelson & Landsman, 1992; Pelton, 1994; Pianta, Egeland, & Erickson, 1989; Zuravin, 1986, 1988).

Studies of the incidence and prevalence of child maltreatment have consistently found a disproportionately high number of low income families (Pelton, 1994), including a study based on parents' self-reports of how they resolve conflicts in their families (Straus, Gelles, & Steinmetz, 1988). However, it is also evident that many poor people are very good parents (Milner, 1994; Pelton, 1994). Examining the effects of parent absence and economic deprivation in over 6,000 households, Gelles (1989) found that children from single-parent households were more likely to be abused than those from two-parent households. However, the poverty of families headed by a single mother was more strongly associated with abuse than was single parenthood.

Poverty, per se, represents a direct and indirect threat to the health and well-being of children (e.g., inferior educational opportunities and inadequate food and shelter). In addition, poverty burdens families with a variety of stresses (e.g., housing problems) that contribute to abuse (Halpern, 1990; Volpe, 1989) and neglect. Any strategy to prevent child maltreatment must address the problem of poverty (Pelton, 1994).

Maltreating families are often socially isolated (Belsky, 1980, 1993; Garbarino, 1980; Polansky, Chalmers, Williams, & Buttenwieser, 1981), and this may be related to maltreatment in three ways. First, the family might not receive material and emotional support from the community (Garbarino, 1980). Second, contact with others in the community can provide role models for acceptable parental behavior and influence parents to conform to these standards. Third, isolated families also may not be pressured to conform to community standards of parenting behavior.

Cultural/Societal Level

The culture and society within which the community resides is the fourth level in the ecological theory. Culture influences the occurrence of maltreatment through its "attitudes toward violence, corporal punishment, and children" (Belsky, 1980, p. 328; Garbarino, 1980). In the United States, violence is widely accepted, as evidenced by the amount of violence in television programming and the acceptance of physical punishment for disciplining children, including the legal use of corporal punishment by schools in many states (Holmes, 1987).

Three other cultural/societal factors also are related to child maltreatment. First, in the United States, parenting is seen as a private matter, with societal/community oversight seen as an unwelcome intrusion on parents' rights. Balancing this perspective with our interest in protecting children and helping families is a necessary step in the effort to prevent child maltreatment. With this change, services could be framed as "family support initiatives rather than child abuse prevention efforts" (Daro & McCurdy, 1994, p. 409), perhaps reducing the stigma often attached to receiving services. Second, prevention efforts need to be culturally sensitive and incorporate minority group experiences as a component (Asbury, Chapter 6, this volume; Daro & McCurdy, 1994; Hay & Jones, 1994). Third, public policies and laws that affect families may contribute to child maltreatment. For example, welfare reform and changes to the Child Abuse Prevention and Treatment Act (CAPTA) may jeopardize the well-being of many children.

Ecological theory suggests that maltreatment is determined by some or all of the factors discussed above, which often interact with each other (Belsky, 1980, 1993). An understanding of the factors contributing to maltreatment is necessary to design and implement prevention programs. Although research on the etiology of child maltreatment has been limited by many methodological problems (Rosenberg & Reppucci, 1985), the ecological model is widely accepted in the field of child maltreatment. Nevertheless, in many areas, our understanding of the exact factors leading to child maltreatment remains limited.

Ecological theory is also useful because it suggests resources to promote positive outcomes among families experiencing child maltreatment, such as social support from extended family members and neighbors. It is worth noting that tackling some and not necessarily all of the risk factors in a given family may prevent maltreatment. For example, giving a mother antidepressants might treat her depression, enabling her to cope with difficult circumstances and consequently reducing the risk of child maltreatment.

Levels of Prevention

Prevention efforts occur at three levels (Dubowitz, 1990; Helfer, 1982; Newman & Lutzker, 1990). Primary prevention, such as providing pediatric care for all children, targets the general population. Secondary prevention is directed at groups thought to be at high risk for child maltreatment; an example is home visiting programs for young, unmarried mothers (e.g., Olds, Henderson, Chamberlin, & Tatelbaum, 1986). Tertiary prevention, or treatment, occurs after the condition has been identified; the goal is to prevent further abuse or neglect as well as or neglect as well as to reduce the negative sequelae of maltreatment. An example is protective services intervention following a substantiated report for child maltreatment.

This chapter will focus mostly on examples of primary and secondary prevention efforts. Some prevention efforts are much less expensive than others (e.g., public awareness messages as compared with providing families multiple home visits). Economic constraints and cost-effectiveness are important considerations for prevention efforts. However, inadequate prevention efforts result in the enormous price we are currently paying as a result of child maltreatment.

Prevention Efforts Directed at the Individual Level

Early research examining the causes of child maltreatment focused on parental factors. However, the ecological model clearly indicates many other potential causes of maltreatment, and even in situations where a parental contributory factor exists, family, community, and cultural/societal components may still be involved. Therefore, although the individual-level prevention efforts described here may be adequate to prevent child maltreatment in some situations, in others, these efforts need to be offered along with other services.

Parenting Education

Parenting education is often provided in group settings. In one study, 30 families with children involved with protective services were randomly assigned to two groups (Wolfe, Edwards, Manion, & Koverola, 1988). All of the families participated in an informational group that met for 2 hours twice a week for an average of 18 weeks. Group sessions included informal discussions on family- and health-related topics, as well as social activities. In addition, half of the families received additional training in child-management skills, including videotaped sessions of mother-child interactions that allowed the mothers to critique their own behavior. Training lasted an average of 20 weeks.

At the three-month follow-up, the mothers who received the additional training reported less intense and fewer child behavior and adjustment problems than those who received the more limited intervention (Wolfe et al., 1988). However, direct observation using the Home Observation for Measurement of the Environment (HOME) did not reveal significant differences between the two groups. Wolfe et al. concluded that the combination of training in child management techniques and family support can address the needs of families at risk for child maltreatment. However, this conclusion is uncertain given that the differences were only found with parental self-report and not by more objective, direct observation.

Whipple and Wilson (1996) found that providing an array of self-selected services to parents, including drop-in child care, parent support groups, parent nurturing programs, and early childhood development classes, was related to decreased parental depression and stress over time. Furthermore, parents with higher levels of involvement benefitted more.

Substance Abuse Problems

Despite methodological shortcomings in the research on parental substance abuse and child maltreatment (i.e., based on retrospective and clinical data), the ecological model and existing data suggest that addressing substance abuse should also reduce child maltreatment. Pregnant women may be more likely to seek treatment for their addiction because of concern for the baby (Deren, 1986). Providing a combination of substance abuse treatment and parenting groups may be especially effective in promoting recovery from substance abuse and improving parenting abilities (Plasse, 1995). However, to date, no studies have evaluated the potential impact of specialized prevention efforts that focus on both parenting and substance abuse treatment (Guterman, 1997). Substance abuse needs to be addressed through a variety of strategies. Primary prevention should occur in schools, through public service announcements, and with routine health care, especially in obstetric clinics. The availability of all types of substance abuse treatment programs, including outpatient and residential programs with child care facilities, needs to be greatly expanded, especially for pregnant women.

Prevention Efforts Directed at the Family Level

Maintaining family relationships is difficult, as evidenced by the high rates of divorce and domestic violence in the United States. Although some families may have extensive informal support (per-

extended family), many other families have few such supports. The amount of formal support needed by a family also depends on a number of situational factors; for example, the birth of a baby can be a particularly stressful time. Family-level prevention efforts may be sufficient to prevent child maltreatment for some families, whereas other families may require parent- and community-level assistance. Family-level programs often include components for helping families access other individual (e.g., drug treatment) and community (e.g., financial support such as welfare) services.

Home Visiting Services

Several studies suggest that home visiting may effectively help families and reduce the incidence of child maltreatment (Wasik, Bryant, & Lyons, 1990). Olds, Henderson, Chamberlin, and Tatelbaum (1986) conducted a randomized study of home visitation designed "to prevent a wide range of childhood health and developmental problems, including child abuse and neglect" (p. 66). Women who were pregnant for the first time could participate in the study; in addition, young (< 19 years), single, and low income women were actively recruited. Women were enrolled in the study prior to the 30th week of pregnancy and were randomly assigned to one of four interventions. Children in one group received developmental screenings at 1 and 2 years of age, and those with problems were referred for intervention. Families in the second group received the screening provided to the first group, as well as transportation for prenatal and well-child care. Families in the third group received the transportation and screening services, as well as an average of nine nurse home visits during pregnancy. Families in the fourth group received the services provided to the third group, as well as nurse home visits until the child was 2 years old. The postnatal visits focused on infant development education, informal support, and health and human services linkages. It should be noted that all families could have obtained standard prenatal care and pediatric primary care, aside from the intervention.

The children of poor, unmarried teenagers were considered to be at greatest risk for child maltreatment. Of these highest risk children, 19% of the group receiving developmental screening only were abused or neglected compared with 4% of the group who received the most comprehensive services. There were also several related differences between these two groups. Compared with the developmental screening-only group, the latter group of mothers reported that their infants were happier and less irritable. They were more concerned about their children's behavior problems, reported more positive interactions with their children, and had more toys available. Their infants also tended to have higher developmental scores. In general, among the highest-risk mothers, those who received the most comprehensive intervention appeared to be functioning significantly better as parents than the mothers whose children received developmental screenings only (Olds et al., 1986).

Unlike Olds et al., the Good Start Project found that families at moderate risk of child maltreatment are most responsive to a variety of services, including developmental assessments, counseling, medical care, social advocacy, and parent-child enrichment sessions in both clinic and home settings (Ayoub & Jacewitz, 1982; Kowal, Kottmeier, Ayoub, Komives, Robinson, & Allen, 1989; Willett, Ayoub, & Robinson, 1991). Certain types of problems were more amenable to change than others. For example, little improvement was achieved with families that initially had problems with discipline, difficult child behavior, learning-disabled children, or parent-child conflict, and fewer than 7% of the families with substance abuse problems improved. However, more than half the families showed improvement in the areas of parent-child interaction during play, communication, and encouragement of the child (Kowal et al., 1989). The Good Start Project demonstrates how a variety of services can be integrated to support families.

The Family Crisis Care (FCC) project, based on the Homebuilders model, was designed to serve "families at imminent risk of child placement out of the home for child abuse and neglect" (Amundson, 1989, p. 286). The FCC was a tertiary prevention program for families identified for child maltreatment, providing intensive services in three phases. The first phase provided intensive crisis intervention over 6 weeks, during which problems and goals were identified and families were referred for appropriate services. The second phase consisted of 2 to 6 weeks of regular in-home visits by therapists with master's degrees. Families were provided with support and concrete services, such as food, clothing, and shelter. The third phase was 4 to 12 weeks of follow-up services, including therapy and assistance in obtaining services from community agencies. The therapists were on call 24 hours a day.

Forty-two families were followed for 6 months after treatment. Ninety percent of the families that received services were able to keep their children at home, avoiding out-of-home placement. Communication and problem-solving skills, as rated by the therapists, were improved for 80% of the families. Ninety-five percent of the families had reduced rates of physical punishment and other problem behaviors. Furthermore, 85% of the families had used suggested community resources (Amundson, 1989). Amundson concluded that "home-based, intensive services delivered by interdisciplinary co-therapists are an effective alternative to out-of-home placement for many abused children" (p. 295). The findings of this study are limited by the lack of a comparison group, making it difficult to assess how the families might have done without intervention.

These studies suggest that home visiting may be an effective intervention for child maltreatment, particularly for certain types of families, such as poor, unmarried, first-time teen mothers (Olds & Henderson, 1989) or families with young children (Nelson, Landsman, & Deutelbaum, 1990). Home visiting might be effective because it assists families at several levels of the ecological theory. At the individual level, the home visitor can provide support and counseling and model good parenting. At the family level, the involvement of extended family members in the care of a child might be enhanced. At the community level, the home visitor can make suitable referrals, helping the family obtain assistance from local resources. Although not all studies have found home visitors to be effective (U.S. General Accounting Office, 1990), overall, home visiting appears to be a promising strategy for serving high-risk families and preventing child abuse and neglect (Cohn Donnelly, 1991; Daro, 1996; Garbarino, 1986).

Support for Working Parents

Working parents need child care for their young children. The quality and availability of child care could be improved in several ways. To ensure quality child care, standards should be established and implemented. Salaries for child care providers should be increased. Employers and governments need to subsidize child care. Finally, flexible work schedules could also help some families obtain child care.

Public policies, such as those concerning parental leave, may influence the relationships within families. Policies that do not allow parents to spend time with newborn children may interfere with bonding, impeding the process of attachment between the infant and parent. Many child development specialists believe that the time after birth is especially important for bonding between parents and children (White, 1985).

Secure attachment in turn is important for developing a sense of security and an ability to trust others. Maltreated children have been found to be less securely attached to their parents than nonmaltreated children (Egeland & Sroufe, 1981).

Recently, several public policy changes have enhanced support for families. The minimum wage has been increased. The new Federal Child Care and Development Block Grant will provide money for states to provide "low- and moderate-income families [with] increased access to affordable care" and improved referral and resource systems (Children's Defense Fund, 1991). In addition, many corporations have been showing more sensitivity to the needs of families, as demonstrated by the increased availability of child care facilities at the work site. The Family Leave Bill, which was passed in 1993, provides up to 12 weeks of unpaid leave per year for parents of a new infant or in the event of illness of a family member. Although this provides some job security, most families still cannot afford to take unpaid leave.

Prevention Efforts Directed at the Community Level

"Socially impoverished neighborhoods contain a disproportionate number of families with multiple needs competing for scarce resources" (Hay & Jones, 1994, p. 387). General services to families, such as housing, child care, and drug treatment, help parents provide better care for their children. Although there have been no clinical trials testing the efficacy of these prevention efforts, it is likely that they help reduce the risk of child maltreatment (Leventhal, 1996). Community-level services need to be available to all eligible families, and access to these programs can be enhanced by ensuring that individual- and family-level service providers know how to help families obtain them.

Social Isolation

Maltreating families are often described as socially isolated (Belsky, 1980, 1993; Garbarino, 1980; Polansky et al., 1981), which may increase the likelihood that they will not have access to available community resources (Thompson, 1995). However, it is not clear whether the families actually have less access to support or whether they simply are unable to use the assistance that is available (Thompson, 1995). Coohey

(1995) found that neglectful and nonneglectful mothers were equally likely to live close to their own mothers; however, the neglectful mothers reported fewer positive relationships and received less emotional support from their mothers. This finding suggests that availability of resources may not adequately represent the actual support received by a family and that it is important to consider perceived support. Service providers need to ask about the resources the family knows about and uses; families may not be aware of available services or know how to obtain them.

A number of prevention strategies, including the home visiting programs discussed above, can be used to reduce social isolation (Thompson, 1995). In addition, family support resource information can be made available through local schools; provision of preschool or day care services could help involve families with young children (Thompson, 1995). In some areas, medical clinics are placed in schools, increasing access to health care services. School programs designed for pregnant and parenting teenagers can provide a range of services that may decrease social isolation. By keeping teens in school, such programs can enhance the educational and occupational achievement of parenting teens while also allowing these teens to maintain contact with their peers.

Programs that may appear to be narrowly focused may actually serve broader needs. For example, in the program described by Plasse (1995), women in a drug treatment day program were also offered parenting classes. This combination was associated with improvements in drug recovery and parenting. Providing multiple services in one setting makes it more convenient for families to access resources.

Poverty

Several programs are designed to reduce the impact of poverty, including Temporary Assistance to Needy Families [TANF] (which recently replaced Aid to Families with Dependent Children [AFDC]), WIC, Food Stamps, School Lunch and Breakfast, and Medical Assistance. Although these programs were not designed to prevent child maltreatment, they provide crucial assistance to low-income families, supporting the functioning of these families. However, many eligible families do not receive these benefits, while others receive inadequate support.

A study by Barth (1989) evaluated a task-oriented prevention program. Ninety-seven women at high risk for child maltreatment were recruited prenatally and then provided with a parent aide who provided in-home services. The mothers identified various goals, such as contacting community service agencies, taking care of themselves and their children, and preparing food. Barth found that the mother's achievement of these goals was associated with reduced scores on the Child Abuse Potential Inventory (Milner, 1980, cited in Barth, 1989). Although this intervention was not designed to reduce poverty, many of the tasks helped reduce the impact of poverty, such as contacting community agencies for assistance and food. Barth cautions that this intervention was not effective for the highest-risk families.

Poverty is a complex problem for which there is no simple solution. However, several aspects of poverty are amenable to change, such as increasing the availability of low-income housing, reducing unemployment, and raising the minimum wage and benefits for those who are employed ("making work pay"). Funding for programs that provide crucial support to low-income families, such as Head Start, WIC, Food Stamps, and Medical Assistance, should be increased so that all eligible families can receive these services or benefits. Fuchs and Reklis (1992) suggest that children could be helped by child allowances and tax credits provided by the government. Reducing poverty should substantially reduce the incidence of child maltreatment (Olds & Henderson, 1989; Pelton, 1994; Wolock & Horowitz, 1984).

Although it is important to provide increased benefits to more families, several other factors should also be addressed. Job training programs should be expanded to serve more families (National Commission on Children, 1991). More emphasis could also be placed on encouraging adolescents to remain in school and on providing them with basic job skills.

Prevention Efforts Directed at the Cultural/Societal Level

The best individual-, family-, and community-level child maltreatment prevention efforts may not be enough to substantially reduce the enormous problem of child maltreatment in the United States. Efforts targeting the broad cultural and societal contributors to maltreatment are also needed.

Attitudes Toward Violence

As a society, the United States sanctions the use of physical punishment of children (Belsky, 1980; Helfer, 1982; Stein, 1984). Corporal punishment is still permitted in schools in the majority of states (Limber & Wilcox, 1996; National Child Abuse Coalition, 1991). However, in many states that still allow corporal punishment, individual counties and cities have banned this practice. Teachers are considered to be experts in understanding and teaching children. When they hit children, they serve as negative role models for parents. Belsky (1980) suggests that maltreatment may occur as an escalation of "acceptable" levels of physical punishment. The message often communicated to parents is that it is all right to hit children, as long as no bruises are left. As a society, our attitudes toward the physical punishment of children need to change (Belsky, 1980; Garbarino, 1996; Helfer, 1982; Stein, 1984). There are many more effective ways than physical punishment to teach and socialize children. Teachers and schools should set an example by rejecting the use of corporal punishment, using preferable forms of discipline, and modeling effective alternatives to physical punishment.

Societal Policies That Affect Children

Two major pieces of recent federal legislation may substantially diminish services to families and increase their vulnerability to child maltreatment: welfare reform and reauthorization of the Child Abuse Prevention and Treatment Act (CAPTA; Pub. L. No. 104-235) (American Humane Association, 1996; Children's Defense Fund, 1996a, 1996b; National Child Abuse Coalition, 1996a, 1996b).

Welfare Reform

A conservative Congress, a president committed to "ending welfare as we know it," and a widely held public view that the welfare system is not working, led to a dramatic dismantling of the long-standing safety net for disadvantaged families. Pub. L. No. 104-93, the Personal Responsibility and Work Opportunity Reconciliation Act of 1996, cut federal funds for a variety of programs by $54 billion over 6 years and replaced many national guarantees for low-income families with optional state programs, via block grants. In many areas, authority is transferred from the federal government to the states, and a previously open-ended entitlement is now a capped block grant with $16.4 billion appropriated annually for the next 6 years.

There is still uncertainty about how exactly many of the changes will be implemented, but there is concern that many children and families may lose vital supports. In general, because the new law allows states enormous latitude, it seems likely that some will provide adequate benefits whereas others will not. There is broad concern that the resources such as jobs, job training, and child care required to move people from welfare to work will not be adequate. Withdrawal of benefits and services might substantially increase the number of families and children in poverty.

Under welfare reform, TANF has replaced AFDC and its associated employment and training program (Job Opportunity and Basic Skills Training [JOBS]) and Emergency Assistance. Previously, all eligible individuals were guaranteed aid at state-established benefit levels, states received federal matching dollars for expenditures without a cap, and there was no time limit for benefits as long as recipients met program eligibility criteria. Under the new law, benefits are no longer guaranteed and cash assistance will be limited to 5 cumulative years at most. The new law also includes stringent work requirements; individuals must work after a maximum of 2 consecutive years on assistance, and states can choose a much shorter period. States must have "objective criteria for delivery of benefits and determining eligibility" (Pub. L. No. 104-235), and they can opt for time limits of less than 5 years. States may exempt 20% of their caseload, such as kinship care providers and victims of domestic violence, from the time limits.

There were also major cuts in the Food Stamps program ($27.7 billion over 6 years), with half of these cuts to be absorbed by families at less than half the poverty line ($7,800 for a family of four) (Center on Budget and Policy Priorities, cited in Children's Defense Fund, 1996c). The Thrifty Food Plan, a low-cost budget used to calculate the amount of food stamps a family receives, will be adjusted to reduce aid. In the past, families receiving financial assistance were automatically able to participate in nutrition programs, such as WIC and the free school lunch program; under welfare reform, eligibility for these programs will be determined by individual states.

In the past, child care was guaranteed for working AFDC recipients, those participating in the JOBS program, and for up to 1 year during the transition from welfare to work. The new law eliminates these guarantees; however, there is some protection for parents with children under 6 years old, who cannot be penalized if they do not work because they cannot find affordable child care. Although child care funds have been increased by $4 billion with an allocation of $22 billion over 7 years, the Office for Management and the Budget estimates a $2.4 billion shortfall in child care funding if all states meet their welfare work targets (Children's Defense Fund, 1996c).

There are also a number of miscellaneous restrictions under welfare reform that may affect services for families with children. First, a minor parent can only receive block grant funds if she lives with an adult or in an adult-supervised setting, and once her child is 12 weeks old, she must be in an educational/training program. Second, childhood disability is more stringently defined, limiting Supplemental Security Income (SSI) to children who have a "medically determinable physical or mental impairment which results in marked and severe functional limitations, which can be expected to result in death or which have lasted or can be expected to last at least 12 months" (American Academy of Pediatrics, 1996). Maladaptive behavior will no longer be a criterion for determining medical disabilities in children. The Congressional Budget Office estimates that over 300,000 children will be denied SSI by the year 2002 (Children's Defense Fund, 1996c). Children with mental retardation, diabetes, autism, cerebral palsy, and epilepsy are at risk of losing their benefits. Third, convicted adult drug felons may be prohibited, for life, from receiving welfare benefits, although states can opt out of this provision or limit the duration of the sanction. Although this does not apply directly to children, there is little doubt that children are likely to be affected by the withdrawal of benefits to their parents. Child abuse and neglect may increase, along with the demand for more foster care and adoptive homes. Fourth, the new law cuts billions of dollars of support to legal immigrants, who will lose SSI and food stamps; other benefits (e.g., Medicaid, TANF block grants) will become optional for states to provide.

The Child Abuse Prevention and Treatment Act (CAPTA)

Vigorous efforts by the House of Representatives to dismantle the federal role in child abuse and neglect by block-granting the modest national program failed, and a substantially weakened version of CAPTA was reauthorized in 1996 (National Child Abuse Coalition, 1996a). Many of the key functions of CAPTA are continued, including a federal role in funding research, training, technical assistance to the states, data collection, and dissemination of information. Also continued are the state grant programs for Child Protective Services improvements, community-based efforts to prevent child maltreatment, and the children's justice program (National Child Abuse Coalition, 1996a). The new CAPTA replaces the National Center on Child Abuse and Neglect with an optional lower level Office on Child Abuse and Neglect, makes the U.S. Advisory Board on Child Abuse and Neglect optional, weakens the recommended definition of abuse and neglect, weakens the criteria for states to obtain federal funding, and appears sympathetic to religious practices that may be construed as medical neglect. The new CAPTA adds an appeals process for findings of child maltreatment and establishes citizen review panels, new state requirements addressing good-faith reporting, and expungement of child protective services records (National Child Abuse Coalition, 1996a).

Under the new CAPTA, child abuse and neglect is now defined as "at a minimum, any recent act or failure to act on the part of a parent or caretaker, which results in death or serious physical or emotional harm, or sexual abuse or exploitation, or presents an imminent risk of serious harm" (Pub. L. No. 104-235). Although this definition establishes a minimum standard, there is concern that states will follow suit and limit their involvement to recent incidents resulting in serious and imminent harm, thereby excluding many less severe cases.

Medical neglect may be a concern when certain religious groups deny children necessary medical attention, relying instead on prayer or other forms of healing. For the first time, CAPTA does not require that parents provide their children with medical care against their religious beliefs or that states deal with such situations as abuse or neglect. However, states are required to allow child protective services to intervene and pursue legal remedies to provide medical care "for a child when such care or treatment is necessary to prevent or remedy serious harm to the child" (Pub. L. No. 104-235).

A variety of demonstration projects to improve child protective services and community prevention efforts will be supported. These include resource centers, self-help support programs to support families, triage systems to assess abuse and neglect reports, intensive interventions to protect children, and kinship care programs for children removed from home. All such demonstration projects need to be evaluated for their effectiveness.

As with welfare reform, the impact of the revised CAPTA remains to be seen. However, the diminished status of the small national agency addressing child maltreatment, the signal emitted by the narrowed definition of abuse and neglect, and several other aspects of the new legislation raise concerns for the safety and well-being of children, particularly in light of the stresses many families are likely to experience resulting from welfare reform.

Children's Rights

The United States helped draft the U.N. Convention on the Rights of the Child but is one of a handful of countries that have not yet ratified it (Murphy-Berman & Weisz, 1996). A number of aspects of the Convention are relevant to the prevention of child maltreatment, including the need to provide assistance and support to parents and guardians to prevent child maltreatment (Melton, 1996). Although then-U.N. Ambassador Madeleine Albright was directed by President Clinton to sign the treaty on February 16, 1995, the treaty must now be approved by a two-thirds vote of the U.S. Senate (Limber & Wilcox, 1996).

There has been extensive grassroots opposition to the Convention for a number of reasons, including the belief that it would prohibit corporal punishment (Limber & Wilcox, 1996). From the perspective that corporal punishment should be prohibited,

> The Convention may be a most powerful tool in encouraging change in U.S. law. In recent years, the U.S. Congress has rejected several attempts to legislate on this matter, even on the more limited issue of the use of corporal punishment in school programs for students with disabilities. (Limber & Wilcox, 1996, p. 1249)

Perhaps following Garbarino's (1996) suggestion and using the term *assault* instead of *corporal punishment* would help change attitudes on this issue.

Conclusion

Child maltreatment is associated with risk factors at each level of the ecological theory: for example, poor parenting skills at the individual level, conflict between parents at the family level, social isolation at the community level, and acceptance of hitting children at the societal level. In many cases, maltreatment results from the interaction of factors at various levels. Clearly, the problem of child maltreatment needs to be addressed through a variety of prevention strategies; no single approach will be sufficient.

Research in the prevention field has progressed (Cohn Donnelly, 1997). More research is being done with more rigorous, longer-term evaluations, as the illustrative examples in this chapter indicate. Research is also beginning to provide answers about targeting specific types of prevention strategies to specific types of families (Guterman, 1997). For example, the home visitors provided by Olds et al. (1986) were particularly effective for poor, single, teenage mothers.

Although progress has been made, much remains to be done. In the past several decades, much has been learned about the etiology and prevention of child maltreatment (Cohn Donnelly, 1997). However, more information is needed about what prevention strategies are most effective and cost-effective for which families. In addition, child maltreatment prevention research has not included the roles of fathers, other family members, and culture; future efforts will need to address these oversights (Guterman, 1997). There are a number of excellent demonstration prevention efforts that need to be thoroughly evaluated and replicated in other locations. However, excellent prevention programs are probably not enough. There also needs to be a national commitment to addressing the underlying problems, such as poverty, that compromise the functioning of families and contribute to child maltreatment.

References

American Academy of Pediatrics. (1996, November 22). *Supplemental security income (SSI) program for children* [Special Alert]. Washington, DC: Author.

American Humane Association. (1996, October). Welfare reform: What it means for children at risk. *Child Protection Leader,* pp. 1-2.

Amundson, M. J. (1989). Family crisis care: A home-based intervention program for child abuse. *Issues in Mental Health Nursing, 10,* 285-296.

Ayoub, C., & Jacewitz, M. M. (1982). Families at risk of poor parenting: A descriptive study of sixty at risk families in a model prevention program. *Child Abuse & Neglect,* 6, 413-422.

Barth, R. P. (1989). Evaluation of a task-centered child abuse prevention program. *Children and Youth Services Review, 11,* 117-131.

Beatty, C. (1996). Parents' rights versus children's rights: A fair contest? *Children's Voice, 5*(3), 10-11.

Belsky, J. (1980). Child maltreatment: An ecological integration. *American Psychologist, 35,* 320-335.

Belsky, J. (1993). Etiology of child maltreatment: A developmental-ecological analysis. *Psychological Bulletin, 114,* 413-434.

Belsky, J., & Vondra, J. (1989). Lessons from child abuse: The determinants of parenting. In D. Cicchetti & V. Carlson (Eds.), *Child maltreatment: Theory and research on the causes and consequences of child abuse and neglect.* New York: Cambridge University Press.

Child Abuse Prevention and Treatment Act of 1996, 42 U.S.C. 5101 *et seq*; Pub. L. No. 104-235.

Children's Defense Fund. (1991). Child care in the states: New plans promise better care for children. *CDF Reports, 13*(3), 1-3.

Children's Defense Fund. (1996a). Child poverty declining, but rates still far too high. *CDF Reports, 17*(12), 5-6.

Children's Defense Fund. (1996b). Most children's services spared; Children lose national safety net. *CDF Reports, 17*(12), 1-15.

Children's Defense Fund. (1996c). Summary of the new welfare legislation. *CDF Reports, 17*(9), 1-7.

Cohn Donnelly, A. H. (1991). What we have learned about prevention: What we should do about it. *Child Abuse & Neglect, 15,* 99-106.

Cohn Donnelly, A. H. (1997). We've come a long way, but the challenges ahead are mighty. *Child Maltreatment, 2,* 6-11.

Coohey, C. (1995). Neglectful mothers, their mothers, and partners: The significance of mutual aid. *Child Abuse and Neglect, 19,* 885-895.

Culbertson, J. L., & Schellenbach, C. J. (1992). Prevention of maltreatment in infants and young children. In D. J. Willis, E. W. Holden, & M. Rosenberg (Eds.), *Prevention of child maltreatment: Developmental and ecological perspectives* (pp. 47-77). New York: John Wiley.

Daro, D. (1988). *Confronting child abuse: Research for effective program design.* New York: Free Press.

Daro, D. (1996). Preventing child abuse and neglect. In J. Briere, L. Berliner, J. A. Bulkley, C. Jenny, & T. Reid (Eds.), *The APSAC handbook on child maltreatment.* Thousand Oaks, CA: Sage.

Daro, D., & McCurdy, K. (1994). Preventing child abuse and neglect: Programmatic interventions. *Child Welfare, 73,* 405-430.

Deren, S. (1986). Children of substance abusers: A review of the literature. *Journal of Substance Abuse Treatment, 3,* 77-94.

Dodge, K. A., Bates, J. E., & Pettit, G. S. (1990). Mechanisms in the cycle of violence. *Science, 250,* 1678-1683.

Dubowitz, H. (1987). *Child maltreatment in the United States: Etiology, impact, and prevention* (Contractor Document; Health Program, Office of Technology Assessment). Washington, DC: U.S. Congress.

Dubowitz, H. (1990). Pediatrician's role in preventing child maltreatment. *Pediatric Clinics of North America, 37,* 989-1002.

Egeland, B., Jacobvitz, D., & Sroufe, L. A. (1988). Breaking the cycle of abuse. *Child Development, 59,* 1080-1088.

Egeland, B., & Sroufe, L. A. (1981). Developmental sequelae of maltreatment in infancy. In R. Rizley & D. Cicchetti (Eds.), *New directions for child development.* San Francisco: Jossey-Bass.

Fuchs, V. R., & Reklis, D. M. (1992). America's children: Economic perspectives and policy options. *Science, 255,* 41-46.

Garbarino, J. (1980). What kind of society permits child abuse? *Infant Mental Health Journal, 1,* 270-280.

Garbarino, J. (1986). Can we measure success in preventing child abuse? Issues in policy, programming, and research. *Child Abuse & Neglect, 10,* 143-156.

Garbarino, J. (1994). Can most child maltreatment be prevented? Yes. In E. Gambrill & T. J. Stein (Eds.), *Controversial issues in child welfare* (pp. 49-52). Boston: Allyn & Bacon.

Garbarino, J. (1996). CAN Reflections on 20 years of searching. *Child Abuse and Neglect, 20,* 157-160.

Garbarino, J., & Crouter, A. (1978). Defining the community context for parent-child relations: The correlates of child maltreatment. *Child Development, 49,* 604-616.

Gelles, R. J. (1989). Child abuse and violence in single-parent families: Parent absence and economic deprivation. *American Journal of Orthopsychiatry, 59,* 492-501.

Gomby, D. S., & Shiono, P. H. (1991). Estimating the number of substance-exposed infants. *The Future of Children, 1*(1), 17-25.

Goodman-Campbell, S. (1979). Mother-infant interactions as a function of maternal ratings of temperament. *Child Psychiatry and Human Development, 10,* 67-76.

Guterman, N. B. (1997). Early prevention of physical child abuse and neglect: Existing evidence and future directions. *Child Maltreatment, 2,* 12-34.

Halpern, R. (1990). Poverty and early childhood parenting: Toward a framework for intervention. *American Journal of Orthopsychiatry, 60,* 6-18.

Hay, T., & Jones, L. (1994). Societal interventions to prevent child abuse and neglect. *Child Welfare, 73,* 379-403.

Helfer, R. E. (1982). A review of the literature on the prevention of child abuse and neglect. *Child Abuse and Neglect, 6,* 251-261.

Holmes, C. P. (1987). Prevention of child abuse: Possibilities for educational systems. *Special Services in the Schools, 3,* 139-153.

Houldin, A. D. (1987). Infant temperament and the quality of the childrearing environment. *Maternal-Child Nursing Journal, 16,* 131-143.

Kaufman, J., & Zigler, E. (1989). The intergenerational transmission of child abuse. In D. Cicchetti & V. Carlson (Eds.), *Child maltreatment: Theory and research on the causes and consequences of child abuse and neglect.* New York: Cambridge University Press.

Kowal, L. W., Kottmeier, C. P., Ayoub, C. C., Komives, J. A., Robinson, D. S., & Allen, J. P. (1989). Characteristics of families at risk of problems in parenting: Findings from a home-based secondary prevention program. *Child Welfare, 68,* 529-538.

Kumpfer, K. L. (1991). Treatment programs for drug-abusing women. *The Future of Children, 1*(1), 50-60.

Leventhal, J. M. (1996). Twenty years later: We do know how to prevent child abuse and neglect. *Child Abuse and Neglect, 20,* 647-653.

Limber, S. P., & Wilcox, B. L. (1996). Application of the U.N. Convention on the Rights of the Child to the United States. *American Psychologist, 51,* 1246-1250.

Main, M., & Goldwyn, R. (1984). Predicting rejection of her infant from mother's representation of her own experience: Implications for the abused-abusing intergenerational cycle. *Child Abuse & Neglect, 8,* 203-217.

Mangelsdorf, S., Gunnar, M., Kestenbaum, R., Lang, S., & Andreas, D. (1990). Infant proneness-to-distress temperament, maternal personality, and mother-infant attachment: Association and goodness of fit. *Child Development, 61,* 820-831.

Martin, M. J., & Walters, J. (1982). Familial correlates of selected types of child abuse and neglect. *Journal of Marriage and the Family, 44,* 267-276.

Mayer, J., & Black, R. (1977). Child abuse and neglect in families with an alcohol or opiate addicted parent. *Child Abuse & Neglect, 1,* 85-98.

McCullough, C. B. (1991). The child welfare response. *The Future of Children, 1*(1), 61-71.

Melton, G. B. (1996). The child's right to a family environment: Why children's rights and family values are compatible. *American Psychologist, 51,* 1234-1238.

Merrick, J. (1985). Addicted mothers and their children: A case for coordinated welfare services. *Child: Care, Health, and Development, 11,* 159-169.

Milliones, J. (1978). Relationship between perceived child temperament and maternal behaviors. *Child Development, 49,* 1255-1257.

Milner, J. S. (1980). *The Child Abuse Potential Inventory: Manual.* Webster, NC: Psytec Corp.

Milner, J. S. (1994). Is poverty a key contributor to child maltreatment? No. In E. Gambrill & T. J. Stein (Eds.), *Controversial issues in child welfare* (pp. 23-26). Boston: Allyn & Bacon.

Murphy-Berman, V., & Weisz, V. (1996). U.N. Convention on the Rights of the Child: Current challenges. *American Psychologist, 51,* 1231-1233.

National Association of Community Health Centers. (1991). *Access to community health centers.* Washington, DC: Author.

National Center for Children in Poverty. (1991, Fall). Number of poor children growing. *News and Issues,* p. 1.

National Child Abuse Coalition. (1991, June 28). Federal bill to prohibit corporal punishment. *National Child Abuse Coalition Monthly Newsletter,* pp. 3-4.

National Child Abuse Coalition. (1996a, September 30). Congress passes CAPTA reauthorization. *Information Sheet.*

National Child Abuse Coalition. (1996b, August 30). Welfare reform impact on abuse/neglect. *Information Sheet.*

National Commission on Children. (1991). *Beyond rhetoric a new American agenda for children and families: Final report of the National Commission on Children.* Washington, DC: Government Printing Office.

Nelson, K. E., & Landsman, M. J. (1992). *Alternative models of family preservation: Family-based services in context.* Springfield, IL: Charles C Thomas.

Nelson, K. E., Landsman, M. J., & Deutelbaum, W. (1990). Three models of family-centered placement prevention services. *Child Welfare, 69,* 3-21.

Newman, M. R., & Lutzker, J. R. (1990). Prevention programs. In R. T. Ammerman & M. Hersen (Eds.), *Children at risk: An evaluation of factors contributing to child abuse and neglect.* New York: Plenum.

Olds, D. L., & Henderson, C. R. (1989). The prevention of maltreatment. In D. Cicchetti & V. Carlson (Eds.), *Child maltreatment: Theory and research on the causes and consequences of child abuse and neglect.* New York: Cambridge University Press.

Olds, D. L., Henderson, C. R., Chamberlin, R., & Tatelbaum, R. (1986). Preventing child abuse and neglect: A randomized trial of nurse home visitation. *Pediatrics, 78,* 65-78.

Pelton, L. H. (1994). Is poverty a key contributor to child maltreatment? Yes. In E. Gambrill & T. J. Stein (Eds.), *Controversial issues in child welfare* (pp. 16-22). Boston: Allyn & Bacon.

Pianta, R., Egeland, B., & Erickson, M. F. (1989). The antecedents of maltreatment: Results from the Mother-Child Interaction Research Project. In D. Cicchetti & V. Carlson (Eds.), *Child maltreatment: Theory and research on the causes and consequences of child abuse and neglect.* New York: Cambridge University Press.

Plasse, B. R. (1995). Parenting groups for recovering addicts in a day treatment center. *Social Work, 40,* 65-74.

Polansky, N. A., Chalmers, M. A., Williams, D. P., & Buttenwieser, E. W. (1981). *Damaged parents: An anatomy of child neglect.* Chicago: University of Chicago Press.

Reddick, S., & Goodwin, D. (1991, September). *A community response to drug affected babies: A cooperative effort.* Paper presented at the Ninth National Conference on Child Abuse and Neglect, Denver, CO.

Rodwell, M. K., & Chambers, D. E. (1994). Can most child maltreatment be prevented? No. In E. Gambrill & T. J. Stein (Eds.), *Controversial issues in child welfare* (pp. 53-57). Boston: Allyn & Bacon.

Rosenberg, M. S., & Reppucci, N. D. (1985). Primary prevention of child abuse. *Journal of Consulting and Clinical Psychology, 53,* 576-585.

Schorr, L. B. (1988). *Within our reach: Breaking the cycle of disadvantage.* New York: Anchor Press–Doubleday.

Sedlak, A. J., & Broadhurst, D. D. (1996). *Third National Incidence Study of Child Abuse and Neglect: Final report.* Washington, DC: U.S. Department of Health and Human Services, National Center on Child Abuse and Neglect.

Spears, L. (1996). Domestic violence is a child welfare issue. *Children's Voice, 5*(3), 4-5.

Stein, T. J. (1984, June). The child abuse prevention and treatment act. *Social Service Review,* pp. 302-314.

Straus, M. A., Gelles, R. J., & Steinmetz, S. K. (1988). *Behind closed doors: Violence in the American family.* Newbury Park, CA: Sage.

Thompson, R. A. (1995). *Preventing child maltreatment through social support: A critical analysis.* Thousand Oaks, CA: Sage.

Trickett, P. K., Aber, J. L., Carlson, V., & Cicchetti, D. (1991). Relationship of socioeconomic status to the etiology and developmental sequelae of physical child abuse. *Developmental Psychology, 27,* 148-158.

U.S. General Accounting Office. (1990, July). *Home visiting: A promising early intervention strategy for at-risk families* (Report GAO/HRD-90-83). Washington, DC: Author.

Volpe, R. (1989). *Poverty and child abuse: A review of selected literature.* Toronto: The Institute for the Prevention of Child Abuse.

Wasik, B. H., Bryant, D. M., & Lyons, C. M. (1990). *Home visiting: Procedures for helping families.* Newbury Park, CA: Sage.

Weisz, V. G. (1994). Consequences of placement for children who are abused. In J. Blacher (Ed.), *When there's no place like home: Options for children living apart from their natural families.* Baltimore, MD: Paul H. Brookes.

Werner, E. E. (1994). Commentary: A social policy perspective. In J. Blacher (Ed.), *When there's no place like home: Options for children living apart from their natural families.* Baltimore, MD: Paul H. Brookes.

Whipple, E. E., & Webster-Stratton, C. (1991). The role of parental stress in physically abusive families. *Child Abuse & Neglect, 15,* 279-291.

Whipple, E. E., & Wilson, S. R. (1996). Evaluation of a parent education and support program for families at risk of physical child abuse. *Families in Society: The Journal of Contemporary Human Services, 77,* 227-239.

White, B. (1985). *The first three years of life: The revised edition.* New York: Prentice Hall.

Widom, C. S. (1989a). Child abuse, neglect, and adult behavior: Research design and findings on criminality, violence, and child abuse. *American Journal of Orthopsychiatry, 59,* 1-13.

Widom, C. S. (1989b). The cycle of violence. *Science, 244,* 160-166.

Willett, J. B., Ayoub, C. C., & Robinson, D. (1991). Using growth modeling to examine systematic differences in growth: An example of change in the functioning of families at risk of maladaptive parenting, child abuse, or neglect. *Journal of Consulting and Clinical Psychology, 59,* 38-47.

Wolfe, D. A. (1984, August). *Behavioral distinctions between abusive and nonabusive parents: A review and critique.* Paper presented at the Second Family Violence Research Conference, University of New Hampshire.

Wolfe, D. A., Edwards, B., Manion, I., & Koverola, C. (1988). Early intervention for parents at risk of child abuse and neglect: A preliminary investigation. *Journal of Consulting and Clinical Psychology, 56,* 40-47.

Wolock, I., & Horowitz, B. (1984). Child maltreatment as a social problem: The neglect of neglect. *American Journal of Orthopsychiatry, 54,* 530-543.

Zuckerman, B. (1991). Drug-exposed infants: Understanding the medical risk. *The Future of Children, 1*(1), 26-35.

Zuravin, S. J. (1986). Residential density and urban child maltreatment: An aggregate analysis. *Journal of Family Violence, 1,* 307-322.

Zuravin, S. J. (1988). Child maltreatment and teenage first births: A relationship mediated by chronic sociodemographic stress? *American Journal of Orthopsychiatry, 50,* 91-103.

• *CHAPTER 6* •

What Do We Know *Now* About Spouse Abuse and Child Sexual Abuse in Families of Color in the United States?

JO-ELLEN ASBURY

Almost 20 years ago, Khatib (1980) called for more "black studies" and less "study of black people." By this, he meant that more scholarship from the relevant cultural perspective (black studies) was needed, and less that subscribed to majority group values and perspectives (study of black people). Khatib's distinction could be appropriately applied to research on all people of color, and violence in families of color in particular. In the first edition of this volume, I criticized research on violence in families of color for focusing almost exclusively on the comparative rates of occurrence (study of black people). Fortunately, many sources published since 1993 acknowledge the unique impacts of race or culture on family violence. Many of the sources cited here attempt to explore each group's unique cultural expressions, how those expressions may affect the nature of violence in the family, and the potential effectiveness of intervention strategies.

It is perhaps worth noting that roughly one third of articles published since 1993 focusing on violence in families of color were published in special issues of a variety of journals. But, it is hard to know how to interpret this. On the one hand, it is commendable that editors are motivated to place special emphasis on issues of family violence in general, and violence in families of color in particular. On the other hand, one wonders if this indicates that such concerns are still not part of the mainstream, thus requiring a special issue.

At any rate, although the state of the literature is certainly better than it was, it is still not what it needs to be (see also Hampton & Yung, 1996). Attention to race in the context of family violence is uneven at best. Most studies or reviews that address families of color include information about African Americans. Some include information on Hispanic *or* Asian American families, but rarely both. Few, if any, address Native American families.

Yee, Fairchild, Weizmann, and Wyatt (1993) have highlighted some problems in defining and applying race as a concept in psychological research. For the purposes of this chapter, race/culture/ethnicity will be defined quite broadly, although admittedly there is some imprecision in such a strategy. The purpose here is to call attention to the differences that must be acknowledged. As the title of West's (1994) book points out, *Race Matters*.

Minority Experiences in America

A 1993 report of the American Psychological Association (APA) notes that 38% of Hispanic, 44% of Asian and Pacific Islanders, 45% of African Americans, and up to 90% of Native American children grow up in poverty. The APA further notes that poverty is not just a lack of money but defines the very context in which people live. People living in poverty experience relative as well as absolute deprivation and higher unemployment rates, even in good economic times. This is of particular interest here as poverty and unemployment tend to discourage family stability. And, although family violence occurs at all income levels, it seems to be more prevalent in lower income families.

The following subsections will highlight some of the unique experiences of the four predominate ethnic minority groups in America (in alphabetical order), particularly as they may relate to family violence. Kanuha (1994) cautions, however, that ethnic group generalizations must be understood as approximations. Otherwise, one runs the risk of perpetuating the very stereotypes one is trying to dispel.

African Americans

Although all minority groups discussed here have been the objects of discrimination, African Americans are unique in their history of more than 200 years of enslavement, a time when they were viewed as inferior human beings at best and property at worst. Although slavery legally ended over 100 years ago, Akbar (1973) notes the continuing influence.

As Table 6.1 shows, African Americans were just under 13% of the population of the United States in 1995. Although African Americans have historically been the major minority group in the United States, population projections suggest their numbers will remain relatively stable (between 15% and 16% of the population in 2050) while the proportions of other ethnic minority groups will increase substantially. African Americans' median income and levels of educational achievement are below those of European and Asian Americans. More African Americans than European Americans live in poverty, and more African American babies are born to unwed mothers than to any other group reported here (U.S. Bureau of the Census, 1996).

In general, African American cultural values have been described as including: harmony and interrelatedness with nature, spirituality and strong religious nature, communalism rather than individualism, focus on the importance of children to ensure the continuity of the family, and flexibility of roles (APA, 1993). Hill (1972) notes that flexibility of roles is one of the strengths of African American families, and Nobles (1980) traces this back to their African roots. Children are likely to be reared without strict differences determined by sex and are likely to be reared to consider competence in interpersonal relationships more important than competence in dealing with the physical environment.

Brice-Baker (1994) cautions that too often all people of the African diaspora are treated as a homogeneous group. She notes that some people of African descent in America may have roots in the Caribbean. Thus, those individuals face issues that other African Americans do not, such as: adjustment to extreme cold weather, unfamiliarity with foods, language differences, and in some cases, difficulties securing employment, particularly to match level of education and experience. They also face the stresses associated with having spouses or family members who came to the United States earlier and may be at a different point in acculturation. Abney and Priest (1995) point out, however, that all people of African descent in America do share one solidifying factor—the experience of racism perpetuated by the majority group culture.

Given the oppression endured, it is not surprising that literature reviewed by Thompson and Smith (1993) suggests that African Americans may have a negative attitude toward mental health services, perhaps because of a mistrust of white therapists. This attitude was more

Table 6.1 Demographic Sketch of Racial Groups in America

	Race				
	European American	*African American*	*Asian American*	*Hispanic*	*Native American*
Population					
Percentage of population (1995)	82.9	12.6	3.5	10.2	0.8
Life expectancy	76.3	69.2	82.3	78.6	75.8
Economic indicators					
Median income	$34,028	$21,027	$40,482	$23,421	N/A
Percentage in poverty	11.7	30.6	14.6	30.7	N/A
Family status (in percent)					
Never married	24.8	43.4	N/A	N/A	N/A
Married	59.8	39.8	N/A	58.3	N/A
Widowed	6.7	6.9	N/A	N/A	N/A
Divorced	8.6	10.0	N/A	N/A	N/A
Births to unwed mothers	23.6	68.7	15.7	40.0	55.8[a]
Female-headed household	14.0	47.9	N/A	24.0	45.0[a]
Male-headed household	4.0	5.6	N/A	7.7	N/A
Education (among those age 25 and older, in percent)					
High school graduate	82.0	67.7	N/A	53.4	N/A
College graduate or higher	24.0	13.2	38.2	9.3	N/A

SOURCE: U.S. Bureau of the Census (1996) except as below.
a. Source is LaFromboise et al. (1994).

pronounced in low-income African Americans than middle-income ones. As a result, they may use available social services only in the more extreme cases. Therefore, available data may actually be more representative of those more extreme cases, not all cases of African American intrafamilial violence.

Asian Americans

Asian Americans were 3.5% of the population in 1995, as Table 6.1 shows. By the year 2050, they are expected to be between 7% and 10% of the population, making them one of the fastest-growing ethnic groups in America. Of those over 25 years of age, 38.2% of Asian Americans have a college degree or more, the highest proportion of any group reported here, including European Americans (U.S. Bureau of the Census, 1996). Yet, Huang and Ying (1989) report that 11% of Chinese Americans are illiterate, seven times the national average. On a more positive note, their median income exceeds that of all other groups included here, and their percentage of births to unwed mothers and percentage of female-headed households is lowest.

Many different groups are generally included under this label (Ho, 1990), a practice that may hinder attention to some important differences. For example, Chao (1992) relates the following incident which she calls "We don't even eat rice the same":

> A H'Mong coworker placed a straw basket with "sticky rice" in the center of the table; a Japanese counselor added short-grained rice from a rice cooker; a Chinese American clinician added a bowl of long-grained rice. The different varieties of rice silently spoke to the different philosophical, ethnic, cultural, historical, and religious traditions. And yet we were all considered to be "Asian." (p. 158)

Ho (1990) notes that whether or not Asian Americans are fairly recent immigrants or second- or third- (or more) generation Americans is also important in understanding their experiences and perspectives.

Keeping in mind the differences Chao and Ho outlined above, a number of sources have noted that in general, Asian American culture is characterized by pacificism, self-control and self-discipline, internal locus of control, strong work ethic and achievement motivation, and strong cultural bonds (APA, 1993). In fact, Huang and Ying (1989) and Nagata (1989) note that some inappropriately label Asians as a "problem free" minority group because of their apparent smooth assimilation into mainstream American culture. However, although Asian Americans have the highest median family income among minorities, they are also underemployed and receiving lower wages than others doing comparable work.

Asian culture has been described as "face" oriented (Huang & Ying, 1989; Zane, 1992). Family appearance and status are extremely important, and the group's desires or priorities take precedence over those of the individual (Chao, 1992; Huang & Ying, 1989; Nagata,1989). Asian families tend to be hierarchical, with parents having status superior to that of the children and men to that of women (APA, 1993; Huang & Ying, 1989). Extended families are often considered the primary family unit (Huang & Ying, 1989; Nagata,1989). If violence is exhibited within the family, it may be difficult for an individual member to admit such a condition to outsiders, out of fear of bringing shame on the family.

Furthermore, some Asian Americans may have a language other than English as their primary one. This may present yet another barrier to effective intervention when one must interact with the dominant culture.

Hispanics

As Marin and Marin (1991) note, the term *Hispanic* is one of convenience, used to refer to those who reside in the United States and trace their origins to Spain or one of the Spanish-speaking nations of Latin America. It is a term that connotes ethnicity, not race. Marin and Marin (1991) note that not all accept this term in reference to themselves. It is also acknowledged that those from Spain have a different culture, history, and demography than other Spanish-speaking Americans. Kaufman Kantor, Jasinski, and Aldarondo (1994) identify the three major Hispanic subgroups in the United States as: Puerto Rican, Mexican, and Cuban. Mexican Americans make up 65% of the Hispanic population (U.S. Bureau of the Census, 1996).

As Table 6.1 shows, Hispanics were just over 10% of the population in 1995. Projections indicate that they will be between 22% and 26% of the population by the year 2050, making them the other fastest-growing ethnic group in America. Hispanics have a median income below that of European Americans and Asian Americans and have a larger proportion of their group in poverty than either of those groups. Their percentage of births to unwed mothers is higher than European and Asian Americans, but not African Americans. Their educational attainment is the lowest of the groups reported here, with just over 9% having a college degree or higher. Kaufman Kantor et al. (1994) cite 1992 Census Bureau data that suggest the unemployment rate among Hispanics is 11.3% (in comparison to 7.5% for non-Hispanics). Unemployment is 22 to 32 times greater among Hispanics than Anglos.

As with Asian Americans, Kaufman Kantor et al. (1994) propose that individual level of acculturation or recency of immigration may be factors for consideration in addressing the needs of Hispanic families. These authors suggest that level of acculturation is highest among Puerto Ricans and Mexican Americans.

Many demographic characteristics that put all groups at greater risk for violence (all forms, not just family violence) are high among Hispanics (APA, 1993). For example, the Hispanic group is young (half of the population is under 26), and just over half have completed high school (APA, 1993).

Marin and Marin (1991) review literature suggesting that Hispanics, like other minority groups already discussed, value a willingness to place the welfare of the group above that of the individual (see also APA, 1993). Hispanics identify with and are attached to the nuclear and extended family and exhibit strong feelings of loyalty, reciprocity, and solidarity with their family members (APA, 1993; Marin & Marin, 1991). Hispanics may also exhibit reluctance to involve outsiders in familial conflicts.

Simpatia, according to Marin and Marin (1991), is a Hispanic cultural script that emphasizes the need for behaviors that promote smooth and pleasant social relationships. As such, simpatia encourages a certain level of conformity and empathy for the feelings of others and de-emphasizes negative behaviors in conflictive circumstances, which may also inhibit their tendency to acknowledge and report violence in the family (APA, 1993; Marin & Marin, 1991).

Kaufman Kantor et al. (1994) explored the possibility of Hispanics being more or less likely to engage in violence as a function of their cultural heritage but found no evidence for such an assertion. On the one hand, Hispanics experience more unemployment and economic stress and tend to have male-dominated families—factors that seem to contribute to greater family violence. On the other hand, Hispanics traditionally have close-knit family units and are very dependent on one another for economic and social support—factors that seem to diminish the tendency for violence.

Like Asian Americans, Hispanics may have a primary language other than English. This may further inhibit their involvement with police or social service agencies.

Native Americans

Those referred to as "American Indians" include all North American native people, including Alaskan Natives, Aleuts, Eskimos, and Metis (mixed bloods) (LaFromboise & Low, 1989). LaFromboise, Berman, and Sohi (1994) report that there are 587 Indian tribal entities and

Alaskan Native Villages. And, despite past eradication efforts, 200 indigenous languages are spoken by Native Americans today.

The U.S. Bureau of the Census (see Table 6.1) indicates that Native Americans were less than 1% of the population in 1995. Projections indicate they will be 1% of the population in 2050. LaFromboise et al. (1994) estimates the Native American population can generally be characterized as growing, with the rise perhaps due to more people acknowledging their Indian identity and to interracial marriages, and birth rates greater than 79%. They also report that Native Americans' median age is 22.6 years (compared to 30 years for other races) with 32% of population under the age of 15. Native Americans' average family size is 4.6, larger than any other U.S. ethnic group. Women, many of whom never married, head 45% of Indian households.

LaFromboise et al. (1994) note that intertribal diversities can make it somewhat difficult to generalize about Native American culture. However, chief among the common values are harmony with and respect for nature, emphasis on family traditions, and emphasis on group cooperation rather than on individual achievement (APA, 1993).

Although tribes differ, traditionally, many live in relational networks that emphasize strong bonds of mutual assistance (LaFromboise & Low, 1989). "To be poor in the Indian world is to be without relatives" (LaFromboise et al., 1994, p. 33). Given their experiences, Native Americans may also exhibit a group loyalty and distrust of outsiders that could result in not bringing incidents of family violence to the attention of legal or social service agents of the dominant culture (Long, 1986).

LaFromboise et al. (1994) note that, "Native Americans are generally reluctant to seek professional therapeutic help, perhaps because of the cultural emphasis on endurance and noninterference and mistrust toward non-Indian providers" (p. 42).

Family Violence

Below, cultural issues regarding spouse abuse and child sexual abuse are explored. Within each category of abuse, studies are reviewed that address: causes or contributing factors; victims' response to the abuse, including tendency to seek some form of outside intervention; and unique factors that may need to be considered in any planned intervention. The reader is referred to Chapter 1 in this volume, by Richard Gelles, for a general overview of the different forms of family violence.

Here, the focus will be on how those issues may vary for people of color in the United States.

Spousal Abuse

Contributing Factors

Taken together, the following sources highlight important differences in the reasons spouse abuse occurs in families of color. For example, Gelles and Straus (1988) propose that status inconsistency is an important factor in the profile of an abusive husband. This occurs when a man's educational background is much higher than his occupational attainment. It may also occur when the husband does not have as much occupational or educational status as his wife. Given the lower median incomes reported in Table 6.1, this is likely to be an important consideration for males heading minority families. Willis (1994) and Marsh (1993) similarly suggest that for African American men, the sense of powerlessness and lack of control that results from racism in the United States may be important factors.

Although some factors may suggest a greater likelihood for violence, other cultural factors may inhibit the male's tendency to abuse his mate. Because African American women have typically been a part of the paid labor force, their employment is not as likely to contribute to the stress that sometimes results in violence. This may not be the same, however, for all women of color.

Given social and historical factors, Brice-Baker (1994) notes that African American men were not taught to expect to dominate or be in charge, so mainstream ideas about causes of spouse abuse may not "fit" entirely. Lewis (1975, cited in Brice-Baker, 1994) suggests that male and female socialization among African Americans is not as divergent as among European Americans. Willis (1994) reviews the unique historical experiences that African Americans had during slavery and explores how that history still affects the lives of African Americans today. Willis proposes that the roles of male and female were influenced by the forced instability of families.

Ucko (1994) notes that the differences in gender socialization between African Americans and European Americans can be traced to differences in traditional African and European cultures. Traditional African expectations of strong, independent women conflict with the European-derived heritage of sexuality as a male status symbol and of male control of women's lives. She notes that the stress created by this conflict may be a significant contributor to violence toward African American women.

Victim's Response to Abuse

Not only must we consider cultural differences in analyzing factors that contribute to violence against women, but such differences are also important in understanding women's response to the abuse. Presumably, people's perception of an act will influence their response to that act.

Kanuha (1994) suggests that being the objects of institutional racism is one such issue. As a result of that institutional racism—negative societal attitudes and discriminatory behaviors toward people of color—Kanuha (1994) surmises that women of color may be reluctant to bring attention to themselves, their families, and by extension to their racial or ethnic communities for fear of contributing to the stigmatization and stereotyping of people of color. Brice-Baker (1994) refers to this as the Anita Hill-Clarence Thomas syndrome. That is, many members of the African American community believed her but took exception to the fact that she brought his misconduct to light, "the implication being that, in a racist society which already holds and perpetrates so many pejorative stereotypes about Black people, it is the job of all the cultures' members to collude in not besmirching images any further" (p. 32).

Sullivan and Rumptz (1994) present data that may corroborate Brice-Baker's point. They found that African American women recruited for their study from domestic violence shelters experienced significantly more severe abuse in the 6 months prior to entering the shelter (compared to European American women). Sullivan and Rumptz suggest that African Americans may be less likely to turn to shelters unless the abuse is severe.

Taken together, sources imply that women of color may delay or avoid seeking assistance due to their perceptions of available services. Kanuha (1994) suggests that women of color may perceive helping professionals as insensitive to the racial and cultural contexts of their lives; they may not view such service as a real option. Their anticipation of a lack of culturally appropriate services contributes to a perception of limited options for them.

Therefore, Ho (1990) and Kanuha (1994) note that feminist mental health providers must be sensitive to the alliances some battered women of color must establish with their batterers against mainstream domestic violence programs that are perceived to have a feminist perspective. Kanuha reviews literature suggesting that the narrow focus on the battered woman, to the exclusion of needs of batterers and others, may in part be responsible for the reluctance of battered women of color to seek help in abusive situations. It may be that for some battered women of color, the need to preserve the family unit in the face of a racist, genocidal society is in direct contradiction to the admonishment of battered women's advocates to "just leave him."

Kanuha (1994) surmises that biased societal perceptions may also influence the woman's self-perceptions. Willis (1994) comments that the media purvey such stereotypes about African American families. Thus, even women not living in stressful environments may find it difficult to escape the negative influence of such images. And those self-perceptions may in turn influence a woman's response to the abuse. For example, the image that women of color are stalwart and resilient in the face of all odds (see also White, 1985) may inhibit an individual woman's tendency to seek help. Brice-Baker (1994) concludes that it is important to increase awareness of the stereotypes among African American women who have been abused and explore the impact on the women in question. The social class, geographic location, and sensitivity of professional caregivers to women who are both battered and nonwhite also appear to be important factors that affect real and perceived options that battered women of color may elect to employ (Kanuha, 1994).

Peterson-Lewis, Turner, and Adams (1988) suggest that African American women may attribute the causes of their abuse externally to the larger society (but not to the abuser) or internally. Therefore, an African American woman may be less likely to involve the police because of her belief that African American males are more likely to be arrested and to be the victims of police maltreatment than their European American counterparts. Furthermore, she might also rationalize that the abuse she received from her mate is merely a reflection of the treatment he received from the dominant culture. Pejorative perceptions that African American women are stronger (physically and emotionally) than other women may add to the belief that she should endure the abuse (see, for example, Young, 1993). African American women may also succumb to the belief that they have few options in terms of other relationships or economic survival based on the implications of media portrayals. Focusing on the experiences of African American women, Peterson-Lewis et al. (1988) propose that their attributional analysis may be adapted to women of all cultures.

Buddhism and Confucian philosophy may have had a significant influence on the role of some women in Asian American or Asian immigrant populations (Ho, 1990). Ho (1990) suggests that spouse abuse in Asian families tends not to come to the attention of authorities and suggests that low statistics regarding rates of occurrence could be due to Asians' lack of use of available resources or lack of adequate mental health services.

Ho's (1990) focus group study gives further insight into Asians' views toward and potential responses to domestic violence. Participants were Laotians, Khmers, Vietnamese, and Southeast Asian Chinese, who did not have to have experience with domestic violence. They were asked to discuss: What are the power differentials between sexes? What is the role of physical violence? What are factors and resources that affect women's ability to leave the battering relationship. Male and female groups were conducted separately. Attitudes about physical violence toward a spouse varied, with Chinese finding it less acceptable and the other three groups having more tolerant attitudes. Even women who felt that it was appropriate to leave (mainly the Chinese women) felt that is was important not to get help outside the family because it could bring shame to the family. Women who saw leaving the home as problematic noted that doing so would cause a woman to break from her traditional expectation of caring for home and husband under any circumstances. The women also noted limited financial resources as a factor, particularly the refugee and immigrant women.

Intervention

A number of sources (e.g., Chao, 1992; Williams, 1995; Willis, 1994) stress the importance of a culturally sensitive approach. For example, Chao describes traditional Asian American family hierarchies as well as traditional remedies that must be understood and incorporated into the therapeutic approach. Williams (1995) proposes that a lack of cultural competence on the part of the practitioner may hinder the effectiveness of treatment.

In addition to differences that may be attributed to cultural perspective are some situational differences that must also be acknowledged. Sullivan and Rumptz (1994) report that African American women are more likely to have children with them when coming to the shelter, more likely to have been living below poverty level, and more likely to have been the sole provider for their family. The authors suggest, therefore, that African American women may need to remain in the shelter longer than majority group women, given the greater severity of abuse experienced prior to entering the shelter and the institutional racism she will have to combat to get on her feet.

Regarding intervention with the abuser, Willis (1994) suggests that it is first necessary to help the offender to understand the present and sociohistorical context and its impact on the family. Then, it is important to help him with conflict resolution. Williams (1994) similarly suggests an Afrocentric approach with African American men who have battered.

Child Sexual Abuse

In 1993, I reported that many studies compared rates of occurrence of child sexual abuse by ethnic group and little more, and that there were significant inconsistencies resulting from those comparisons (Asbury, 1993). Today, such inconsistencies remain (perhaps primarily for the same reasons: nonequivalent samples, nonequivalent methodologies), but many authors have gone beyond that to address the unique cultural experiences as they affect child sexual abuse.

Nature of Abuse

Regarding the question of rates of occurrence, Urquiza and Goodlin-Jones (1994) report data from a rare and commendable multiethnic sample. They suggest that rates of abuse were similar for African American and European American women and lower for Hispanic and Asian American women. Wyatt, Newcomb, and Riederle (1993) report that African Americans are at greater risk for sexual abuse than European Americans. Abney and Priest (1995) surmise that African Americans may be more vulnerable due to stereotypes about their supposed hypersexuality and permissiveness. Abney and Priest (1995) also note that African American mothers are more likely to be unmarried or remain unmarried for longer periods of time than European American mothers. Thus, young African American girls are more likely to be exposed to their mother's boyfriends, a potential source of abuse.

Rao, DiClemente, and Ponton (1992), in a multiethnic chart review study, report that Asian victims of child sexual abuse showed a demographic profile distinct from European Americans, African Americans, and Latinas. Asian victims tended to be older, were more likely to live with both parents, and were more likely to be abused by a male relative. They were also more likely to be immigrants.

Mennen (1994) reports that Hispanic, African American, and European American women were similar in their relation to the perpetrator, their age when the abuse began, and the kind of abuse experienced. The only ethnic difference reported here is that European American girls tended to have been abused longer than Latinas or African Americans. Mennen cautions, however, that some sampling limitations may have contributed to finding few racial differences where others have reported them.

Sanders-Phillips, Moisan, Wadlington, Morgan, and English (1995) compared Latina to African American girls ages 8 to 13 years old who had experienced sexual abuse. They report that Latinas tended to be higher in depression, abused at a younger age, more likely to be abused by a relative, and more likely to have a sibling abused. Latinas also had larger families and enjoyed less maternal support regarding their allegations.

Wyatt, Guthrie, and Notgrass (1992), Urquiza and Goodlin-Jones (1994), and Wyatt and Riederle (1994) note that once sexually victimized, chances of subsequent revictimization are high. Reporting data from their multiethnic sample, Urquiza and Goodlin-Jones (1994) indicate that of those (adult) women who reported having been raped, nearly 65% had previously experienced sexual assault prior to age 18. For nonvictimized women, just over 35% reported a history of childhood sexual abuse.

Wyatt and Riederle (1994), comparing African American and European American women, report that regardless of ethnicity, those more likely to be sexually harassed in work and social settings were women with contact sexual abuse histories. However, the harassers of European American women tended to be their superiors, whereas harassers of African American women also included coworkers, peers, clients, or subordinates.

Victim's Response to Abuse

Obviously, before a victim can report abuse, incidents must be recognized as abusive. Whether or not there are variations by culture as to what is perceived as acceptable and what isn't has not yet been fully explored. However, the studies reviewed directly below give examples of some of the cultural or ethnic differences that must be considered.

Thompson and Smith (1993) conducted interviews with a sample of African Americans representative of the African American population in their city and found that rates of recognizing scenarios presented as incidents of abuse were high (95%). However, participants were not as adept at identifying short-term reactions to the abuse, such as behavioral acting out. The authors surmise that this lack of awareness may result in delays in seeking treatment, as the behaviors may be misunderstood or mislabeled. Thompson and Smith (1993) also suggest that African American families may be concerned about the legal, judicial, and societal implications for African American men when sexual assault allegations are made public and may therefore be reluctant to bring such charges to the authorities.

In addition to Thompson and Smith (1993), a number of studies have explored the victim's propensity to report the abuse. For example, Rao et al. (1992) notes that because Asians are more likely to be abused by a relative, there may be a greater tendency to disbelieve the victim, which may inhibit the victim's tendency to report the abuse.

In an introspective study, Wyatt (1990) reports that, in general, African Americans and European Americans did not differ significantly when all types of abuse were considered (contact versus noncontact; less severe versus more severe). Although she found no ethnic differences in three of four levels of nondisclosure, she does point out some ethnic differences that should be considered. Wyatt speculates that African Americans are more likely to fear the consequences of disclosure because of their awareness of the financial hardships if a stepfather or the mother's boyfriend were to leave the house. Furthermore, with the strong extended family tradition among African Americans, it may be more difficult for a young woman to report the abuse.

Levy (1988) reports a number of patterns that he observed to be specific to child abuse in the Hispanic community and that may hinder a young victim's tendency to report the abuse: (a) a general attitude that sexual attitudes are too intimate to discuss, even within the family; (b) the expectation that women will marry as virgins, which complicates the issue for young victims, as reporting her abuse brings attention to the fact that she is no longer a virgin; and (c) a general expectation that women must "suffer in silence." Levy notes, however, that these attitudes may vary as a function of acculturation.

Abney and Priest (1995) allude to some level of denial in African American communities, which would certainly have an impact on a victim's tendency to report the abuse. They note that African Americans have a tendency to believe that sexual abuse of children is something that happens in other ethnic groups. This is coupled with a predilection not to talk about the abuse (once it is known) because acknowledgment could further damage the image of African Americans and further exclude them from the American mainstream. In addition, Abney and Priest (1995) suggest that tolerance for or endurance of suffering is highly valued in the African American culture, and African American women are particularly noted for their strength. These authors suggest that this may lower disclosure rates and impede victims' pursuit of treatment. Finally, reporting may also be hindered by African Americans' negative experiences with the criminal justice system and the victim's desire not to want to compound the societal plight of African American men.

Regarding the manner of reporting the abuse, Wyatt (1990) reports that African Americans tended to report the abuse to someone in the extended family, whereas European Americans used friends and authority figures.

In terms of long-range effects, Wyatt (1990) reports that African American women who experience severe abuse were more likely (than African American women who experienced less severe abuse) to report health-related problems. And African American women were significantly more likely to report avoiding men who look like their abuser.

Intervention

A number of authors (e.g., Abney & Priest, 1995; Hampton & Yung, 1996; Levy, 1988; Rao et al, 1992; Thompson & Smith, 1993) stress the importance of a culturally sensitive approach. However, what that culturally sensitive approach might look like seems to be less well articulated. Abney and Priest (1995) suggest that much more is needed in terms of sound theory, research, and clinical practice. Fontes (1995) proposes that a culturally sensitive sexual abuse intervention must be user friendly. Clients should feel welcomed, respected, and understood. Services, paperwork, and outreach should be readily available in the client's language. And services must fit the schedules, finances, and geographic locations of the population one is trying to serve. Fontes (1995) advocates treatment teams with representatives of all major cultures in a given area.

Thompson and Smith (1993) and Rao et al. (1992) add that therapists working with families of color may need to be prepared to do more than strictly therapy, perhaps needing to help and nurture the family in a variety of ways, including negotiating with schools or other public service agencies. Abney and Priest (1995) add that degree of assimilation into the dominant culture must also be considered.

A number of sources point out certain cultural factors that may inhibit effective intervention and that therapists must be prepared to handle. For example, Thompson and Smith (1993) found that participants' attitudes toward seeking treatment were significantly associated with their attitudes toward the agencies providing treatment. And negative attitudes toward treatment agencies were primarily among low-income African Americans. Low-income African Americans were also less likely to seek treatment if they anticipated police involvement. Thompson and Smith (1993) also report that participants selected pediatricians as the most preferred provider if child abuse was suspected or identified. The authors speculate that this might be because medical resources are generally more accessible.

Of course, the best intervention is prevention. Levy (1988) reports on a primary prevention program designed for implementation in Hispanic communities. Levy notes that one must consider their added vulnerability to exploitation and victimization due to their limited access to resources and limited control over their own environment. Presentations to parents and children (separate sessions) were made in Spanish and focused on susceptibility, severity, prevention, and coping. The generalizability of this approach to other people of color apparently has not been determined.

Summary

In general, families of color in the United States have less money and less education and are more likely to be living in poverty. People of color in the United States have experienced various forms of discrimination that may make them more reluctant to seek professional help, should violence occur within the family. Furthermore, certain within-group norms may further encourage victims to avoid outside intervention. Consequently, victims of color may only seek help under extreme circumstances. Therefore, future efforts—both empirical and clinical—should be designed with these factors in mind.

Perhaps the ideas presented here are best summarized by the following, gleaned from the APA (1993):

- All research should be conceptualized, designed, and conducted with attention to traditions, beliefs, attitudes, and behaviors of the group being studied as well as the circumstances under which they are living.
- Investigators are urged to examine their own racial and cultural assumptions for bias in conceptualization, design, methodology, and selection of participants.
- It is recommended that members of the study population participate at every stage of the research, from planning through execution and publication.
- Development of new and improved gender-sensitive and culturally sensitive measures, psychological tests, and assessment instruments is encouraged. These instruments should be normed on different ethnic and racial groups and the subcultures that make up each group.

References

Abney, V. D., & Priest, R. (1995). African Americans and sexual child abuse. In L. A. Fontes (Ed.), *Sexual abuse in nine North American cultures* (pp. 11-30). Thousand Oaks, CA: Sage.

Akbar, N. (1973). *The psychological legacy of slavery.* Unpublished manuscript, Norfolk State University.

American Psychological Association. (1993). *Violence and youth.* Washington, DC: Author.

Asbury, J. E. (1993). Violence in families of color in the United States. In R. L. Hampton, G. R. Adams, E. H. Potter, III, & R. P. Weissberg (Eds.), *Family violence: Prevention and treatment* (pp. 159-178). Newbury Park, CA: Sage.

Brice-Baker, J. R. (1994). Domestic violence in African American and African Caribbean families. *Journal of Social Distress and the Homeless, 3*(1), 23-38.

Chao, C. M. (1992). The inner heart: Therapy with Southeast Asian families. In L. A. Vargas & J. D. Koss-Chioino (Eds.), *Working with culture: Psychotherapeutic interventions with ethnic minority children and adolescents* (pp. 157-181). San Francisco: Jossey-Bass.

Fontes, L. A. (1995). Culturally informed interventions for sexual child abuse. In L. A. Fontes (Ed.), *Sexual abuse in nine North American cultures* (pp. 259-266). Thousand Oaks, CA: Sage.

Gelles, R. J., & Straus, M. A. (1988). *Intimate violence.* New York: Simon & Schuster.

Hampton, R. L., & Yung, B. R. (1996). Violence in communities of color: Where we were, where we are, and where we need to be. In R. L. Hampton, P. Jenkins, & T. P. Gullotta (Eds.), *Prevention violence in America* (pp. 53-86). Thousand Oaks, CA: Sage.

Hill, R. (1972). *The strengths of black families.* New York: Emerson-Hall.

Ho, C. K. (1990). An analysis of domestic violence in Asian American communities: A multicultural approach to counseling. *Women and Therapy,* 9(1-2), 129-150.

Huang, L. N., & Ying, Y.-W. (1989). Chinese American children and adolescents. In J. T. Gibbs, L. N. Huang, & associates (Eds.), *Children of color* (pp. 30-66). San Francisco: Jossey-Bass.

Kanuha, V. (1994). Women of color in battering relationships. In L. Comas-Diaz & R. Greene (Eds.), *Women of color* (pp. 428-454). New York: Guilford.

Kaufman Kantor, G., Jasinski, J. L., & Aldarondo, E. (1994). Sociocultural status and incidence of marital violence in Hispanic families. *Violence and Victims,* 9(3), 207, 222.

Khatib, S. M. (1980). Black studies or the study of black people: Reflections on the distinctive characteristics of black psychology. In R. L. Jones (Ed.), *Black psychology* (2nd ed., pp. 48-55). New York: Harper & Row.

LaFromboise, T. D., Berman, J. S., & Sohi, B. K. (1994). American Indian women. In L. Comas-Dias & B. Greene (Eds.), *Women of color* (pp. 30-71). New York: Guilford.

LaFromboise, T. D., & Low, K. G. (1989). American Indian children and adolescents. In J. T. Gibbs, L. N. Huang, & associates (Eds.), *Children of color* (pp. 114-147). San Francisco: Jossey-Bass.

Levy, B. (1988). "Taking care of me": Preventing child sexual abuse in the Hispanic community. In L. E. A. Walker (Ed.), *Handbook on sexual abuse of children* (pp. 387-401). New York: Springer.

Long, K. L. (1986). Cultural considerations in the assessment and treatment of intrafamilial abuse. *American Journal of Orthopsychiatry, 56*(1), 131-136.

Marin, G., & Marin, B. V. (1991). *Research with Hispanic populations.* Newbury Park, CA: Sage.

Marsh, C. E. (1993). Sexual assault and domestic violence in the African American community. *Western Journal of Black Studies, 17*(3), 149-155.

Mennen, F. E. (1994). Sexual abuse in Latina girls: Their functioning and a comparison with White and African American girls. *Hispanic Journal of Behavioral Sciences, 16*(4), 475-486.

Nagata, D. K. (1989). Japanese American children and adolescents. In J. T. Gibbs, L. N. Huang, & Associates (Eds.), *Children of color* (pp. 67-113). San Francisco: Jossey-Bass.

Nobles, W. W. (1980). Africanity: Its role in black families. *Black Scholar, 9,* 10-17.

Peterson-Lewis, S., Turner, C. W., & Adams, A. M. (1988). Attributional processes in repeatedly abused women. In G. W. Russell (Ed.), *Violence in intimate relationships* (pp. 107-130). New York: PMA.

Rao, K., DiClemente, R. J., & Ponton, L. E. (1992). Child sexual abuse of Asians compared with other populations. *Journal of the American Academy of Child and Adolescent Psychiatry, 31*(5), 880-886.

Sanders-Phillips, K., Moisan, P. A., Wadlington, S., Morgan, S., & English, K. (1995). Ethnic differences in psychological functioning among black and Latino sexually abused girls. *Child Abuse and Neglect, 19*(6), 691-706.

Sullivan, C. M., & Rumptz, M. H. (1994). Adjustment and needs of African American women who utilized a domestic violence shelter. *Violence and Victims,* 9(3), 275-286.

Thompson, V. S., & Smith, S. W. (1993). Attitudes of African American adults toward treatment in cases of child sexual abuse. *Journal of Child Sexual Abuse,* 2(1), 5-19.

Ucko, L. G. (1994). Culture and violence: The interaction of Africa and America. *Sex Roles, 31*(3-4), 185-204.

Urquiza, A. J., & Goodlin-Jones, B. L. (1994). Child sexual abuse and adult revictimization with women of color. *Violence and Victims, 9*(3), 223-232.

U.S. Bureau of the Census. (1996). *Statistical abstract of the United States* (116th ed.). Washington, DC: Government Printing Office.

West, C. (1994). *Race matters.* New York: Vintage.

White, E. C. (1985). *Chain, chain, change.* Seattle, WA: Seal Press.

Williams, O. J. (1994). Group work with African American men who batter: Toward a more ethnically sensitive practice. *Journal of Comparative Family Studies, 25*(1), 91-103.

Williams, O. J. (1995). Black males and violence. *Proceeding of the Institute on Domestic Violence in the African American Community.* Washington DC: U.S. Department of Health and Human Services.

Willis, J. T. (1994). A conceptual model for counseling the violent offender in black domestic relations. *Family Therapy, 21*(2), 139-148.

Wyatt, G. E. (1990). The aftermath of child sexual abuse of African American and White American women: The victim's experience. *Journal of Family Violence, 5*(1), 61-81.

Wyatt, G. E., Guthrie, D., & Notgrass, C. M. (1992). Differential effects of women's child sexual abuse and subsequent sexual revictimization. *Journal of Consulting and Clinical Psychology, 60*(2), 167-173.

Wyatt, G. E., Newcomb, M. D., & Riederle, M. H. (1993). *Sexual abuse and consensual sex: Women's developmental patterns and outcomes.* Newbury Park, CA: Sage.

Wyatt, G. E., & Riederle, M. (1994). Sexual harassment and prior sexual trauma among African American and White American women. *Violence and Victims, 9*(3), 233-247.

Yee, A. H., Fairchild, H. H., Weizmann, F., & Wyatt, G. E. (1993). Addressing psychology's problem with race. *American Psychologist, 48*(11), 1132-1140.

Young, M. E. (1993). *Mules and dragons.* Westport, CT: Greenwood.

Zane, N. (1992). Health status of Asian Americans. *Focus, 6*(1), 8, 10.

• *CHAPTER 7* •

Physical and Sexual Violence in Marriage

ROBERT L. HAMPTON
PAMELA JENKINS
MARIA VANDERGRIFF-AVERY

Over the last several decades, the research literature on violence in marriage and intimate relationships has increased substantially. Although substantial disagreement and debate about the extent of domestic violence remain, there is an underlying consensus that the home is one of society's most dangerous institutions.

This chapter considers some of the research on physical and sexual violence, discussing the incidence and prevalence of both physical and sexual violence as well as institutional responses to these behaviors. This chapter also explores some of the issues requiring future research and intervention. The authors note high rates of violence, including sexual assaults, during pregnancy. Highlighted is the seriousness of the problem of violence in the home and the need to rethink and redefine intervention techniques, developing more effective ones.

Violence in intimate relationships is a behavior pattern that occurs in physical, emotional, psychological, sexual, and economic forms to perpetuate fear, intimidation, power, and control. Furthermore, violence is defined as "acting with or using great physical force or strength in order to injure, control, or intimidate others . . . , committing harm or doing destruction" (*Oxford English Dictionary,* 1982). It would follow from this definition that violence in a marriage is the abuse of a spouse, usually a woman, to maintain control and power by the abuser, usually a man (Dickstein, 1988; Gelles & Conte, 1990).

Historically, women and children, not men, have been the subject of inquiry or discussion on marital or family violence. Family violence studies (Straus & Gelles, 1986; Walker, 1991) show that large numbers of women are likely to be the intended victims of men's violence, which ranges from simple assault to homicide. For many centuries, women have occupied low status and commanded little respect in the social hierarchy. Such standing in society made them the natural victims of a variety of negative impositions, including violence. Their low status in many instances led to an overt disregard for women in general. Within this context, it is not surprising that many cultures did not have labels for spouse abuse. It was hidden, disguised, ignored, and accepted as "culturally consistent" behavior (Pirsig, 1991). In a 1988 report, a Virginia medical college team of paleopathologists identified a much higher incidence of fractures (30% to 50%) among women than among men (9% to 20%) in mummies that were 2,000 to 3,000 years old. According to Dickstein (1988), these were primarily skull fractures caused by lethal blows inflicted during peacetime acts of personal violence.

The nation's response to domestic violence has been uneven. Some concern was voiced in the late part of the nineteenth century and into this century (Pleck, 1987). Then, again, in the latter part of this century, a battered women's movement awoke societal consciousness about the social problem of domestic violence (Schechter, 1982). In 1981, the first "national day of unity" against domestic violence was observed. This observance continued annually until 1984, when several days in October were designated Domestic Violence Awareness Week. In 1987, the annual violence week was expanded to include observance during the entire month by the National Coalition Against Domestic Violence, an organization of battered women, shelters, and support groups that conducts public education campaigns to continually inform the public about battering.

The public discourse about domestic violence has changed significantly during the last decade. Domestic violence, by any measure, constitutes a social problem and a crime. In 1994, the U.S. Congress passed, and President Clinton signed, the Violent Crime Control and Law Enforcement Act of 1994. The Violence Against Women Act (VAWA), which was part of this act, changed federal laws and grant procedures. The focus of this act and its associated funding have already shifted state and local municipalities' methods of applying for and receiving federal funds to train workers and enact domestic violence policies. As with many other social ills, it is still not clear whether recognition of this as a problem has led to successful prevention and intervention techniques.

Physical Violence in Marriage and Intimate Relationships

Incidence and Prevalence

Our cultural understanding of domestic violence as a social problem has involved a concerted effort to "count" the incidence and prevalence of this behavior. Estimates of the incidence and prevalence of violence vary depending on the definition of the problem and the method used to measure it. For this discussion, violence is defined as an act carried out with the intention, or perceived intention, of causing physical pain or injury to another person.

There are two elements in this definition: act and intention. The first element, the act, is clear. One has only to imagine a husband who takes a knife and throws it at his wife. Although he misses and no one is injured, the throwing of a knife is a serious act of violence. Using an act as the defining criterion of violence results in a higher estimate of incidence rates than one based on injuries. The second element of the definition suggests that the husband must willfully act toward his spouse in a manner that could cause pain or injury. In most instances, accidental injuries are not considered violence.

Even with this definition, the true rates of violence in marriage are unknown. Counting the incidence and prevalence of domestic violence is difficult. The methodological problems associated with access, validity, and reliability are enormous (see Dobash & Dobash, 1979; Dobash, Dobash, Wilson, & Daly, 1992; Kurz, 1993; Straus, 1993). These problems have resulted in a contradictory set of facts. These facts—based on how and who gets counted—have serious implications for funding and policy.

In June 1993, the National Crime Victim Survey was implemented with a new design created to capture more incidents of domestic violence. Again, in 1995, the Bureau of Justice Statistics revamped the estimates from the redesigned surveys. Their figures for violent crimes reported against women are an estimated 4.4 million in 1992, 4.8 million in 1993, and 4.7 million in 1994.

The National Family Violence Surveys are the only nationally representative studies of family violence (Gelles & Straus, 1988; Straus &

Gelles, 1990). These surveys provide a rich source of data on the nature, type, severity, and correlates of violence in the American family. Because the 1985 survey provides the most current data, we will use these data for our estimate of couple violence.

Of every 100 couples in a married or cohabiting relationship, 16 reported a violent incident during the year of the survey. This represents a negligible decrease in the proportion of couples experiencing violence in 1985 compared to 1975 (Straus & Gelles, 1986). Applying the 1985 rate to the 54 million couples in the United States that year results in an estimate of 8.7 million couples who experienced at least one assault during the year.

The 1985 survey indicates that 1-year incidence rates of husband-to-wife violence have declined. Straus and Gelles (1986) estimate that husband-to-wife violence decreased by 6.6% between their 1975 and 1985 surveys. The rate of severe violence by husbands also decreased. The rate declined from 38 per 1,000 couples in 1975 to 30 per 1,000 couples in 1985. This 21% decrease is important because it represents a considerable number of couples. According to Straus and Gelles (1990),

> If the 1975 rate for husband-to-wife severe violence had remained in effect, the application of this rate to the 54 million couples in the U.S. in 1985 is an estimate of a least 2,052,000 severely assaulted wives each year. . . . However, if there has been a 27 percent decrease in the rate, that translates to 1,620,000 beaten wives, which is 432,000 fewer than would have been the case if the 1975 rate prevailed. (p. 119)

However, even with these decreases, Straus and Gelles (1986) found that more than 11% of the women surveyed had experienced at least one act of violence during the study year.

The most important statistic is not the rate of overall violence but the one that measures the risk of injury. Sixty-three of 1,000 couples reported serious assaults such as kicking, punching, biting, or choking. When applied to the number of couples in the United States, this rate implies that an estimated 3.4 million incidents of intimate violence carried a relatively high risk of injury.

In contrast to the 1-year incidence rates, prevalence rates indicate the proportion of couples who, over the course of their relationship, experienced a violent event. About 30% of the couples had experienced at least one such altercation.

Male violence against wives and lovers has been an appropriate focus for most research on couple violence. Although the National Family Violence Surveys and other surveys using the Conflict Tactics Scales (CTS) have found nearly equivalent rates of husband-to-wife and wife-to-husband violence, considerable debate still rages over the degree to which there is sexual symmetry in marital violence (Dobash et al., 1992). In fact, the identification and assessment of perpetrators and victims have been among the most contested findings of the National Family Violence Surveys. It has been argued that many of the methods used to detect family violence are inadequate. The CTS, for example, ignores sexual assaults and rapes. Dobash and colleagues (1992) argue that claims of sexual symmetry in couple violence do not reflect sexually symmetrical motivation or action. Finally, many feminist researchers argue that researchers and service providers cannot ignore the context of the violence, its nature and consequences, the role of obligations of each family member, and the different mechanisms or transactional sequences that lead to various forms of abuse (Bograd, 1988).

Because men are typically larger than their wives and usually have greater access to power, property, and prestige, they do not experience the same physical or social consequences from violence as women do. A considerable proportion of wife-to-husband violence occurs in the context of domestic conflict, either as a preemptive strike or in retaliation for previous wife abuse. Further analysis of two national samples also shows that:

- Men perpetrate more aggressive actions against their female partners than women do against their male partners.
- Men perpetrate more severe actions at least by the name of the action (e.g., punch, kick, choke, beat up, threaten with or use a knife or gun).
- Men are more likely to perpetrate multiple aggressive actions during a single incident.
- Women are much more likely to be injured during attacks by male partners than men are during attacks by female partners. (Browne, 1997, p. 51)

Ethnic and Racial Differences in Physical Intimate Violence

Because families of color have been victims of benign neglect in community-based studies of spousal violence, knowledge gaps riddle our understanding of physical intimate violence in minority families. Much of the problem lies in our cultural myths and beliefs about minority communities and in how these myths play out in service provision (Koss et al., 1994).

Several data sources indicate that couple violence may be more prevalent among African Americans than among whites. The first National Family Violence Survey (Straus, Gelles, & Steinmetz, 1980), which is generally cited as the primary source of data on the prevalence and incidence of spousal violence in African American families, reported that African American husbands had higher rates of overall and severe violence toward their wives than white husbands. In their studies of the relationship between race and spousal violence, Lockhart and White (1989) and Lockhart (1991) found that middle-class African American women were more likely than middle-class European American women to report that they were victims of violence by their marital partners.

However, social and economic factors probably account for much, if not all, of this apparent racial difference. Income inequalities may be one factor explaining differences in rates of violence between black and white families; however, controlling for income does not exclusively account for the racial disparity (Hampton & Gelles, 1994; Hampton, Gelles, & Harrop, 1989). Several additional factors must be considered in assessing domestic violence among black partners (Hampton & Gelles, 1994). The limited research on black spouse abuse reveals several relevant variables, including occupation and income, but also such factors as embeddedness in social networks, unemployment, and violence in one's family of orientation (Asbury, 1987; Uzzell & Peebles-Wilkins, 1989). In their analyses of 1975 National Family Violence Survey data, Cazenave and Straus (1979) found that embeddedness in primary networks is closely associated with lower rates of spousal slapping for African American couples than for white couples. For African American couples, the number of years in the neighborhood, the number of children, and the number of non-nuclear family members in the household were all associated with lower levels of spousal violence.

Using data gathered through a purposive sample in a major southeastern metropolitan area, Lockhart (1991) argues that her data support the claim that African American couples are not inherently more violent than European American couples. Higher levels of violence, when they do exist, may be due in part to the particular social predicament of African Americans in American society. By this reasoning, many African Americans have achieved middle-class positions only recently as a result of relatively recent changes in their lives and may have retained the norms, values, and role expectations of their lower-socioeconomic developmental experiences (Lockhart, 1991).

Racial bias in the service system may also contribute to the disproportionately high rates of reported violence among African American families. Although statistics suggest that African American families represent a significant portion of violent families identified and served by agencies, this may in part reflect the actions of gatekeepers and not racial differences in the type, nature, or severity of family violence (Hampton, 1987; Hampton & Newberger, 1985).

The evidence on relative rates of couple violence among Hispanics is mixed. Probably one of the best studies of couple violence among Hispanics was the Los Angeles Epidemiologic Catchment Area (ECA) survey (Sorenson & Telles, 1991), which avoided problems associated with generalizing across Hispanic subgroups by limiting analysis to people of Mexican descent. The sample included 1,243 Mexican Americans and 1,149 non-Hispanic whites. This study found no significant differences between non-Hispanic white and Mexican American families in lifetime rates of self-reported violence toward a spouse. Spousal violence rates for Mexican Americans born in Mexico and non-Hispanic whites born in the United States were virtually equivalent (20.0% and 21.6% respectively). Significantly, spousal violence rates were highest for Mexican Americans born in the United States (30.9%) (Sorenson & Telles, 1991). This research also revealed a gender difference, with women reporting higher rates of hitting or throwing things at their spouse/partner.

One of the major findings that emerged from this study was that rates of spousal violence among Mexican Americans vary according to immigration status. Mexican Americans born in the United States reported rates 2.4 times higher than those born in Mexico did. The higher rates of violence among American-born immigrants may be related to cultural conflicts resulting from exposure to discrepancies between their familial culture of origin and the dominant culture in which they reside (Sorenson & Telles, 1991).

Other social factors—such as economic deprivation, youthfulness, and urban residence—may also help account for higher rates of spouse abuse in Hispanic families (Straus & Smith, 1990). When these factors are controlled, there is no statistically significant difference between Hispanics and non-Hispanic whites. Another study, using information from shelters for abused women, found no differences between Hispanic, African American, and European American women in reported rates of abuse (Gondolf, Fisher, & McFerron, 1988)

Little research exists on domestic violence among Native American women or Asian American women (Norton & Monson, 1995). Most of the data that does exist is anecdotal. In regard to Native Americans, Allen (1990) reports that physical violence against women is at a dangerously high level, whereas Bachman (1992) shows rates of domestic violence in Native American communities that are comparable to the rates in the rest of the population. Chester, Robin, Koss, Lopez, and Goldman (1994) discuss the difficulty of understanding violence within the context of the diversity of Native American cultures.

Much is also unknown about domestic violence among Asian Americans. Using focus groups, Ho (1990) concentrated on the dynamics of the violence in Asian American families rather than collecting data on incidence and prevalence. She found that in many traditional cultures, such as the Asian cultures she was examining, much of the abuse goes unreported because of a reluctance to report incidents to culturally different agencies. Therefore, the available rates of domestic violence in Asian American families may be grossly inaccurate.

Although many methodological challenges surround the ability to count the incidence and prevalence of domestic violence, the enterprise is still worth pursuing. New measures, including ones that consider cultural contexts, need to be developed to help address the knowledge gaps in understanding violence in families of color.

Lethal Violence

Intrafamily homicide is the most severe consequence of family violence. In the United States from 1980 to 1984, about 25% of all one-on-one cases of murder and non-negligent manslaughter—18,712 homicides—occurred between family members over the age of 18 (Browne, 1987; Straus, 1986a). Nine percent of all murders that occurred nationwide between 1976 and 1996 were committed by an intimate (Bureau of Justice Statistics, 1998). Women were at greater risk of being killed by a male partner than by other family members or by any other people outside of the partnership (Frieze & Browne, 1989). In the homicides involving heterosexual partners, most of the victims were women: 58% were women killed by their male partner, whereas 42% were men killed by their female partner.

From 1976 through 1985, the spousal homicide rate in the United States was 1.6 per 100,000 married people, with wives being at 1.3 times the risk of husbands (Mercy & Saltzman, 1989). Between 1976 and 1996, 30% of female murder victims were killed by an intimate partner compared to only 6% of male murder victims (Bureau of Justice Statistics, 1998).

Previous research demonstrates that female victims of marital homicide are more likely to be killed at home than in any other setting (Goetting, 1991; Mann, 1991). Using homicide data from Detroit in the early 1980s, Goetting found that almost 40% of homicides occurred in the bedroom, 21% in the living room, and 10% in the kitchen. Husbands were twice as likely to kill in a bedroom as were wives. Nearly 60% of the homicides occurred on weekends.

The location of the homicide plays an important role in the circumstances associated with the homicide event (Rose & McClain, 1990). The home is not only the place where female victims are more likely to be killed, it is also the place where they are more likely to kill their marital partners (Goetting, 1991; Jurik & Winn, 1990; Rose & McClain, 1990). When women kill, it is frequently during situations of domestic conflict or in retaliation for previous abuse (Browne, 1987; Goetting, 1991; Jurik & Winn, 1990; Mann, 1991). Several studies have shown that African Americans are overrepresented among female perpetrators (Block, 1988; Jurik & Winn, 1990; McClain, 1982-1983; Valdez & Nourjah, 1988).

According to the most recent data from the federal government (Bureau of Justice Statistics, 1998), the overall number of intimate murders was 36% lower in 1996 than 20 years earlier, in 1976. Although the decline has occurred for both male and female victims of intimate violence, it has decreased at a much higher rate among male victims. In 1996, the number of male intimate murder victims was about 60% lower than it was in 1976. For women, the decline in victimization rate was far less, only dropping about 20%. There has also been a decline in the per capita rate of intimate murders among African Americans. In 1976, the intimate homicide rate was almost 11 times higher among blacks than whites. By 1996, the rate among blacks had dropped to just over 4 times higher than that of whites. As with the overall population, the greatest decrease in intimate partner homicide rates among African Americans has occurred among men. Research done by Browne and Williams (1993), using Supplementary Homicide Report Data from 1976 through 1987, shows similar patterns. Their research points to the difference involving unmarried couples. Although the lethal victimization rate for men in unmarried relationships varied unsystematically over time from 1976 through 1987, the rate of unmarried women being killed by their male partners increased significantly.

Data on prior police contact suggests that family and intimate assaults occur within a context of repeated violence (Browne, 1987; Saltzman et al., 1990; Straus, 1986a). Thus, intrafamily homicides are not unpredictable, or unpreventable, events.

Marital Rape

Marital rape is another form of violence within intimate relationships, one that has only recently been acknowledged as a problem. Marital rape was not considered a crime in the United States until the mid-1970s. With the advent of the 1970s' women's movement, society began to reconsider this concept. Subsequently, social scientists began to investigate sexual assault, forced sex in marriage, and marital rape. By 1980, however, only three states had completely eliminated the marital rape exemption from their laws, and only five states had modified it. The rationale for the marital exemption in rape laws was partly based on the belief that marriage constituted the wife's implicit consent to grant sex to her husband whenever he desired it.

Few women whose husbands have forced them to have sex define themselves as rape victims (Gelles, 1987). Most women see rape as primarily occurring between strangers. Pagelow (1984) reports that women who stated that they had not been raped also reported that they had submitted to sexual demands to prevent beatings or out of fear of their partner. Several women in this study also reported physical assaults during sexual activity so severe that they were injured or lost consciousness, yet they did not define these acts as sexual assaults.

The subject of marital rape has been popularized in media coverage of several significant court cases where efforts were made to criminalize this form of sexual assault. For most of our history, it has been assumed that a husband could not rape his wife. Legal policies based on common law and patriarchy have supported husbands' notions that their wives—and their wives' bodies—belong to them (Pagelow, 1988). Marital rape is still one of the least discussed and researched areas in the family violence field.

The Incidence and Prevalence of Marital Rape

As with all forms of intimate violence, the incidence and prevalence of marital rape are difficult to document. Bachman and Saltzman (1995) found that only 18% of all female rape victims had been assaulted by a complete stranger. About 10% of all victims were raped or sexually assaulted by their husbands or ex-husbands, 16% by boyfriends or ex-boyfriends, 3% by relatives, and 53% by acquaintances or friends. In other words, 26% of all rapes and sexual assaults were committed by a current or former intimate partner.

Diana Russell's (1982) research was among the first to challenge the assumption that marital rape is just another form of abuse suffered by battered wives. Of the 644 married women in the sample, 14% reported sexual assaults by husbands: 12% had been forced to have intercourse, and 2% had experienced other types of sexual assault. Sexual assaults by husbands were the most common type reported, occurring over twice as often as sexual assault by a stranger. In their interviews of 323 Boston-area women, Finkelhor and Yllö (1985) found that nearly 10% had been forced to have sex with their husbands. Gelles and Straus (1988) found that 50 women per 1,000 reported that their husbands attempted to force them to have sex each year and that 80 per 1,000 were forced to have sex by their husbands.

In Russell's sample and others, researchers have found that some men batter their wives but do not rape them, some rape but do not batter them, and others do both (Bowker, 1983; Browne, 1987; Finkelhor & Yllö, 1985; Shields & Hanneke, 1983). The mixture of sexual and nonsexual violence in marriage may be the highest level on a continuum of wife abuse because these victims may have experienced more severe forms of nonsexual violence and stronger reactions (Bowker, 1983; Russell, 1982; Shields & Hanneke, 1983).

Most of the available conceptual knowledge on marital rape comes from surveys of battered women, rape crisis hotlines, and court cases. Although our theoretical knowledge base on the subject of marital rape is limited, public professional awareness and research concern is growing. In addition, there is evidence (Gelles, 1987) to suggest that marital rape afflicts a large number of marriages, whether or not there are any signs of physical battering. Analysis of the definition of marital rape and previously held views regarding its occurrence offer some conceptual understanding of this subject.

Factors in Family Violence

Many factors identified in research and in the popular press attempt to explain why domestic violence is so prevalent in our society. We identify two broad categories of antecedents to family and domestic violence: social and psychological antecedents. Social antecedents include limited access to goods and services; limited opportunities, social and structural constraints, estrangement and social isolation from others; and physical proximity of family members. The anger and despair generated by social structural constraints is acted out with those "nearest and dearest" and most vulnerable to scapegoating.

Psychological antecedents include blocked aspirations, unrestrained anger, faulty regulation of emotional closeness and distance, sado-masochistic relational patterns and generational transmission of learned violence-prone behavior, and low self-esteem.

Structure of the Family

Physical and sexual violence in marriage is perhaps best thought of as an indicator of families in trouble. Many factors can jeopardize a family and lead to violence. This multiplicity of causes complicates the task of understanding the origins of couple violence.

Straus (1991) believes that among the social causes of domestic violence is the high level of conflict that is characteristic of families. Much of this conflict is associated with factors that form the very foundation of family life in this country. According to Gelles and Straus (1979), these factors are: involuntary membership, intensity of involvement, gender and age differences, family privacy, range of activities and interests, right to influence, and shared identity. These factors add up to produce a high level of conflict, which in turn increases the risk that one or another member of the family will try to win the conflict using violence. As the amount of conflict increases, the assault rate also increases dramatically (Straus, 1991).

Gender Inequality: Power and Control

Although conflict can be part of any marriage, the victims are often determined by the imbalance of power in these intimate relationships.

Feminist scholars see male dominance in overt and subtle forms as a major cause of family violence. The feminist analysis of wife beating is in many respects a critique of patriarchy (Yllö & Straus, 1990). Such an analysis concentrates on why women become the most "appropriate" victims of domestic violence (Dobash & Dobash, 1979; Dobash et al., 1992).

Husband violence is associated with nonegalitarian decision making (Yllö & Straus, 1990). Research shows that egalitarian couples have the lowest rates of violence, and husband-dominated couples have the highest rate of spouse abuse (Straus et al., 1980). It can be argued that in male-dominant relationships, many husbands use violence, physical and sexual, as a way to maintain power. It is also true that in many instances where the husband is not dominant, men may resort to violence in response to perceived powerlessness.

Exposure to Violence in Family of Orientation

This proposition suggests that a disproportionate number of individuals who engage in physical assault against their wives were socialized in households in which they observed parental violence. Some studies indicate that there is an association between observation of fathers hitting mothers and subsequent wife abuse (Caesar, 1988; Hampton & Gelles, 1994; Pagelow, 1981; Rosenbaum & O'Leary, 1981; Straus et al., 1980).

Although the experience one has with violence as a child is a powerful contributor to adult attitudes toward violence, this variable explains only a small percentage of the variance in couple violence. For most couples, there is no direct transfer of behaviors observed in childhood to the marital relationship.

Alcohol and Substance Abuse

Several studies report a strong association between substance abuse, especially abuse of alcohol, and marital violence (Browne, 1987; Dutton, 1992; Hayes & Emshoff, 1993; Rosenbaum & O'Leary, 1981; Walker, 1984). Abusive men with a history of alcohol or drug problems are apt to abuse their spouses when both drunk and sober. They tend to be violent more frequently and with greater severity. They also are more likely to attack their partners sexually (Browne, 1987; Frieze & Knoble, 1980; Roy, 1977; Walker, 1984).

Sociological Explanations

Sociological investigations represent the most prevalent attempts to understand the nature of marital violence. This is ironic, because practice professions such as psychology and social work have most often been called on to address the problems. From a sociological perspective, marital violence moves beyond the exterior of the marriage, which deals with offspring, security, and caretaking. It emanates from the underlying architecture and symbolizes the very complex problems encountered by couples. The marriage is expected to provide all things to both spouses, that is, love, sexual compatibility, companionship, togetherness, and all other expressive as well as instrumental needs. A great deal is requested from each spouse, and the greater the burden that is placed on the intimate relationship, the more stressed and fragile it becomes. Contemporary couples are trying to cope with vast and widespread changes in societal patterns. People bring to marriage disparate expectations and values. Dreams and visions are often based more on wishes and fantasies than on what reality can offer. Considering these conditions, it is no wonder that marital violence develops or that it originates from the intimate emotional realm perhaps as often as from social structural and societal patterns. Sooner or later, many couples will become angry when unmet needs or unrealistic demands surface. Long-standing anger is often projected onto the partner, and repetitive violence may erupt in the marriage.

Marital violence experts, giving attention to the complex nature of intimacy and marital relationships, must wonder about the extent to which this violence is reported. They have made serious attempts to understand the complex nature of intimate relationships in developing effective clinical models that concurrently address the social attitudes and relationship patterns that underlie the perpetuation and underreporting of marital violence.

Consequences of Family Violence

The response to family violence on the part of individuals who are battered is negative and extensive. At the first level are the physical consequences of domestic violence. We know that physical assaults range from pushing and shoving to homicides. Many of the injuries go unreported and untreated throughout the relationship. In a large, community-based family clinic, Hamberger, Saunders, and Hovey

(1992) found that 25% of female clients reported at least one injury by their male partner. The emotional and psychological response to the injury or threat of injury is as serious as the physical injuries. Victims of domestic violence often experience feelings of disbelief, fear, and withdrawal (Herman, 1992). Because many of these threats continue over the period of a relationship, many victims learn to analyze their situation differently in light of threats and possible injuries (Koss et al., 1994).

Women's responses to battering include the development of general negative attitudes toward marriage and intimate relationships. Psychosomatic reactions create alarming health problems. Depression and suicide attempts increase with a corresponding increase in the use of drugs and alcohol. Social isolation, child battering, and retaliatory violence may develop. Studies have noted the lack of psychological and emotional well-being among battered women who have sought help or refuge in a shelter or agency. These studies have shown that battered women frequently suffer a lack of self-esteem (Rieker & Carmen, 1986; Roark & Vlahos, 1983), feelings of loss and inadequacy (Turner & Shapiro, 1986), depression (Hilberman & Munson, 1977), and learned helplessness (Walker, 1979).

Several psychological distress items were included in the second National Family Violence Survey with the intent of measuring the three aspects of mental health that have been shown to be related to violent victimization: depression, stress, and somatic symptoms. Women who reported experiencing violence and abuse also reported higher levels of moderate and severe psychological distress. The multivariate analysis indicated that violence made an independent and nonspurious contribution to the psychological distress experienced by women (Gelles & Harrop, 1989).

Learned Helplessness or Active Survival?

At least two views from the literature describe the consequences of violence on battered women. The first view sees the battered woman as an active survivor of an abusive situation (see Bowker, 1993). The second view categorizes the battered woman as a helpless and passive victim (Gondolf et al., 1988; Walker, 1993).

The concept of learned helplessness has been used to illustrate the victimization process. Walker (1979) suggests that repeated battering diminishes the woman's motivation to respond. As a result, women show a tendency to be submissive in the face of intermittent punishments or abuse. As the abuse continues, the battered woman becomes immobilized, feels a loss of emotion over the battering experience, and begins to blame herself for the abuse inflicted on her by another.

Contrary to the learned helplessness hypothesis is the view of women as survivors who actively work to protect their safety and the safety of their families (Bowker, 1993; Dobash & Dobash, 1979). This hypothesis views the battered woman as an active survivor rather than as a helpless victim. Many battered women remain in abusive situations due not to passivity but to repeated unsuccessful attempts to escape. These women increase their help-seeking efforts in face of increased violence. They try in a logical, consistent way to assure themselves and their children protection and survival. Such efforts supersede fear, giving up, depression, or the passivity of the learned helplessness state. The surviving battered woman is heroic, assertive, and persistent (Gondolf & Fisher, 1988). She fails at these attempts not because she is unsuccessful, but because the systems fail her. This research based on a comprehensive survey of more than 6,000 women in Texas shelters provides the largest database on the subject to date. The findings challenge the existing paradigm of learned helplessness and offer new modes of thinking about victimization and survival, help seeking, battered women and their batterers, and the community system of resources and support services. The implications for clinical treatment and intervention are extensive.

Institutional Responses to Domestic Violence

The response of the social system to the battered woman's cry for help historically has been insufficient. There are serious barriers and deficiencies in the help sources that must be addressed to support the help-seeking efforts of battered women.

Why is there such an observable breakdown in the social support network designed to aid individuals in crisis? Family violence scholars have elucidated several assumptions about the battered woman. The first relates to a system of male dominance and subsequent insensitivity to the impact of the larger social order on individual problems. Second, there is the prevalent, unquestioned assumption that domestic violence stems from the pathology of individuals and families rather than from social structural constraints and impingements. Third, the privatization of family life holds the position that families are expected to fend for themselves for adequate housing, child care, economic sufficiency, protection, adequate employment, and support.

To address the social problems and consequences of family violence substantially and realistically, efforts should seek to assess the problem in a social structural way and to increase the social status and power of the battered woman. The social structural constraints identified earlier must be relaxed, and attitudes, thinking, actions, and resources of the social system must be addressed to alter the battering position in which many women find themselves.

A thorough clinical assessment needs to be conducted at the same time as the social structural assessment. Intense family violence and battering situations nearly always involve serious and intense emotional reactions. Long-standing battering situations often produce clinical levels of depression, low self-concept, anger, and other underlying problems that require the understanding and skills of good clinicians. Clinical intervention, when coupled with systematic intervention, can often move individuals swiftly toward a stable plateau.

Historically, interventions to aid physically abused children originated in the medical community in the 1950s. Formal programs for victims of marital violence began in the early 1970s. These programs assumed, in most cases, that survivors of wife assault are adults and that they are able to make their own decisions. Among the crisis intervention services that have received considerable attention in the past decade are medical settings, the police, and treatment programs for male batterers. Because male batterers are being addressed elsewhere in this volume (see Bennett & Williams, Chapter 9), we will direct our attention to interventions by hospitals and the police.

Medical Settings

Hospitals and other medical settings play important roles in recognizing, reporting, and treating victims. Despite the frequency with which health care professionals see cases of family violence, it is widely accepted that health care professionals are likely to either ignore or minimize the abuse or they are likely to scapegoat or disbelieve the victims (Klingbeil, 1986).

The available data suggest that health care professionals treat a large number of women for injuries that resulted from interpersonal violence. A study of a representative sample of 1,793 women in Kentucky

(Shulman, 1979) found that 1 out of 10 had been physically assaulted by her partner during the year, and 79 of the assaults were serious enough to require medical attention. About 43% of the injured women required treatment, and 44% of these needed two or more treatments. About 59% sought treatment in a hospital emergency room. Taking these data to estimate spouse abuse, Straus (1986b) calculated an annual incidence rate of 4.4 injuries requiring medical attention per 100 married women in Kentucky.

Two hospital-based studies also concluded that battered women are seen frequently in emergency rooms. In a study conducted at a large general hospital emergency department in Detroit, 25% of the women examined were known victims of domestic violence (Goldberg & Tomlanovich, 1984). Similar results were reported by research done in San Francisco, which concluded that 36% of admissions to the county trauma center resulted from interpersonal violence (Sumner, Mintz, & Brown, 1986). On a national level, 37% of female emergency room patients were injured by an intimate in 1994, with 16% being injured by a current or former spouse and 21% being injured by a current or former boyfriend (Rand, 1997).

There is also evidence that physicians frequently ignore the initial signs of battering. Through their examination of emergency department records, Flitcraft, Frazier, and Stark (1980) found that many women seen once for inflicted injuries subsequently returned with inflicted injuries. Stark and Flitcraft (1985) found that only 1 in 25 battered women was identified as battered in the emergency department they studied. McLeer and Anwar (1989) found that when a protocol to identify battered women was introduced to an emergency department, in which they asked female trauma patients if they had been injured by someone, almost 30% of all female trauma patients were battered women.

There is much variability in staff responses to victims, based on their medical specialty, their perception of the victim, and their training. Many medical personnel tend to focus on the injury itself while ignoring the process and circumstances of the incident that produced it. Health care advocates for victims of wife abuse have proposed that health care personnel learn to identify battered women and intervene on their behalf (Hampton, 1988).

A recent study reveals two important caveats to our discussion of battered women in health care settings. First, battered women who present to emergency departments have a diverse set of behavioral characteristics: The majority present like other patients. A significant minority, 39%, had traits that medical staff found discrediting and difficult—26% of this group had alcohol on their breath or had used drugs, whereas 13% were, as the medical literature suggests, "evasive" (Kurz, 1990). Although there was no stereotypical "abused woman," this study suggests that health care personnel should be prepared to encounter many battered women who appear similar to other patients. The study also suggests that the majority of abused women respond to direct questioning.

An ongoing education and concrete intervention program can produce positive responses to battered women (Kurz, 1990). This study suggests, however, that we cannot automatically assume that the presentation of information to health care personnel will lead to completed interventions. Health care personnel, like other professionals in the field, often give conditional responses to victims. Staff are less responsive to women with discrediting attributes. They sometimes do not respond because they feel they do not have the time for interventions and often prefer to give other cases priority. Occasionally, they do not see responding to battered women as a central part of their medical role (Kurz, 1990).

The Police

One of the recommendations that emerged from the study done by the Attorney General's Task Force on Family Violence (1984) was that the criminal justice system should become more actively involved in punishing perpetrators of domestic violence. In its Law Enforcement Recommendation 2, the report states that "consistent with state law, the chief executive of every law enforcement agency should establish arrest as the preferred response in cases of family violence" (p. 17).

Drawing heavily from the results of the Minneapolis Police experiment, this report called for police departments and criminal justice agencies to recognize battering as a criminal activity and respond accordingly. This position was supported by the case of Tracy Thurman, a battered wife who had regularly sought assistance from the Torrington, Connecticut, police to protect her from the violent attacks of her estranged husband. Thurman was severely battered and left permanently injured in June 1983 while police officers stood by and did nothing.

Subsequently, she filed a civil suit against the City of Torrington and 29 police officers (*Thurman v. City of Torrington,* 1985). Thurman won her case and later settled out of court for $1.9 million. Because of the ever-present threat of similar suits, a number of communities adopted the policy of mandatory arrest for cases of family violence.

In general, police respond to domestic violence calls reluctantly and with a sense of futility (Berk & Loseke, 1980; Caputo, 1991; Elliot, 1989). Although the early 1980s was a period in which the "arrest the perpetrator" approach was the preferred response by many law enforcement agencies, recent evidence sheds new light on this type of intervention strategy. Based on his assessment of data collected through seven National Institute of Justice experiments, Sherman (1992) found that:

- Arrest increases domestic violence among people who have nothing to lose, especially the unemployed.
- Arrest deters domestic violence in cities with higher proportions of white and Hispanic suspects.
- Arrest deters domestic violence in the short run but escalates violence later on in cities with higher proportions of unemployed black suspects.
- A small but chronic portion of all violent couples produce the majority of domestic violence incidents.
- Offenders who flee before police arrive are substantially deterred by warrants for their arrest, at least in Omaha. (p. 247)

This suggests that arrest as an intervention does not produce a uniform result. It can, in some cases, produce unintended negative consequences for victims. Consequently, this intervention is conditional and limited.

The debate about the benefits of arrest continues. Another unintended consequence is the occurrence of dual arrest. Also, the consequence of dual arrest is that in some areas, both men and women are attending mandatory counseling and anger prevention groups.

McCord (1992) points out that whether or not arrest policies stop the violence, consequences may still be beneficial. McCord calls into question evaluation procedures that do not take into account other benefits and outcomes from mandatory and pro-arrest policies. These other benefits include whether or not suspects find new victims or increase the severity of crimes. These arrest studies also do not take into account the possible benefits to the victim and possible long-term benefits for police.

Compassion Versus Control

Alvin Rosenfeld and Eli Newberger (1977), two physicians, described two competing philosophies that have been applied to treating child abuse. These philosophies are equally applicable to other forms of family violence interventions.

A compassionate intervention may focus on mediation, education, training, and treatment. It often involves providing additional resources for the family. The agent of social control who applies a compassionate intervention is guided to approach each case with understanding and a nonpunitive outlook (Mederer & Gelles, 1989). Outcomes of the intervention are thought to be attitude change, improved skills at coping with stress, and, ultimately, the cessation of wife battering. The underlying philosophy is humane and compassionate attitudes toward both the victim and the abuser (Rosenfeld & Newberger, 1977).

A control model is based on the assumption that deviant behavior is controlled when punishment is both certain and severe. Individuals are in effect coerced, threatened, and sanctioned into conformity. This occurs formally and informally. Paternoster and Iovanni (1986) found that deterrence works primarily through informal processes and that, once these are controlled, perceptions of severity and certainty of punishment have no effect on deviant behavior. The threat of arrest and public exposure as a wife beater might deter potentially violent men from abusing their wives (Mederer & Gelles, 1989).

The control model involves aggressive use of intervention to limit, and, if necessary, punish the perpetrator. Abusers are held accountable for their actions. Preferred options include the arrest and criminal prosecution of the aggressor.

Mederer and Gelles (1989) discuss several advantages and disadvantages to interventions based on either philosophy. It is probably wise to heed the advice given by Rosenfeld and Newberger (1977) in that they suggest that effective treatment involves both compassion and control. This advice is supported by an empirical examination of the effectiveness of battered women's shelters (a compassion approach) in preventing future battering (Berk, Newton, & Berk, 1986). The shelters appeared to have a beneficial effect for 8 out of 10 women who stayed in them. They reported no new violence after they left the shelter. For other women, shelters either had no impact or, worse, triggered new episodes of violence. Washburn and Frieze (1981) compared three groups of battered women: those going to a shelter, those who filed orders of protection, and those who responded to an advertisement seeking subjects for a study of battered women. Women from the shelter were about twice as likely as the others to be unemployed. These women and those filing protection orders tended to have experienced more severe violence, particularly marital rape. The women who filed protection orders felt the least powerful and defined their actions as helping themselves to change their situations.

It is possible to use control interventions (arrest, prosecution, and sentencing) to motivate perpetrators to participate in treatment programs. Diversion programs are another way of combining both control and compassion (Mederer & Gelles, 1989). In an era when the police are the only institution that can command substantial public funds to combat domestic violence, it is important to acknowledge that control and compassion can be linked. It is also important to note that domestic violence can be better addressed through a wide range of nonpolice programs, from industrial policy to Head Start to counseling and therapy for victims and batterers (Sherman, 1992).

In the best of all worlds, appropriate legal controls, humane support, and primary prevention programs to address wife abuse would be present in all communities. These programs not only would address individual-level variables that might contribute to violent episodes but, where possible, would also address social structural issues as well. In the final analysis, violence is a dynamic series of interactions between perpetrators and survivors, wherein one party ultimately wins, one ultimately loses, or there is a draw. Because all parties are influenced by dynamics within and without, both groups are victims needing intervention and assistance. Violence is more than an overt act, it is an end product of complex psychological and social forces.

We cannot assume that simply presenting information to professionals working in the field will lead to appropriate interventions. It will continue to be necessary for hospitals and the police, for example, to make referrals to battered women's programs, and vice versa. It is only through cross-agency and cross-disciplinary efforts on many levels that we can hope to reduce and eventually alleviate the pain and suffering related to marital violence.

Future Issues in Domestic Violence

Although the research in this area has grown enormously in the last two decades, there is still much work to be done. How the questions are developed and answered is not just an academic exercise (see Pagelow, 1992). As researchers, our ethical responsibilities toward this subject are intricate and complex. Whether we work with advocates, which advocates we work with, and how our findings are used have serious consequences for policy. Following are some of the issues that need further research and new intervention strategies.

Certain categories of victims need further study and intervention because they may find themselves at particular risk for serious injury. First, divorced, separated, and single women face risks. We know that women who announce they are leaving a relationship and those women who actually leave are sometimes at great risk (Ptacek, 1997). Another set of women who face unique risks are pregnant women. Research cannot answer whether or not battering increases during pregnancy, only that the violence does not stop. Helton, McFarlane, and Anderson (1987) found that up to 37% of obstetric patients were physically attacked by an intimate partner.

Another particularly vulnerable group of women needing further research and intervention are elderly victims of domestic violence. Elder abuse has often been viewed as abuse between an elderly parent and adult child. Although this certainly describes a portion of the abuse, there is some evidence that elder abuse also includes elderly women as victims of spouse abuse. Vinton (1992) points out that the needs of elderly women are often not met in traditional shelter programs and that other intervention strategies need to be developed.

Another aspect for future research and programming is the relationship of children in homes where domestic violence is present. Edleson (1977) refers to this phenomenon as the overlap between child maltreatment and woman abuse. In his review of the literature, he found that studies show that children are abused in about half the families where the mother is a known victim of domestic violence, and other studies show that mothers are battered in about half the families where the child is a known victim of physical abuse. Osofsky (1995) discusses the effects on children who witness violence. The effects on the children in any development stage are staggering, especially when the children are related to the perpetrators and victims of violence. Both Edleson and Osofsky point out the need for more analytic, less descriptive research.

One of the most significant developments in domestic violence is the advent of shelters, which first opened in this country in 1974. There are now about 2,000 shelters nationwide, most providing a variety of services for battered women and their children. Certain groups, such as lesbians, some older women, and women from different cultures, do not use shelters. The focus in this country remains on the crisis psychological model emphasizing the individual education of individual women who enter shelters. The issue of shelters and their ability to provide safety for all women constitutes a major area of concern for research and intervention.

Further research also needs to be done investigating the impact that recent policies have had on the lives battered women. Two recent policies that are ripe for this kind of inquiry are the 1994 Violence Against Women Act and the 1996 Personal Responsibility and Work Opportunity Act (PRWOA). Although the 1994 Violence Against Women Act appears to be an exciting and much needed policy that protects battered women and penalizes their batterers, research needs to be done to evaluate its effectiveness and to determine the act's strengths and weaknesses. After a thorough evaluation, changes to the policy could be made, if necessary.

Even though some research has been done examining the effects of the PRWOA on battered women (see Raphael & Tolman, 1997), more needs to be done. One major premise of this policy is moving people "off of welfare and into work." States have set up time guidelines determining how long welfare recipients have to make this move. After examining four recent studies on the relationship between welfare and domestic violence, Raphael and Tolman (1997) found that a relatively large and consistent percentage of women on welfare were currently abused by their partners (ranging from 14.6% to 32%) and that the majority of them had been victims of domestic violence at some point in their lives (33.8% to 64.9%). The problems associated with being a victim of domestic violence may interfere with a woman's ability to work, as a result of the physical or psychological damage of the violence or out of fear of future violence. As a result, some battered women may be placed at a greater risk as a result of the strict employment requirements and time limitations of the PRWOA. The Wellstone/Murray Family Violence Amendment has been passed in response to this possibility. It "gives state welfare departments the flexibility to provide battered women on welfare more time to remove the domestic violence barrier by obtaining specialized domestic violence services" (Raphael & Tolman, 1997, p. iv). Although this is definitely a positive step, states may or may not choose to use it. The ramifications of the 1996 PRWOA and the Wellstone/Murray Family Violence Amendment on the lives of battered women need to be continuously explored.

Finally, violence against women is an international issue. As growing feminist movements emerge across the globe, domestic violence is increasingly recognized as a problem throughout the world (Alexander, 1993; Fernandez, 1997; Kahn, 1993; Romken, 1997). Shelters and other programs for battered women now exist in many countries. The barriers to collaboration between countries to protect and save women are enormous. Future research should investigate the ways in which communities across the globe might work to understand the issues of intimate violence.

References

Alexander, R. (1993). Wife battering: An Australian perspective. *Journal of Family Violence, 8,* 229-251.

Allen, P. G. (1990). *Violence and the American Indian woman. The speaking profits us: Violence in the lives of women of color.* Seattle, WA: SAFECO Insurance Company.

Asbury, J. (1987). African American women in violent relationships: An exploration of cultural difference. In R. L. Hampton (Ed.), *Violence in the black family: Correlates and consequences* (pp. 89-105). Lexington, MA: Lexington Books.

Attorney General's Task Force on Family Violence. (1984). Report. Washington, DC: U.S. Department of Justice.

Bachman, R. (1992). *Death and violence on the reservation: Homicide, family violence, and suicide in American Indian population.* New York: Auburn House.

Bachman, R., & Saltzman, L. E. (1995). *Violence against women: Estimates from the redesigned survey.* Washington, DC: Bureau of Justice Statistics, U.S. Department of Justice.

Berk, R. A., & Loseke, D. (1980). Handling family violence: The situated determinants of police arrest in domestic disturbances. *Law and Society Review, 15*(2), 317-346.

Berk, R. A., Newton, P. J., & Berk, S. F. (1986). What a difference a day makes: An empirical study of the impact of shelters for battered women. *Journal of Marriage and the Family, 48,* 431-490.

Block, C. (1988). Lethal violence in the Chicago Latino community, 1965 to 1981. In J. F. Kraus, S. B. Sorenson, & P. D. Juarez (Eds.), *Proceedings from the research conference on violence and homicide in Hispanic communities* (pp. 31-65). Los Angeles: UCLA Publication Services.

Bograd, M. (1988). Feminist perspectives on wife abuse: An introduction. In K. Yllö & M. Bograd (Eds.), *Feminist perspectives on wife abuse* (pp. 11-26). Newbury Park, CA: Sage.

Bowker, L. H. (1983). *Beating wife-beating.* Lexington, MA: Lexington Books.

Bowker, L. H. (1993). A battered woman's problems are social, not psychological. In R. J. Gelles & D. Loseke (Eds.), *Current controversies on family violence* (pp. 154- 166). Newbury Park, CA: Sage.

Browne, A. (1987). *When battered women kill.* New York: Free Press.

Browne, A. (1997). Violence in marriage: Until death do us part? In A. P. Cardarelli (Ed.), *Violence between intimate partners: Patterns, causes, and effects* (pp. 48-69). Needham Heights, MA: Allyn & Bacon.

Browne, A., & Williams, K. R. (1993). Gender, intimacy, and lethal violence: Trends from 1976-1987. *Gender and Society, 7,* 78-98.

Bureau of Justice Statistics. (1998). *Violence by intimates: Analysis of data on crimes by current or former spouses, boyfriends, and girlfriends.* Washington, DC: U.S. Department of Justice.

Caesar, P. L. (1988). Exposure to violence in the families of origin among wife abusers and maritally nonviolent men. *Violence and Victims, 3,* 49-56.

Caputo, R. K. (1991). Police classification of domestic violence calls: An assessment of program impact. In D. D. Knudsen & J. L. Miller (Eds.), *Abused and battered* (pp. 147-152). New York: Aldine de Gruyter.

Cazenave, N. A., & Straus, M. A. (1979). Race, class, network embeddedness, and family violence: A search for potent support systems. *Journal of Comparative Family Studies, 10*(3), 79-90.

Chester, B., Robin, R., Koss, M., Lopez, J., & Goldman, D. (1994). Grandmothers dishonored: Violence against women by male partners in American Indian communities. *Violence and Victims, 9,* 249-258.

Dickstein, L. (1988). Spouse abuse and other domestic violence. *Psychiatric Clinics of North America, 2,* 611-625.

Dobash, R. E., & Dobash, R. P. (1979). *Violence against wives: A case against patriarchy.* New York: Free Press.

Dobash, R. P., Dobash, R. E., Wilson, M., & Daly, M. (1992). The myth of sexual symmetry in marital violence. *Social Problems, 39,* 71-91.

Dutton, M. A. (1992). *Empowering and healing the battered woman.* New York: Springer.

Edleson, J. L. (1977). *The overlap between child maltreatment and woman battering.* Unpublished manuscript, University of Minnesota School of Social Work, St. Paul.

Elliot, D. (1989). The evaluation of criminal justice procedures in family violence crimes. In L. Ohlin & M. Tonry (Eds.), *Family violence* (pp. 427-480). Chicago: University of Chicago Press.

Fernandez, M. (1997). Domestic violence by extended family members in India. *Journal of Interpersonal Violence, 12,* 433-455.

Finkelhor, D., & Yllö, K. (1985). *License to rape: Sexual abuse of wives.* Beverly Hills, CA: Sage.

Flitcraft, A., Frazier, W. D., & Stark, E. (1980). *Medical encounters and sequelae of domestic violence.* Final report to the National Institute of Mental Health, Bethesda, MD.

Frieze, I. H., & Browne, A. (1989). Violence in marriage. In L. Ohlin & M. Tonry (Eds.), *Family violence* (pp. 163-218). Chicago: University of Chicago Press.

Frieze, I. H., & Knoble, J. (1980, August). *The effects of alcohol on marital violence.* Paper presented at the annual meeting of the American Psychological Association, Montreal.

Gelles, R. J. (1987). *Family violence* (2nd ed.). Newbury Park, CA: Sage.

Gelles, R. J., & Conte, J. (1990). Domestic violence and sexual abuse of children. *Journal of Marriage and the Family, 52,* 1045-1058.

Gelles, R. J., & Harrop, J. W. (1989). Violence, battering, and psychological distress among women. *Journal of Interpersonal Violence, 4*(4), 400-420.

Gelles, R. J., & Straus, M. A. (1979). Determinants of violence in the family: Toward a theoretical integration. In W. R. Burr, F. I. Nye, S. K. Steinmetz, & M. Wilkinson (Eds.), *Contemporary theories about the family* (pp. 549-581). New York: Free Press.

Gelles, R. J., & Straus, M. A. (1988). *Intimate violence: The causes and consequences of abuse in the American family.* New York: Simon & Schuster.

Goetting, A. (1991). Patterns of marital homicide: A comparison of husbands and wives. In R. L. Hampton (Ed.), *Black family violence: Current research and theory* (pp. 147-160). Lexington, MA: Lexington Books.

Goldberg, W., & Tomlanovich, M. C. (1984). Domestic violence victims in the emergency department. *Journal of the American Medical Association, 251*(25), 3259-3264.

Gondolf, E. W., & Fisher, E. R. (1988). *Battered women as survivors: An alternative to treating learned helplessness.* Lexington, MA: Lexington Books.

Gondolf, E. W., Fisher, E. R., & McFerron, J. R. (1988). Racial differences among shelter residents: A comparison of Anglo, black, and Hispanic battered. *Journal of Family Violence, 3,* 39-51.

Hamberger, L. K., Saunders, D. G., & Hovey, M. (1992). The prevalence of domestic violence in community practice and rate of physician inquiry. *Family Medicine, 24,* 283-287.

Hampton, R. L. (1987). Race, ethnicity, and child maltreatment: An analysis of cases recognized and reported by hospitals. In R. E. Staples (Ed.), *The black family essays and studies* (4th ed., pp. 178-191). Belmont, CA: Wadsworth.

Hampton, R. L. (1988). Physical victimization across the lifespan: Recognition, ethnicity, and deterrence. In M. Straus (Ed.), *Abuse and victimization: Across the lifespan* (pp. 203-222). Baltimore, MD: Johns Hopkins University Press.

Hampton, R. L., & Gelles, R. J. (1994). Violence toward black women in a nationally representative sample of black families. *Journal of Comparative Family Studies, 25*(1), 105-119.

Hampton, R. L., Gelles, R. J., & Harrop, J. W. (1989). Is violence in black families increasing: A comparison of 1975 and 1985 national survey rates. *Journal of Marriage and the Family, 51,* 969-980.

Hampton, R. L., & Newberger, E. H. (1985). Child abuse incidence and reporting by hospitals: The significance of severity, class, and race. *American Journal of Public Health, 75*(1), 56-60.

Hayes, H. R., & Emshoff, J. G. (1993). Substance abuse and family violence. In R. L. Hampton, T. P. Gullotta, G. R. Adams, E. H. Potter, III, & R. P. Weissberg (Eds.), *Family violence: Prevention and treatment* (pp. 281-310). Newbury Park, CA: Sage.

Helton, A., McFarlane, J., & Anderson, E. (1987). Battered and pregnant: A prevalence study. *American Journal of Public Health, 77,* 1337-1339.

Herman, J. L. (1992). *Trauma and recovery.* New York: Basic Books.

Hilberman, E., & Munson, K. (1977). Sixty battered women. *Victomology: An International Journal, 2,* 460-470.

Ho, C. K. (1990). An analysis of domestic violence in Asian American communities: A multistructural approach to counseling. In L. S. Brown & M. F. P. Root (Eds.), *Diversity and complexity in feminist therapy* (pp. 129-150). New York: Haworth.

Jurik, N., & Winn, R. (1990). Gender and homicide: A comparison of men and women who kill. *Violence and Victims, 5*(4), 227-242.

Kahn, W. J. (1993). Battered spouse as a social concern in work with families in two semi-rural communities in Nigeria. *Journal of Family Violence, 8,* 361-372.

Klingbeil, K. S. (1986). Interpersonal violence: A comprehensive model in a hospital setting from policy to program. In *Homicide, suicide, and unintentional injuries* (Department of Health and Human Services, Report of the Secretary's Task Force on Black and Minority Health, Vol. 5, pp. 245-263). Washington, DC: Government Printing Office.

Koss, M. P., Goodman, L., Browne, A., Fitgerald, L., Keita, G. P., & Russon, N. F. (1994). *No safe haven: Male violence against women at work, at home, and in the community.* Washington, DC: American Psychological Association.

Kurz, D. (1990). Interventions with battered women in health care settings. *Violence and Victims, 5*(4), 243-256.

Kurz, D. (1993). Physical assaults by husbands: A major social problem. In R. J. Gelles & D. Loseke (Eds.), *Current controversies on family violence* (pp. 88-103). Newbury Park, CA: Sage.

Lockhart, L. L. (1991). Spousal violence: A cross-racial perspective. In R. L. Hampton (Ed.), *Black family violence: Current research and theory* (pp. 85-102). Lexington, MA: Lexington Books.

Lockhart, L. L., & White, B. (1989). Understanding marital violence in the black community. *Journal of Interpersonal Violence, 4,* 421-436.

Mann, C. R. (1991). Black women who kill their loved ones. In R. L. Hampton (Ed.), *Black family violence: Current research and theory* (pp. 129-146). Lexington, MA: Lexington Books.

McClain, P. D. (1982-83). Black families and lethal violence: Has time changed the circumstances under which they kill? *Omega, 13*(1), 3-25.

McCord, J. (1992). Deterrence of domestic violence: A critical view of research. *Journal of Research in Crimes and Delinquency, 29,* 229-239.

McLeer, S. V., & Anwar, R. (1989). A study of women presenting in an emergency department. *American Journal of Public Health, 79,* 65-67.

Mederer, H., & Gelles, R. J. (1989). Compassion or control: Intervention in cases of wife abuse. *Journal of Interpersonal Violence, 4*(1), 25-34.

Mercy, J. A., & Saltzman, L. E. (1989). Fatal violence among spouses in the United States, 1976-1985. *American Journal of Public Health, 79,* 595-599.

Norton, I., & Monson, S. (1995). A silent majority: Battered American Indian women. *Journal of Family Violence, 10,* 307-318.

Osofsky, J. D. (1995). The effect of exposure to violence on young children. *American Psychologist, 50,* 782-788.

Pagelow, M. (1981). *Women battering: Victims and their experience.* Beverly Hills, CA: Sage.

Pagelow, M. D. (1984). *Family violence.* New York: Praeger.

Pagelow, M. D. (1988). Marital rape. In V. B. Van Hasselt, R. L. Morrison, A. S. Bellack, & M. Hersen (Eds.), *Handbook of family violence* (pp. 207-232). New York: Plenum.

Pagelow, M. D. (1992). Adult victims of domestic violence. *Journal of Interpersonal Violence, 7*(1), 87-120.

Paternoster, R., & Iovanni, L. (1986). The deterrent effect of perceived severity: A reexamination. *Social Forces, 64*(3), 751-770.

Pirsig, R. (1991). *LILA: An inquiry into morals.* New York: Bantam.

Pleck, E. (1987). *Domestic tyranny: The making of American social policy against family violence from colonial times to the present.* New York: Oxford University Press.

Ptacek, J. (1997). The tactics and strategies of men who batter: Testimony from women seeking restraining orders. In A. P. Cardarelli (Ed.), *Violence between intimate partners* (pp. 104-124). Needham Heights, MA: Allyn & Bacon.

Rand, M. R. (1997). *Violence-related injuries treated in hospital emergency departments.* Washington, DC: Bureau of Justice Statistics, U.S. Department of Justice.

Raphael, J., & Tolman, R. M. (1997). *Trapped by poverty, trapped by abuse: New evidence documenting the relationship between domestic violence and welfare.* Chicago: Taylor Institute.

Rieker, P. P., & Carmen, E. H. (1986). The victim-to-patient process: The disconfirmation and transformation of abuse. *American Journal of Orthopsychiatry, 56*(3), 360-370.

Roark, M. L., & Vlahos, S. (1983). An analysis of the ego status of battered women. *Transactional Analysis Journal, 13,* 164-167.

Romken, R. (1997). Prevalence of wife abuse in the Netherlands: Combining quantitative and qualitative methods in survey research. *Journal of Interpersonal Violence, 17,* 99-125.

Rose, H. M., & McClain, P. D. (1990). *Race, place, and risk: Black homicide in urban America.* Albany: State University of New York Press.

Rosenbaum, A., & O'Leary, K. D. (1981). Marital violence: Characteristics of abusive couples. *Journal of Counseling and Clinical Psychology, 49,* 63-71.

Rosenfeld, A., & Newberger, E. (1977). Compassion versus control: Conceptual and practical pitfalls in the broadened definitions of child abuse. *Journal of the American Medical Association, 237,* 2086-2088.

Roy, M. (1977). *Battered women.* New York: Van Nostrand Reinhold.

Russell, D. E. H. (1982). The prevalence and incidence of forcible rape of females. *Victimology, 7,* 81-93.

Saltzman, L. E., Mercy, J. A., Rosenberg, M. L., Elsea, W. R., Naper, G., Sikes, R. K., Waxweiler, R. J., & the Collaborative Working Group for the Study of Family and Intimate Assaults in Atlanta. (1990). Magnitude and patterns of family and intimate assault in Atlanta, Georgia 1984. *Violence and Victims, 5*(1), 3-17.

Schechter, S. (1982). *Women and male violence.* Boston: South End Press.

Sherman, L. W. (1992). *Policing domestic violence.* New York: Free Press.

Shields, N. M., & Hanneke, C. R. (1983). Battered wives' reactions to marital rape. In D. Finkelhor, R. J. Gelles, G. T. Hotaling, & M. A. Straus (Eds.), *The dark side of families: Current family violence research* (pp. 131-148). Beverly Hills, CA: Sage.

Shulman, L. (1979). *The skills of helping individual and groups.* Itaska, IL: F. E. Peacock.

Sorenson, S. B., & Telles, C. A. (1991). Self-reports of spousal violence in a Mexican American and non-Hispanic white population. *Violence and Victims, 6,* 3-16.

Stark, E., & Flitcraft, A. (1985). Spouse abuse. In *Surgeon General's workshop of violence and public health: A sourcebook* (pp. SA1-SA43). Atlanta, GA: Centers for Disease Control.

Straus, M. A. (1986a). Domestic violence and homicide antecedents. *Bulletin of the New York Academy of Medicine, 62,* 446-465.

Straus, M. A. (1986b). Medical care costs of intra-family assault and homicide to society. *Bulletin of the New York Academy of Medicine, 62,* 556-561.

Straus, M. A. (1991). Physical violence in American families: Incidence, rates, causes, and trends. In D. D. Knudsen & J. L. Miller (Eds.), *Abused and battered* (pp. 17-33). New York: Aldine de Gruyter.

Straus, M. A. (1993). Physical assault by wives: A major social problem. In R. J. Gelles & D. R. Loseke (Eds.), *Current controversies on family violence* (pp. 67-87). Newbury Park, CA: Sage.

Straus, M. A., & Gelles, R. J. (1986). Societal change in family violence from 1975 to 1985 as revealed by two national surveys. *Journal of Marriage and the Family, 48,* 465-479.

Straus, M. A., & Gelles, R. J. (1990). *Physical violence in American families: Risk factors and adaptations to violence in 8,145 families.* New Brunswick, NJ: Transaction Publishers.

Straus, M. A., Gelles, R. J., & Steinmetz, S. K. (1980). *Behind closed doors: Violence in the American family.* Garden City, NY: Anchor Press, Doubleday.

Straus, M. A., & Smith, C. (1990). Violence in Hispanic families in the United States: Incidence rates and structural interpretations. In M. A. Straus & R. J. Gelles (Eds.), *Physical violence in American families: risk factors and adaptations in 8,145 families* (pp. 341-368). New Brunswick, NJ: Transaction Publishers.

Sumner, B. B., Mintz, E. R., & Brown, P. L. (1986). Interviewing persons hospitalized with interpersonal violence-related injuries: A pilot study. In *Homicide, suicide, and unintentional injuries* (Department of Health and Human Services, Report of the Secretary's Task Force on Black and Minority Health, Vol. 5, pp. 267-317). Washington, DC: Government Printing Office.

Thurman v. City of Torrington, 595 F. Supp. 1521 (USDC No. H-84120, 1985).

Turner, S. F., & Shapiro, C. H. (1986). Battered women: Mourning the death of a relationship. *Social Work, 30,* 372-376.

Uzzell, O., & Peebles-Wilkins, W. (1989). Black spouse abuse: A focus on relational factors and intervention strategies. *Western Journal of Black Studies, 13,* 10-16.

Valdez, R. B., & Nourjah, R. (1988). Homicide in Southern California, 1966-1985: An examination based on vital statistics data. In J. F. Kraus, S. B. Sorenson, & P. D. Juarez (Eds.), *Proceedings from the research conference on violence and homicide in Hispanic communities* (pp. 85-100). Los Angeles: UCLA Publication Services.

Vinton, L. (1992). Battered women's shelters and older women: The Florida experience. *Journal of Family Violence,* 7(1), 63-72.

Walker, L. E. (1979). *The battered woman.* New York: Harper & Row.

Walker, L. E. (1984). *The battered woman syndrome.* New York: Springer.

Walker, L. E. (1991). Posttraumatic stress disorder in women: Diagnosis and treatment of battered woman syndrome. *Psychotherapy, 28,* 21-29.

Walker, L. E. (1993). The battered woman syndrome is a psychological consequence of abuse. In R. J. Gelles & D. Loseke (Eds.), *Current controversies on family violence* (pp. 133-153). Newbury Park, CA: Sage.

Washburn, C., & Frieze, I. H. (1981). *Methodological issues in studying battered women.* Paper presented at the First National Conference for Family Violence Researchers, University of New Hampshire, Durham.

Yllö, K. A., & Straus, M. A. (1990). Patriarchy and violence against wives: The impact of structural and normative factors. In M. A. Straus & R. J. Gelles (Eds.), *Physical violence in American families: Risk factors and applications to violence in 8,145 families* (pp. 283-399). New Brunswick, NJ: Transaction Publishers.

• *CHAPTER 8* •

Psychological Abuse in Marriage and Dating Relationships

CHRISTOPHER M. MURPHY
MICHELE CASCARDI

As a topic of investigation, psychological abuse is relatively new. Although strongly related to physical aggression in marriage, it has received far less attention. Psychological abuse does not result in serious physical injuries requiring medical or legal intervention. Its costs to society are less obvious, and it is less sensational than physical abuse. Consequently, psychological abuse has not garnered the same sort of media coverage and public awareness. Researchers, as well, have given only limited attention to psychological abuse, in part due to the ambiguities in defining and measuring it. The emerging evidence, however, provides several compelling reasons to investigate this topic.

Why Study Psychological Abuse?

Available data suggest that psychological abuse may be more emotionally devastating than physical abuse. This is, at least in part, because psychological abuse is often directed at the recipient's basic sense of self, and it can have a profound negative impact on the self-concept. Newly emerging research documents a significant negative impact of psychological abuse on anxiety and stress-related symptoms and depression among battered women.

Psychological abuse may also be very important in understanding the development of physical violence in relationships. Psychological aggression is highly correlated with physical aggression (Straus, 1974) and is a strong longitudinal predictor of physical aggression in early marriage (Murphy & O'Leary, 1989; O'Leary, Malone, & Tyree, 1994). By studying psychological abuse, we may uncover important clues to the development and prevention of physical violence in intimate adult relationships.

Psychological abuse is also very important in understanding the dynamics of abusive relationships. In fact, psychological abuse may be the mainstay of coercive control within physically violent relationships. It occurs much more frequently and in many more forms than physical abuse and may serve similar functions.

In brief, there are a number of reasons to investigate psychological abuse. It is pervasive and frequent, has a negative impact on the emotional and physical well-being of abuse victims, is associated with the development of physical aggression, and plays an important role in the dynamics of battering relationships.

What Is Psychological Abuse?

Like many social science constructs, psychological abuse has been difficult to define and quantify. Rather than providing one precise definition, this chapter examines the various ways that psychological abuse has been defined in the literature. These different definitions are associated with different assessment strategies and research traditions. A careful review of these traditions and the current state of knowledge will help us to refine our definitions and theoretical predictions. The goal of this chapter is to provide a framework to guide further development of the nomological net surrounding this hypothetical construct (Cronbach & Meehl, 1955).

Definitional Challenges

Abuse Versus Aggression. As a first step toward developing a working model of psychological abuse, it is helpful to distinguish the terms *aggression* and *abuse.* Traditionally, American and European scholars have described the origins of aggressive behavior in natural selection (Darwin & Wallace, 1858/1970), characterizing aggression as an instinctual trait (James, 1890) or instinctual energy (Freud, 1920/1959). Although aggression has been conceptualized in many ways, most social scientists define it as behavior intended to produce injury or harm (e.g., Dollard, Doob, Miller, Mowrer, & Sears, 1939). Finer discriminations include the mode of expression, for example, in the distinction between verbal and physical aggression; the interpersonal dynamics, for example, in the distinction between passive/indirect and overt/direct aggression; and the functional significance, for example, in the distinction between instrumental aggression (directed toward specific interpersonal goals) and expressive aggression (communicating anger or frustration).

Although the term abuse, like aggression, implies harmful intentions, abuse also refers to harmful effects of behavior. Most important, abuse connotes unequal power or dominance relations, as in the abuse of children by adults or the instrumental control of a battered woman by an abusive husband, whose behavior is supported by the values and practices of the larger society.

Activist/Feminist and Social Science Traditions. These differences between abuse and aggression parallel distinctions between the activist/feminist and social science traditions. Feminist scholarship on abuse has emphasized the subjective experience of victims (e.g., Walker, 1979, 1984). Emphasis is placed on the negative effects that abuse has on the victim's sense of self, interpersonal relationships, and autonomy. Abuse is understood as a systematic pattern of control and domination, with psychological, physical, and sexual dimensions. The assessment of abuse often involves in-depth, qualitative victim interviews. From the feminist perspective, abuse is derived from social and historical traditions that promote men's dominance over women and children in the domestic sphere (Breines & Gordon, 1983; Dobash & Dobash, 1979). Abuse is seen as instrumental in nature and perpetrated by men against women and children.

Operational definitions of psychological aggression by social survey researchers, in contrast, often begin with a list of aversive behaviors that can occur during conflicts or disagreements between intimate partners (e.g., insulted or swore at the partner, stomped out of the room or house or yard). These definitions focus on discrete behaviors that an observer could recognize as aggressive, rather than subjective reactions of the target. The expressive dimension is often emphasized, as aggression is thought to represent a breakdown in conflict resolution or communication. Aggressive behaviors are assessed without regard to their effects (e.g., Straus, 1979, 1990). The measures can be used to characterize the behavior of either member of a couple, without regard to differences in physical size and strength, power and dominance relations, gender, or the historical and social context in which the behavior occurs.

The varied conceptualizations of psychological abuse may have a profound influence on its definition and measurement. For example, the assumption that psychological abuse is instrumental (i.e., directed toward specific interpersonal goals) would result in very different behavioral measures than would the assumption that psychological abuse is expressive (i.e., an outburst of anger or frustration). Terms like *cold, calculating, vindictive,* and *controlling* would be applied to the former, and terms like *impulsive, rash, unpremeditated,* and *reflexive* to the latter. Different behaviors would fit these different constructs, as exemplified in the difference between a mean, controlling glance that says "you better shut up or else" versus an exasperated exclamation of hostility that says "you don't care about my feelings."

Interpersonal Context. Problems may also arise from inadequate appreciation of interpersonal and social contexts in the definition and measurement of psychological abuse (e.g., Breines & Gordon, 1983). For example, communication theorists demonstrate how similar behaviors can be playful or aggressive depending on the frame, or metacommunication context (Bateson, 1972). Subtle shifts in voice tone, posture, or facial expression can render the same phrase "harmless ribbing" in one context and "character assault" in another. Some behaviors may be abusive because they occur in the context of violence or intimidation. Hostile sarcasm, for example, may be annoying or disheartening in the context of a healthy relationship, but quite frightening if it has been previously accompanied by physical violence.

Ethnic and Cultural Context. To add even greater complexity, a similar behavior may be abusive in certain social or cultural contexts, and not in others. For example, some behaviors that are acceptable or even normative in certain cultures (e.g., loud expressions of negative emotions) may be perceived as abusive in a different cultural milieu.

Power and Dominance. Differences in role definition and power relations are also important in defining psychological abuse. For example, when aggression occurs in a relatively symmetrical power relationship, such as a boxing match or with childhood peers of roughly equal strength, it is not generally considered abusive. Aggressive behavior is considered abusive if it takes place in a relationship that is asymmetrical by tradition (e.g., parent and child). It may also alter the symmetry of a relationship over time. In either case, abuser and victim roles can be clearly identified.

Asymmetries in dominance and power characterize most adult heterosexual relationships. The traditions and ideology of male dominance in the family, and the economic hardships faced by women who leave abusive relationships, provide social and cultural support for power imbalance (Murphy & Meyer, 1991). The asymmetry of power may also increase over time, as aggressive actions by a man toward a woman typically yield more severe consequences than aggressive acts by a woman toward a man, due to men's relatively greater size, greater weight, and more extensive socialization in the use of violence. As with physical abuse, it is also likely that the consequences of psychological abuse vary on the basis of gender, but this issue has received relatively little empirical attention.

Topography, or Consequences of Behavior. Many child abuse researchers define psychological abuse in terms of its consequences, that is, as behaviors that produce psychological harm (e.g., Garbarino, Guttman, & Seeley, 1986; Grusec & Walters, 1991). Adult relationship researchers, in contrast, define psychological abuse on the basis of topography, or the form of aggressive behavior expressed (i.e., in contrast to physical abuse). The current review maintains this distinction. Psychological abuse is conceptualized as a category of behaviors, rather than a category of effects.

A Working Definition

The following working definition is offered to integrate insights and complexities described above: Psychological abuse consists of coercive or aversive acts intended to produce emotional harm or threat of harm. In contrast to physical abuse, these coercive behaviors are not directed toward the target's bodily integrity but are instead directed at the recipient's sense of self. The specific forms of psychological abuse and its effects can vary across interpersonal, social, and cultural contexts. Subjectively, psychological abuse has several common effects on the recipient—producing fear, increasing dependency on the abuser, and damaging the self-concept.

Assessment

Overview

Available assessment methods reflect the diversity in conceptualizations of psychological abuse. Some investigators have used in-depth, qualitative interviews with battered women to describe and assess abuse (e.g., Hoffman, 1984; Marshall, 1996; Walker, 1979). Some have used brief checklists of aggressive behaviors (e.g., Straus, Gelles, & Steinmetz, 1980). Others have devised more extensive behavior checklists derived from qualitative research on battered women (e.g., Tolman, 1989).

Forms of Psychological Abuse

Qualitative studies have identified consistent themes in the experiences of battered women, with an emphasis on the ways in which abusive behavior represents an attempt to control and dominate the partner (Pence, 1989; Walker, 1979). These researchers have described a number of specific expressions of psychological abuse. Isolating and restricting behaviors track, monitor, and control the partner's activities and social contacts. Humiliating and degrading behaviors denigrate, ridicule, or degrade the partner. Threats include harm to self, partner, friends, relatives, pets, and so on. Property violence reflects damage or destruction of personal property, often highly valued objects. Economic deprivation refers to behaviors that establish unilateral control over family finances or increased financial dependency on the abuser. Some qualitative accounts also include exploitation of male privilege involving demands of subservience or forced adherence to rigid sex roles; emotional withholding, the refusal of emotional contact or support; and minimization and denial, reflecting efforts to downplay the extent or impact of violence and abuse, often through questioning the partner's perceptions, feelings, or sanity. Further description and subtypes can be found in work by Hoffman (1984), Marshall (1996), Pence (1989), and Tolman (1992).[1]

Strengths and Weaknesses of Qualitative Studies

In-depth, qualitative interview studies of battered women have offered important insights. They accentuate the subtlety and complexity of psychological abuse, uncovering a central theme of domination and control. These investigations have offered an integrative framework to understand how physical and psychological abuse operate in tandem to establish an atmosphere of intimidation, devaluation, and control. Qualitative researchers have also emphasized the often devastating effects of psychological abuse, such as disorientation and self-doubt associated with tactics of mind control (Andersen, Boulette, & Schwartz, 1991) and extreme terror experienced by many battered women. These findings regarding severely battered women, however, may not generalize to other settings and populations. The experiences of battered women in shelters, or other women who self-identify as battered, may differ in important ways from the experiences of women who are participating in population surveys or who are seeking relationship therapy. Aggressive or controlling behaviors may be experienced quite differently in the context of a mutually satisfactory nonviolent relationship, a distressed nonviolent relationship, or a violent relationship. The unstructured format of qualitative interviewing is helpful in uncovering patterns of experience and behavior (Murphy & O'Leary, 1994). Some research questions, however, require a more structured and systematic data collection strategy (e.g., when aggregating data from multiple interviewers) or a briefer format (e.g., when surveying large samples).

Quantitative Research Strategies

Objective quantitative assessments of abusive behaviors have been used to study the prevalence and correlates of psychologically aggressive acts in populations outside of domestic violence facilities. These instruments have also been used to examine the association between psychological and physical abuse, the putative effects of psychological abuse, and the association of psychological abuse with other hypothesized correlates and causes.

Behavior Checklist Measures

The most widely used measure of relationship aggression is Straus's (1979) Conflict Tactics Scale (CTS), an 18-item behavior checklist designed to assess three conflict resolution strategies: reasoning, verbal (or psychological) aggression, and physical aggression. Factor analyses consistently locate a dimension labeled psychological aggression, as distinct from physical aggression (Barling, O'Leary, Jouriles, Vivian, & MacEwen, 1987). This factor contains some items that reflect verbal aggression (e.g., insulted or swore at partner) and some nonverbal aggressive acts (e.g., stomped out of the room or house or yard).

The CTS was designed for large-scale survey studies, which have dramatized the high prevalence of violence in the American family (Straus & Gelles, 1990; Straus et al., 1980). With respect to many other research problems, however, the CTS has important limitations as a measure of psychological abuse. In particular, the subjective experience of victims was not considered in item development (Stets, 1991). As a result, the range of psychologically abusive behaviors is quite narrow and focused on aggressive behaviors during conflict. Consequently, the original CTS contains relatively few items to assess psychological aggression, with no further breakdown of its forms or subtypes.

A recent revision of the CTS, the CTS2, contains eight psychological abuse items, is two more than the original version (Straus, Hamby, Boney-McCoy, & Sugarman, 1996). These items are separated into minor and severe subscales. The severe subscale items discriminated severe physical violence cases from minor physical violence cases in the scale development sample of U.S. adults in the community. The minor subscale items discriminated physically violent cases from nonviolent cases only. No factor analyses or other discriminant validity data were provided to support the minor and severe distinction. Although the items in general appear to be face-valid indicators of psychological abuse, the distinction between minor and severe subscales has not been adequately validated. The respective items do not appear qualitatively different. For example, "called my partner fat or ugly" and "accused my partner of being a lousy lover" are severe psychological abuse items, whereas "insulted or swore at my partner" is a minor psychological abuse item, even though it would appear to subsume these severe items.

Other measures have attempted to redress some of the limitations of the CTS as a measure of psychological abuse. The Index of Spouse Abuse (ISA) was designed for use with clinical samples (Hudson & McIntosh, 1981). It contains a checklist of behaviors that is more extensive than the CTS and more reflective of the severe end of emotional abuse. The scale consists of two factors: physical abuse (11 items) and nonphysical abuse (19 items). The authors provide a weighting scheme to reflect normative perceptions of the seriousness or severity of the scale items. Despite potential improvements over the CTS, particularly with regard to severity weighting and relevance for clinical domestic violence samples, the ISA has not been widely adopted in the field. One major problem is that the physical abuse scale, derived by factor analysis, contains items that are not face-valid indicators of physical abuse (e.g., "my partner screams and yells at me").

O'Leary and Curley (1986) developed a measure of spouse-specific aggression (SSAG) to assess behavior that is distinguished conceptually from assertiveness. This measure includes 12 items reflecting both passive aggression (e.g., I'll often give my mate the "silent treatment" when I am mad at him/her) and direct psychological aggression (e.g., "I often say nasty things to my mate, especially when I'm angrily discussing something with him/her"). Subjects endorse the items as personal tendencies (e.g., "highly descriptive of me"), rather than reporting on the frequency of specific behaviors. The SSAG response format may have advantages in comparing behavior across unequal time intervals, for example, if different intervals are assessed before, during, and after a treatment program. A possible limitation of the response format, however, is that it asks about characteristic behavioral styles. Reports of behavioral styles may be less sensitive to change over time than reports of specific behavioral frequencies.

Strengths and Weaknesses

These four measures, the CTS, CTS2, ISA, and SSAG, are all face-valid assessments for the general domain of psychological aggression in adult relationships. Each can be administered in questionnaire format in 5 to 10 minutes. They all meet general psychometric standards for internal consistency and, with the exception of the newly developed CTS2, have shown predicted correlations with various criteria (e.g., physical aggression). The ISA and SSAG measures have some advantages over the CTS with respect to psychological aggression. Both have more items, which may increase reliability. The ISA weights the perceived severity of aggressive behaviors, although further research is needed to validate the distinction between severity and frequency dimensions of psychological abuse. The SSAG includes items to assess passive aggression, and it asks respondents to report general response tendencies, rather than the frequency of specific behaviors. Biased subjective estimation of event frequency and distorted time perception of past events are common problems in self-report measures of behavior (Sudman, Bradburn, & Schwartz, 1996). The response format of the SSAG may reflect a more manageable cognitive task than the other measures, which purport to assess behavior frequency in a given interval of time. None of these measures, nor any measures of physical abuse in marriage, has been validated against independent behavioral observations during the interval covered by the assessment.

All of these measures share certain limitations. They assess a relatively small sample of psychologically aggressive behaviors (or styles) with no carefully validated breakdown of subscales or factors. For measures like the CTS and ISA to be considered accurate estimates of behavior frequency, some untenable assumptions must be made, namely, that respondents interpret the meaning of items consistent with the researchers' definition (e.g., what is considered "yelling," "insulting," etc.) and that they can accurately recall the frequency of such events over a lengthy time frame (usually a 1-year period).

Incorporating Qualitative Insights into Quantitative Assessments

Some measures incorporate insights from qualitative research with battered women into a structured assessment format. Tolman (1989) specified 58 abusive behaviors in a self-report questionnaire called the Psychological Maltreatment of Women Inventory (PMWI). Items were drawn from existing measures and developed from the clinical and qualitative literatures on battered women. The PMWI excludes items involving physical contact, threats of violence, or aggression toward objects. Although the items represent several abuse subtypes, factor analysis uncovered only two subscales: *Dominance-isolation* and *Emotional-verbal.* The author found high internal consistency for the subscales, but low agreement between spouses' reports. Although the PMWI is the most comprehensive questionnaire measure of psychological abuse, the subscales are conceptually unclear and do not adequately reflect the forms of abuse described by battered women. Clear evidence of discriminant validity for the subscales is lacking. Although it provides wider domain sampling of abusive behavior than the other measures, the PMWI requires similarly untenable assumptions about the accuracy of behavior frequency reports over lengthy time intervals. Because many of the items assess severe forms of abuse, the endorsement rates of behaviors covered by the PMWI may be quite low in nonclinic samples such as dating relationships (Kaisan & Painter, 1992; Molidor, 1995). Scales such as the CTS or SSAG may have better distributional properties in nonclinical samples, whereas the PMWI may offer a more extensive assessment tool for samples with known or suspected domestic violence.

Marshall (1992) developed the 46-item Severity of Violence Against Women Scales (SVAWS) to reflect the seriousness, abusiveness, aggressiveness, violence, and threat value of abusive behaviors. The goal was to develop a measure that includes threatened, attempted, and completed behaviors likely to cause physical injury or pain (Weis, 1989), including both indirect acts (threats or acts that limit well-being) and direct acts (resulting in physical or emotional harm; Gondolf, 1987).

The SVAWS was developed using two large samples of college ($n >$ 700) and community ($n > 200$) women who rated, on a 10-point scale, how serious, abusive, aggressive, violent, and threatening were each of 46 acts against a woman. The mean score for each item was submitted to factor analysis to reveal distinct severity scales. Factor analyses in both samples yielded nine factors, listed in order of severity rating: serious physical violence, sexual violence, moderate physical violence, minor physical violence, threats of serious violence, mild physical violence, threats of moderate violence, symbolic violence, and threats of mild violence. Four of these nine factors can be classified as psychological abuse: threats of serious violence (e.g., threatened to hurt her, kill himself, kill her), threats of moderate violence (e.g., destroyed something, threatened to destroy something), symbolic violence (e.g., hit or kicked a wall or door, drove dangerously, threw an object), and threats of mild violence (e.g., shook a finger at her, made threatening gestures, acted like a bully). Although the severity ratings support the separation of these nine factors, it is not clear whether ratings of actual behavior would conform to this factor structure (i.e., whether the factors reflect behavioral patterns). The recommended response format involves a 4-point frequency scale for each item (*never, once, a few times, many times*), which requires fewer assumptions about the accuracy of recall for event frequency but requires some ambiguous subjective judgment about the difference between a few and many times. The SVAWS is still in very early stages of development. Few data are available with regard to the scale's reliability and validity.

The Measure of Wife Abuse (MWA) contains four factors measuring physical, sexual, verbal, and psychological abuse (Rodenburg & Fantuzzo, 1993). The 15 psychological abuse items include such things as harassment, stealing from the partner, and following the partner around. The 14 verbal aggression items consist mostly of self-esteem attacks (e.g., called partner stupid; called the partner ugly) and threats of violence. The verbal and psychological scales correlated .46 in the development sample of battered women, and the scales had good internal consistency.

Factor loadings suggest that the verbal and psychological abuse items form distinct factors, but the factor analysis was conducted on severity ratings (asking how often the victim was hurt by each behavior) rather than frequency ratings. As with the SVAWS, it is possible that the factors cohere due to differences in perceived item severity, rather than coherent patterning in the abuser's behavior. Like the PMWI and SVAWS, the MWA may provide a more robust assessment of verbal/psychological abuse than briefer measures like the CTS, especially with clinical samples. Further validation research, however, is needed for all of these measures, with specific attention to independent indicators of abusive behavior frequency, such as informant data from other household members, observational or time-sampling measures of in-home behavior, and daily or weekly assessments of abusive behavior frequency.

Structured interview methods also exist. Marshall and colleagues present respondents with a dictionary of definitions for 44 categories of psychological abuse and then combine an interview and self-report questionnaire to assess these categories. This method was devised to increase the likelihood that respondents and researchers would share the same definition or meaning of the behaviors assessed. Similarly, Follingstad and colleagues had interviewers interpret or categorize experiences described by battered women (Follingstad, Rutledge, Berg, Hause, & Polek, 1990). Using semistructured phone interviews, they coded women's experiences into several predetermined categories of psychological abuse, along with information about the frequency of abuse in each category and the perceived severity of pain that each caused. These interview methods allow battered women to describe their own experiences and reactions in an open-ended fashion, while the information is quantified for statistical analysis. The reliability of these interview measures, and their convergent validity with questionnaire measures, are unknown.

Response Bias

One persistent issue in the assessment of relationship abuse concerns the tendency to bias responses in a socially desirable fashion (Arias & Beach, 1987; Saunders, 1991). With regard to interpartner physical violence, evidence suggests that perpetrator reports of aggression are associated with measures of social desirability, whereas victim reports of aggression are not (Arias & Beach, 1987; Dutton & Hemphill, 1992). Individuals are more willing to report aggression by a partner than by themselves (Riggs, Murphy, & O'Leary, 1989). Initial evidence suggests that aggressive men may underreport physical violence and may blame the partner, both to create a positive impression to others and to maintain or enhance self-esteem (Dutton, 1986; Murphy, Cascardi, Ginsburg, & O'Leary, 1991; Ptacek, 1988; Waltz, Babcock, Jacobson, & Gottman, 1991).

As with physical abuse, self-reports of psychological abuse are also affected by social desirability bias. Men admit to less psychological abuse than their partners report (Tolman, 1989). Men's self-reports of both physical and psychological abuse are associated with measures of conscious impression management (lying). Men's self-reports of psychological abuse are also associated with measures of self-deception, reflecting self-enhancing beliefs and denial of negative personal qualities (Dutton & Hemphill, 1992). Perhaps because behaviors such as slapping or hitting a spouse are obvious, a conscious lie is required for socially desirable responding. Honest reporting of psychological abuse, on the other hand, apparently requires self-awareness, which can be affected by more subtle forms of self-deception. For example, a respondent may believe that excessive monitoring of his partner's whereabouts and activities reflects concern for her welfare, whereas the partner may see it as intrusive and controlling.

Research Findings

Prevalence of Psychological Abuse in Intimate Adult Relationships

Table 8.1 contains prevalence estimates for a set of psychologically aggressive behaviors from the CTS (Straus, 1979) in different samples. For distressed partners seeking marital therapy, 89% to 97% have enacted each behavior during the preceding 12 months. Over two thirds of engaged partners reported that these aggressive behaviors occurred in the year prior to marriage. The high rates were not surprising for the marital clinic group. For the engaged couples, however, almost all of whom report a high level of satisfaction with the relationships, the normative nature of psychological aggression is somewhat surprising. This result is consistent with the relatively high rates of physical aggression found among dating and engaged couples (O'Leary et al., 1989; Sugarman & Hotaling, 1989).

Table 8.1 Yearly Prevalence Estimates for Psychologically Aggressive Behaviors

Behavior (During a Disagreement or Conflict)	*Sample*				
	Marital Therapy Clinic (N = *187*)[a]		*Engaged Couples (Sexes Combined)* (N = *398*)[a]	*National Survey*[b] (N = *1,461 Males; 1,909 Females)*	
	M → F	*F → M*		*M → F*	*F → M*
Insulted or swore[c] at partner	94%	92%	77%	43%	54%
Did or said something to spite partner	94%	95%	67%	44%	54%
Stomped out of the room, house or yard	90%	89%	74%	33%	39%
Sulked or refused to talk about an issue	97%	97%	87%	52%	58%

NOTES: M → F = male to female aggression; F → M = female to male aggression.
a. Source is Barling et al. (1987). Estimates combine both partners' reports (i.e., husband and wife each report on their own and their partners' behavior); *N* = number of couples.
b. Source is Stets (1990). Estimates by self-report only.
c. In the national survey, this item was shortened to "insulted partner."

Interestingly, prevalence rates from a representative survey of U.S. households are lower than from newlywed and clinic samples, with somewhere between 30% and 60% of spouses reporting each behavior (Stets, 1990) and with about 25% reporting none of these behaviors during the year prior to the survey (Straus & Sweet, 1992). These different rates are most likely due to the use of different measurement procedures as well as age effects. The national figures rely on reports from one partner only, whereas the newlywed and marriage clinic studies combine both spouses' reports about each partner's aggression. Differences between newlyweds and the national survey samples may also be due to the reduction in aggressive behavior over the life span, as negative correlations between age and psychological aggression on the CTS (in the .25 to .40 range) were observed for both men and women in two national family violence surveys (Suitor, Pillemer, & Straus, 1990).

Using a different set of items and a different response set in a large stratified representative sample of the Canadian population, Johnson and Sacco (1995) found relatively low rates of psychological abuse experiences among adult women who had been married at some point in life. Only 17% of Canadian women who had ever been married

controlling or emotionally abusive behaviors surveyed. As a specific comparison, only 7% of ever-married Canadian women reported that their current partner "calls her names to put her down or make her feel bad," whereas 43% of U.S. respondents on Straus's CTS reported that the male partner had insulted or sworn at the female partner in the prior 12 months. It is unlikely that cultural differences account for these widely divergent findings. More likely explanations derive from the emphasis on violent experiences in the Canadian survey as a whole (rather than on relationship conflict), the wording of controlling behavior items to include perpetrator intentions (e.g., "to put her down or make her feel bad"), the narrow focus of the behaviors covered (e.g., "called her names" versus "insulted or swore at her"), and the inclusion of subjects who were not currently involved in a relationship. Given the double-barreled nature of these items and the survey context, respondents may have avoided reporting many psychologically aggressive behaviors due to the perception that they were not intentional, not sufficiently harmful, or not exact examples of the behavior covered (e.g., "he doesn't really mean it when he says those things"; "it doesn't really hurt me"; "I wouldn't say that it was name calling").

In contrast to aggressive behavior surveys, Lebov-Keeler and Pipes (1990) examined self definitions of psychological abuse for female college students in exclusive heterosexual relationships using the following definition:

> Being psychologically abused means that your boyfriend *repeatedly* used one or more of the above verbal and/or nonverbal tactics [from the CTS] with the result that you *frequently* feel hurt or fearful, or feel badly about yourself following his use of these tactics. (p. 36, emphasis in original).

Of 175 women surveyed, 11% identified themselves as psychologically abused on this basis, suggesting that a more general perception of abuse is considerably less common than the aggressive behaviors composing this pattern.

Other research has examined the prevalence of psychological abuse in violent relationships. Follingstad et al. (1990) located women with a history of physical abuse through advertisements, shelters, and social service agencies. Of 234 women interviewed, 99% reported experiencing at least one type of emotional abuse at some time during the marriage. Ridicule and verbal harassment was the most common form (reported by 90% of the sample), followed by behaviors designed to isolate or restrict their activities (reported by 79%), threats of abuse (74%), severe jealousy or possessiveness (73%), property damage (59%), and threats to change or end the marriage (49%). In addition, the abuse was very frequent for most women studied. For restriction, jealousy/possessiveness, and ridicule/harassment, over 60% of the women who had experienced each form of abuse reported that it occurred at least once a week.

Tolman (1989) administered 58 items covering a wide range of psychologically abusive behaviors to over 200 women at shelter intake. A very high proportion of the women reported that each behavior occurred at least once in the past 6 months. Very few items were endorsed by less than half of the women, and the vast majority of items were endorsed by over 75% of them. Some example item endorsement frequencies were: partner swore at her (95%), tried to blame her for causing the violence (90%), ordered her around (89%), called her names (86%), insulted her in front of others (85%), monitored her time (85%), did not allow her to socialize with friends (79%) or see family (60%), restricted her use of the car (54%) or telephone (56%), tried to convince her that she was crazy (55%), threatened to have her committed (33%), and kept her from medical care (29%) (Tolman, 1989, p. 165).

Men's reporting rates at batterers' program intake were considerably lower than women's rates at shelter intake. Although only a small number of those studied were from the same marriages, there was relatively little correspondence between partners' reports. Even so, the men reported perpetrating a wide range of psychologically abusive behaviors (Tolman, 1989).

In summary, certain forms of psychological aggression are very common in adult relationships, whether or not physical abuse is present. In normative samples, there is an age-related decline in psychological aggression that is similar to the decline across the life span in other forms of aggression. In samples of battered women, virtually all experience a pervasive pattern of psychological abuse in addition to the physical violence.

Associations With Physical Aggression

Several cross-sectional studies have documented a moderate to strong correlation between psychological aggression and physical aggression, assessed retrospectively over a 1-year interval (Straus, 1974; Straus et al., 1980, 1996). This association is also apparent in retrospective recall studies of specific conflict episodes, which reveal greater levels of psychological aggression by both spouses in conflicts that escalate to physical aggression when compared to the conflicts of nonviolent couples (Cascardi & Vivian, 1995; Infante, Chandler, & Rudd, 1989; Sabourin, Infante, & Rudd, 1993). Similar results have been found in observational studies of problem discussions conducted in a laboratory setting, during which physically violent couples display higher levels of aversive and defensive communication than do nonviolent distressed and nondistressed couples (Cordova, Jacobson, Gottman, Rushe, & Cox, 1993; Margolin, John, & Gleberman, 1988).

Straus (1974) used the correlation between verbal and physical aggression to argue against ventilationist therapies that promote openly hostile expression of feelings to "let off steam." His claim was that verbal aggression, rather than serving as a release valve, actually increases the likelihood of physical aggression.

Longitudinal evidence provides further support for this point. Murphy and O'Leary (1989) found that prior levels of psychological aggression predicted initial reports of physical aggression during the first 30 months of marriage. Marital satisfaction did not significantly predict physical aggression longitudinally, even though it was correlated with physical aggression cross-sectionally. These findings support an escalation model in which high levels of psychological aggression precede the initiation of physical aggression.

An important question that arises from these observations is whether psychological and physical aggression reflect the same underlying psychological process or whether they reflect separate processes. One way to examine this is to ask whether there are one or two dimensions in the measurement instruments that combine psychological and physical aggression. Factor analyses from a variety of samples suggest that psychological and physical aggression, as measured by the CTS and other scales, form distinct latent variables (Barling et al., 1987; Caulfield & Riggs, 1992; Shepard & Campbell, 1992). Some investigators, however, have questioned whether the latent variable of physical aggression also contains less severe behaviors such as threats of violence (Schafer, 1996).

Stets (1990) approached this question by asking whether psychological and physical aggression could be best represented by a two-stage model or as different thresholds along a single continuum of aggression. She examined two patterns of correlates: one that optimally distinguished nonaggressive individuals from psychologically aggressive but nonviolent individuals, and one that optimally distinguished psychologically aggressive individuals from physically aggressive individuals. Because these patterns were different, she argued in favor of a two-stage escalation process, rather than a single underlying process with different thresholds. Although this evidence does not strictly refute the notion of a single underlying dimension of aggression, it suggests that there is something to gain by examining separately the correlates of psychological and physical abuse.

Some recent research has also examined whether various types of psychological abuse have differential correlations with physical abuse. In a study of college dating relationships, psychologically abusive behaviors that reflect domination and intimidation (e.g., "raised voice to yell and scream at the partner") were more highly correlated with physical aggression than were behaviors reflecting hostile withdrawal (e.g., "acted cold or distant when angry") or efforts to isolate the partner and maintain dependency in the relationship (e.g., "tried to stop the partner from seeing certain friends or family members") (Murphy, Hartman, Muccino, & Douchis, 1995). Greater specificity in the assessment of psychological abuse may prove helpful in understanding the development of physical aggression and the more comprehensive pattern of abuse associated with clinical spouse battery.

In summary, there is a high correlation between psychological and physical aggression in intimate adult relationships, yet they are distinct phenomena, with somewhat distinct correlates. Longitudinal research has identified an escalation process from psychological to physical aggression in early marriage. Different forms of psychological abuse may have different associations with physical abuse, but more research is needed to clarify the distinct patterns of psychological abuse and their role in the development of physical violence.

Other Correlates and Presumed Causes

A number of recent studies have identified correlates of psychological abuse. In surveys of the U.S. population, levels of psychological aggression by both males and females were positively correlated with marital conflict (disagreements), frequency of alcohol intoxication, verbal aggression outside of the home, and approval of the use of physical aggression. Psychological aggression was negatively correlated with age for both males and females, and husband-to-wife psychological aggression was negatively correlated with the number of children in the home (Stets, 1990; Straus & Sweet, 1992). Race and gender were not correlated with psychological abuse when physical abuse and relationship conflict had been controlled statistically (Straus & Sweet, 1992).

In a community study of women in unhappy relationships, women's relationship satisfaction was negatively correlated with male partners' use of emotional control tactics. In addition, women's decisions to leave a relationship were associated with male partners' attempts to control or degrade them (Vitanza, Walker, & Marshall, 1990). Not surprisingly, other research has also found that both males and females who are more dissatisfied with their relationship engage in higher rates of psychological aggression (Edleson, Eisikovits, Guttmann, & Sela-Amit, 1991).

In research on college dating samples, longer relationships with more frequent contact appear to have somewhat elevated rates of psychological aggression (Mason & Blankenship, 1987; Stets, 1991). Stressful life events were associated with psychological aggression (both experienced and perpetrated) for women but not for men (Mason & Blankenship, 1987). Witnessing interparental violence predicted psychologically abusive behavior by males but not females in Stets's (1991) study of college students, but it predicted psychological aggression by females but not males in national survey data (Stets, 1990).[2] Virtually all of these associations are modest in magnitude ($r < .30$).

The role of interpersonal control in psychological abuse has been examined from a number of perspectives. Stets (1991) defined interpersonal control as "the act of managing or regulating another's thoughts, feelings, or actions" (p. 98) and reported that it was correlated with psychological abuse in dating relationships (Stets, 1991). Unfortunately, however, this definition of interpersonal control may be confounded with abusive behavior, and the effects of abuse may be misconstrued as causes.

As an alternative, some researchers have defined the need for power as a stable personality trait reflecting the motivation to influence and control others. This trait can be assessed independent of relationship behavior through a projective test (Winter, 1973). In a college dating sample, males' need for power was associated with their use of physical aggression but not psychological aggression (Mason & Blankenship, 1987). The need for power discriminated male batterers from a mixed sample of discordant and happily married men and was highly correlated with the level of physical violence within the sample of batterers (Dutton & Strachan, 1987). The association with psychological abuse, however, remains unclear.

Using self-report ratings, Ronfeldt, Kimerling, and Arias (in press) found that dissatisfaction with the level of control in the relationship was significantly associated with males' psychological abuse in dating relationships. These investigators concluded that the perceived dissatisfaction with power arrangements, rather than the perception of actual control, contributes to the motivation for abusive behavior. Taken together, these studies highlight the importance of further research on the motivational dynamics of control as an important avenue for understanding psychological abuse.

Communication researchers have developed a model that explains verbal aggression as an argumentative skills deficit (Infante et al., 1989). Argumentativeness, in this model, is defined as "a skill for defending and attacking positions rather than persons" (Sabourin et al., 1993, p. 247), whereas verbal aggressiveness is defined as a tendency to attack the partner's self-concept. As predicted by the model, higher levels of verbal aggressiveness and lower levels of argumentative skill distinguish maritally violent couples from nonviolent controls (Infante et al., 1989). These results suggest that individuals revert to verbally aggressive tactics when they lack more constructive skills for handling disagreements.

Gender Differences in Reporting and Perpetrating Psychological Abuse

Available data suggest that psychological aggression is often reciprocal in nature, as the levels reported by, or about, relationship partners are highly correlated (O'Leary & Curley, 1986; Sabourin et al., 1993; Stets, 1991). In national survey data, the rates of psychological aggression on the CTS were almost identical for males and females (Straus & Sweet, 1992). Despite this gender similarity in rates of psychological aggression, there was a substantial gender difference in the frequency with which psychological aggression was reported. Whether reporting on themselves or on their female partners, males report lower frequencies of psychological aggression than do females. Females, in contrast, report higher frequencies of psychological aggression by themselves and their partners, suggesting that females employ a more inclusive definition for the behaviors on the CTS or that they are more open in reporting psychologically aggressive behaviors on the survey.

Psychological abuse appears to be more unilateral in the relationships of battered women. Sabourin (1991) asked battered women in a shelter to describe specific violent episodes. Raters coded the women's verbal aggression and the severity of men's violence from these accounts. The results showed that the more violent a man was during an incident, the less verbally aggressive the woman was.

In brief, regardless of the gender of the reporter, population survey data reveal no gender differences in the frequency of common psychologically aggressive behaviors. A strong gender difference is apparent, however, in reporting. When compared to men, women report higher frequencies of psychological aggression by both themselves and their partners. Data from battered women in shelters reveal a different picture, in which the abusive male more unilaterally perpetrates a wide range of psychologically abusive behaviors.

Effects

Many women perceive psychological abuse to be more painful and damaging than physical abuse. Walker (1979) began her interview studies by equating battering with physical violence but later downplayed this distinction because so many women claimed that psychological abuse was more harmful. Most of the women "described incidents involving psychological humiliation and verbal harassment as their worst battering experiences, whether or not they had been physically abused" (Walker, 1979, p. xv). Along similar lines, Follingstad et al. (1990) sampled over 200 women with a history of physical abuse and found that 72% rated psychological abuse as having had a more severe impact on them than physical abuse.

Follingstad and colleagues (1990) also asked women which form of emotional abuse was the worst one for them. In their data, attacks on self-esteem and self-concept appeared to be even more painful and damaging than attempts to provoke fear and intimidation. Most likely, there is a synergistic effect on self-esteem when women are also isolated from social supports or encouraged to feel responsible for the violence. Because these data were gathered retrospectively, they may also reflect battered women's efforts to sort out long-lasting effects of the more insidious forms of abuse. Clinical accounts demonstrate how abuse can systematically erode self-esteem and create confusion, self-blame, and self-doubt (e.g., Nicarthy, 1986; Walker, 1979). Some of these effects may depend on subtle cues from batterers, friends, relatives, authorities, or the culture at large. For example, women often wonder if what they are experiencing is in fact abuse, after having been convinced that they "deserved" it, "provoked" it, or that "it was not that bad." Abusive men commonly try to convince a partner that she is crazy, question her view of events or reality, and minimize the degree or effects of violence (Dutton, 1986; Tolman, 1989). Unfortunately, health professionals may reinforce these notions by failing to diagnose the cause of injuries in cases of spouse assault or by providing battered women with a diagnosis and medication but no social service or shelter referrals (Kurz & Stark, 1988).

Some authors have compared battered women to prisoners of war (Romero, 1985) or political hostages (Graham, Rawlings, & Rimini, 1988). Romero (1985) noted many similarities between strategies used to brainwash POWs in Korea and patterns of psychological and physical abuse. Both involve concerted efforts to produce terror, dependency, and debility in the context of a life-and-death situation over an extended period of time. Like hostages in life-threatening situations, battered women sometimes display intense attachments to their captors (called traumatic bonding) and efforts to protect captors from outside intervention (Dutton & Painter, 1981; Graham et al., 1988).

Relatively little research has examined the specific effects of psychological abuse, because it is often seen as inseparable from physical abuse (Walker, 1979), or as part of relationship conflict in general (e.g., Peterson, 1983). Available evidence, however, suggests that many effects commonly observed in battered women may be due to psychological abuse or its combined effects with physical abuse. The most commonly described sequelae of physical abuse include alcohol problems (Bergman, Larsson, Brismar, & Klang, 1987), post-traumatic stress disorder (PTSD) and related anxiety symptoms (Houskamp & Foy, 1991), and low self-esteem or depression (Cascardi & O'Leary, 1992; Walker, 1984), all of which have been empirically associated with psychological abuse as well.

Among battered women, studies have found that psychological abuse is associated with a range of anxiety, stress, trauma, and depression symptoms. Saunders (1994), for example, found that verbal abuse was significantly associated with PTSD in battered women. Dutton and Painter (1993) reported that the overall severity of battered women's trauma symptoms was strongly associated with batterers' dominance and isolation tactics. Similarly, Anguilar and Nightingale (1994) found that batterers' emotional abuse and controlling tactics predicted lower levels of self-esteem among abused women.

The associations between psychological abuse experiences and distress symptoms generalize to women seeking help for marital problems, and to community samples as well, although the associations may be smaller in magnitude than in samples of battered women. Among women seeking marital treatment, acts of dominance and isolation predicted symptoms of traumatic stress (Cascardi, O'Leary, & Schlee, 1997). Similarly, in a sample of over 200 married women from the community, Arias, Street, and Brody (1996) reported that psychological abuse was significantly, albeit modestly, correlated with depressive symptoms and symptomatic drinking.

The association between psychological abuse and distress symptoms appears to be somewhat independent of the effects of physical abuse. Arias (1995) found that psychological abuse experiences among battered women were correlated with self-reported depression, anxiety symptoms, and stress symptoms, even after statistically controlling for physical abuse. In another study, 63% of women recruited from various sources (e.g., community, shelter) who experienced only verbal abuse met diagnostic criteria for PTSD using a self-report instrument (Kemp, Green, Hovanitz, & Rawlings, 1995).

It is also quite possible that the negative effects of psychological abuse are stronger in the context of physical abuse, as suggested by the strong associations between psychological abuse and emotional distress found among battered women. Among women seeking marital treatment, the combined experience of physical and verbal abuse was associated with higher levels of depression than verbal abuse alone (Vivian & Malone, in press). Similarly, among women in bad or stressful relationships who were recruited from the community, those who experienced only psychological abuse were less emotionally distressed and less likely to have attempted suicide than those who experienced serious physical abuse (Vitanza, Vogel, & Marshall, 1995). Note, however, that these studies did not directly test the hypothesis that physical violence potentiates the effects of psychological abuse. Delineation of the psychological processes by which various forms of abuse are linked to distress and trauma symptoms, and the relative contribution of psychological and physical assaults in this process, remain important topics for future investigations.

Future Research Directions

Several important directions for future research might bolster efforts to understand and prevent domestic violence. First, more descriptive and psychometric research is needed to illuminate the different forms and patterns of psychological abuse. Although there is a rich clinical literature describing many forms of psychological abuse, existing measures are quite limited in scope and interpretability. Preliminary work suggests that certain patterns of psychological abuse are highly related to physical abuse.

In a related vein, further research on the motivational dynamics of psychological abuse may prove very important in intervention with both severely abusive individuals and with distressed relationships more generally. Promising initial work has suggested that psychological aggression results when individuals are dissatisfied with the power arrangements in their relationships, and when individuals lack sufficient argumentative skills to handle disagreements. These hypothesized causes, however, characterize a large proportion of the population. Many additional factors may be at work in the pervasive and comprehensive patterns of psychological abuse that accompany severe spouse battery.

Finally, more research is needed on psychological abuse in nonviolent relationships, in early stages of relationship formation, and in youthful samples. Much of the available knowledge derives from samples for whom physical violence and psychological abuse have been present for a considerable period of time. However, potentially problematic relationship patterns often begin in adolescence or early adulthood, and escalating coercive processes often begin near the onset of intimate relationships. More research on specific patterns of abuse as they emerge and develop over time may further illuminate the processes of coercive escalation that result in severe spouse battery.

Summary

Psychological abuse in intimate adult relationships is an important new area of inquiry. Psychologically aggressive or hostile acts occur in the vast majority of intimate relationships. Moreover, psychological aggression is highly correlated with physical aggression and predicts the onset of physical aggression among newlywed couples. Despite these strong associations, these constructs can be reliably distinguished, both conceptually and empirically.

Severely battered women experience a wide array of intimidating and controlling behaviors. The majority of battered women report that psychological abuse is more painful and damaging than physical abuse. Recent empirical studies have found that psychological abuse is associated with anxiety, trauma, and depression symptoms in battered women, and its effects are somewhat independent from the effects of physical abuse.

Relatively little research has examined the causes and correlates of psychological abuse. Relationship distress, dissatisfaction with power arrangements, alcohol consumption, and a lack of argumentative skills have been empirically related to psychological aggression. Further research is needed to clarify the forms and patterns of psychological abuse, and to understand its role in the development and maintenance of severely abusive relationships.

Notes

1. Two additional forms of abuse often go together with the above but are not considered in the current review because they have distinct research traditions. One is the manipulation of, threat to, or abuse of children, and the other is sexual coercion and violence.

2. Correlates from Stets's (1990) study were presented in a multivariate prediction context. We assumed that variables with highly significant beta weights also had significant univariate correlations (a safe assumption unless there were strong suppression or moderator effects in the regression equation).

References

Andersen, S. M., Boulette, T. R., & Schwartz, A. H. (1991). Psychological maltreatment of spouses. In R. T. Ammerman & M. Hersen (Eds.), *Case studies in family violence* (pp. 293-327). New York: Plenum.

Anguilar, R. J., & Nightingale, N. N. (1994). The impact of specific battering experiences on the self-esteem of abused women. *Journal of Family Violence, 9*, 35-45.

Arias, I. (1995, October). *The impact of psychological abuse on battered women.* Paper presented at the National Violence Prevention Conference of the Centers for Disease Control and Prevention, Des Moines, IA.

Arias, I., & Beach, S. R. H. (1987). Validity of self-reports of marital violence. *Journal of Family Violence, 2*, 139-149.

Arias, I., Street, A. E., & Brody, G. H. (1996, September). *Depression and alcohol abuse: Women's responses to psychological victimization.* Paper presented at the American Psychological Association's National Conference on Psychosocial and Behavioral Factors in Women's Health, Washington, DC.

Barling, J., O'Leary, K. D., Jouriles, E. N., Vivian, D., & MacEwen, K. E. (1987). Factor similarity of the Conflict Tactics Scales across samples, spouses, and sites: Issues and implications. *Journal of Family Violence, 2*, 37-54.

Bateson, G. (1972). *Steps to an ecology of mind.* San Francisco: Chandler.

Bergman, B., Larsson, G., Brismar, B., & Klang, M. (1987). Psychiatric morbidity and personality characteristics of battered women. *Acta Psychiatrica Scandinavica, 76*, 678-683.

Breines, W., & Gordon, L. (1983). The new scholarship on family violence. *Signs: Journal of Women in Culture and Society, 8,* 490-531.

Cascardi, M., & O'Leary, K. D. (1992). Depressive symptomatology, self-esteem, and self-blame in battered women. *Journal of Family Violence, 7,* 249-259.

Cascardi, M., O'Leary, K. D., & Schlee, K. A. (1997). *Major depression and PTSD in physically abused women: Distinct entities or one underlying dimension of emotional distress?* Manuscript under review.

Cascardi, M., & Vivian, D. (1995). Context for specific episodes of marital violence: Gender and severity of violence differences. *Journal of Family Violence, 10,* 265-293.

Caulfield, M. B., & Riggs, D. S. (1992). The assessment of dating aggression: Empirical evaluation of the Conflict Tactics Scale. *Journal of Interpersonal Violence, 7,* 549-558.

Cordova, J. V., Jacobson, N. S., Gottman, J. M., Rushe, R., & Cox, G. (1993). Negative reciprocity and communication in couples with a violent husband. *Journal of Abnormal Psychology, 102,* 559-564.

Cronbach, L. J., & Meehl, P. E. (1955). Construct validity in psychological tests. *Psychological Bulletin, 52,* 281-302.

Darwin, C., & Wallace, A. R. (1970). The Linnean Society Papers. In P. Appleman (Ed.), *Darwin: A Norton critical reader* (pp. 81-97). New York: Norton. (Original work published 1858)

Dobash, R. E., & Dobash, R. (1979). *Violence against wives: A case against the patriarchy.* New York: Free Press.

Dollard, J., Doob, L., Miller, N., Mowrer, O., & Sears, R. (1939). *Frustration and aggression.* New Haven, CT: Yale University Press.

Dutton, D. G. (1986). Wife assaulters' explanations for assault: The neutralization of self-punishment. *Canadian Journal of Behavioral Science, 18,* 381-390.

Dutton, D. G., & Hemphill, K. J. (1992). Patterns of socially desirable responding among perpetrators and victims of wife assault. *Violence and Victims, 7,* 29-39.

Dutton, D. G., & Painter, S. L. (1981). Traumatic bonding: The development of emotional attachments in battered women and other relationships of intermittent abuse. *Victimology, 6,* 139-155.

Dutton, D. G., & Painter, S. L. (1993). Emotional attachments in abusive relationships: A test of traumatic bonding theory. *Violence and Victims, 8,* 105-120.

Dutton, D. G., & Strachan, C. E. (1987). Motivational needs for power and spouse-specific assertiveness in assaultive and nonassaultive men. *Violence and Victims, 2,* 145-156.

Edleson, J. L., Eisikovits, Z. C., Guttmann, E., & Sela-Amit, M. (1991). Cognitive and interpersonal factors in woman abuse. *Journal of Family Violence, 6,* 167-182.

Follingstad, D. R., Rutledge, L. L., Berg, B. J., Hause, E. S., & Polek, D. S. (1990). The role of emotional abuse in physically abusive relationships. *Journal of Family Violence, 5,* 107-120.

Freud, S. (1959). *Beyond the pleasure principle* (J. Strachey, Trans.). New York: Bantam Books. (Original work published 1920)

Garbarino, J., Guttman, E., & Seeley, J. W. (1986). *The psychologically battered child.* San Francisco: Jossey-Bass.

Gondolf, E. W. (1987). Evaluating programs for men who batter: Problems and prospects. *Journal of Family Violence, 2,* 95-108.

Graham, D. L. R., Rawlings, E., & Rimini, N. (1988). Survivors of terror: Battered women, hostages, and the Stockholm Syndrome. In K. Yllö & M. Bograd (Eds.), *Feminist perspectives on wife abuse* (pp. 217-233). Beverly Hills, CA: Sage.

Grusec, J. E., & Walters, G. C. (1991). Psychological abuse and childrearing belief systems. In R. H. Starr & D. A. Wolfe (Eds.), *The effects of child abuse and neglect* (pp. 186-202). New York: Guilford.

Hoffman, P. (1984). Psychological abuse of women by spouses and live-in lovers. *Women and Therapy, 3,* 37-47.

Houskamp, B. M., & Foy, D. W. (1991). The assessment of posttraumatic stress disorder in battered women. *Journal of Interpersonal Violence, 6,* 367-375.

Hudson, W. W., & McIntosh, S. R. (1981). The assessment of spouse abuse: Two quantifiable dimensions. *Journal of Marriage and the Family, 43,* 873-888.

Infante, D. A., Chandler, T. A., & Rudd, J. E. (1989). Test of an argumentative skill deficiency model of interspousal violence. *Communication Monographs, 56,* 163-177.

James, W. (1890). *The principles of psychology* (Vol. 2). New York: Henry Holt.

Johnson, J., & Sacco, V. F. (1995). Researching violence against women: Statistics Canada's national survey. *Canadian Journal of Criminology, 37,* 281-304.

Kaisan, M., & Painter, S. L. (1992). Frequency and severity of psychological abuse in a dating population. *Journal of Interpersonal Violence, 7,* 350-364.

Kemp, A., Green, B. L., Hovanitz, C., & Rawlings, E. I. (1995). Incidence and correlates of posttraumatic stress disorder in battered women: Shelter and community samples. *Journal of Interpersonal Violence, 10,* 43-55.

Kurz, D., & Stark, E. (1988). Not-so-benign neglect: The medical response to battering. In K. Yllö & M. Bograd (Eds.), *Feminist perspectives on wife abuse* (pp. 249-266). Beverly Hills, CA: Sage.

Lebov-Keeler, K., & Pipes, R. B. (1990, August). *Psychological abuse among college women in exclusive heterosexual dating relationships.* Paper presented at the American Psychological Association, Boston, MA.

Margolin, G., John, R. S., & Gleberman, L. (1988). Affective responses to conflictual discussions in violent and nonviolent couples. *Journal of Consulting and Clinical Psychology, 56,* 24-33.

Marshall, L. L. (1992). Development of the Severity of Violence Against Women Scales. *Journal of Family Violence, 7,* 103-121.

Marshall, L. L. (1996). Psychological abuse of women: Six distinct clusters. *Journal of Family Violence, 11,* 369-399.

Mason, A., & Blankenship, V. (1987). Power and affiliation motivation, stress, and abuse in intimate relationships. *Journal of Personality and Social Psychology, 52,* 203-210.

Molidor, C. E. (1995). Gender differences of psychological abuse in high school dating relationships. *Child and Adolescent Social Work Journal, 12,* 119-134.

Murphy, C. M., Cascardi, M., Ginsburg, E., & O'Leary, K. D. (1991, November). *Responsibility attributions for aggression in dating relationships.* Paper presented at the Association for the Advancement of Behavior Therapy, New York.

Murphy, C., Hartman, J., Muccino, L., & Douchis, K. (1995, November). *Dependency characteristics and abusive behavior in dating relationships.* Washington, DC: Association for the Advancement of Behavior Therapy.

Murphy, C. M., & Meyer, S. L. (1991). Gender, power, and violence in marriage. *Behavior Therapist, 14,* 95-100.

Murphy, C. M., & O'Leary, K. D. (1989). Psychological aggression predicts physical aggression in early marriage. *Journal of Consulting and Clinical Psychology, 57,* 579-582.

Murphy, C. M., & O'Leary, K. D. (1994). Research paradigms, values, and spouse abuse. *Journal of Interpersonal Violence, 9,* 207-223.

Nicarthy, G. (1986). *Getting free: A handbook for women in abusive relationships* (2nd ed.). Seattle, WA: Seal Press.

O'Leary, K. D., Barling, J., Arias, I., Rosenbaum, A., Malone, A., & Tyree, A. (1989). Prevalence and stability of physical aggression between spouses: A longitudinal analysis. *Journal of Consulting and Clinical Psychology, 57,* 263-268.

O'Leary, K. D., & Curley, A. D. (1986). Assertion and family violence: Correlates of spouse abuse. *Journal of Marital and Family Therapy, 12,* 281-289.

O'Leary, K. D., Malone, J., & Tyree, A. (1994). Physical aggression in early marriage: Prerelationship and relationship effects. *Journal of Consulting and Clinical Psychology, 62,* 594-602.

Pence, E. (1989). Batterer programs: Shifting from community collusion to community confrontation. In P. L. Caesar & L. K. Hamberger (Eds.), *Treating men who batter* (pp. 24-50). New York: Springer.

Peterson, D. R. (1983). Conflict. In H. H. Kelley, E. Bersheid, A. Christensen, J. H. Harvey, T. L. Huston, G. Levenger., E. McClintock, L. A. Peplau, & D. R. Peterson (Eds.), *Close relationships* (pp. 169-219). New York: W. H. Freeman.

Ptacek, J. (1988). Why do men batter their wives? In K. Yllö & M. Bograd (Eds.), *Feminist perspectives on wife abuse* (pp. 133-157). Newbury Park, CA: Sage.

Riggs, D. S., Murphy, C. M., & O'Leary, K. D. (1989). Intentional falsification in reports of interpartner aggression. *Journal of Interpersonal Violence, 4,* 220-232.

Rodenburg, F. A., & Fantuzzo, J. W. (1993). The measure of wife abuse: Steps toward the development of a comprehensive assessment technique. *Journal of Family Violence, 8,* 203-228.

Romero, M. (1985). A comparison between strategies used on prisoners of war and battered wives. *Sex Roles, 13,* 537-547.

Ronfeldt, H., Kimerling, R., & Arias, I. (in press). Relationship power satisfaction and perpetration of dating violence in the context of paternal marital violence. *Journal of Marriage and the Family.*

Sabourin, T. C. (1991). Perceptions of verbal aggression in interpersonal violence. In D. D. Knudsen & J. L. Miller (Eds.), *Abused and battered* (pp. 135-145). New York: Aldine de Gruyter.

Sabourin, T. C., Infante, D. A., & Rudd, J. E. (1993). Verbal aggression in marriages: A comparison of violent, distressed but nonviolent, and nondistressed couples. *Human Communication Research, 20,* 245-267.

Saunders, D. G. (1991). Procedures for adjusting self-reports of violence for social desirability bias. *Journal of Interpersonal Violence, 6,* 336-344.

Saunders, D. G. (1994). Posttraumatic stress symptom profiles of battered women: A comparison of survivors in two settings. *Violence and Victims, 9,* 31-44.

Schafer, J. (1996). Measuring spousal violence with the Conflict Tactics Scale: Notes on reliability and validity issues. *Journal of Interpersonal Violence, 11,* 572-585.

Shepard, M. F., & Campbell, J. A. (1992). The abusive behavior inventory: A measure of psychological and physical abuse. *Journal of Interpersonal Violence, 7,* 291-305.

Stets, J. E. (1990). Verbal and physical aggression in marriage. *Journal of Marriage and the Family, 52,* 501-514.

Stets, J. E. (1991). Psychological aggression in dating relationships: The role of interpersonal control. *Journal of Family Violence, 6,* 97-114.

Straus, M. A. (1974). Leveling, civility, and violence in the family. *Journal of Marriage and the Family, 36,* 13-29.

Straus, M. A. (1979). Measuring intrafamily conflict and violence: The Conflict Tactics Scales. *Journal of Marriage and the Family, 41,* 75-88.

Straus, M. A. (1990). The Conflict Tactics Scales and its critics: An evaluation and new data on validity and reliability. In M. A. Straus & R. J. Gelles (Eds.), *Physical violence in American families* (pp. 49-73). New Brunswick, NJ: Transaction.

Straus, M. A., & Gelles, R. J. (Eds.). (1990). *Physical violence in American families.* New Brunswick, NJ: Transaction.

Straus, M. A., Gelles, R. J., & Steinmetz, S. K. (1980). *Behind closed doors: Violence in the American family.* Garden City, NY: Anchor Press.

Straus, M. A., Hamby, S. L., Boney-McCoy, S., & Sugarman, D. B. (1996). The revised Conflict Tactics Scales (CTS2): Development and preliminary psychometric data. *Journal of Family Issues, 17,* 283-316.

Straus, M. A., & Sweet, S. (1992). Verbal/symbolic aggression in couples: Incidence rates and relationships to personal characteristics. *Journal of Marriage and the Family, 54,* 346-357.

Sudman, S., Bradburn, N. M., & Schwartz, N. (1996). *Thinking about answers: The application of cognitive processes to survey methodology.* San Francisco: Jossey-Bass.

Sugarman, D. B., & Hotaling, G. T. (1989). Dating violence: Prevalence, context, and risk markers. In M. A. Pirog-Good & J. E. Stets (Eds.), *Violence in dating relationships: Emerging social issues.* New York: Praeger.

Suitor, J. J., Pillemer, K., & Straus, M. A. (1990). Marital violence in life course perspective. In M. A. Straus & R. J. Gelles (Eds.), *Physical violence in American families* (pp. 305-317). New Brunswick, NJ: Transaction.

Tolman, R. M. (1989). The development of a measure of psychological maltreatment of women by their male partners. *Violence and Victims, 4,* 159-177.

Tolman, R. M. (1992). Psychological abuse of women. In R. T. Ammerman & M. Hersen (Eds.), *Assessment of family violence* (pp. 291-310). New York: John Wiley.

Vitanza, S., Vogel, L. C. M., & Marshall, L. L. (1995). Distress and symptoms of posttraumatic stress disorder in abused women. *Violence and Victims, 10,* 23-34.

Vitanza, S., Walker, F., & Marshall, L. L. (1990). *The effect of psychological abuse on women's relationships and health.* Unpublished manuscript, University of North Texas.

Vivian, D., & Malone, J. (in press). Relationship factors and depressive symptomatology associated with mild and severe husband-to-wife physical aggression. *Violence and Victims.*

Walker, L. E. (1979). *The battered woman.* New York: Harper & Row.

Walker, L. E. (1984). *The battered woman syndrome.* New York: Springer.

Waltz, J., Babcock, J. C., Jacobson, N. S., & Gottman, J. M. (1991, November). *Husband and wife reports of interspousal violence: Sex differences in minimization.* Paper presented at the Association for the Advancement of Behavior Therapy, New York.

Weis, J. G. (1989). Family violence research methodology and design. In L. Ohlin & M. Tonry (Eds.), *Family violence.* Chicago: University of Chicago Press.

Winter, D. G. (1973). *The power motive.* New York: Free Press.

• *CHAPTER 9* •

Men Who Batter

LARRY W. BENNETT
OLIVER J. WILLIAMS

Attention directed toward men who batter women has increased dramatically the past few years. The criminal and civil trials of popular athlete and actor O. J. Simpson for the murder and wrongful death of his ex-wife focused public attention not only on femicide, but also on a justice system that failed to stop domestic violence. Print and electronic media inundated domestic violence agencies and experts with requests for interviews, information, and stories about battered women and their plight. For a brief time, the public cared about battered women and wondered why men batter and what could be done to stop them. There have been other episodes of public attention to battering. The bruised, swollen face of Hedda Nussbaum looking out from the cover of periodicals in 1987 was such an episode. The stories of Nussbaum's enslavement by her abuser, Joel Steinberg, and the murder of their child, Lisa, clearly portrayed the link between child abuse and woman abuse for all to see.

Although the stories of victims such as Hedda Nussbaum and Nicole Brown Simpson serve to awaken a public that usually does not think about battered women or their abusers, interest soon fades, and the reality of the daily abuse suffered by many thousands of women recedes from public view. Why are we not outraged as a people that horrific violence occurs on a daily basis in every community? In part, it is because we are able to view the perpetrators of these offenses as monsters, deviates, and most of all, different from us. Over 1,400 women die every year at the hands of their abusers (Bachman & Saltzman, 1995), and these particular woman abusers are murderers. Over 1,000 times that number of women are battered every year, and probably 10,000 times that many women suffer extreme dominance, control, and emotional abuse by men who may rarely batter them. Just how different batterers are from nonbatterers depends on how much of men's behavior we include in our definition of woman abuse.

Like Joel Steinberg and O. J. Simpson, men who batter are often respectable men with responsible careers and appear otherwise unremarkable. Men who batter do not carry the mark of a batterer, and their violence is usually concealed. It is less easy for a victim to conceal her injuries, and battered women are always more visible than batterers. For their own safety, battered women frequently attempt to conceal the fact of their victimization. The public has had a far greater fascination with "why she stays" than with "why he abuses." Rather than seeing the actions of battered women as choosing when it is safe to leave, which for many of them is never, people often see her remaining with her abuser as evidence of her own pathology. All of these reasons have permitted the batterer to remain in relative obscurity.

Whether a special focus on men who batter is desirable depends on our beliefs about domestic violence. On one hand, an increased focus on men who batter may ultimately result in an improvement in our ability to evaluate, refer, retain, and help batterers choose nonviolence. On the other hand, a focus on men who batter may detract attention from helping the victims of violence and drain funding from programs designed to serve victims. In this chapter, we will review various perspectives on men who batter, knowledge about their characteristics, and the effectiveness of efforts to prevent their violence. We will use the terms *men who batter* and *woman abuse* because available data support a view of partner abuse as primarily the activity of offenders who are men and victims who are women (Bachman & Saltzman, 1995). Although women use physical violence against men (Straus, 1993) and domestic abuse occurs in gay and lesbian relationships (Island & Letellier, 1991; Renzetti, 1992), our focus will remain on men who are physically or nonphysically abusive of women partners or ex-partners.

Perspectives on Men Who Batter

Discussions about the causes of woman abuse and appropriate interventions for men who batter encompass a number of viewpoints and often elicit strong opinions. What we see and what we do about woman abuse depends on whether we choose to focus on the cultural norms that incubate and legitimate woman abuse, on the interpersonal context of violence in a relationship, or on the characteristics and beliefs of men who batter (Margolin & Burman, 1993). In our society, violence is usually viewed as individual deviancy. From such a psychological perspective, woman abuse is an outcome of an individual man thinking, behaving, and choosing poorly. Individual men learn to be violent in their families of origin, from the media, in interaction with peers, and by successful practice. Men also learn violence by reinforcement of their violent behavior through its desirable effects, through a lack of sanction, and in some cases, through overt support. A few researchers believe batterers' behavior is associated with physical pathology (Elliot, 1982; Rosenbaum, Hoge, & Adelman, 1994). Those employing a psychological view of battering do not usually disagree that woman abuse is criminal, nor that social and gender factors are important, but they do emphasize the need for personal counseling (O'Leary, 1993).

Sociologists and feminists have expanded our view of woman abuse from the level of individual deviancy. The most recent women's movement is responsible for making woman abuse a public issue. With the growing prominence of feminism and the shelter movement of the 1970s, domestic violence came to be viewed as violence against women in a patriarchal society (Martin, 1976). This view emphasizes gender, power, and the social supports for male dominance (Yllö, 1993). Although woman abuse is the responsibility of the individual and individual factors play a role in determining which men will be violent under which conditions, the larger concerns are the social engines that create, empower, and maintain the high level of violence against women in our society. Feminists emphasize the criminal nature of woman abuse (Hart, 1988). Feminists do not usually oppose interventions for batterers, but they have been opposed to programs that de-emphasize the criminality of battering, or that drain attention and resources from battered women's programs. Feminists also oppose interventions in which victims appear to share responsibility for their abuse. Shared responsibility includes some forms of couples' counseling (Lane & Russell, 1989) or therapy that views victims as co-dependent (Lindquist, 1986).

From our perspective, individual deviancy as an explanation for woman abuse appears to be gaining support. Several factors may account for the increasing emphasis on individual men and their personal dysfunction in the latter 1990s. Overall, a focus on individual deviancy reflects the conservative tenor of our times. Conservative thinking emphasizes an individual's responsibility to society over society's responsibility to its citizens. If men were violent with women because society supported such violence, something would be wrong with the foundation of our society. Conservatives prefer to view society's ills as residing within individuals. A positive view of society is much easier to maintain if we view batterers as having disorders.

A second reason for the increasing focus on the psychological contribution to woman abuse is the trend toward medicalization of our society. The paperback version of the second edition of the American Psychiatric Association's *Diagnostic and Statistical Manual of Mental Disorders* (*DSM-II*), which was used between 1968 and 1980, was 134 pages. In 1980, the third edition of the *DSM* was 494 pages, and in 1994, the fourth edition was a hefty 886 pages. The 561% increase in *DSM* pages over a 14-year period is both symbolic of, and proportional to, the medicalization of human behavior. During the same era, community mental health became behavioral health care, with a concomitant shift in health emphasis from community action to individual behavior, and from prevention to treatment (DuMont, 1992). During the last 25 years, woman abuse has gone from a private matter to a public matter. Men who batter, however, have remained private, psychological anomalies.

There are, however, several advantages to the current emphasis on the psychological view of men who batter. Focusing on individuals permits us to examine variations more closely. By understanding which men batter, the types of batterers, and other variants, perhaps we can construct better assessment protocols and better match intervention to the person, escaping the "one size fits all" approaches that have dominated batterer intervention programs to date. In the age of accountability, we should welcome the opportunity to hold policymakers and practitioners accountable for describing what they do and for knowing the effects of their interventions. However, we believe accountability will be far more useful when it focuses not on numbers reported to faceless agents of health care organizations, but rather on the safety of battered women reported to the women themselves, to their advocates, and to the criminal justice system.

Characteristics of Men Who Batter

It is not easy to distinguish men who batter from men who do not batter. Moreover, men who batter tend to be as different from one another as they are from men who do not batter. Violence in a man's family of origin, psychopathology, and substance abuse patterns are three of the parameters that may be used to differentiate batterers from nonbatterers and from one another.

Violence in the Family of Origin

One of the primary ways cultural beliefs about violence are transmitted is through the family of origin. Violence in the family of origin—either observing a parent-figure battering or else being the victim of parent-figure abuse—has been consistently associated with men battering across a number of scientific studies (Hotaling & Sugarman, 1986). Men who batter are more likely than nonbattering men to report a history of parental violence in their families of origin (Caesar, 1988; Murphy, Meyer, & O'Leary, 1993). Although rates of family of origin violence as high as 75% have been reported in some batterer programs (Fitch & Papantonio, 1983), violence in the family of origin of men who batter may not be as invariable as many believe. In a recent study of 840 batterers in four U.S. batterer programs, 33% of the men reported observing parental battering and 26% reported being physically harmed by their parents (Gondolf, 1996).

Because violence in the family of origin is not universal among batterers, other factors must modify these early experiences. One good candidate for a modifier is alcohol abuse or dependency. Hamberger and Hastings (1991) compared alcoholic batterers, nonalcoholic batterers, community (nonreferred) batterers, and community nonviolent men, and found that only the alcoholic batterers differed from nonbatterers in family of origin violence. In a national study of 723 nonabstinent men, Kantor and Asdigian (1993) identified three pathways linking violence and abuse in the family of origin to current woman abuse: (a) the direct effect of observing parental violence, (b) a low level of education, and (c) multigenerational heavy drinking. This research suggests that violent socialization in the family of origin increases the risk of alcohol abuse, which in turn increases the risk for woman abuse.

Psychopathology

There is a continuum of thought regarding batterer pathology. On one end of this continuum are those who believe a focus on psychopathology is unrelated to the criminal act of woman abuse. From this perspective, a focus on psychopathology is, at best, irrelevant, and at worst, dangerous. On the other end of this continuum of thought are those who argue that almost all batterers have psychiatric disorders. Dinwiddie (1992) interviewed a nonclinical sample of 380 married men and found 61 (16%) who indicated they had beat up, cut, or injured their female partner. Of the 61 batterers, 46% met the criteria for antisocial personality disorder, 33% met the criteria for major depression, 87% met the criteria for alcoholism, 49% met the criteria for two of the three disorders, and 11% met the criteria for all three disorders. Researchers using other community samples have also found that batterers have higher rates of personality disorder and dysphoria than nonbatterers (Hastings & Hamberger, 1988). About 9 of 10 batterers fall above a 75 cut-off score on at least one personality disorder scale of the Millon Clinical Multiaxial inventory (Gondolf, 1996; Hamberger & Hastings, 1991). Dutton (1995) argues that many emotionally abusive men who batter exhibit an abusive personality. Borderline personality organization, a much broader construct than the behaviorally anchored borderline personality disorder in the *Diagnostic and Statistical Manual* (DSM-IV; American Psychiatric Association, 1994) is viewed as a central feature of abusive men. One key to their unstable affect may be perception of separation and abandonment, a perception that becomes both very real and very dangerous when a partner actually leaves or threatens to leave a relationship (Dutton & Starzomski, 1993).

There is also a recurrent emphasis on possible organic origins and manifestations of violence. An early proponent of organic origins for battering was Elliot (1982), who reviewed the records of 286 batterers and found evidence of brain trauma or other brain insult such as encephalitis in 102 (36%) of them. More recently, head injury was found to be a significant correlate of being a batterer (Rosenbaum et al., 1994). Unfortunately, this research cannot determine whether these head injuries came before or after the men became woman abusers.

Overall, research findings suggest that batterers who come to the attention of law enforcement officials and batterers programs exhibit substantially greater levels of pathology than nonbatterers. To date, however, there is no evidence that psychopathology plays a direct, causal role in woman abuse.

Substance Abuse

The annual rate of man-to-woman violence in the United States increases proportionately with the frequency with which men get drunk, from about 2% of men who never get drunk to 9% of white-collar men and 40% of blue-collar men who are drunk often (Coleman & Straus, 1983). The average amount of alcohol used prior to intimate violence, however, is about 1 ounce, an amount of alcohol equivalent to one beer (Pernanen, 1991). Furthermore, most episodes of woman abuse do not involve alcohol. Using data from the 1985 National Family Violence Survey, Kantor and Straus (1987) found that, in three out of four episodes of woman abuse, neither party was intoxicated.

Given these relatively low rates for the co-occurrence of drinking and woman abuse, why does alcohol have the reputation of having a strong influence on domestic violence? One reason is the assumption of malevolence associated with alcohol and drugs (Hamilton & Collins, 1981). Whenever alcohol or drugs are involved in any problem, they are assumed to be a cause of the problem. A second reason is that alcohol use and alcohol abuse are different phenomena. A man who drinks heavily does not have to be drinking to be affected by alcohol. Alcohol abuse is more strongly related to woman abuse than alcohol use. In one study of male factory workers, a diagnosis of alcohol abuse or dependency was a better predictor of woman abuse than was the frequency with which a man used alcohol or the quantity he usually drank (Leonard, Brommet, Parkinson, Day, & Ryan, 1985). In clinical and forensic studies, rates of alcohol abuse or intoxication in woman abuse are well above 50% (Hamilton & Collins, 1981; Leonard & Jacob, 1988).

Abstinence from alcohol or drugs is neither a necessary nor a sufficient condition for men being nonviolent. Recovering alcoholics and addicts, some with many years of sobriety, are well represented in batterers programs. Nine percent of 840 batterers in Gondolf's (1996) multisite study of batterer characteristics reported being recovering alcoholics or addicts, and 26% reported being in alcohol or drug treatment at some point. Research to date does not support the belief that men who batter are "out of control" when they do so. Despite the impairment in men's lives caused by alcohol, woman abuse remains a matter of choice and a "guided doing" (Pernanen, 1991).

Batterer Typology

One commonly hears the terms *batterer* or *men who batter,* but there has been little mention that batterers may not be a homogenous group. On one extreme, at the case end, every batterer is different from every other batterer in terms of personality, experience, motivation to violence, violence employed, and so forth. On the other end of this continuum, there is a single type—the batterer. Between these two typological extremes is a growing consensus that there are several types of batterers, although there is considerable overlap between types, and some batterers are not classifiable.

A number of studies have identified types or clusters of batterers (e.g., Gondolf, 1988b; Hamberger & Hastings, 1986; Saunders, 1992). The earliest typology for batterers was two-fold and found men who were violent only with their families different in important ways from men who were violent both in and outside of families (Shields, McCall, & Hanneke, 1988). Key factors differentiating family-only batterers were lower levels of alcohol consumption and less criminal behavior outside the family (Cadsky & Crawford, 1988). Generally violent batterers account for about 10% of a national sample of self-identified batterers (Kandel-Englander, 1992). For court-referred samples, the proportion of batterers who are generally violent is nearer 25%.

The two-fold typology is supported by a recent, well-designed study of 60 married couples where the husband had used moderate to severe violence against his partner in the past year (Gottman et al., 1995). The researchers used various physiological measures to divide the men into two groups, which they labeled Type 1 and Type 2 batterers: the heart rate reactivity of Type 1 batterers (20% of the men) decreased from the baseline rate during experimentally induced marital conflict, whereas the heart rate reactivity of Type 2 batterers increased from the baseline rate during conflict with their wives. A larger proportion of Type 1 batterers had experienced violence in the family of origin (56% v. 13%) and were violent outside the marriage (44% v. 3%). Type 1 batterers also scored substantially higher on antisocial and aggressive-sadistic personality measures. During experimentally induced marital conflict, Type 1 batterers were more belligerent and contemptuous of their wives. The wives of Type 1 batterers expressed less anger than the wives of Type 2 batterers. Two years later, the couples were recontacted. None (0%) of the Type 1 men and 27% of the Type 2 men were divorced or separated after 2 years. The authors conclude that there is a physiologically based typology of men who batter. Type 1 batterers are more antisocial, are generally violent, and instill greater levels of fear in their victims. The authors speculate that the lower levels of anger by wives and the lower separation rate for the wives of Type 1 batterers was due to the greater danger in arguing with, or leaving, this type of batterer.

Other studies find evidence for a three-fold typology of men who batter. Gondolf (1988b) used shelter intake data from a random sample of battered women to describe three clusters of batterers: typical batterers (50%), antisocial batterers (about 40%), and sociopathic batterers (about 10%). Saunders (1992) used evaluations of 165 men in batterers treatment to generate a similar typology of family-only aggressive (52%), generally aggressive (29%), and emotionally volatile (19%) batterers. Because the typology studies use data from different sources, there is no clear fit between them. Nevertheless, much of the same data were collected in all the studies. At present, research supports a tentative tripartite typology of family-only, dysphoric/borderline, and antisocial/generally violent batterers (Holtzworth-Munroe & Stuart, 1994). Family-only or typical batterers, probably half of those seen in batterers programs, usually have a lower level of violence severity, do not have significant levels of psychopathology, are less likely to abuse alcohol or drugs, and are usually not violent to people outside their family. The dysphoric/borderline batterers, roughly a quarter of the men seen in batterers programs, are often emotionally unstable, particularly at times when they sense their partner moving too close or too far away from them. Dysphoric batterers may abuse alcohol and drugs to regulate their mood. The third type of batterer, perhaps one fourth of batterers seen in batterers programs, are men whose violence against women is a variation on their violence toward society. The generally violent, antisocial, or Type 1 batterer is more likely to abuse drugs and alcohol and is more likely to injure his victims seriously. His abuse of alcohol or drugs may reflect a need to relieve boredom and provide stimulation.

Typing batterers is controversial. There is overlap and exclusion with all typologies, but particularly with batterer typologies. Definitive research has yet to be conducted. Typologies are only useful if they lead to better understanding of cause and better interventions. Some observers are concerned that the focus on mental disorders or personality disorders associated with typing batterers might divert responsibility from their crime to their disorders, detracting from issues of gender and power. A focus on disorders also ignores the largest group of batterers: those who have no disorders. A potentially more interesting and useful group, yet relatively unstudied, is men who do not batter. Information on how some men who are otherwise dysphoric, antisocial, alcoholic, or normal manage to choose nonviolence may better instruct us how to prevent violence against women than the pathology-based approaches, which are more interesting to therapists and researchers.

Interventions for Men Who Batter

In the 1970s, early programs for men who batter were provided by profeminist men's groups seeking to support the actions of the women's antiviolence movement (Adams & McCormick, 1982). Groups such as EMERGE in Boston and RAVEN in St. Louis were based on an analysis of men's privilege as the cause of woman abuse. At the same time, family therapists were providing services for couples where men had battered their partners (Margolin, 1979). Today, we see variations on these twin themes of gender-specific programs for batterers and domestic abuse programs for couples. A broader response is the emergent community-based systems for prevention of violence (Hart, 1995). Coordinated community responses to family violence seek to provide unified, coordinated, and accountable approaches to domestic violence. Many of the problems associated with parallel, fragmented, and sometimes conflictual violence prevention efforts are minimized with a coordinated community-based approach. Key components of coordinated community responses would include the criminal justice and medical systems, victim advocates, shelters and women's programs, child protection services, senior services, other social service and mental health providers, clergy, and batterer intervention programs (Witwer & Crawford, 1995)

In this chapter, we will focus on three overlapping types of intervention with men who batter: criminal justice interventions, batterer programs, and couples programs. First, however, we must recognize that much of the assistance to batterers is provided by professionals or programs who either do not know they are helping a man who batters or else have decided that the reason he batters is due to another problem, and that problem is the focus of their intervention. Interventions provided by mental health professionals, such as medication and psychotherapy, are often targeted at symptoms bundled with woman abuse and classified as a disorder. Woman abuse may be labeled as a psychiatric disorder such as intermittent explosive disorder or else directly named as a nonpsychiatric problem, such as physical abuse of an adult. The abusive behavior is not infrequently viewed as symptomatic of other disorders, which are seen as either more pervasive or more explanatory of the symptom picture, such as major depression, post-traumatic stress disorder (PTSD), alcohol dependency, or partner relational problem. Another source of intervention for men who batter, either independent of or in conjunction with mental health intervention, is the self-help group. Groups such as Alcoholics Anonymous and Parents Anonymous are heavily populated by men who batter. These men either do not accept their violence as a problem or believe their violence originates in another problem, such as stress or alcohol.

Criminal Justice Interventions

Criminal justice interventions include protective orders, arrest, prosecution, and sentencing. The criminalization of domestic violence in the United States began in the 1970s (Zorza, 1992). With few exceptions, the criminalization of domestic violence has developed with little empirical evidence for its effectiveness and very little effort to examine the underlying assumption that violence can be prevented by legal sanction (Fagan, 1996). Although domestic violence is illegal, enforcement of laws and justice is a different story. Drawing from a number of empirical studies, Dutton (1995) estimated that, for every 1,000 domestic violence events, 14 result in arrest; of those 14, only 4 result in some form of punishment. Although these figures are based on data that are over a decade old, and recent changes in criminal justice responses to woman abuse may have doubled the proportion of arrests and punishments, the still-low rates support feminists' belief that there is social support for violence against women.

A protective order is a judicial order regulating the behavior of the batterer (and the victim) when violence has been alleged or documented. The typical order of protection enforces a separation between the individuals involved. Orders are useful for women who want to be protected but do not want their partner or ex-partner in jail (Finn, 1991). This is particularly helpful when the batterer's income or protection is critical to the well-being of the battered woman and her children. Like arrest and prosecution, protective orders may be useful to battered women in ways other than those intended. The media have dramatically portrayed the failure of protective orders in cases of femicide, but consumers have been, in general, satisfied with orders of protection (Horton, Simonidis, & Simonidis, 1987). Studies of the effects of orders of protection are mixed. In one study of 300 women receiving orders of protection, 60% of the women reported being abused in the year after the order was granted (Harrell, Smith, & Newmark, 1993). In another study, orders of protection, in conjunction with services from a battered women's program, increased the rate of completed prosecutions (Weisz, Tolman, & Bennett, 1996).

Police intervention may result in arrest, or it may result in crisis counseling, victim referral, and batterer referral without arrest. Because domestic violence is a crime, women's advocates prefer arrest to diversions such as counseling, separation, and crisis interruption. Recently, policies mandating arrest in cases of domestic violence have proliferated, and the arrest rates of women charged with domestic violence have increased proportionately. In Kenosha, Wisconsin, for example, a mandatory arrest law led to a 12-fold increase in women's arrest rates and a two-fold increase in men's arrest rates (Hamberger & Potente, 1994).

In the first experimental study of the effect of arrest on recidivism, Minneapolis police officers either arrested, counseled, or separated batterers and victims. Arrest produced significantly lower rates of recidivism (Sherman & Berk, 1984). Early optimism about the beneficial effects of arrest based on the Minneapolis experiment has been modified in light of equivocal results in later replications (Schmidt & Sherman, 1993). Although arrest, by itself, is not a panacea, as was once believed, nothing has been found that, by itself, is better than arrest in preventing batterer recidivism (Berk, 1993).

The limitations of arrest may reside both with the motivation of the arresting officer and with the characteristics of the batterer. Police often react more to the characteristics of subjects in cases of domestic violence—for example, resistance to questioning, drunkenness, and so forth—than to the criminal act of wife abuse (Gondolf & McFerron, 1989). Despite the belief that men who batter are "out of control," batterers are renowned for their ability to control themselves when necessary, such as during a police officer's visit. Arrest may be more effective for batterers who have something to lose—job, face, freedom, wife, and so on—than for batterers who are already at the social margin. Arrest is more effective, on the average, if the batterers are white, middle-class, employed, married, cohabiting men who have pushed, restrained, or shoved their victim and subsequently felt bad about it. In other words, if the batterer has a "stake in conformity" (Toby, 1957), he is more likely to respond to criminal justice interventions—or any interventions, for that matter. Unfortunately, the batterers most likely to be arrested are those who are poor, minorities, and at greater risk of public exposure, such as alcoholics, addicts, and the mentally ill. These are precisely the type of batterers that intervention programs, as currently configured, often fail to help. Although arrest, by itself, may not deter woman abuse, as proponents had argued, when combined with other interventions under conditions of a community-based prevention effort, arrest is probably a deterrent for most men (Gelles, 1993).

Once a batterer is arrested, he can be prosecuted, or the charges can be dropped. Aggressive prosecution of batterers reflects a drastic policy change from only a few years ago when prosecution of domestic violence cases was sporadic. A current debate is whether victims should be permitted to control prosecutions or whether prosecutors should proceed independent of the victim's wishes. Research on the effectiveness of prosecution is mixed. In the most comprehensive prosecution study to date, victim-controlled prosecution significantly reduced severe physical violence compared to traditional prosecution (Ford & Regoli, 1993). Many prosecutors do not believe in victim-controlled prosecution, however. In a metropolitan Chicago county, a battered woman was recently jailed by a state's attorney after she refused to cooperate with the prosecution of her batterer. In a logic reminiscent of Vietnam-era assurances that villages had to be burned to save them, the prosecutor reasoned that the jailing was for her own protection.

Once a batterer is convicted of domestic abuse or a similar crime, a range of punishment may be applied. Dutton (1995) estimates that 25 of every 100 arrests lead to some sort of punishment for the batterer. Because incarceration may be harmful to the batterer's victim in terms of lost economic support and loss of relationship, Tolman (1996) suggests a variety of sanctions that may reduce some of these incongruities, including day incarceration, weekend incarceration, home confinement, intensive probation, community service, batterer intervention programs, and restitution.

Increasingly officials and advocates are discussing the dual facts that battering is a crime that deserves punishment and that victims should not suffer further effects of a batterer's behavior secondary to his punishment. Further refinements are being implemented, such as assertive case management and use of intermediate sanctions to enforce batterer compliance with orders and with program demands.

Batterers Intervention Programs

At present, gender-specific programs for men who batter, or batterers intervention programs, are shaped by the twin forces of feminist philosophy and the need for practical thinking and behaving skills necessary to choose nonviolence. The battered women's movement and feminism have contributed an analysis of gender and power to batterers intervention programs, forming the basis for the challenges to men's attitudes and beliefs about male dominance and privilege. The cognitive-behavioral paradigm informing anger management and stress reduction skills has been equally influential in batterers programs. Almost all programs are some combination of these two elements, whether they are providing profeminist cognitive-behavioral therapy (Ganley, 1989), working within a community intervention model popularized by the Domestic Abuse Intervention Project in Duluth (Pence & Paymar, 1993), or using an ecological model (Edleson & Tolman, 1992).

Feminists have criticized programs that emphasize the development of anger management skills (Adams, 1988; Gondolf & Russell, 1986). On the other hand, Donald Dutton (1994) wonders what actual force patriarchy carries if 90% of the men growing up in patriarchal society are not violent toward women. It is beyond the scope of this chapter to extend these debates here, but such discussions, and the program evaluations that might illuminate them, are ongoing at the present time.

Regardless of the theoretical perspective, groups are the preferred mode of service delivery for batterers intervention programs. Groups may be open- or close-ended, structured or unstructured. Groups are most often structured and time-limited, ranging from 8 to 32 meetings of 2 to 3 hours each, and average 8 to 12 men per group (Edleson & Tolman, 1992). Some programs are as long as 52 weeks. Time has been the principal criterion for deciding when a man has completed a batterers program, but competency-based programs are now being implemented. In a time-limited program, completion is signaled by attendance during the required period of time. In a competency-based program, completion depends both on whether the batterer has attended for the required time and also whether he has achieved criterion behaviors before completion. Criterion behaviors could include nonviolence reports from the victim, statements by the batterer that he is responsible for his violent acts, completion of out-of-session tasks and homework, and so forth. Safety of the victim and reliability of observations are paramount considerations, along with the logistical problem of processing batterers through a program within the constraints of court sentencing.

Groups have the potential to decrease a batterer's sense of isolation and beliefs in his exceptionality, improve his interpersonal skills, offer mutual aid, identify and develop expertise in critical areas, maximize confrontation of denial and inappropriate behavior, develop a norm for personal and social change, and maximize rewards for change (Stordeur & Stille, 1989). On the other hand, groups have the potential to increase negative male bonding, provide a celebration of men's dominance over women, enhance misogyny, promote collusion between therapist and batterer, and increase the risk to victims (Hart, 1988). Most current intervention programs propose that nonviolence requires an examination of male dominance and a change in attitude toward women, in addition to learning to manage anger, solve problems, reduce stress, improve social skills, express feelings, and so on. In a coordinated community approach to preventing violence, these changes must occur at the community as well as at the personal level.

Issues With Batterer Intervention Programs

Attrition. Men's departure prior to program completion has always been a problem associated with batterers intervention programs. Attrition is usually computed as the ratio of men who drop out of a program to the total of men who began the program. Attrition might more accurately be figured by including in the denominator all those men who were referred to the program, but who never attended. In one metropolitan program, for example, of 200 batterers referred, only 14% actually attended any of the program sessions, and less than 1% completed the 8-month program (Gondolf & Foster, 1991). This reflects either a 93% or a 99% attrition rate. In another batterers intervention program, of over 500 men contacting the program over a 12-month period, 283 attended at least one group, and 153 completed the program, reflecting an attrition rate of either 45% or 70% (Edleson & Syers, 1990, 1991).

Attrition may be a critical factor in the effectiveness of batterer intervention programs. One study found that batterers must attend at least 75% of the program before noticing an effect (Chen, Bersani, Myers, & Denton, 1989). This finding may reflect the "planned behavior" and efficacy that some experts believe are important in preventing recidivism (Tolman, Edleson, & Fendrich, 1995). Men who attend at least 75% of a program most likely believe they can benefit from it, establish a stronger attachment to the program and to the people in the program, and experience a greater degree of self-efficacy. Also, they probably have a greater stake in maintaining the relationship and in their life. Batterers who are better educated, are employed, and have children are more likely to complete batterers intervention programs (Gruszinski & Carrillo, 1988).

Effectiveness of Batterers Intervention Programs. Using partner-reported physical abuse as a criterion, program studies report nonviolence rates of between 53% to 85% when men are followed up between 4 and 26 months after the program (Tolman & Edleson, 1995). In a 5-year follow-up using criminal justice records, Shepard (1992) found 60 of 100 men had not re-offended. Three factors were associated with recidivism in the Shepard study: evidence of substance abuse, a history of violence in the family of origin, and a criminal record. On the other hand, when comparing batterers in court-mandated groups with batterers not mandated to treatment, Harrell (1991) found no difference in recidivism at 6-month follow-up and concluded that batterer intervention programs had no discernable effect. A secondary analysis of Harrell's data found a recidivism rate of 44% (Tolman et al., 1995). These researchers found that perceived behavioral control (self-efficacy) played a significant role in predicting actual abusive behavior. They speculate that intervention failed to significantly increase the perceived behavioral control of batterers who attended intervention programs in Harrell's study because they were not successful in bringing about meaningful changes in perceived self-efficacy. This is not surprising, because the full intervention in Harrell's study was 12 to 18 hours, a level of intervention that would not meet many state standards for batterer intervention programs.

Edleson and Syers (1990, 1991) studied three types of batterers programs under short-term and longer-term conditions (12- and 32-week) and followed up at 6 months and again at 18 months. The types of programs studied were a structured psychoeducational group, a self-help program, and a combined psychoeducational/self-help program. Although the majority of men in all six groups were nonviolent at 6 and 18 months, the shorter structured programs had the lowest recidivism. For the 153 men who completed the program, two of three were nonviolent at follow-up. There may be other considerations for determining the length of a batterers program, but short-term programs appear to be as effective as longer ones.

Overall, batterers intervention program outcomes are modest. To evaluate such programs fairly, outcomes should be compared to other programs targeting similar populations. When compared, for example, to therapy with men with personality disorders and to men with addiction problems, batterers intervention programs have a similar effect (Jacobson, 1994). Batterers programs demonstrate dropout rates similar to those of drug and alcohol programs, programs for sex offenders, and check-forging intervention programs (Gondolf, 1997). The debate about the effectiveness of batterers' programs must continue. We anticipate that such programs will become more effective as they improve their connections to community-based violence prevention efforts, provide differential programming for different kinds of batterers, attend to problems that foster noncompliance such as cultural insensitivity and substance abuse, and incorporate feedback and accountability systems into their daily practice.

Coordinated Community Responses. As a result of the advocacy of battered women's programs, many communities are organizing to prevent violence against women. To prevent duplicate, parallel, or conflicting efforts between various systems and agencies, coordinated community responses are replacing autonomous, isolated responses to woman abuse. Barbara Hart (1995) describes four alternate forms of organization for coordinated community approaches to domestic violence: community partnerships, community intervention, coordinating councils, and training/technical assistance projects. Community partnering begins with a domestic violence program that develops a strategic plan of action and engages individuals and groups in the community to work on the plan. Community intervention programs are private-sector programs designed to enhance the functioning of the criminal justice and mental health response to domestic violence. Task forces or coordinating councils focus on studying and enhancing the criminal justice response to domestic violence. Training and technical assistance projects produce manuals, certification, training, videotapes, procedure guides, clearinghouses, protocols, model policies, and any other general support for violence prevention.

As coordinated community approaches to violence take shape, batterers intervention programs will be modified. Dealing with batterers who are substance abusers, are noncompliant, or have mental disorders is a much easier task when all relevant agencies are fully networked. We anticipate that these coordination efforts will greatly enhance program effectiveness.

Accountability and Safety. Batterers are accountable for their behavior, theoretically, both to their victim and to the community, through the criminal justice system. Most people who work with victims of domestic violence believe that programs and individuals who work with men who batter also need an avenue of accountability. One reason for program accountability is that participation in a batterers program is one of the best predictors that a battered woman will leave a domestic violence shelter and return to her batterer (Gondolf, 1988a). In the same way that battered women use orders, arrest, and prosecution informally to meet goals other than those held forth by the criminal justice system, battered women use batterers intervention programs, counseling, and other forms of assistance to meet those same informal goals. A battered woman may believe that after attending an initial interview or a group, the batterer will change his behavior, and some batterers do change. Batterers may also use their attendance at a batterers program as a form of partner control, in a quid pro quo fashion: "I did this program, now you must do something for me."

Many experts believe that batterers intervention programs have a responsibility to inform battered women about the structure and process of the program, what can realistically be expected from such a program based on research and evaluation, alternatives to the program, the findings from the preliminary interview, any risk factors that become apparent during the program, and any emergent threats or other behaviors that could pose a risk to her safety. Furthermore, a batterers intervention program is obligated not only to assess these threats, but to take action to ensure the victim's safety (Hart, 1988). Concern about program accountability has led to the development of batterer program standards.

Standards for Batterers Intervention Programs. There is considerable variation in programs, particularly newer ones that are not affiliated with more established model programs (Gondolf, 1990). Despite relatively few outcome studies on program effectiveness, over half of U.S. states have standards either in place or under development (Battered Women's Justice Project, 1994). In those states regulated by law, the regulatory body may be a local judicial board, a criminal justice body, or another state code agency, such as public health or child protection. Although in some areas there is near consensus between protocols (e.g., group treatment as modality of choice, treatment providers' duty to warn victims of impending violence, use of contracting, and mandatory substance abuse assessments), there are other areas where there is little consensus between standards (e.g., provision of affordable services, community service requirements, use of mental status examinations, professional credentials, and evaluation of outcomes).

Some mental health professionals view standards as premature, infringing on their right to practice according to their professional training. When these professionals encounter program standards, they see politically driven government regulations operating without a scientific basis for their dictates. In opposition to these mental health professionals are advocates for battered women, who view regulation as a necessary step to ensure accountability to the victims of violence. The criticism and discussion of batterers intervention standards have become progressively polarized in the domestic violence literature (cf. Adams, 1994; Geffner, 1995a, 1995b; Goldman, 1991; Gondolf, 1995b; Hessmiller-Trego, 1991; Rosenbaum & Stewart, 1994). Due to accountability issues in most standards, licensed mental health professionals are sometimes forced to be trained by uncredentialed paraprofessionals, advocates, and shelter workers. Standards committees are viewed by some professionals as closed bodies that have systematically excluded the mental health professions, academics, and researchers (Geffner, 1995a). A second criticism of batterers intervention standards evokes positivist arguments about the quality and quantity of research in the field. In this view, there is no empirical support for a particular way of preventing or treating domestic abuse. Because there is no empirical evidence that one intervention works better than another, critics argue that standards should not constrain practice (Geffner, 1995b; Goldman, 1991; Rosenbaum & Stewart, 1994). The authority of standards is also questioned. In most states there is no legislative authority to enforce standards. Some batterers programs argue that standards ask too much of programs in terms of compliance, when, in most cases, the regulatory body is not providing funding for the program. Profeminist men's groups are concerned that standards may falsely suggest that those programs that meet standards are safe and that the staff working in those programs are free of violence in their own lives (NOMAS, 1992).

The last, and most fundamental criticism of batterer program standards is that they were written by feminists and attempt to force practitioners to conform to this ideology. From a conservative perspective, standards are believed to inhibit free enterprise in service of a feminist agenda. Standards are also regarded by some conservatives as the product of "big government." The entrepreneurial paradigm regards regulation suspiciously, particularly regulation based on feminist, collaborative values. Due to the rising frequency of court-mandated batterer treatment (and the money that accompanies mandated treatment), proprietary agencies and practitioners have become increasingly involved in services to court-referred batterers.

Culturally Competent Programs. The first responsibility of batterers programs must be protecting battered women and ending men's violence. A secondary responsibility is to present program content relevant to minority men. Minority men complete batterers programs at lower rates than their white counterparts (Williams, 1994). Why do minority men not fare as well as white men in batterer programs? Service delivery methods can account for some of this disparity due to the gap in culturally congruent services for men of color. This is a vital issue to the safety of battered women. A program that is unable to engage men who, under the best of conditions, are resistant to cooperating increases the risk to battered women by engendering a man's resistance to get help. After a culturally insensitive program ignores the African American or Latino experience, for example, a batterer subsequently feels more justified in rejecting help and labeling programs racist or insensitive, which they may be. In a national study of batterers intervention programs, Williams and Becker (1994) found that most programs do not design service delivery with minority clients in mind. Most services are deliberately color-blind, and this often means that services do not address realities or concerns of men of color. People who design and conduct batterer programs are often mirror images of the people who complete programs—white, middle class, and educated.

How might batterer interventions become more culturally competent? A link must be made between a batterer's social realities and his behavior toward his partner. hooks (1995) believes practitioners must learn to confront African American men's scapegoating of African American women. If, as African American men often believe, oppression and environment produce violent behavior, why is their target women who, in most cases, experience the same oppressive environment?

Although many of the factors linked to violence by men are universal, there are important differences for African American men. Much of the content that is important to address with men of color is not included in batterers intervention programs (Williams, 1998). In fact, there may be resentment in addressing this content because of its apparent nonrelevance for white batterers. Both counselors and men who batter may doubt the truth or significance of necessary minority representations. But if minority men detect that they are being marginalized, they will disengage from the treatment process. Definitions of racism, community structure and environment, social context, power, control, sexism, and masculinity are often based on a Euro-American perspective rather than a minority reality. Staples (1982) urges that sexism and power dynamics be presented to African American men, but in an authentic and accurate manner.

In a study that compared men who completed treatment in either racially mixed or African American groups, race was a significant influence on trust, comfort, willingness to discuss critical subjects, and participation in treatment (Williams, 1998). Men in the African American group felt more positive about their experiences and more willing to discuss issues associated with race that they considered as influences on their behavior.

Batterers intervention programs can address cultural and racial differences in at least four ways (Williams, in press). In a color-blind group, differences do not make a difference. The group culture suggests that there are no color or culture differences. In a healthy heterogeneous group, differences due to race and culture are addressed. *Culturally specific milieu* refers to a program where a critical mass of one minority group is present, with no explicit mechanism or attempt to address concerns raised due to diversity. If concerns are raised, practitioners will not address them or do not know how to address them. Finally, in a culturally focused group, issues associated with diversity and the intersection of race, culture, gender, and violence are specifically addressed with a specific race/cultural group.

Substance abuse. For some men, alcohol use may alter their risk of violence or increase its severity. For others, alcohol may have no effect on their violence. Only a careful history of substance use and violence can determine the relationship between alcohol and woman abuse at the case level. Recognizing the confluence between substance abuse and men who batter has resulted in increased efforts to link treatment for substance abuse and batterers programs. Dual diagnosis programs are usually arranged in either sequential, parallel, or integrated patterns (Minkoff, 1989). In a sequential approach, batterers are referred to a substance abuse agency after an initial evaluation. When substance abuse treatment is completed, the recovering substance abuser rejoins the batterers program. We believe it ill-advised to refer batterers to substance abuse treatment and provide no batterer intervention program while they are in substance abuse treatment. Many men who batter remain involved with a female partner while they are in substance abuse treatment, which is currently provided on a mostly outpatient basis. There is no reason to believe a man will quit battering when he enters substance abuse treatment. The sequential model also fails when batterers do not re-enter batterers treatment, having either never made it to substance abuse treatment, dropped out of substance abuse treatment, or else chosen not to return to the batterers program. Assertive case management is one possible solution to these flaws in sequential programs, but the effectiveness of case management in retaining batterers has never been evaluated. Moreover, most agencies lack adequate staff to provide the level of professional case management required.

The parallel model of serving substance-abusing batterers is one alternative to sequential interventions. In the parallel model, batterers intervention and substance abuse treatment occur during the same time frame but in different agencies. To be successful, the parallel model requires active linkage and networking between the relevant agencies to prevent conflicting messages about power, control, codependency, triggers, and other problematic concepts (Bennett & Lawson, 1994).

An alternative to sequential and parallel models is an integrated model. In this approach, substance abuse treatment and batterers intervention occur in the same setting. In less integrated programs, substance abuse modules and violence modules are interwoven or "separate but equal" within the program (e.g., Conner & Ackerley, 1994; Manzano, 1989). In a fully integrated model, interventions for woman abuse and interventions for substance abuse would be based on a common theoretical perspective, such as power (Gondolf, 1995a; McClelland, 1975).

Batterer-Program Fit. Batterers may differ not only in the violence-based typologies discussed earlier in this chapter, but also in other stage markers that could be used to refine interventions. Four markers that have drawn attention are levels of moral development, stages of motivation, attachment characteristics, and chronicity. Gondolf (1987) argues that Kolberg's six-stage theory of moral development may be applicable to batterers and batterers intervention programs. Interventions for batterers who see their participation in a program as an inappropriate punishment that requires their obedience could be different than interventions for batterers who understand not only that they broke the law but that they need to learn how to regard and relate to women as equal partners. So far, research has not been directed at moral development and batterers intervention.

Several observers have suggested that Prochaska, DiClemente, and Norcross's (1992) stages of motivational change might be employed to better fit intervention to a batterers' readiness to change (Edleson, 1996; Gelles, 1994; Murphy & Baxter, in press). Men who deny they have a problem (other than getting caught), men who accept their behavior as criminal and want to change, and men who have successfully changed and want to maintain their success might benefit from different programming. Confrontation-oriented programs (e.g., Pence & Paymar, 1993) use interventions that assume batterers are uniformly in the precontemplation or denial stage of change, whereas cognitive-behavioral programs use interventions more appropriate to the action stage of change (Murphy & Baxter, 1997). By using interventions targeting only one stage of change, batterers intervention programs run the risk of failing to engage a substantial proportion of the men in their programs, a risk confirmed by the rates of attrition reviewed earlier. Application of the motivational model to batterer programs has not yet been studied.

Men with different attachment characteristics may do better with an approach that differs substantially from typical batterer programs in the 1990s. To date, only one study has examined the relationship between program type and batterer type. Saunders (1994) randomly assigned batterers to 20 week, 2.5 hours of either profeminist cognitive behavioral program or psychodynamic, process-oriented program. Partner and police reports showed no difference by treatment, except that men with dependent personality features did substantially better in the psychodynamic condition. This research presents an interesting challenge to the way we currently conceptualize programs for batterers.

Another way to characterize batterers is by chronicity. First-time batterers may respond to programs differently than men who have prior battering offenses. One of the most important points about generally violent, antisocial batterers, a point that is usually overlooked, is that other interventions have already failed to deter them from violence. To us, it seems naive to think that a standard batterers intervention program will succeed where other, often many, programs have failed. Gondolf (1988b) suggests that long-term treatment or some form of residential treatment might be considered with these batterers. Conversely, a 52-week program may miss the mark with a man who has shoved his partner against the wall once and is horrified at his behavior. Although such a man would be a distinct minority in the groups of court-referred batterers with which we are familiar, he is much more likely to be found in voluntary (partner-referred) or couples programs.

Maintenance of gains is an important aspect of the change process (Prochaska, Norcross, & DiClemente, 1994), but few batterers programs have addressed the issues of continuing care or relapse prevention. Relapse prevention has proved useful in the treatment of substance abuse (Marlatt & Gordon, 1985; Prochaska et al., 1992). Relapse prevention or continuing care programs for batterers are in the early stages of development (Daniels & Murphy, 1996; Jennings, 1990).

Programs for Couples

With the exception of discussing the meaning and extent of women's violence toward men, the debate that has evoked more animation than any other is the issue of providing counseling to couples where the man has been violent. It seems logical to believe that working with a couple, if a functional couple were available, would be a more systematic and effective intervention because the man was violent toward the woman in the context of couple interaction. But critics of couples counseling in cases of woman abuse argue that conjoint counseling forces women to share in the responsibility for violence and increases the risk to women of further violence. Historically, systems-oriented therapists have been myopic and frequently ignored larger, more influential systems outside the nuclear family (Bograd, 1984). Cautions and opposition for couples counseling in cases of woman abuse come from many quarters, including experts on men who batter (Adams, 1988), most state standards for batterers intervention programs (Battered Women's Justice Project, 1994), and some family therapists (Bograd, 1984; Jacobson, Gottman, & Shortt, 1995; Kaufman, 1992).

There are more than philosophical reasons to be concerned about counseling couples. A major concern is that those providing counseling to couples either ignore violence for other issues, or else fail to see violence at all. Practitioners are known to greatly underestimate the existence of woman abuse in their couple clients unless they proactively screen for it. Of 132 couples seeking counseling at one university-based clinic, only 6% of the women indicated abuse to be a problem in their relationship at intake (O'Leary, Vivian, & Malone, 1992). When asked a direct question about violence in a private interview, however, 44% of the women acknowledged they had been victims at some time in the marriage. When the assessment expanded to using a checklist of abusive behaviors, the proportion of women in this sample who could be classified as victims of abuse had gone from 1 in 16 to over half (53%). In addition to the problem of detection, marriage and family therapists may be unprepared to intervene, even when violence is identified. A sample of members of the American Association of Marriage and Family Therapists were presented with two actual cases of severe woman abuse taken from court records (Hansen, Harway, & Cervantes, 1991). The therapists were asked to evaluate the case and make recommendations for intervention. About 40% of the therapists did not indicate that domestic violence was an issue in the case, 55% did not believe the case required immediate action, and only 8 of 362 therapists recognized the potential for lethality.

On the other hand, some battered women prefer couples counseling (Brannen & Rubin, 1996; Sirles, Lipchik, & Kowalski, 1993). Current thinking in much of the domestic violence field is that battered women know what is best for them. After all, battered women have a track record of survival, and they—more than professionals—are able to judge their own safety. This line of thinking leads us to an interesting question: What if a battered woman requests couples counseling? Does she still know what is best?

Promoters of couple groups for men who batter and their partners now attend more to victim safety, largely because of criticism by advocates that couples counseling puts battered women at risk. Often, men in couples counseling are staked in conformity, less violent, and not violent outside the family; consequently, they are more motivated to complete the program.

Early reviews of couples programs for abuse were not encouraging (e.g., Tolman & Bennett, 1990). Couples programs are now beginning to report results from improved studies. In one recent report, 42 couples were randomly assigned to either gender-specific or couples groups (Brannen & Rubin, 1996). The gender-specific groups employed the Duluth curriculum (Pence & Paymar, 1993), and the couples program used Neidig and Friedman's (1984) model for couples groups. Unlike many couples programs, which screen out serious batterers, this program targeted court-referred batterers, a third of whom had severely abused their partners. Weekly individual contact with the victim checked for fear and safety issues. During the program, six instances of abuse were reported, with four of the six being in the gender-specific program.

At posttest, there were no differences in any physical abuse measure. At 6-month follow-up, 26 of 42 couples were re-interviewed. One man of the 12 couples group participants had been violent by victim self-report, and one man of the 14 gender-specific group participants had been violent. Program satisfaction was highest in the couples group (Brannen & Rubin, 1996). Of course, this is but a single small study. Other studies comparing gender-specific and couples groups are under way.

How does one decide whether couples counseling is appropriate? Our own perspective is that counseling for couples where the man has battered is not a safe alternative unless the following conditions are present: (a) the woman, when not in the man's presence, and not in response to a question about couples counseling, initiates a request for couples counseling; (b) the woman has a separate domestic violence counselor and a safety plan; (c) the man has either completed a batterers program or has been nonviolent for 6 months by the woman's report; (d) the man accepts responsibility for his violence and demonstrates regret by words and action; (e) nonviolence remains one of the foci of the conjoint work; (f) non-physical abuse and controlling behavior are included in the discussion of violence; and (g) the couples therapist has a working relationship with a battered women's program. By suggesting these criteria for couples counseling, we do not mean to imply that other forms of counseling are safe, or that similar safeguards are not needed. At this point, we do believe that evidence demands such precautions be met prior to couples counseling.

Summary

Understanding and intervening with men who batter can only occur by understanding the male dominant cultures that support men to control the lives of women. The extent to which an individual man incorporates male dominant thinking, practices controlling behavior, and emotionally or physically abuses his partner depends on personal experience, which often begins in the family of origin, moves through peer culture indoctrination and reinforcement, extends to the very moment he decides to act, and also incorporates the response of the local culture of accountability. Attempts to punctuate, emphasize, and typify these sequences of behavior are worthwhile, but a micro-approach to men's violent behavior, divorced from the culture in which it incubates, may increase the risk to battered women.

We believe that knowing more about batterers and batterers intervention is worth the effort: Knowing more about batterers and batterer interventions will help reduce violence against women. In the extreme, however, the various perspectives on men who batter run the risk of becoming "nothing buts": A batterer is nothing but mentally ill, nothing but a criminal, nothing but part of a couple, nothing but controlling. These are simplifications that have lost their capacity to explain. Woman abuse is a complex phenomenon with many causes. We do battered women no favors by reducing the discussion to the level of slogans.

Batterers intervention programs are as effective as other programs that target difficult men, be they alcoholics, men with mental disorders, or other types of criminals. The development and evaluation of batterers programs is relatively recent. Early models have had some limited success, and there is reason to believe that the next generation of batterer interventions will have greater success. The "one size fits all" approach to batterer programs provided by lone agencies will be replaced by modularized or differential programming that is fully networked with criminal justice and health services, services for battered women, and other human service agencies. The complexity of woman abuse and men who batter demands a complex response, one that is far too difficult for singular, simple efforts. The safety of battered women is the criterion around which programs for batterers must be organized.

References

Adams, D. (1988). Treatment models for men who batter: A profeminist analysis. In K. Yllö & M. Bograd (Eds.), *Feminist perspectives on wife abuse* (pp. 176-199). Newbury Park, CA: Sage.

Adams, D. (1994). Point/counterpoint: Treatment standards for abuser programs. *Violence Update, 5*(1), 5, 9.

Adams, D., & McCormick, A. (1982). Men unlearning violence: A group approach. In M. Roy (Ed.), *The abusive partner: An analysis of domestic battering* (pp. 170-197). New York: Van Nostrand Reinhold.

American Psychiatric Association. (1994). *Diagnostic and Statistical Manual* (4th ed.). Washington, DC: Author.

Bachman, R., & Saltzman, L. E. (1995, August). *Violence against women: Estimates from the redesigned survey* (NCJ-154348). Washington, DC: U.S. Department of Justice.

Battered Women's Justice Project. (1994). *State batterers programs.* Unpublished manuscript, 4032 Chicago Avenue South, Minneapolis, MN 55407.

Bennett, L., & Lawson, M. (1994). Barriers to cooperation between domestic violence and substance abuse programs. *Families in Society, 75*, 277-286.

Berk, R. A. (1993). What the scientific evidence shows: On average, we can do no better than arrest. In R. J. Gelles & D. R. Loseke (Eds.), *Current controversies on family violence* (pp. 323-336). Thousand Oaks, CA: Sage.

Bograd, M. (1984). Family systems approaches to wife battering. *American Journal of Orthopsychiatry, 54,* 558-568.

Brannen, S. J., & Rubin, A. (1996). Comparing the effectiveness of gender-specific and couples groups in a court-mandated spouse abuse treatment program. *Research on Social Work Practice, 6,* 405-424.

Cadsky, O., & Crawford, M. (1988). Establishing batterer typologies in a clinical sample of men who assault their female partners. *Canadian Journal of Community Mental Health, 7,* 49-63.

Caesar, P. L. (1988). Exposure to violence in the family of origin among wife abusers and maritally nonviolent men. *Violence and Victims, 3,* 49-63.

Chen, H., Bersani, C., Myers, S. C., & Denton, R. (1989). Evaluating the effectiveness of a court sponsored abuser treatment program. *Journal of Family Violence, 4,* 309-322.

Coleman, D. H., & Straus, M. A. (1983). Alcohol abuse and family violence. In E. Gottheil, K. A. Druley, T. E. Skoloda, & H. M. Waxman (Eds.), *Alcohol, drug abuse, and aggression* (pp. 104-124). Springfield, IL: Charles C Thomas.

Conner, K. E., & Ackerley, G. D. (1994). Alcohol-related battering: Developing treatment strategies. *Journal of Family Violence, 9,* 143-155.

Daniels, J. W., & Murphy, C. M. (1996). *Stages and process of change in batterers' treatment.* Paper submitted for publication, University of Maryland Baltimore County.

Dinwiddie, S. H. (1992). Psychiatric disorders among wife batterers. *Comprehensive Psychiatry, 33,* 411-416.

DuMont, M. P. (1992). *Treating the poor.* Belmont, MA: Dympha Press.

Dutton, D. G. (1994). Patriarchy and wife assault: The ecological fallacy. *Violence and Victims, 9,* 167-182.

Dutton, D. G. (1995). *The domestic assault of women: Psychological and criminal justice perspectives* (2nd ed.). Vancouver: University of British Columbia Press.

Dutton D. G., & Starzomski, A. J. (1993). Borderline personality in perpetrators of psychological and physical abuse. *Violence and Victims, 8,* 327-337.

Edleson, J. L. (1996). Controversy and change in batterers' programs. In J. L. Edleson & Z. C. Eisikovits (Eds.), *Future interventions with battered women and their families* (pp. 154-169). Thousand Oaks, CA: Sage.

Edleson, J. L., & Syers, M. (1990). The relative effectiveness of group treatments for men who batter. *Social Work Research and Abstracts, 26,* 10-17.

Edleson, J. L., & Syers, M. (1991). The effects of group treatment for men who batter: An 18-month follow-up study. *Research in Social Work Practice, 1,* 227-243.

Edleson, J. L., & Tolman, R. M. (1992). *Intervention for men who batter: An ecological approach.* Newbury Park, CA: Sage.

Elliot, F. (1982). Biological contributions to family violence. In J. C. Hansen & L. R. Barnhill (Eds.), *Clinical approaches to family violence* (pp. 37-58). Rockville, MD: Aspen.

Fagan, J. (1996). *Criminalization of domestic violence: Promises and limits.* Rockville, MD: National Institute of Justice.

Finn, P. (1991). Civil protection orders: A flawed opportunity for intervention. In M. Steinman (Ed.), *Woman battering: Policy responses* (pp. 155-190). Cincinnati, OH: Anderson.

Fitch, F., & Papantonio, A. (1983). Men who batter: Some pertinent characteristics. *Journal of Nervous & Mental Disease, 17,* 190-192.

Ford, D. A., & Regoli, M. J. (1993). The criminal prosecution of wife assaulters: Process, problems, and effects. In N. Hilton (Ed.), *Legal responses to wife assault: Current trends and evaluations* (pp. 96-126). Newbury Park, CA: Sage.

Ganley, A. L. (1989). Integrating feminist and social learning analyses of aggression: Creating multiple models for intervention with men who batter. In P. L. Caesar & L. K. Hamberger (Eds.), *Treating men who batter: Theory, practice, and programs* (pp. 196-235). New York: Springer.

Geffner, R. (1995a). Standards for batterer intervention: Editor's response. *Family Violence and Sexual Assault Bulletin, 11*(3-4), 29-32.

Geffner, R. (1995b). Standards in the family violence field. *Family Violence and Sexual Assault Bulletin, 11*(1-2), 3.

Gelles, R. J. (1993). Through a sociological lens: Social structure and family violence. In R. J. Gelles & D. R. Loseke (Eds.), *Current controversies on family violence* (pp. 31-46). Newbury Park, CA: Sage.

Gelles, R. J. (1994, July). *Common features of violence in and out of the family.* Invited address, National Conference on Family Violence Research and Practice, University of Nebraska, Omaha.

Goldman, J. (1991). Protect us from the protectors. *Family Violence and Sexual Assault Bulletin, 7*(3), 15-17.

Gondolf, E. W. (1987). Changing men who batter: A developmental model for integrated interventions. *Journal of Family Violence, 2,* 335-349.

Gondolf, E. W. (1988a). The effect of batterer counseling on shelter outcome. *Journal of Interpersonal Violence, 3,* 275-289.

Gondolf, E. W. (1988b). Who are those guys? Toward a behavioral typology of batterers. *Violence & Victims, 3,* 187-203.

Gondolf, E. W. (1990). An exploratory study of court-mandated batterer programs. *Response to the Victimization of Women & Children, 13,* 7-11.

Gondolf, E. W. (1995a). Alcohol abuse, wife assault, and power needs. *Social Service Review, 69,* 275-283.

Gondolf, E. W. (1995b). Gains and process in state batterer programs and standards. *Family Violence and Sexual Assault Bulletin, 11*(3-4), 27-28.

Gondolf, E. W. (1996, November). *Characteristics of court-mandated batterers in four cities.* Paper presented at the annual meeting of the American Society of Criminology, Chicago.

Gondolf, E. W. (1997). Expanding batterer program evaluations. In G. Kaufman Kantor & J. Jasinski (Eds.), *Out of darkness: Contemporary research perspectives on family violence* (pp. 208-218). Thousand Oaks, CA: Sage.

Gondolf, E. W., & Foster, R. A. (1991). Wife assault among VA alcohol rehabilitation patients. *Hospital and Community Psychiatry, 42,* 74-79.

Gondolf, E. W., & McFerron, J. R. (1989). Handling battering men: Police action in wife abuse cases. *Criminal Justice & Behavior, 16,* 429-439.

Gondolf, E. W., & Russell, D. (1986). The case against anger control treatment for batterers. *Response to the Victimization of Women & Children, 9,* 2-5.

Gottman, J. M., Jacobson, N. S., Rushe, R. H., Shortt, J. W., Babcock, J., LaTaillade, J. J., & Waltz, J. (1995). The relationship between heart rate reactivity, emotionally aggressive behavior, and general violence in batterers. *Journal of Family Psychology, 9*, 227-248.

Gruszinski, R. J., & Carrillo, T. P. (1988). Who completes batterers treatment groups? An empirical investigation. *Journal of Family Violence, 3*, 141-150.

Hamberger, L. K., & Hastings, J. E. (1986). Personality correlates of men who abuse their partners: A cross-validation study. *Journal of Family Violence, 1*, 323-341.

Hamberger, L. K., & Hastings, J. E. (1991). Personality correlates of men who batter and nonviolent men: Some continuities and discontinuities. *Journal of Family Violence, 6*, 131-147.

Hamberger, L. K., & Potente, T. (1994). Counseling heterosexual women arrested for domestic violence: Implications for theory and practice. *Violence and Victims, 9*, 125-137.

Hamilton, C. J., & Collins, J. J. (1981). The role of alcohol in wife beating and child abuse: A review of the literature. In J. J. Collins (Ed.), *Drinking and crime: Perspectives on the relationship between alcohol consumption and criminal behavior* (pp. 253-287). New York: Guilford.

Hansen, M., Harway, M., & Cervantes, N. N. (1991). Therapists perceptions of severity in cases of family violence. *Violence & Victims, 4*, 275-286.

Harrell, A. (1991). *Evaluation of court-ordered treatment for domestic violence offenders: Summary and recommendations.* Washington, DC: The Urban Institute.

Harrell, A. V., Smith, B., & Newmark, L. (1993). *Court processing and the effects of restraining orders for domestic violence victims.* Washington, DC: The Urban Institute.

Hart, B. (1988). Beyond the "Duty to Warn": A therapist's duty to protect. In K. Yllö & M. Bograd (Eds.), *Feminist perspectives on wife abuse* (pp. 234-248). Newbury Park, CA: Sage.

Hart, B. (1995, March). *Coordinated community approaches to domestic violence.* Paper presented to the Strategic Planning Workshop on Violence Against Women, National Institute of Justice, Washington, DC.

Hastings, J. E., & Hamberger, L. K. (1988). Personality characteristics of spouse abusers: A controlled comparison. *Violence and Victims, 3*, 31-48.

Hessmiller-Trego, J. (1991). Letter to the editor. *Family Violence and Sexual Assault Bulletin, 7*(4), 24-25.

Holtzworth-Munroe, A., & Stuart, G. L. (1994). Typologies of male batterers: Three subtypes and the differences between them. *Psychological Bulletin, 116*, 476-497.

hooks, b. (1995). *Killing rage: Ending racism.* New York: Owl Books.

Horton, A. L., Simonidis, K. M., & Simonidis, L. L. (1987). Legal remedies for spousal abuse: Victim characteristics, expectations, and satisfaction. *Journal of Family Violence, 2*, 265-279.

Hotaling, G. T., & Sugarman, D. B. (1986). An analysis of risk markers in husband to wife violence: The current state of knowledge. *Violence and Victims, 1*, 101-124.

Island, D., & Letellier, P. (1991). *Men who beat the men who love them: Battered gay men and domestic violence.* Binghamton, NY: Haworth.

Jacobson, N. (1994, July). *Typology of batterers.* Invited address, National Conference on Family Violence Research and Practice, University of Nebraska, Omaha.

Jacobson, N. S., Gottman, J. M., & Shortt, J. W. (1995). The distinction between Type 1 and Type 2 batterers—Further consideration: Reply to Ornduff et al. (1995), Margolin et al. (1995), and Walker (1995). *Journal of Family Psychology, 3*, 272-279.

Jennings, J. L. (1990). Preventing relapse versus "stopping" domestic violence: Do we expect too much from battering men? *Journal of Family Violence, 5,* 43-60.

Kandel-Englander, E. (1992). Wife battering and violence outside the family. *Journal of Interpersonal Violence, 7,* 464-470.

Kantor, G. K., & Asdigian, N. (1993, October). *Socialization to alcohol-related family violence: Disentangling the effects of family history on current violence.* Paper presented at the Annual Meetings of the American Society of Criminology, Phoenix, AZ.

Kantor, G., & Straus, M. A. (1987). The drunken bum theory of wife beating. *Social Problems, 34,* 213-230.

Kaufman, G. (1992). The mysterious disappearance of battered women in family therapists' offices: Male privilege colluding with male violence. *Journal of Marital and Family Therapy, 18,* 233-243.

Lane, G., & Russell, T. (1989). Second-order systemic work with violent couples. In P. L. Caesar & L. K. Hamberger (Eds.), *Treating men who batter* (pp. 135-162). New York: Springer.

Leonard, K. E., Brommet, E. J., Parkinson, D. K., Day, N. L., & Ryan, C. M. (1985). Patterns of alcohol abuse and physically aggressive behavior in men. *Journal of Studies on Alcohol, 46,* 279-282.

Leonard, K. E., & Jacob, T. (1988). Alcohol, alcoholism, and family violence. In V. B. VanHasselt, R. L. Morrison, A. S. Bellack, & M. Hersen (Eds.), *Handbook of family violence* (pp. 383-406). New York: Plenum.

Lindquist, C. (1986). Battered women as co-alcoholics: Treatment implications and case studies. *Psychotherapy, 23,* 622-628.

Manzano, T. A. (1989, April). *Domestic violence and chemical dependency: A dual track program design (The Tulsa Model).* Paper presented at Second National Working With Batterers Conference, Baltimore, MD.

Margolin, G. (1979). Conjoint marital therapy to enhance anger management and reduce spouse abuse. *American Journal of Family Therapy, 7,* 13-24.

Margolin, G., & Burman, B. (1993). Wife abuse versus marital violence: Different terminologies, explanations, and solutions. *Clinical Psychology Review, 13,* 59-73.

Marlatt, G. A., & Gordon, J. R. (1985). *Relapse prevention: Maintenance strategies in the treatment of addictive behaviors.* New York: Guilford.

Martin, D. (1976). *Battered wives.* New York: Pocket Books.

McClelland, D. C. (1975). *Power: The inner experience.* New York: John Wiley.

Minkoff, K. (1989). An integrated treatment model for dual diagnosis of psychosis and addiction. *Hospital & Community Psychiatry, 40,* 1031-1036.

Murphy, C. M., & Baxter, V. A. (1997). Motivating batterers to change in the treatment context. *Journal of Interpersonal Violence, 12,* 607-619.

Murphy, C. M., Meyer, S. L., & O'Leary, K. D. (1993). Family of origin violence and MCMI-II psychopathology among partner assaultive men. *Violence & Victims, 8,* 165-176.

Neidig, P. H., & Friedman, D. H. (1984). *Spouse abuse: A treatment program for couples.* Champaign, IL: Research Press.

NOMAS. (1992, July). *Position paper of the Ending Men's Violence Network.* Chicago: National Organization of Men Against Sexism.

O'Leary, K. D. (1993). Through a psychological lens: Personality traits, personality disorders, and levels of violence. In R. J. Gelles & D. R. Loseke (Eds.), *Current controversies on family violence* (pp. 7-30). Newbury Park, CA: Sage.

O' Leary, K. D., Vivian, D., & Malone, J. (1992). Assessment of physical aggression against women in marriage: The need for multimodal assessment. *Behavioral Assessment, 14,* 5-14.

Pence, E., & Paymar, M. (1993). *Education groups for men who batter: The Duluth model.* New York: Springer.

Pernanen, K. (1991). *Alcohol in human violence.* New York: Guilford.

Prochaska, J. O., DiClemente, C. C., & Norcross, J. C. (1992). In search of how people change: Applications to addictive behavior. *American Psychologist, 47,* 1102-1114.

Prochaska, J. O., Norcross, J. C., & DiClemente, C. C. (1994). *Changing for good.* New York: Morrow.

Renzetti, C. (1992). *Violent betrayal: Partner abuse in lesbian relationships.* Newbury Park, CA: Sage.

Rosenbaum, A., Hoge, S. K., & Adelman, S. A. (1994). Head injury in partner-abusive men. *Journal of Consulting and Clinical Psychology, 62,* 1187-1193.

Rosenbaum, A., & Stewart, T. P. (1994). Point/counterpoint: Treatment standards for abuser programs. *Violence Update, 5*(1), pp. 9, 11.

Saunders, D. G. (1992). A typology of men who batter: Three types derived from cluster analysis. *American Journal of Orthopsychiatry, 62,* 264-275.

Saunders, D. G. (1994, November). *Cognitive-behavioral and process-psychodynamic treatments for men who batter: Interactions between offender traits and treatment.* Paper presented at the Association for the Advancement of Behavior Therapy.

Schmidt, J. D., & Sherman, L. W. (1993). Does arrest deter domestic violence? *American Behavioral Scientist, 36,* 601-609.

Shepard, M. (1992). Predicting batterer recidivism five years after community intervention. *Journal of Family Violence, 7,* 167-178.

Sherman, L. W., & Berk, R. A. (1984). The specific deterrent effects of arrest for domestic assault. *American Sociological Review, 49,* 261-272.

Shields, N. M., McCall, G. J., & Hanneke, C. R. (1988). Patterns of family and nonfamily violence: Violent husbands and violent men. *Violence and Victims, 3,* 83-97.

Sirles, E. A., Lipchik, E., & Kowalski, K. (1993). A consumer's perspective on domestic violence interventions. *Journal of Family Violence, 8,* 267-276.

Staples, R. (1982). *Black masculinity: The black male's role in American society.* San Francisco, CA: The Black Scholar Press.

Stordeur, R. A., & Stille, R. (1989). *Ending men's violence against their partners.* Newbury Park, CA: Sage.

Straus, M. A. (1993). Physical abuse by wives: A major social problem. In R. J. Gelles & D. R. Loseke (Eds.), *Current controversies on family violence* (pp. 67-87). Newbury Park, CA: Sage.

Toby, J. (1957). Social disorganization and stakes in conformity: Complimentary factors in the predatory behavior of hoodlums. *Journal of Criminal Law, Criminology, and Political Science, 48,* 12-17.

Tolman, R. M. (1996). Expanding sanctions for batterers: What can we do besides counseling them? In J. L. Edleson & Z. C. Eisikovits (Eds.), *Future interventions with battered women and their families* (pp. 170-185). Thousand Oaks, CA: Sage.

Tolman, R. M., & Bennett, L. (1990). A review of quantitative research on men who batter. *Journal of Interpersonal Violence, 5,* 87-118.

Tolman, R. M., & Edleson, J. L. (1995). Intervention for men who batter: A review of research. In S. Stith & M. A. Straus (Eds.), *Understanding partner violence: Prevalence, causes, consequences, and solutions* (pp. 262-274). Minneapolis, MN: National Council on Family Relations.

Tolman, R. M., Edleson, J. L., & Fendrich, M. (1995, July). *The application of the theory of planned behavior to abusive men's cessation of violent behavior.* Paper presented at the Fourth International Family Violence Research Conference, University of New Hampshire, Durham, NH.

Weisz, A. N., Tolman, R. M., & Bennett, L. W. (in press). An ecological study of nonresidential services for battered women within a comprehensive community protocol for domestic violence. *Journal of Family Violence.*

Williams, O. J. (1994). Group work with African American men who batter: Toward more ethnically sensitive practice. *Journal of Comparative Family Studies, 25,* 91-103.

Williams, O. J. (1995). Treatment for African American men who batter. *CURA Reporter, 25,* 6-10.

Williams, O. J. (1998). Healing and confronting the African-American man who batters. In R. A. Carrillo & J. Tello (Eds.), *Family violence and men of color: Healing the wounded male spirit* (pp. 74-94). New York, NY: Springer.

Williams, O. J., & Becker, L. R. (1994). Partner abuse programs and cultural competence: The results of a national study. *Violence and Victims, 9,* 287-295.

Witwer, M. B., & Crawford, C. A. (1995). *A coordinated approach to reducing family violence: Conference highlights* (NCJ155184). Washington, DC: U.S. Department of Justice.

Yllö, K. (1993). Through a feminist lens: Gender, power, and violence. In R. J. Gelles & D. R. Loseke (Eds.), *Current controversies on family violence* (pp. 47-61). Newbury Park, CA: Sage.

Zorza, J. (1992). The criminal law of misdemeanor domestic violence, 1970-1990. *Journal of Criminal Law and Criminology, 83,* 240-279.

• *CHAPTER 10* •

Understanding Elder Abuse

LINNER WARD GRIFFIN

Although literature and research on elder abuse or elder maltreatment have received increased attention during the 1980s and 1990s, research on elder abuse is still sparse, when compared with the attention given to child abuse and spouse abuse. This chapter presents an overview of the most recent research on the subject. Some information about elder abuse is presented; lingering unanswered questions and issues also are raised.

The first part of the chapter introduces the reader to the growing number of elders in the population and to the rights reserved for them by the national government. The second part recognizes the lack of valid data about abuse among older people. The third part defines elder abuse and presents the characteristics of both victims and perpetrators of elder maltreatment. The fourth part looks at abuse among minority elders, recognizing differences between the majority and minority populations and their respective support networks. Abuse in institutions is examined in the fifth part. The next section reviews states' enacted responses to elder abuse and examines the public's use of laws to address elder maltreatment. Concerns regarding access and use of social services are raised in the seventh part. The chapter concludes with a summary of facts about elder abuse and recommendations by the author for interim measures that have the potential to reduce elder maltreatment.

Who Are the Elderly?

The elderly represent an unusual segment of the population in this country and in the world. One reason for this statement is the lack of clarity about when one becomes elderly. Programs and organizations that serve older adults use different age designations to define their clientele. The American Association for Retired Persons, the premier advocacy group for aged people, invites individuals to become members when they reach the age of 50. Older Americans Act services become available to some spouses of elders at age 55. Services funded by Title 20 and other sources of funding through the U.S. Department of Health and Human Services become available to people who have reached 60 years of age. However, individuals may retire with reduced Social Security benefits at age 62 or with full benefits at age 65. As part of these services, Medicare becomes available for retirees at age 65. Recently passed federal legislation has pushed back the "full benefit" retirement age for some younger people until age 68, and it will later be pushed back to age 70. Indeed, determination of exactly when one becomes elderly is unclear. The determination seems dependent on organizations or programs with different agendas.

Some things are known. According to U.S. Bureau of the Census projections, there were 33.5 million people age 65 or older in the United States in 1995, a number that represented 12.8% of the nation's population. This number represents one of every eight Americans, 19.8 million of whom are older women and 13.7 million of whom are older men. The oldest of the elderly—or people age 85 or older—are the most rapidly growing elderly age group. The oldest of the elderly numbered 3 million in 1994, or 10% of all people over 65. This number represents over 1% of the total population. It is expected that by 2050, the number of individuals age 85 or older will reach 19 million (Administration on Aging [AoA] & American Association of Retired Persons [AARP], 1996). It is a sad commentary that as the number of elderly increases, so do the pressures that surround growing old. One very real societal concern is the negative behaviors associated with abuse of the elderly.

The Rights of the Elderly

Elders are adult citizens or residents of the United States. As such, the aged have rights and privileges afforded all adults within this country. Although their physical and/or mental conditions may make them dependent on others to survive, they are not children. The 1981 White House Conference on Aging defined the following as the rights of aged people:

To have basic needs met,
To have adequate medical care,
To feel respected,
To obtain employment based on merit,
To have both moral and financial support from the family and the community,
To share in community recreational and educational resources,
To live and die with dignity, and
To have access to knowledge regarding how to improve later life and to the resources that enable improvement.

Unique Distinctions of Elder Abuse

The issue of aging should be of great concern to us all because everyone and everything ages. We all will be affected by society's views and behaviors toward its older citizens. Aging issues may attract more interest in the future because there will be more older citizens. By the year 2000, half of the population will be near 50 years of age (Butler, Lewis, & Sunderland, 1991). The life spans of men and women are increasing also. During the eighteenth century, the average life span was only 35 years; by the 1900s, the life span had lengthened to 50 years (Steinmetz, 1988). In 1995, people reaching the age of 65 had an average life expectancy of an additional 17.4 years—18.9 years for females and 15.6 years for males. During that year (1995), about 2.0 million people celebrated their 65th birthday (5,575 per day). In that same year, almost 1.7 million people 64 or older died, resulting in a net increase of 352,000, or 964 per day (AoA & AARP, 1996). As a result, there are more elderly people. Moreover, people are allowed to work as long as they desire, reducing their need to depend on others for support (Steinmetz, 1978). At the turn of the century, individuals were members of larger families, which provided whatever help their members needed. This type of support system, which stressed interdependence, responded to the needs of older sick relatives because there were more relatives to share the various responsibilities.

Today, the life span is longer (70-plus years), and the trend is to have smaller families. Smaller numbers in the nuclear family have strained the traditional support system, as fewer are asked to do more for the older members and for longer periods of time. Health and human service professionals have become increasingly aware of abuse of the elderly in response to familial strain and stresses.

Furthermore, societal attitudes toward aged people have tended to put the aged on the borders rather than in the mainstream of our society. The facts that we are living longer and that there will be more aged people in the future are but two reasons why elder abuse requires our attention today. Contemporary circumstances and attitudes may predispose caregivers and other adults to be abusive with the elderly. Elder abuse is an important issue for the entire population because as the number of elderly people increases, the number of abuse cases will likely increase unless something is done to address the problem.

Although elder abuse has much in common with other types of abuse, it also has some differences. An examination of these similarities and differences follows.

Similarities

Elder maltreatment researchers and adult protection workers have identified several similarities between elder abuse and other types of domestic violence. Although the cycle of violence (tension–explosion–honeymoon) is usually associated with battered women (Walker, 1985), it may also be a common experience for elderly women and men who are abused. Another similarity between elder abuse and other types of abuse is the family context within which this problem has been viewed. Nonfamily members may perpetrate abuse of the elderly, but most of the abuse of the aged individual occurs within the family. Often, unresolved conflicts among family members manifest themselves through violent behavior inflicted on the older family member. Prior use of violence in the family's history also may manifest itself as a recurring theme through elder abuse.

Differences

Although these similarities exist, there are also issues unique to the abuse of elders. A list of these differences follows.

One difference is that ageism and the aging process in and of itself may result in attitudes and stresses on potential caregivers that could predispose them to use abuse against aged people.

The role of being contributors to society may be reduced as individuals age. The ability to function and contribute may be replaced by societal and individual definitions of ability. These societal definitions may influence how even close family relatives, such as siblings, nephews, nieces, and children, view their aging family member. These are potential caregivers, especially when one recalls that only about 5% of the elderly population live in institutions. Most are either living alone or with relatives.

The tendency toward ageism promotes the real possibility that when and/or if the functioning of older people is reduced, potential support systems and caregivers could take greater control of their lives. This tendency also reduces the amount of personal control exercised by the elderly and the life choices they are able or allowed to make. Older people may need assistance, but many are not totally disabled. The help provided by caregivers could be stressful to them, even though it may also be useful. Rebellion against help could be viewed by caregivers as being uncooperative or ungrateful and as further proof of the elder's inability to make good choices rather than a desire to remain independent. Caregivers may use abuse as a mean of maintaining control over the elder or to release tension. Abuse may take several forms: physical violence, overmedication, neglect, or isolation. Types of elder abuse will be discussed later in this chapter.

An aged individual may still be very capable of functioning independently. The perpetrator may victimize the aged person because the perpetrator is financially dependent and the victim is physically vulnerable. In such cases, the victim is both physically abused and financially exploited.

Stress on the traditional family support system in combination with negative attitudes and a lack of respect toward the older and more dependent, vulnerable family member may also be factors that predispose some to be abusive with aged men and women.

Maltreatment of older people must be examined within a social and familial context. There must be a clear message accepted by all age groups that the elderly have rights, deserve support, and deserve to be protected from abuse.

Definition of Abuse

That elders are abused is a confusing and tragic reality. The actual incidence of this abuse among older Americans is unclear. Projections include 4% (Crystal, 1987), 5% (Poertner, 1986), 7.1% (Pierce &

Trotta, 1986), and 1.57 million people annually (Tatara, 1994b; U.S. Bureau of the Census, 1994). Helping professionals are dedicated to helping older people resolve their problems, reduce their pain, and eliminate the threat of maltreatment. To be helpful and eradicate abuse, practitioners must understand the concept of maltreatment, and they must have a clear definition of the term. Definitions give researchers and service providers guidance in framing and responding to problems such as elder maltreatment. If the definitions are either faulty or noninclusive of diversity, one's perceptions and professional capacity to accurately address the problem are restricted (Lucas, 1989). A critical review of the literature indicates that a comprehensive understanding of elder maltreatment is lacking. Also apparent is a limited understanding of maltreatment of the aged among diverse cultural groups.

The Senate Special Committee on Aging (U.S. Congress, 1977) and the U.S. Select Committee on Aging (U.S. Congress, 1980) provided a framework to define elder abuse, including such categories as physical, emotional, psychological, verbal, and sexual abuse; financial exploitation; neglect by caregiver; and self-neglect. These definitions were broad, offering a sweeping description of each category of maltreatment but they ignored such issues as degree of maltreatment, ethnic diversity, or cultural context. Specifically, there were no criteria to determine when a situation was not elder maltreatment or to explain the extent to which African Americans and other minorities differed from European Americans in experience or perception of elder abuse. Attention to these items could provide more precise guidance about when maltreatment occurs and when intervention is appropriate. Opinions about what constitutes maltreatment differ and, in the absence of contextually specific criteria, services are unavoidably haphazard and often ineffective.

Even a broad general definition can provide a basis for extreme cases. When things are less clear, which is often the case, a more precise operational definition is needed. Thus, many practitioners find themselves in a broad middle ground of uncertainty. This often results in the mislabeling of adult protection cases. When cases are mislabeled, inappropriate actions may be taken. Such activity results in outcomes that are unresponsive to the needs and wants of aged clients.

In addition, abuse has different meanings to different groups of people. "Definitions vary among professional affiliations, across cultural, ethnic and religious groups and by geographical locations" (Valentine & Cash, 1986, p. 19). Psychologists, physicians, social workers, lawyers, and other professionals have problems defining abuse. The issue of elder abuse includes many different phenomena, which may or may not be related. The term "is confusing because it covers many types of abuse [and] there is no consensus . . . about its parameters" (Straus & Gelles, 1986, pp. 470-471). Elder abuse is most often a "catch-all" term that includes physical maltreatment, financial exploitation, neglect/self-neglect, misuse of medication, violation of rights, and psychological abuse (Crystal, 1987; Moore & Thompson, 1987; Sengstock & Hwalek, 1987). Abuse, as used in this chapter, is modified from a definition proposed by Valentine and Cash (1986). It is defined as caretaker behavior directed toward the aged person, which can either be an act of commission (abuse) or omission (neglect) and either physical or mental. It must also meet these criteria:

Demonstrable physical or psychological harm to the elder or prognosis that harm is likely to occur

Causal link between caregiver behavior and harm to the elder

Determination by the social worker that maltreatment is sufficiently severe to warrant intervention

Hudson (1989), Kosberg (1988), and Johnson (1989) note the lack of uniformity in identifying the behavioral manifestations of elder maltreatment, whether it is elder abuse (physical, emotional, verbal, sexual, spiritual, or financial exploitation) or neglect (by caregiver or self-neglect). Blanton (1989), Hall (1986), Johnson (1989), Griffin and Williams (1992), and Williams and Griffin (1996) also question the applicability of instruments used to capture and measure abuse and neglect from one region of the United States to another. Yet, information from such research is used in the training of practitioners and applied in adjudication and treatment of clients despite the aforementioned gaps in knowledge.

Definitions of Elder Abuse

Presently, elder abuse can be described through the following categories: physical abuse, psychological abuse, financial exploitation, neglect, and violation of rights.

Physical Abuse involves interactions or exchanges that may result in battering or other types of physical harm. Examples include restrictions on freedom of movement, sexual abuse, purposeful physical behaviors by the perpetrator that cause emotional distress to the victim, unjustified denial of an individual's rights, or physical assault. Physically restraining a victim to a room or to a bed, overmedicating an elder to keep him/her calm, withholding food, and punching or slapping an elderly person are all examples of elder abuse.

Psychological Abuse is the dehumanization of the victim through fear or violence or other consequences of angering the perpetrator, such as isolation, threats, verbal assaults, and name-calling. If the aged person doesn't do as he or she is told, the caregiver may threaten to withhold a privilege or the like. In addition to a purposeful psychological attack, there may be an insensitivity to the life changes the aged person has experienced, that is, deaths of friends and relatives or a reduction in physical capacities. Caregivers may not have noticed that the aged person may be experiencing some emotional distress and/or is having difficulty adjusting to changes in his/her life.

Patronizing the aged, treating them like children, or limiting their control over their own lives through decision making can be considered forms of psychological abuse. It is also important to note that once physical abuse has occurred (as in the case of battered women), psychological abuse—or fear of a reoccurrence of the violence—follows it.

Financial Exploitation is the misuse or theft of property. Examples of property include personal property, savings accounts, real property, checking accounts, retirement accounts, public assistance income, Social Security checks, and the like. Financial exploitation can be accompanied by force or misrepresentation. An example of financial exploitation occurs when someone takes an older person's money and uses it without the older person's permission. If aged people confront the exploiter or complain, their complaints may be ignored or they may be physically or psychologically abused until they relent or are silent.

Neglect is the lack of responsible behavior on the part of the caregiver in addressing the needs of the aged person. This may include not providing adequate nutrition, medication, proper hygiene, or medical care. Neglect may include not doing those things for aged people that the older people increasingly find difficult to do for themselves, such as bathing, cooking, cleaning, paying bills, getting dressed, and so on. These are examples of active neglect by a caregiver. There is also passive neglect, which involves an unintentional lack of action by the caregiver or self-neglect. In the case of self-neglect, the aged people cannot or will not provide the above services for themselves.

Violation of Rights is the active disregard for the rights that every aged person has, which were outlined earlier.

Characteristics of Perpetrators and Victims

Although abuse occurs in households of varying incomes, most victims of elder abuse are reported to be white and living in middle-class families. Whereas some perpetrators are described as "short of money," many also are reported to be white middle-class women whose children are ready to leave home. The white middle-class perpetrator may be ready to rediscover her relationship with her spouse, find a new career, or return to school. It is at this time, when she may be anxiously anticipating a difference in her life, that she may be forced to take on the responsibility of an elder parent or an in-law who comes into the home. This phenomenon describes what has been called the "sandwich generation" by Miller (1981) and Brody (1985).

At a national Adult Protective Services Conference in San Antonio, Texas, in 1987, the typical victim of abuse was described as: (a) a white female, who resides with the perpetrator, (b) middle class, (c) having a severe mental or physical impairment, and (d) 75 years of age or older.

The typical perpetrator was described as: (a) a relative of the victim, (b) an adult child, (c) a female, (d) middle aged, (e) sharing a common residence with the aged person, and (g) having other conflicts—internal or external stresses in her life (Myers & Shelton, 1987).

More recently, Decalmer (1993) integrated the work of Tatara (1994a, 1994b) and others to develop a profile of the typical abused elder. The abused elder was described as

Female,
Over 75 years old,
Physically impaired, often chair- or bedridden,
Mentally impaired,
Socially isolated,
Depressed,
Ready to adopt the sick role,

[Having] thwarted many attempts to help in the past,
[Having] been an abusing parent in the past,
Too poor to live independently, and
Stubborn—last attempt to have some independence. (Decalmer, 1993, p. 60)

Typical elder abusers were described as:

A relative who has looked after the elder for many years
(an average of 9.5 years),
Lives with victim,
50 to 70 years old,
Short of money, stressed,
Socially isolated,
Past violent behavior—at least to property,
[Exhibited] depression, hostility, or anger,
Alcohol or drug addiction, and
Parent-child hostilities early in life. (Decalmer, 1993, pp. 60-61)

Intergenerational Violence

Murray Straus and Richard Gelles (1986) note that there is an intergenerational cycle to violence. Supporting Straus and Gelles, Myers and Shelton (1987) noted that "some cases of elder abuse occur in homes where there [are] lifelong patterns of abuse and violent relationships," a phenomenon called the "intergenerational transmission of violent behavior" (Anetzberger, 1987; Godkin, Wolf, & Pillemer, 1989; Mindel & Wright, 1982). Although a few studies do not support this premise, Suzanne Steinmetz (1978) completed a study that does. She found that only 1 out of 400 children raised in nonviolent homes was abusive to an elder parent when the child became an adult. In contrast, she found that 1 of every 2 adults who were abused as children abused their elderly parents when they became adults. This finding suggests that unresolved conflicts may result in the victimization of the older people when they become vulnerable in later years. The abusers may see, through intergenerational learning, sanctions or justification for the abuse. It is important, therefore, to break this intergenerational transmission of violent behavior in order to end it.

Abuse Among Minority Elders

The above-stated description of victims and perpetrators may have several discrepancies with what is commonly found in minority communities. Much of the sparse existing research identifies characteristics of elder abuse in the majority population group and surmises that the same conditions exist among minority elders. There is no evidence to directly support or refute this grouping practice. However, researchers do acknowledge that housing patterns and dependency patterns of Caucasians frequently differ from those of minority populations (Morycz, Malloy, Bozich, & Martz, 1987).

Minorities do not necessarily fit the typical profile of the victim or perpetrator. Although there may be several similarities between Caucasian families and families of minorities with regard to abuse, there also may be several differences. To what extent are there differences? The answer is unclear. More research is needed to determine the incidence of elder abuse among minority populations, the characteristics or circumstances of elder abuse among them, and if and/or how abuse among minority elderly differs from the traditional criteria cited in the literature. For example, any discussion of African American elderly must necessarily begin with a recognition of their unique racial experience in this country (Cazenave, 1981). A dependent adult child may live with an economically more stable elder in African American households. Abuse may not be a result of male or female socialization to violence, long-standing familial conflicts, or stress on the primary caretaker due to the needs of the frail elder family member as has been proposed in the literature (Myers & Shelton, 1987). Although it is believed that many of these concepts and characteristics have universal application, sociocultural influences also may contribute to violence and abuse of the minority aged. These sociocultural influences have directed patterns of behavior among minorities and shape their experiences in this country. African American elders share a unique heritage that differs from other aged in the United States. They share the anger and humiliation of a history of slavery and a geographic regional southeastern U.S. ancestry. Both experiences have created for them an identity as a people with common attitudes and shared values generic to the race. Other historical influences that have impressed the African American experience include poverty, the search for uniform civil rights, and the biased political interpretation of laws.

Likewise, Latino elders have experienced the effects of more recent immigration to the United States from a homeland. Many have not chosen to become acculturated to the United States, preferring to speak their native language and to maintain separate holidays, festivals, dietary choices, and social groups. These choices separate them further from the majority (Caucasian) population. Suspicions, frustrations, and underlying biases describe relationships between Latinos and other minorities and the majority culture. These emotions also describe intracultural relations within the Latino minority groups. These frustrations have the potential to surface and erupt violently with little provocation.

Historically, minority groups have been acted on violently through racism and other biases, either personally or institutionally. Violent social influences may predispose some members of minority families to behave violently (Griffin & Williams, 1992). When examining the etiology of minority family abuse, the societal experiences of some who abuse may be likened to those victims of abuse who in turn become abusers themselves (Steinmetz, 1978). When victims become abusers, it is widely accepted that they have undergone a social learning experience that occurs as a result of victimization. The exposure to abuse teaches some victims how to be abusive. The prior victim may become abusive of others in an effort to exercise control over his/her social environment (Griffin, 1994; Pillemer & Finklehor, 1989; Williams & Griffin, 1991). Minorities directly or collectively experience systemic bias in many forms. This can include verbal or physical attacks, lack of access to quality education or equal employment, lack of access to equal housing, lack of economic opportunities, poor health services, and so on. The oppressive behaviors that reduce or prevent options for minority elders may be seen as a violation of individuals' rights, which is a form of abuse. They also are subject to sociological and psychological attacks that result when victims are often blamed for their own conditions (Thomas & Sillen, 1976).

Abuse in Institutions

Although this chapter has focused on adult abuse within the family context, it is important to include as victims of abuse those individuals who reside in adult foster care homes, group or personal care homes, intermediate and skilled care facilities, and other types of group care facilities. The client groups in such settings can include people ranging from the very young to the aged.

Victims of abuse in institutions suffer forms of abuse similar to those of victims of family violence. The categories of institutional abuse include neglect, exploitation, physical abuse, emotional or psychological abuse, and sexual abuse. The definitions of abuse in institutions are similar to definitions of abuse within the family context. One important difference, however, is that family members are not the only possible perpetrators in institutions. Administrators, staff, and other residents of the facilities can perpetrate abuse.

Criteria for evaluating the various forms of abuse in institutions are similar to those used to evaluate violence in the family context; but the range of perpetrators and the fact that the abuse is occurring within a group in a protective institutional setting are important considerations to remember. For example, evaluating abuse can include observing whether there is evidence of physical and emotional attacks by the caregivers. In addition, human service workers must evaluate evidence of injury to the victim, even when the suspected perpetrators are the institutional caregivers (responsible staff) and/or other residents within a facility, who may or may not be cognitively alert.

The evaluation of neglect and exploitation also uses criteria similar to those used in the family context; however, there are differences that deserve to be mentioned. In an institutional setting, the result of staff neglecting a patient may result in that patient exploiting other residents physically, sexually, or emotionally. Conversely, the neglect of a patient also may result in that person being left vulnerable to various forms of abuse by other residents.

In the area of institutional exploitation, it is important to evaluate in what ways a resident's funds are being spent by the organization and whether the patient is receiving what he or she is eligible to receive. Records should be monitored periodically to determine if staff or other residents are taking funds from a vulnerable client.

Sexual abuse may occur between staff and resident, resident and resident, and/or visiting family members and resident. The Maine Adult Protective Services Training Guide for Facility Staff (Maine Department of Human Services, 1987) presents a definition of sexual abuse and indicators of sexual abuse in institutions. Sexual abuse is "a particular form of physical abuse in which sexual activity that is harmful to the resident, emotionally or physically, is initiated by and/or accepted by staff." Common indicators of sexual abuse can include the following:

You notice that a staff member offers affectionate gestures to a resident that are too lingering and seductive or become centered on the sex organs, anus, and breasts.

You observe injury to a resident's genitals, anus, breast, or mouth following an overnight visit with family.

You overhear a resident making openly sexual remarks to or about an incapacitated resident or attempting to talk an incapacitated resident into sexually intimate acts.

A young female resident tells you that her father touches her body in places that make her uncomfortable during his visits to the boarding home.

You happen upon a staff member exposing his/her genitals to a resident.

You learn of a staff member taking nude photographs of residents.

Such observations are indicative of sexual maltreatment and can be reasons to notify the director, nurses, or others about the incident(s).

Preventing Abuse in Institutions

Prevention of abuse in hospitals, group care facilities, and other health facilities is a primary concern of the legal, social service, and health care systems. Recommendations for preventing abuse in institutional settings include the following:

Administration and supervisors should be visible, available, and supportive of staff. They must communicate clearly and consistently that all residents must be treated with dignity and respect.

Training programs must be provided that develop appropriate attitudes in new employees and teach staff about resident behavior and needs.

Administration and supervisors must impress on staff and residents the importance of reporting suspected abuse, neglect, and exploitation. A confidential means of reporting must be developed within the facility to protect reporters and reduce pressures imposed by a peer group.

Minor incidents must be dealt with immediately. Any level of abuse, no matter how "minor," should not be tolerated.

Supervision of employees must be supportive and competent. Staff who are becoming angry with a particular patient need to report their feelings to their supervisor for consideration of alternatives in providing care or reassignment.

> Counseling services for employees with significant personal problems should be available by referral as part of the employee's health services. (Maine Department of Human Services, 1987)

Regardless of the context or the setting, abuse has the same effect with respect to the suffering of victims. It is harmful, demoralizing, and dangerous to dependent individuals within our society. Efforts to understand and eradicate abuse in institutions and all forms of abuse are a high priority.

Elder Maltreatment and the Law[1]

Abuse of the elderly who live in the community among friends and family emerged as a serious national concern in the mid-1970s. Since then, elder maltreatment has been the focus of regular federal congressional deliberation and state legislative activity. In 1977, the Senate Special Committee on Aging proposed a framework for the definition and treatment of elder abuse. The report examined social work and legal interventions and suggested "pragmatic solutions" (p. v). The committee's report also provided model acts for adult protective services, public guardianship, and civil commitment. Additional hearings held by the House Select Committee on Aging in 1981 led to its recommendation that states enact protective laws that include mandatory reporting requirements (Velick, 1995). By 1991, all 50 states and the District of Columbia had enacted elderly abuse statutes or had amended already existing protective services laws to bring the aged or elderly within the ambit of their protection. The existence of these protective laws "substantiates society's value of all individuals and its commitment to protect vulnerable older people" (Williams & Griffin, 1996, p. 6).

Adult Protective Services Legislation

Publicly funded programs established to implement the objectives of state protective statutes are generally referred to as adult protective services (APS) (Gottlich, 1994; Mixson, 1995). Despite the periodic reviews and recommendations of Congress, there is no federal legislation creating a national APS system; each state has developed its own laws and programs to respond to the needs of vulnerable populations. Many of the resulting programs were funded through Title XX of the Social Security Act and, more recently, social service block grants

(Mixson, 1995). Perhaps because there is no underlying or unifying legislation, no commonly accepted definition of elder abuse or maltreatment has been formulated. There is little consistency in terminology from state to state, and critical provisions in many statutory schemes are fraught with ambiguity. Due to the lack of clarity in the law, elders may be denied services because they fail to meet a statutory definition, or they may be exposed to intrusive interventions based on behavior that does not rise to the level of abuse intended by the legislation (Macolini, 1995, citing Pillemer & Suitor, 1988).

A review of state laws reveals substantial variation in criteria for protection, reporting and investigative procedures, classification of violations as civil or criminal, and available remedies. Several states specify a minimum age for protection (usually 60 or 65); in most of those states, the statutes also protect younger "disabled" or "incapacitated" adults who are unable to protect themselves (e.g., Florida). Many other jurisdictions use age 18 and "vulnerability to mistreatment" as the criteria for reporting and intervention (Kapp, 1995). As Williams and Griffin (1996) observed, the able-bodied elderly are excluded from protection in some jurisdictions. Pursuant to the recommendations of Congress, 42 states and the District of Columbia mandate reporting of suspected elder abuse and neglect by designated professionals; 15 of those states require *anyone* with such suspicions to file a report. Furthermore, 24 states specifically encourage voluntary or discretionary reporting by concerned others (Kapp, 1995; Macolini, 1995; Velick, 1995). In 30 of the mandatory reporting states, failure to report abuse carries sanctions ranging from a minimal fine to imprisonment for up to 6 months (Polisky, 1995). In reality, however, penalties for noncompliance are rarely imposed. Typically, state or local social service agencies are designated to receive the reports of elder abuse; less frequently, law enforcement agencies or state programs on aging may be authorized to receive the information.

Legal Remedies for Maltreatment

Traditional Criminal and Tort Law

Although there is no uniformity among the states in defining penalties for elder abuse, Polisky (1995) identified four ways in which states criminalize elder maltreatment. They:

Do *not* impose criminal liability for elder abuse apart from traditional criminal law

Only impose criminal liability for *physical* elder abuse

Impose criminal liability for physical elder abuse and for emotional elder abuse but require proof of *mental suffering* by the victim

Impose criminal liability for physical as well as emotional elder abusive *acts*, regardless of proof of mental suffering by the victim. (pp. 392-393)

In more than half the states, elderly victims of maltreatment must rely on traditional criminal law (e.g., assault, attempted murder, extortion) or civil tort claims (e.g., negligence, intentional infliction of emotional distress) in seeking redress against an abuser. A few of those states have enhanced criminal penalties for common-law crimes when they are committed against the aged or disabled (e.g., Florida). The harm inflicted on the elderly may fit criminal definitions, but older people—especially minorities—are frequently intimidated by the court system. They may be reluctant to prosecute a friend or family member and may be unable or unwilling to testify about the abusive acts. Tort actions present even greater obstacles in that their pursuit generally requires the elder to retain counsel and incur the expense of sometimes protracted litigation, without any guarantee of success. Elders frequently suffer psychological or emotional harm at the hands of their caregivers. However, statutes requiring proof of mental anguish to establish emotional abuse are of limited effectiveness because successful prosecution requires the testimony of the victim. Elders suffering from mental impairments due to advanced age or disease may not understand or remember the incident or may be unable to testify on their own behalf. Only three states—Delaware, Arkansas, and Rhode Island—have criminalized both physical and emotional abusive acts regardless of whether mental suffering exists. Polisky (1995) reports that Delaware has been particularly successful in prosecuting cases of emotional abuse based on a statute that requires the state to prove only that someone has acted in an abusive manner.

Other State Laws

Domestic violence and guardianship statutes may provide appropriate solutions in particular cases of elder maltreatment. Domestic violence statutes may provide an alternative form of protection if the relationship between the elder and the abuser fits the statutory definition. Many state statutes only protect victims against spouses or former spouses, or people with whom they have lived as if married or with whom they have children. Thus, the elder sharing a residence with a friend, child, grandchild, or other kin or nonkin would not be covered under such a scheme. Furthermore, protection under these statutes generally requires the cooperation of the victim. It may also require some affirmative action, such as seeking a restraining order or filing for separation or divorce, which is often not feasible or appropriate in cases of elder abuse. An important consideration in seeking assistance under these statutes is that domestic violence remedies typically rely on restraint or removal of the abuser who, in a case of elder maltreatment, may be the primary caregiver.

Guardianship and conservatorship statutes are used most frequently in cases of self-neglect, where it becomes necessary to intervene on behalf of elders who lack the capacity to consent to services, or who refuse assistance (Gottlich, 1994). Conservatorship protects only the property of the elder; guardianship may protect property and/or the person and is the more commonly used form. Guardianship should be pursued only in those cases where the incapacity of the adult to manage his or her own affairs is clearly demonstrated. If the petition is granted, decision making for the elder is placed in the hands of the guardian, who may acquire more control over the elder than is necessary to eliminate the abusive situation (Heisler & Quinn, 1995). For an elder who is otherwise competent, a more appropriate alternative may be the execution of a durable power of attorney through which the elder may be protected while retaining a degree of personal autonomy.

Many of the provisions intended to define or distinguish the various forms of abuse are vague or contradictory, resulting in their inconsistent interpretation and application. Generally, it is the function of the courts to interpret laws and to determine whether or not they are fair in their application. Yet, despite the array of protective laws and the range of potential proceedings involving the elderly, courts are rarely called on to review or resolve elder abuse cases (Stiegel, 1996). Absent judicial interpretation, operational definitions of abusive behavior and situations are constructed by APS workers, health care providers, law enforcement personnel, concerned citizens, victims, perpetrators, and others.

Elder abuse laws present significant practical and ethical dilemmas for medical, mental health, and social service providers. For example, mandatory reporting laws, arguably important mechanisms for fighting elder maltreatment (Velick, 1995), may create conflicts between adhering to the legal duty to report suspected abuse and the professional/ethical responsibility to respect the elderly client's right to confidentiality and self-determination (Gottlich, 1994; Macolini, 1995). An additional conflict for minority professionals may be a sense of ethnic loyalty, a wish to protect a perpetrator from the ethnic group from public condemnation by the criminal justice system, which historically has been dominated by Caucasian lawyers and judges.

The laws also allow for significant invasion of privacy and infringement of individual rights of those whom they are designed to protect. Remedies, that is, services or procedures intended to prevent further abuse, typically include removal from the home, civil commitment, and conservatorship or guardianship proceedings. In some cases, these interventions may be imposed involuntarily and may fail to include effective procedural safeguards for the protection of the elder's rights (Staudt, 1985). These laws are necessary and well-intended. But the acknowledged variation in their interpretation by professionals and others involved in the process raises serious concerns regarding their application.

The potential for different or conflicting interpretations is even greater when the people involved in a case are from different cultural backgrounds, for example, African American and European American (Williams & Griffin, 1996). The issues involved in elder maltreatment are complex; and, as Hudson (1991, p. 2) notes, the "meanings of the concepts are culturally determined, value-laden and emotionally charged, and have ethical ramifications." As several authors have observed (Griffin, 1998; Hudson, 1991; Moon & Williams, 1993; Williams & Griffin, 1996), the role that cultural diversity plays in definition, assessment, and intervention in the area of elder abuse has not been adequately examined. Without specificity in elder maltreatment laws, the perceptions of the designated professional will determine the need to report suspected abuse or neglect; those of the APS provider will determine the need to investigate, the existence of an abusive situation, and the appropriate intervention. A study by Moon and Williams (1993) of African American, Caucasian American, and Korean American elderly women suggests that considerable ethnic group differences exist in the perceptions of abuse by elderly women. It is likely that the subjective determinations of maltreatment are similarly influenced by the cultural norms and values of professionals. Without common definitions and interpretations of the law among professionals, and without an understanding of cultural differences, APS providers assume a responsibility that carries with it the potential for causing inadvertent harm to the populations they serve (Mixson, 1995).

The law, as examined in this chapter, classifies people and types of abuse but provides few descriptions to aid in identification of either. It grants authority for intervention, but with little guidance toward matching a listed remedy to appropriate situations or problems. But the law, whether drafted with precision or ambiguity, is merely a framework within which professionals must apply their expertise. In current practice, the law and the legal system are underused by service providers and mistrusted by minority elders. For the law to be effective it must be recognized by both groups as a community resource and as a potentially powerful mechanism for prevention and treatment of elder abuse.

Access to and Use of Social Services

Myers and Shelton (1987) propose that an important ingredient in remedying the problem of elder abuse is increasing the services available to help primary caregivers. Social and health problems have been responsible for generating numerous services during the 1970s and 1980s that were aimed at relieving caregivers of some of the ongoing responsibilities of providing continual care to their aged loved ones and, thereby, relieving caregivers' stress. But what kinds of services make a difference? Which services affect elder abuse?

Getting services into and accepted by the aged communities have posed a problem. Several reasons are indicated. First, service providers consistently cite resistance of elder victims to involvement with them or the agencies they represent. When encountered, such resistive behaviors are sometimes attributed to shame, embarrassment, and fear. Susan Tomita (1990) offers neutralization theory to explain this denial process. She notes the tendency for victims and perpetrators to neutralize, that is, minimize or rationalize, what is happening to them. An older person may be unable to acknowledge forms of abuse that would prompt an accusation against his or her adult child. What would such an accusation imply about the elder's skills at child rearing? Rearing a child capable of maltreatment would represent a personal failure. Tomita warns service providers not to become triangulated in the denial process with their clients.

Still another view is that denial and/or resistance may be psychological defense mechanisms that both victims and perpetrators use to protect themselves emotionally. Or, as with battered women in an unsafe environment, the victim may believe that to feel or behave any differently might increase the potential for harm. So elderly victims may employ such defense mechanisms to protect themselves from their abusers. The practitioner is called on to be able to distinguish between neutralization, denial, and reality.

Second, the use of traditional research instruments has caused some researchers to believe that minority cultural values dictate heavy reliance on the informal helping network instead of the formal service system (Krischef & Yoelin, 1981). Another concern is that many minorities are uneasy and unsure about support offered from the traditional public or private agencies; they may only feel comfortable using informal support networks (Barresi, 1990; Carlton-LaNey, 1991, 1992; Neighbors & Jackson, 1984; Taylor & Chatters, 1986; Taylor, Neighbors, & Broman, 1989). The greater truth may be that minority aged rely more on family because of the absence of formal community services. Third, when one thinks of increasing services to white middle-class caregivers, certain types of support programs come to mind, for example, home health care, private physician-delivered medical care, adult day care/adult day health (Griffin, 1993). Such may not be the case when one thinks of services in minority communities. Waring and Kosberg (1984), Jackson (1978), and Johnson (1978) note racial disparities in medical and social services. If, as Jackson (1980) proposed, part of what contributes to elder abuse among African Americans is the lack of community services, which can cause caregivers/perpetrators to be overwhelmed with caring for an infirm elder, then as Liu and Yu (1985) note, minority aged are singled out for "differential and inferior treatment" regarding social services. When one suggests providing services to a population whose needs have been historically underestimated, as in the African American community, one questions where to begin. The community has been systematically underserved. Multiple needs, such as financial, medical, housing, and acquiring medications, exist (Sengstock, Hwalek, & Petrone, 1989). The needs are overwhelming whereas services are inadequate in types and amounts.

The enormity of the task of providing services should not cause scholars and program planners to avoid making an attempt to address the needs. Such avoidance, benign neglect, is a common form of abuse that is cited by professionals who simply do not know where to begin.

The issues of traditional support networks, gaps in research, and poverty with regard to older adults should be reasons enough to encourage further studies of elder maltreatment.

Recommendations and Conclusion

This chapter has presented and discussed several themes and facts about elder abuse. Child-to-parent abuse is but one possibility regarding perpetrators and victims. Other forms include elder-to-elder or partner abuse, parent-to-child abuse, and associate (neighbor, friend, etc.) to elder abuse.

Available research stresses the family connection in abuse, the cycle of abuse, and the intergenerational elements connected with abuse. It is important to remember Steinmetz's study (1978), which demonstrated that 1 in 2 adults who were abused as children grew up to abuse their aged parents, compared to 1 in 400 adults who were not abused as children. Family patterns of abuse and unresolved conflicts among family members often play a role here. Abusive caregivers may harbor resentment toward an elderly family member.

Elderly family members may behave violently toward caregivers, depending on their physical or emotional impairments. Aged people may also use violence as a means of demonstrating their level of frustration because of reduced independence or ability to function. This explosive behavior directed at the caregiver may result in the caregiver responding with violence.

There may be other stresses in the caregiver's nuclear family that contribute to the abuse, such as marital problems, substance abuse, or emotional problems. Caring for elders can create financial problems for caregivers. If any one of these issues is experienced by the caregiver, caring for the elder family member could be viewed as another stress. Lack of family or community support may also enhance the level of stress experienced by the caregiver.

The stress of caring for someone who is physically and/or mentally impaired can increase the risk of abuse. The more helpless and dependent a person is, or perceives himself/herself to be, the higher the risk of family violence.

Diversity is an essential element in conceptualizing elder maltreatment. Without allowing for ethnic and cultural diversity, any definition is ungeneralizable and narrow, with limited implications for all concerned. It is important that the helping professions respond to the real problems of elder maltreatment. Completion of recent research in several states has provided pertinent information about the character and nature of elder abuse. Additional future research must be undertaken to explore the unique characteristics of abuse in families. Acquiring empirical information is a necessary first step in improving services to this underserved population.

Recommendations

Although much remains to be learned from research, research requires time for completion and assimilation. How to effectively and expeditiously break the cycle of violence remains a concern of social workers, counselors, psychiatrists, and other helping professionals today. Some helpful measures can be undertaken by the human service community in the interim. The following interim recommendations are offered.

First, community-based education about the existence of elder abuse as a problem should be provided to the informal and formal networks within the community. Such efforts would affect kin and nonkin relationships and could be provided through neighborhood groups, churches, senior citizen centers, mental health centers, and health care centers.

Second, shared definitions and consistent interpretations of the law are needed. Discussions must be encouraged among APS professionals and a dialogue must begin between professionals and elders. Groups can be urged to contribute perceptions and insights regarding forms and patterns of potentially abusive behavior as it exists in the community.

Third, in addition to providing information about the existence of elder maltreatment, attention must be directed toward developing nonjudgmental attitudes among the helpers of both the victims and perpetrators of elder maltreatment. Nonjudgmental attitudes are important if professionals are to cultivate trust in the community and, by doing so, encourage both victims and abusers to share and to involve themselves in treatment and recovery processes.

Fourth, education and discussions must occur to overcome distrust of the legal system and the reluctance to seek assistance from legal service providers. Courts are underused by professionals; legal services are underused by elders. Service providers and elders need guidance in understanding the legal system and what the law can and cannot do.

Elders need information regarding the availability of legal and treatment services for both victims and perpetrators.

Finally, recognizing that education may be one form of primary prevention, other forms of prevention and assistance should be present in communities to provide treatment to clients in need of services. Many private and public service agencies are available to the community at large. Research has shown that elders make better use of such agencies and programs when the programs are placed within their immediate neighborhoods—in senior citizens centers and in nutrition sites for elders.

Conclusion

It is important for service practitioners and the community at large to gain knowledge, skills, and empathy in the area of elder maltreatment. They must end the cycle of abuse and not deny its strong family connection. In doing so, they may prevent future abuse. Although the most prevalent type of abuse does occur in families, it is important to recognize that abuse also occurs in institutions. Practitioners must become effective in working with elder abuse, not only because aged people need assistance, but also because the family and the person in the violent environment are both at risk.

Appendix

Here is a list of some state laws affecting abusive acts.

Arkansas Code Ann. 5-28-103 (Michie Supp. 1993) (criminalizing physical and emotional abusive acts).

Delaware Code Ann. tit. 31, 3902 (Michie Supp. 1994) (criminalizing physical and emotional abusive acts).

Florida Stat. Ann. 415.102(10) (West Supp. 1997) ("'disabled adult' means a person 18 years of age or older who suffers from a condition of physical or mental incapacitation. . .").

Florida Stat. Ann. 415.102(11) (West Supp. 1997) ("'elderly person' means a person who is 60 years of age or older. . .").

Florida Stat. Ann. 784.08 (West Supp. 1997) (Assault or battery on person 65 years of age or older, reclassification of offenses; minimum sentence).

Georgia Code Ann. 30-5-3(7.1) (Michie 1997) ("'elder person' means a person 65 years of age or older. . .").

Rhode Island Gen. Laws 23-17.8-10 (Michie Supp. 1994) (criminalizing physical and emotional abusive acts).

Note: For expanded discussion and citation of elder abuse statutes, reporting provisions, and penalties, see Kapp (1995), Macolini (1995), Polisky (1995), and Velick (1995).

Note

1. This section is adapted from Griffin, L.W., Williams, O. J. & Reed, J. G. (1998). Abuse among African-American elders. In R. Kennedy-Bergen (Ed.), *Issues of Intimate Violence* (chap. 18). Thousand Oaks, CA: Sage.

References

Administration on Aging & American Association of Retired Persons. (1996). *A profile of older Americans: 1996.* Washington, DC: U.S. Department of Health and Human Services.

Anetzberger, G. (1987). *The etiology of elder abuse by adult offspring.* Springfield, IL: Charles C Thomas.

Barresi, C. M. (1990). Diversity in black family caregiving: Implications for geriatric education. In *Minority aging: Essential curricula content for selected health and allied health professionals* (DHHS Publication No. HRS-P-DV-90-4). Washington, DC: U.S. Department of Health and Human Services, Public Health Service.

Blanton, P. G. (1989). Zen and the art of adult protective services: In search of a unified view of elder abuse. *Journal of Elder Abuse and Neglect, 1*(1), 27-35.

Brody, E. M. (1985). Parent care as a normative to family stress. *Gerontologist, 25,*19-29.

Butler, R. N., Lewis, M. I, & Sunderland, T. (1991). *Aging and mental health* (4th ed.). New York: Macmillan.

Carlton-LaNey, I. (1991). Some considerations of the rural elderly black's underuse of social services. *Journal of Gerontological Social Work, 16*(1/2), 3-17.

Carlton-LaNey, I. (1992). Elderly black farm women: A population at risk. *Social Work, 37*(6), 517-523.

Cazenave, N. A. (1981, October 13-17). *Elder abuse and black Americans: Incidence, correlates, treatment, and prevention.* Paper presented at the Annual Meeting of the National Council on Family Relations, Milwaukee, WI.

Crystal, S. (1987, Summer). Elder abuse: The latest "crisis." *The Public Interest, 88,* 56-66.

Decalmer, P. (1993). Clinical presentation. In P. Decalmer & F. Glendenning (Eds.), *The mistreatment of elderly people* (pp. 35-61). Newbury Park, CA: Sage.

Godkin, M. A., Wolf, R. S., & Pillemer, K. A. (1989). A case-comparison analysis of elder abuse and neglect. *International Journal on Aging and Human Development, 28,* 207-225.

Gottlich, V. (1994). Beyond granny bashing: Elder abuse in the 1990s. *Clearinghouse Review, 28*(4), 371-381.

Griffin, L. W. (1993). Adult day care and adult protective services. *Journal of Gerontological Social Work, 20,* (1-2), 115-133.

Griffin, L. W. (1994). Elder maltreatment among rural African Americans. *Journal of Elder Abuse and Neglect, 6*(1), 1-27.

Griffin, L. W. (in press). You just don't hit your momma. In T. Tatara (Ed.), *Understanding elder abuse among minority populations.* Washington, DC: Taylor & Francis.

Griffin, L. W., & Williams, O. J. (1992). Abuse among African American elderly. *Journal of Family Violence, 7*(1), 19-35.

Griffin, L.W., Williams, O. J. & Reed, J. G. (1998). Abuse among African-American elders. In R. Kennedy-Bergen (Ed.), *Issues of intimate violence* (chap. 18). Thousand Oaks, CA: Sage.

Hall, P. A. (1986). Minority elder maltreatment: Ethnicity, gender, age, and poverty. *Journal of Gerontological Social Work, 9*(4), 53-72.

Heisler, C. J., & Quinn, M. J. (1995). A legal perspective. *Journal of Elder Abuse & Neglect, 7*(2/3), 131-156.

Hudson, M. F. (1989). Analyses of the concepts of elder mistreatment: Abuse and neglect. *Journal of Elder Abuse and Neglect, 1*(1), 5-27.

Hudson, M. F. (1991). Elder mistreatment: A taxonomy with definitions by Delphi. *Journal of Elder Abuse & Neglect, 3*(2), 1-20.

Jackson, J. J. (1978, September-October). Special health problems of aged blacks. *Aging, 278-279,* 15-20.

Jackson, J. J. (1980). *Minorities and aging.* Belmont, CA: Wadsworth.

Johnson, R. (1978, September-October). Barriers to adequate housing for elderly blacks. *Aging, 278-279,* 33-39.

Johnson, T. F. (1989). Elder mistreatment identification instruments: Finding common ground. *Journal of Elder Abuse and Neglect, 1*(4), 15-37.

Kapp, M. B. (1995). Elder mistreatment: Legal interventions and policy uncertainties. *Behavioral Sciences and the Law, 13*(3), 365-380.

Kosberg, J. I. (1988). Preventing elder abuse: Identification of high risk factors prior to placement decisions. *The Gerontologist, 28,* 43-50.

Krischef, C., & Yoelin, M. L. (1981, Spring). Differential use of informal and formal helping networks among rural elderly and white Floridians. *Journal of Gerontological Social Work, 3,* 45-59.

Liu, W. T., & Yu, E. (1985, September). Asian/Pacific American elderly: Mortality differentials, health status, and use of health services. *Journal of Applied Gerontology, 4,* 35-64.

Lucas, E. T. (1989, May). Elder mistreatment: Is it really abuse? *Free Inquiry in Creative Society, 17,* 95-99.

Macolini, R. M. (1995). Elder abuse policy: Consideration in research and legislation. *Behavioral Sciences and the Law, 13*(3), 349-363.

Maine Department of Human Services. (1987). *A training guide for facility staff: Abuse, neglect, and exploitation in nursing homes, boarding homes, and adult foster homes.* Augusta, ME: State House Station II.

Miller, D. A. (1981). The "sandwich" generation: Adult children of the aging. *Social Work, 26,* 419-423.

Mindel, C. H., & Wright, R. (1982). Satisfaction in multigenerational households. *Journal of Gerontology, 37,* 483-489.

Mixson, P. M. (1995). An adult protective services perspective. *Journal of Elder Abuse & Neglect,* 7(2/3), 69-87.

Moon, A., & Williams, O. J. (1993). Perceptions of elder abuse and help-seeking patterns among African American, Caucasian, and Korean American elderly. *The Gerontologist, 33*(3), 396-394.

Moore, T., & Thompson, V. (1987, Fall). Elder abuse: A review of research, programmes, and policy. *The Social Worker, Travailleur Social, 55,* 115-122.

Morycz, R. K., Malloy, J., Bozich, M., & Martz, P. (1987, January). Racial differences in family burden: Clinical implications for social work. *Journal of Gerontological Social Work, 10,* 133-154.

Myers, J. E., & Shelton, B. (1987). Abuse and older persons: Issues and implications for counselors. *Journal of Counseling Development, 65,* 376-380.

Neighbors, H. W., & Jackson, J. S. (1984). The use of informal and formal help: Four patterns of illness behavior in the Black community. *American Journal of Community Psychology, 12.*

Pierce, R. L., & Trotta, R. (1986). Abused parents: A hidden family problem. *Journal of Family Violence, 1,* 103.

Pillemer, K. A., & Finklehor, D. (1989, April). Causes of elder abuse: Caregiver stress versus problem relatives. *American Journal of Orthopsychiatry, 59,* 179-187.

Pillemer, K. A., & Suitor, J. J. (1988). Elder abuse. In V. B. Van Hasselt, R. L. Morrison, A. S. Bellack, & M. Hersen (Eds.), *Handbook of family violence* (pp. 247-270). New York: Plenum.

Poertner, J. (1986, Spring). Estimating the incidence of abused older persons. *Journal of Gerontological Social Work, 9,* 3-15.

Polisky, R. A. (1995). Criminalizing physical and emotional elder abuse. *The Elder Law Journal, 3*(2), 377-411.

Sengstock, M. C., & Hwalek, M. A. (1987). A review and analysis of measures for the identification of elder abuse. *Journal of Gerontological Social Work, 10,* 21-36.

Sengstock, M. C., Hwalek, M. B., & Petrone, S. (1989). Services for aged abuse victims: Service types and related factors. *Journal of Elder Abuse and Neglect, 1*(4), 37-57.

Staudt, M. (1985). The social worker as an advocate in adult protective services. *Social Work, 30*(3), 204-208.

Steinmetz, S. K. (1978, July-August). Battered parents. *Society, 15,* 54-55.

Steinmetz, S. K. (1988). *Duty bound—Elder abuse and family care.* Newbury Park, CA: Sage.

Stiegel, L. A. (1996). What can courts do about elder abuse? *The Judges' Journal, 35*(4), 38-43.

Straus, M., & Gelles, R. (1986, August). Societal change and change in family violence from 1975-1985 as revealed by two national studies. *Journal of Marriage and the Family, 48,* 465-479.

Tatara, T. (1994a). *Elder abuse: Questions and answers: An information guide for professionals and concerned citizens.* Washington, DC: National Center on Elder Abuse.

Tatara, T. (1994b). Summaries of the statistical data on elder abuse in domestic settings for fiscal year 1990 and 1991. In F. Schick & R. Schick (Eds.), *Statistical handbook on aging Americans* (p. 98). Phoenix, AZ: Oryx Press.

Taylor, R. J., & Chatters, L. M. (1986, November-December). Patterns of informal support to elderly black adults: Family, friends, and church members. *Social Work,* pp. 432-438.

Taylor, R. J., Neighbors, H. W., & Broman, C. L. (1989, May). Evaluation by black Americans of the social services encountered during a serious personal problem. *Social Work,* pp. 205-210.

Thomas, A., & Sillen, S. (1976). *Racism and psychiatry.* Secaucus, NJ: The Citadel Press.

Tomita, S. T. (1990). The denial of elder mistreatment by victims and abusers: The application of neutralization theory. *Violence and Victims, 5*(3), 171-184.

U.S. Bureau of the Census. (1994). *Statistical abstract of the United States, 1993* (110th ed.). Washington, DC: Government Printing Office.

U.S. Congress, Select Committee on Aging. (1980). *Elder abuse.* U.S. House of Representatives. Ninety-sixth Congress, Second Session, June 11, 1980. (Item 1009). Washington, DC: Government Printing Office.

U.S. Congress, Select Committee on Aging. (1981). U.S. House of Representatives. Ninety-seventh Congress, First Session. (Item 277). Washington, DC: Government Printing Office.

U.S. Congress, Senate Special Committee on Aging. (1977, July). *Protective dervices for the elderly: A working paper* (No. 052-070-04120-0). Washington, DC: Government Printing Office.

Valentine, D., & Cash, T. (1986). A definitional discussion of elder maltreatment. *Journal of Gerontological Social Work, 9,* 17-28.

Velick, M. D. (1995). Mandatory reporting statutes: A necessary yet underutilized response to elder abuse. *The Elder Law Journal, 3*(1), 165-190.

Walker, L. (1985). *The battered woman.* New York: Harper & Row.

Waring, M. L., & Kosberg, J. I. (1984). Morale and the differential use among the black elderly of social welfare services delivered by volunteers. *Journal of Gerontological Social Work, 6,* 81-94.

Williams, O. J., & Griffin, L. W. (1991). Elder abuse in the black family. In R. L. Hampton (Ed.), *Black family violence: Current research and theory* (pp. 117-127). Lexington, MA: Lexington Books.

Williams, O. J., & Griffin, L. W. (1996). Elderly maltreatment and cultural diversity: When laws are not enough. *Journal of Multicultural Social Work, 4*(2), 1-13.

• *CHAPTER 11* •

Substance Abuse and Family Violence

H. DAVID BANKS
SUZANNE M. RANDOLPH

Researchers and practitioners have focused increasing attention on the complex relationship between substance abuse and family violence, and they have made substantial progress in understanding the comorbidity of these two phenomena during the past decade. Practitioners from a variety of disciplines have begun to devote resources to prevention and treatment among service populations at risk for both substance abuse and family violence. However, the relationship between substance abuse and domestic violence is difficult to understand, principally because: (a) there are many other factors involved, and (b) the relationship between substance abuse and domestic violence is not always clear or linear.

To date, most of the heuristic research and practice models for understanding and predicting the relationships between relevant variables have been developed within multidisciplinary frameworks. Multidisciplinary teams are most effective in improving our understanding of family violence situations related to substance abuse (American Psychological Association, 1996; Mariano, 1989). Generally, multidisciplinary prevention and treatment efforts have sought to strengthen the ability of family members to seek safety from violence, obtain culturally appropriate substance abuse treatment, and end violent behavior. Along these lines, this chapter combines research and practice literature from the fields of social work, nursing, psychology, medicine, health education, and law to help illustrate some of the key concepts related to situations involving both domestic violence and substance abuse.

Substance Abuse

Definitions and Paradigms

For the purposes of this chapter, substance abuse is defined as a use of alcohol or other drugs that results in cognitive impairment and/or severe affective distortions that affect an individual's ability to perform functions that she or he is ordinarily able to perform. Alcohol's effect on human functioning is similar to the effect of sedatives and hypnotics, whereas the effect of cocaine is similar to that of amphetamines. All together, the *Diagnostic and Statistical Manual of Mental Disorders* (DSM-IV; the American Psychiatric Association, 1994) identifies 11 classes of drug substances that can alter cognitive and affective functioning.

Early research attempted to explain substance abuse by focusing on the individual (Fullilove, Fullilove, Smith, & Winkler, 1993; Leonard & Jacob, 1988; Schwartz, 1989) and investigating the personality traits, family histories, individual belief systems, and communication skills influencing substance abuse (Funkhouser, 1991). Later, attention shifted to identifying environmental attributes such as poverty, social settings, and community norms that might shape individual decisions to abuse substances (Dent & Arias, 1990; Schwartz, 1989). Currently, two major areas of concern stand out in the field: so-called high-risk youth and the rapid increase in cocaine abuse.

High-Risk Youth

Epidemiologic research suggests that early initiation of substance use is an important predictor of later substance abuse. Those who abuse substances most, especially alcohol, may choose to begin use during their teen or young adult years (Martin, 1992).

For this reason, many research and prevention programs have been geared toward high-risk youth. During the 1980s, the federal government began to place a high priority on helping youth at high risk for substance abuse and their families (Funkhouser, 1991). The Anti-Drug Abuse Act of 1986 established the Office for Substance Abuse Prevention (OSAP), which was funded and charged to initiate programs that would provide prevention and early intervention services for youth generally and high-risk youth specifically (Funkhouser, 1991). The Anti-Drug

Abuse Act of 1988 mandated a variety of prevention programs to serve high-risk youth and their families.

High-risk youth is an abbreviation for a more accurate term, *youth from high-risk environments* (Funkhouser, 1991). Contemporary theory examines a wide range of influences—including genetics, parents, and peers—to explain the initiation of substance use among teens and young adults. The youth's family, in particular, has come under scrutiny for its critical role in either preventing or contributing to early substance use. Although some research indicates a genetic predisposition to substance abuse, other studies have shown that positive family environments can serve as an effective protective factor in discouraging the initiation of drug use among youth (Dent & Arias, 1990; Hillbrand, Foster, & Hirt, 1991). Conversely, the child's or teenager's family may also be one of the chief determinants influencing early alcohol and other drug use. The family environment may be high risk for several reasons, including: the presence of adults who are abusing alcohol (McGaha & Leoni, 1995; Pollack et al., 1990), an inadequate household income (Neff, Holamon, & Schluter, 1995), or the existence of violence and other stressors among family members (Somers, Love, Evans-Schaeffer, & Soucar, 1994).

Cocaine Abuse

Much substance abuse/family violence research has focused on the relationship of alcohol to family violence while giving very little attention to other substance use or combination usage (Levy & Brekke, 1990; Martin, 1992; Miller, Downs, & Gondoli, 1990). However, research that is specific to other forms of substance abuse is a pressing need because findings from studies done on alcohol and violence may not be applicable in research and practice settings among populations that are choosing to abuse other drugs.

The abuse of some substances other than alcohol may actually pose a greater risk of violence and other social ills. In an investigation of women and men arrested in eight cities, Kantor and Straus (1989) found that other drug abuse was a better predictor of violence than alcohol abuse. Martin (1992) found that cocaine use was more highly associated with the perpetration of violence than alcohol.

Of all forms of substance abuse, cocaine abuse is one area of particular concern. Nationally, crack/cocaine abuse has surpassed alcohol and heroin abuse in many locales (Leukefeld & Tims, 1993). From an epidemiologic perspective, cocaine abuse has rapidly spread within the United States (Tims & Leukefeld, 1993) and increased dramatically during the 1980s (National Institute on Drug Abuse, 1993). Cocaine abuse is unique among other illegal substance abuse because it is abused by a heterogeneous population and is available in a low-cost and highly addictive form (Tims & Leukefeld, 1993). The discovery of a low-cost smokable cocaine derivative known as crack has led to an increase in cocaine usage among teens and young adults.

Cocaine treatment knowledge is in the preliminary stages (Leukefeld & Tims, 1993). There are no specific empirically validated protocols for cocaine treatment (Leukefeld & Tims, 1993). Leukefeld and Tims (1993) believe that cocaine research should address clients diagnosed as cocaine-dependent, using cocaine either alone or in combination with other drugs (including alcohol). The investigators believe that future studies should include social and demographic characteristics, psychopathology, natural history, and treatment-seeking behavior. Future research and practice will need to examine the use of multiple drugs and violence as well as the impact of cocaine usage and violence.

Family Violence

The connection between substance abuse and family violence is one of the most complicated issues to understand in the family violence literature (Mignon, 1994). Alcohol and other substance abuse is associated with all categories of family violence. Children can abuse alcohol and be violent and/or parents can abuse alcohol and be violent. Therefore, the abuse of alcohol in family violence situations, in particular, does not seem to be related to the relationship of the perpetrator to the victim (Martin, 1992; Slade, Daniels, & Heisler, 1991). Consensus exists that alcohol abuse and its accompanying impairment interfere with the cessation of family violence (Adams, 1990; Minnesota Coalition for Battered Women, 1992; Tolman & Bennett, 1990). However, none of the evidence suggests that alcohol treatment alone will effectively change abusive behavior. This chapter will focus on the relationship between substance abuse and family violence, which is defined here as the emotional, physical and sexual violence perpetrated by: (a) adult males toward adult females, (b) adults toward children, (c) adults toward elders, and (d) adolescent children toward adults.

Adult Male Violence Toward Women

In his 1986 conference on interpersonal violence, which effectively moved violence into the arena of public health, U.S. Surgeon General C. Everett Koop stated that domestic violence was the leading cause of injury to women ages 16 to 44 in the United States. Studies estimate that between 22% and 35% of women who visit hospital emergency rooms are there because of injuries sustained at the hands of a known male assailant (National Coalition Against Domestic Violence, 1996).

Intimate violence against women has received greater attention than similar violence against men because of the greater severity and impact of violence against women. Because men are typically larger than their wives and usually have greater access to power, property, and prestige, men do not experience the same physical or social consequences of family violence as do women (Hampton & Coner-Edwards, 1993). Women surviving family violence are likely to be exposed to attacks on self-esteem, suffer loss of possessions, and be at risk for loss of status in the community.

Research on male violence toward women indicates that there are several different forms of abuse. Paymar and Pence (1993) offer the following typology of the different forms: coercion and threats; intimidation; emotional abuse; isolation; minimizing, denying, and blaming; using children; economic abuse; and male privilege. Woodall-Jones (1994) argues that emotional or psychological abuse is often the most devastating form of abuse for women. Research has begun to investigate the psychological consequences of violence (Flanzer, 1990; Neff et al., 1995; Stith, Crossman, & Bischof, 1991; Wolfe, Reppucci-Dickson, & Hart, 1995). Future research and practice may help inform investigations of any correlations between substance abuse and particular forms of violence among specific populations of men who batter.

Early research helped provide the basis for future investigations regarding substance abuse and male violence toward women (Appleton, 1980; Straus, Gelles, & Steinmetz, 1980). In an analysis of the 1985 National Family Violence Survey, which used responses from approximately 2,000 women, Kantor and Straus (1989) concluded that women who abuse alcohol are more likely to be victims of minor marital violence but that female substance abuse of any type is not a significant factor in severe marital violence. However, the Minnesota Coalition for Battered Women (1992) cautions that it is important never to attribute a man's use of violence to a woman's chemical abuse.

Male batterers who abuse alcohol run a higher risk of being killed by their spouses. In her investigation of female survivors of male battering who had killed their abusers, Browne (1987) found that 78% of the deceased abusers were intoxicated on a regular basis, compared to only 40% of the living abusers.

Although substance abuse in both men and women has often been found to coexist with male violence against women, the reasons for this apparent connection are unclear. At present, relatively little is known about factors that place alcoholic males at risk for marital violence (Murphy & O'Farrell, 1994). For women, other than a violent family of origin, there is no evidence of a battered women's profile (Barnett & Fagan, 1993; Bennett, Tolman, Rogalski, & Srinivasaraghavan, 1994; Blount, Silverman, Sellers, & Seese, 1994; Keller, 1996).

Despite the high correlation between alcohol and spouse abuse, it is doubtful that alcohol or other substances play a direct, causal role in most violent episodes (Bennett, 1995; Kantor & Straus, 1987; Leonard & Blane, 1992; Martin, 1992; Rainbolt & Greene, 1990). Evidence does not exist to support the notion of a simple disinhibition effect of drugs (Neff et al., 1995; Tolman & Bennett, 1990). Tolman and Bennett (1990) conclude that disinhibition is not generally a viable explanation for the relationship between alcohol abuse and family violence. Disinhibition resulting from alcohol abuse may lead men who already approve of the use of violence to endorse wife abuse in specific situations (Kantor & Straus, 1987). Generally, however, research data suggest that psychoactive drugs do not act in isolation to increase the probability of domestic assault (Bennett, 1995; Kantor & Straus, 1989; Levy & Brekke, 1990; Zubretsky & Digirolamo, 1994).

Several factors may help predict the presence of both domestic violence and substance abuse. Women who use drugs appear to be more likely to suffer abuse than those who do not use drugs (Miller et al., 1990). Studies of cocaine use among women have found that women tend to use cocaine initially because it gives them acceptance by their significant others (Hilliard, 1995). Childhood observation of family violence also appears to put families at risk for domestic violence (Miller & Downs, 1993; Straus & Gelles, 1990).

Elder Abuse by Adult Children

Elder abuse is defined as the emotional, financial, or physical maltreatment of an older person by someone with whom the elder has a relationship. The occurrence of elder abusive relationships is further defined by the distribution of power within the relationship, in which the abuser typically has control over a resource that puts the abuser in a position to abuse the elder. The abuser may or may not live with the elder.

Research is very limited; hence, definitive statements about the causes of elder abuse and its epidemiology cannot be made (American Psychological Association, 1996). However, because the majority of elder caregivers are women, it is suspected that women make up the majority of the perpetrators of elder abuse (American Psychological Association, 1996). The most common type of abuse appears to be neglect. As for the causes of elder abuse, a special family violence task force of the American Psychological Association (1996) concluded that a combination of psychological, social, and economic factors combine with the mental and physical conditions of the elderly to contribute to the incidence of elder abuse within families. The person who abuses an elder may have a history of substance abuse or other personal problems (American Psychological Association, 1996).

Adolescent Violence Toward Parents

Adolescents, especially those with histories of substance abuse, may become violent toward their parents and other household caregivers (Pelletier & Coutu, 1992; Schiff & Cavaiola, 1993). There are few empirical investigations of intrafamily abuse by a child (American Psychological Association, 1996; Pelletier & Coutu, 1992); for this reason, the American Psychological Association (1996) calls for additional research to be conducted in this area. However, existing data indicate that the rates of parent abuse by children are related to the frequency of substance abuse and other forms of family violence in the home (American Psychological Association, 1996).

Sons are slightly more likely to be violent than daughters, and the majority of children who attack a parent are in their teenage years (Schiff & Cavaiola, 1993). Mental health professionals explain gender differences in violence toward parents by arguing that violence toward parents initiated by boys may follow social scripts related to male aggression; moreover, adolescent boys might also be taking advantage of puberty-induced increases in their body size (Bronfenbrenner, 1989).

Although data indicate that mothers are more likely to be victims of child violence, fathers seem to be more likely victims of older male children. Older boys are more likely to assault fathers who had used violence or alcohol in the family (Schiff & Cavaiola, 1993). According to clinical observations of adolescents who had abused a parent, the abused parents had often turned over their decision-making authority to the adolescent (Pelletier & Coutu, 1992). Adolescents from substance-abusing families reported more family violence and substance abuse than did adolescents from non-substance abusing families (McGaha & Leoni, 1995).

Explanatory Models

There are several models for explaining the complex connection between the various forms of family violence and substance abuse. The cognitive models examine the role of cognitive processes and learning in explaining the relationship between substance abuse and family violence. One type of cognitive model posits that, through life experiences, people learn that drug use is a societally acceptable excuse for the use of violence. Violence is the result of a perpetrator's cognitive rationalization that any consequences they will meet as a result of the use of violence will be mediated by society's awareness that drugs were involved in the incident (Levy & Brekke, 1990).

Another version of cognitive model seeks to interpret battering behavior from the perspective of cognitive distortions. While intoxicated, an individual's ability to accurately process information may be distorted. This distortion appears to lead some people to use violence toward others, either out of frustration or in an attempt to more accurately process events around them.

The comorbidity model argues that a common cause or set of causes leads to substance-abusing and familial violent behavior. The model does not state that drug abuse and family violence are themselves causally related; but rather, that they are both observable manifestations of a common underlying set of causative factors (Bennett & Lawson, 1994). One version of the model seeks to link the intergenerational transmission of both substance abuse and family violence. This version of a comorbidity model examines patterns within the family of origin as the root cause for both substance-abusing and violent behaviors.

Another version of the model relates to abusers' needs to achieve power and control over others. Substance abusers and those who are violent in families may have exacerbated needs to exercise power and control over others. Gondolf (1995) argues that alcohol abuse and woman abuse may both be the result of an abuser's need for power and control, which occurs within a societal context.

The set of personality-situational models seeks to examine how individual personality characteristics (Hamberger & Hastings, 1994; Kantor & Straus, 1987) or situational variables (Miczek et al., 1994) influence the co-occurrence of violence and substance abuse. There is evidence that alcohol may affect violent behavior for people with specific personality profiles. Also, Miczek and colleagues (1994) argue that situations surrounding the acquisition of drugs, with the accompanying exposure to a violent subculture, may contribute to adult male violence against women.

Substance Abuse and Family Violence Comorbidity

Incidence

Because the behaviors of substance abuse and family violence may go largely unreported, caution should be used when interpreting incidence and prevalence data. The existing studies, however, have demonstrated a relatively high incidence of substance abuse among domestic violence cases. In a study of 232 men arrested for domestic violence, Vanfossen and Bonham (1992) found that 38% of the men reported they were drinking alcohol at the time of their arrest. In their study of substantiated child abuse cases, Wheat and Connors (1991) found that 52% of the adults involved were identified as substance abusers by social work substance abuse assessment protocols.

Gender Differences in Substance Abuse

Research indicates that gender issues need to be considered in the areas of substance abuse and family violence (Hilliard, 1995; McClelland, Davis, Kalin, & Warner, 1972; Woodhouse, 1992; Zubretsky & Digirolamo, 1994). For men, alcohol abuse may be a means of asserting power and feeling "like a man" (McClelland et al., 1972). Among men, alcohol may provide a technique for strengthening a fragile masculine ego (Lemle & Mishkind, 1989). In contrast, women are more likely to use alcohol to sedate the emotional trauma of previous abuse (Lemle & Mishkind, 1989). Research indicates that up to half of all female alcoholism may be precipitated in some way by spouse abuse (Blount et al., 1994; Brown, 1993; Kagle, 1987; Schwartz, 1989). One nursing study found that two thirds of the female alcoholics had been battered (Bergman, Larsson, Brismar, & Klang, 1989). Women may drink in family violence situations to ease the stress of diminished female roles (Wilsnack, 1984) or as a response to depression (Kagle, 1987; Miller et al., 1990; Skrip & Kunzman, 1991).

For some women, alcohol and other drugs may represent a strategy for surviving incidents of family violence. Substance abuse may help ease the emotional and/or physical pain caused by family violence. Women who abuse substances have reported that the fear and anxiety associated with family violence situations may become less difficult to deal with, if only for a short period of time, when alcohol and other drugs are abused (Minnesota Coalition for Battered Women, 1992). Female incest survivors are more likely to abuse substances and may show up in treatment settings for post-traumatic stress disorder (PTSD) problems not directly related to the original abuse (Skrip & Kunzman, 1991). Women in recovery are more likely than women in the general population to have a history of violent trauma (Fullilove et al., 1993; Roberts, 1988; Wilsnack, 1984).

Pregnancy, Substance Abuse, and Domestic Violence

The impact of maternal substance abuse, particularly cocaine abuse, has recently become a major issue in the fields of both substance abuse and family violence. Historically, efforts to work with pregnant women who have abused substances has its roots in the child abuse field. However, professional attention to this problem has spread across disciplines. Andrews and Patterson (1995) attribute the amount of attention to maternal substance abuse to technological innovations permitting increased attention to fetal health and to women's increased use of cocaine, with its devastating effects on a newborn. Such maternal substance abuse cuts across race: Within geodemographically similar groups, the rates of maternal substance abuse are similar among black women and white women (Chasnoff, Landress, & Barrett, 1990). The widespread prevalence of the problem may contribute to the high level of public concern.

Maternal use of substances may begin during pregnancy. The onset of the problem may in turn have its roots in battering, which can set off a cycle of domestic violence and substance abuse during pregnancy. The National Coalition Against Domestic Violence (1996) estimates that between 15% and 25% of pregnant women are battered. Data on women and substance abuse document that women are more likely to abuse substances following violence and other trauma (Fullilove et al., 1993; Skrip & Kunzman, 1991; Thomann, 1992). Domestic violence may, in some cases, trigger substance abuse during pregnancy.

Whatever the cause of maternal substance abuse, longitudinal data demonstrate severe developmental motor, social, and affective impacts from maternal use of tobacco, alcohol, cocaine, cannabis, and opiates (Kaplan-Sanoff & Leib, 1995). Babies born to substance-abusing mothers are more likely to suffer from fetal alcohol syndrome, withdrawal syndrome, child abuse, and neglect (Gaines & Kandal, 1992; McCance-Katz, 1991). Children born to substance-abusing mothers may be at increased risk of eating disorders, antisocial behavior, and stress-related mental and physical disorders in later development (Andrews & Patterson, 1995). Maternal prenatal drug use has also been linked to sudden infant death syndrome (Gaines & Kandal, 1992). Although there is a well-established research history documenting the relationship between alcohol and fetal harm, more research needs to be done on the effects of other forms of maternal substance abuse, particularly cocaine abuse, to establish a similar history between cocaine use and fetal harm (Anderson & Patterson, 1995).

Maternal substance abuse may be a major factor resulting in children being taken from the home. According to Marcenko and Spence (1995), maternal substance abuse is the best predictor of out-of-home living arrangements for children. Women who abuse substances while pregnant have been charged with child abuse in many locales. Such punitive measures are being enforced in many states despite research evidence suggesting that the policy of arresting, indicting, and incarcerating pregnant substance abusers needs reexamination and can actually exacerbate the situation for mother and child (American Psychological Association, 1996; Andrews & Patterson, 1995; Hawk-Norton, 1994; Marcenko, Spence, & Rohweder, 1994). In a policy review, Merrick (1993) argues that policies should focus on rehabilitation rather than criminal prosecution. Policies and programs that focus on rehabilitating substance-abusing pregnant women can address the problem holistically, unlike punitive measures that seek to punish or incarcerate women for their substance-abusing behavior.

Comorbidity of Child Abuse and Substance Abuse

Since 1970, professionals from a variety of disciplines are mandated by law to report any suspicions they have of child maltreatment (Warner & Hansen, 1994). Health professionals such as nurses, health educators, and physicians have worked effectively to identify cases of child abuse (Holtz & Furniss, 1993). Hospitals have been used to analyze child abuse report data (Hampton & Newberger, 1985). Physicians were among the first to document physical manifestations of child abuse (see Caffey, 1946). Physicians may be in ideal positions to detect and prevent family violence (Atwood, 1991; Melvin, 1995). Professionals, including nurses (Rynerson & Fishel, 1993), educators (Caliso & Milner, 1994), physicians (Warner & Hansen, 1994), and social workers (Hegar, Zuravin, & Orme, 1994) have published articles contributing to our understanding of the phenomenon of child abuse. Data on the incidence of child abuse have also been compiled (Straus, 1991).

However, when it comes to the connection between child abuse and substance abuse, the literature is inconsistent and incomplete (Leonard & Jacob, 1988; Martin, 1992; Mignon, 1994). Methodological weaknesses require that the findings to date be regarded as tentative. The most serious shortcoming of existing child abuse studies is the failure to define severity of injury in consistent and useful ways (Hegar et al., 1994).

Despite these limitations, research does suggest that alcoholics or parents under the influence are more likely to maltreat their children. Families in which one or both parents are chemically dependent are at high risk for child abuse (Bijur, Kurzon, Overpeck, & Scheidt, 1992). In the extant literature on child abuse perpetrator characteristics, substance abuse is consistently listed among the behavioral factors (Milner & Chilamkurti, 1991). (See Milner and Crouch, Chapter 2, this volume, for a more comprehensive review of the literature on child abuse perpetrator characteristics.) In a Canadian sample, 27% of the child abuse and neglect cases involved an abuser who was reported to have been intoxicated at the time of the incident (MacMurray, 1979). Compared to a matched control group of nonabusive parents, parents who had abused their children exhibited a significantly higher rate of alcoholism (Famularo, Stone, Barnum, & Wharton, 1986). However, Sorensen, Goldman, Ward, and Albanese (1995) found no apparent impact of parental substance abuse in a Florida study of child abuse custody decisions.

Collaboration in Service Delivery

Despite some inconsistencies in findings regarding the relationship between child abuse and substance abuse, there is support for programs that address both issues simultaneously in an integrated fashion. Schwartz (1989) believes that prevention and education aimed at settings where physicians work must address substance abuse and violence at the same time to be effective. Programs that treat alcohol abuse without also treating domestic violence seem less effective than integrated programs because cessation of substance abuse does not necessarily lead to an end to violent behaviors. In some instances, the termination of substance abuse has actually led to an increase in family violence (Bennett & Lawson, 1994).

Although the evidence seems to indicate that programs need to address both issues in a joint fashion, the dearth of research literature explaining the relationship between substance abuse and family violence has left programs without a reliable set of findings on which to base interventions. However, several common tenets have been traditionally found in both substance abuse and family violence programs, as illustrated in Table 11.1.

In many states, joint service efforts have increased. A growing trend among substance abuse programs is to add family violence components to their services (Gondolf, 1995; Gondolf & Foster, 1991; Manzano, 1990). Several states have also begun to recommend screening for spousal violence among women seeking alcoholism treatment (Miller et al., 1990).

Such coordination still appears to be the exception rather than the norm, however. In their study of substance abuse and domestic violence programs, Bennett and Lawson (1994) found that batterers programs—except for those associated with women's programs—did not screen for addiction. In turn, chemical dependency professionals need to gain a better understanding of battering to discover the signs of battering in a woman's life and to provide culturally appropriate strategies for ending the violence (Minnesota Coalition for Battered Women, 1992).

Differing beliefs about abusers' control over their behavior may be the most important barrier to service coordination between substance abuse and domestic violence programs (Bennett & Lawson, 1994).

Table 11.1 Tenets Used in Both Substance Abuse and Family Violence Programs

Recognition of intergenerational aspects of transmission
Appreciation of how family, friends, and employment are affected
Awareness that the issue may be treated as a family secret
Awareness that the issue is underestimated or misunderstood by larger society
Acknowledgment of the progressive nature of the problem
Understanding of possible associations with other social issues (e.g., poverty, family structure, etc.)
Belief in the cyclical nature of symptom presentation

Substance abuse treatment programs are often based on the disease model (Levy & Brekke, 1990), whereas family violence programs are based on an empowerment model (Bennett & Lawson, 1994). Although Bennett and Lawson (1994) believe that systemic research has not investigated the relationship nor reasons for conflict between substance abuse and domestic violence treatment programs, there is much consensus as to the root of the critical disagreements. The controversies generally arise around the question of whether or not violence is a symptom of addiction and codependency (Kerr, 1992).

Better coordination between family violence and substance abuse treatment programs is needed to provide effective assistance to families struggling with both issues. Funkhouser (1991) recommends a comprehensive approach to substance abuse prevention, one that integrates domestic violence assessment and provides appropriate treatment referrals. In either system, women and men dealing with both substance abuse and family violence should be referred to professionals who are knowledgeable enough about both issues to make appropriate treatment plans (Kerr, 1992). If a person reveals domestic abuse while in treatment for substance abuse, the referral protocol should include at least the following three components: referring children to child protective services, offering batterer counseling and assistance, and referring partners to a domestic violence program. Because of the high correlation between substance abuse and family violence, assessment and intervention for the other problems should be considered a quality assurance issue (Bennett & Lawson, 1994; Conner & Ackerley, 1994). To make this type of coordination smooth, well-coordinated interagency relationships should include formal agreements and written referral procedures between substance abuse and batterer treatment programs (Roberts, 1988).

Collaborative Treatment for Substance-Abusing Mothers

For the substance-abusing mother, research evidence points to a need to explicitly link substance abuse treatment and parent education (Van-Bremen & Chasnoff, 1994). Intervention strategies to increase self-esteem among pregnant substance abusers have also been indicated (Higgins, Clough-Hendel, & Wallerstedt, 1995). Women with substance abuse problems also have more intense needs for basic transportation, housing, and food than women without substance abuse problems (Marcenko et al., 1994). Investigators further argue that the professional delivery systems may need to temporarily serve some of the social network support functions for maternal substance abusers (Marcenko et al., 1994; Steinbock, 1995). Social work literature documents that low-cost prenatal care and substance abuse education for professionals and the public are among the most frequently mentioned initial strategies for dealing with maternal substance abuse (Merrick, 1993).

Prenatal and infant programs offer an ideal communications channel for identifying and reaching families who are at high risk because of maternal substance abuse. Moreover, these programs afford opportunities to prevent child abuse by teaching parents about positive parenting practices and family management (Funkhouser, 1991). However, for long-term success in addressing maternal substance abuse, a coordinated response from medical, child welfare, addictions treatment, family support, and legal systems is essential (Andrews & Patterson, 1995).

Successful treatment programs of all kinds must tailor their interventions to their clients' individual needs and characteristics and must involve their clients in decision making. The Minnesota Coalition for Battered Women (1992) notes that women want to be equal and active participants in the treatment process rather than have decisions forced on them by professionals. The most successful treatment programs also provide an individualized approach (Wekerle & Wolfe, 1993), as well as culturally sensitive programming (Minnesota Coalition for Battered Women, 1992).

Because children from violent and substance-abusing homes are more likely to experience family violence and/or substance abuse as adults, effective treatment should include preventive measures for children. Treatment for children surviving family violence should support bonding with healthy nonviolent role models outside the home. Children should also learn that they can only control their own behavior and not that of their parents, in coping with the violence (Johnson & Montgomery, 1989). Professionals can help to identify survivors of abuse in clinical settings (Skrip & Kunzman, 1991), especially because many women who are survivors of family violence may not remember the abuse (Skrip & Kunzman, 1991).

Conclusion

Great economic, social, and emotional devastation occurs when substance abuse and family violence occur simultaneously. Assault by a known assailant is the leading cause of injury to adult women in the country today, while increasing proportions of youth and adults from all social classes are being lost to substance abuse.

Many of the issues surrounding the relationship between substance abuse and various forms of family violence are not clearly understood. However, teams of individuals from a variety of disciplines can collaborate to develop a better understanding of the network of individual and environmental factors at work in violent and substance-abusing families (Finkelhor, 1988). Some of the research questions that future professionals may address include the following:

- What key societal and familial indicators can explain or predict the comorbidity of substance abuse and family violence?
- How can interventions for either substance abuse or family violence help prevent the onset of the other condition?
- Can recovering addicts and survivors of family violence offer their knowledge to help improve substance abuse and family violence treatment and prevention programs?

There is an urgent need to help develop additional research questions as well as programs that reduce the incidence of substance abuse and keep family members safe from harm. Finally, practice and research can continue to inform policy and legislation designed to diminish impact of substance abuse and family violence nationwide. However, a significant hurdle to any such progress is the difficulty of obtaining accurate and consistent data due to underreporting, ineffective methodologies, and lack of critical analyses. Future research and practice must seek to use culturally appropriate methods of investigating the connections between substance abuse and family violence using data from survivors of these events.

References

Adams, D. (1990). Identifying the assaultive husband in court: You be the judge. *Response to the Victimization of Women and Children, 13,* 13-16.

American Psychiatric Association. (1994). *Diagnostic and Statistical Manual* (4th ed.). Washington, DC: Author.

American Psychological Association. (1996). *Violence and the family* (Report of the American Psychological Association Presidential Task Force on Violence and the Family). Washington, DC: Author.

Andrews, A. B., & Patterson, E. G. (1995). Searching for solutions to alcohol and other drug abuse during pregnancy: Ethics, values, and constitutional principles. *Social Work, 37,* 55-66.

Appleton, W. (1980). The battered woman syndrome. *Annals of Emergency Medicine, 9,* 84-91.

Atwood, J. D. (1991). Domestic violence: The role of alcohol. *Journal of American Medical Association, 265,* 460-461.

Barnett, O. W., & Fagan, R. W. (1993). Alcohol use in male spouse abusers and their female partners. *Journal of Family Violence, 8,* 1-25.

Bennett, L. W. (1995). Substance abuse and the domestic assault of women. *Social Work, 40,* 750-771.

Bennett, L. W., & Lawson, M. (1994). Barriers to cooperation between domestic-violence and substance-abuse programs. *Families in Society,* pp. 277-287.

Bennett, L. W., Tolman, R. M., Rogalski, C. J., & Srinivasaraghavan, J. (1994). Domestic abuse by male alcohol and drug addicts. *Violence and Victims, 9,* 59-68.

Bergman, B., Larsson, G., Brismar, B., & Klang, M. (1989). Battered wives and female alcoholics: A comparative social and psychiatric study. *Journal of Advanced Nursing, 14,* 727-734.

Bijur, P. E., Kurzon, M., Overpeck, M. D., & Scheidt, P. C. (1992). Parental alcohol use, problem drinking, and children's injuries. *Journal of the National Medical Association, 267,* 3166-3171.

Blount, W. R., Silverman, I. J., Sellers, C. S., & Seese, R. A. (1994). Alcohol and drug use among abused women who kill, abused women who don't, and their abusers. *Journal of Drug Issues, 24,* 165-177.

Bronfenbrenner, U. (1989). Toward an experimental ecology of human development. *American Psychologist, 32,* 513-531.

Brown, E. (1993). *Women's assessment procedures.* Paper presented at the Second National Conference on Drug Abuse Research and Practice. Washington, DC: National Institute on Drug Abuse.

Browne, A. (1987). *When battered women kill.* New York: Free Press.

Caffey, J. (1946). Multiple fractures in the long bones of infants suffering from chronic subdural hematoma. *American Journal of Radiology, 56,* 163-173.

Caliso, J. A., & Milner, J. S. (1994). Childhood physical abuse, childhood social support, and adult child abuse potential. *Journal of Interpersonal Violence, 9,* 27-44.

Chasnoff, I. J., Landress, H. J., & Barrett, M. E. (1990). The prevalence of illicit drug or alcohol use during pregnancy and discrepancies in mandatory reporting in Pinellas County, Florida. *New England Journal of Medicine, 322,* 1202-1206.

Conner, K. R., & Ackerley, G. D. (1994). Alcohol-related battering: Developing treatment strategies. *Journal of Family Violence, 9,* 143-155.

Dent, D. Z., & Arias, I. (1990). Effects of alcohol, gender, and role of spouses on attributions and evaluations of marital violence scenarios. *Violence and Victims, 5,* 185-193.

Famularo, R., Stone, K., Barnum, M., & Wharton, R. (1986). Alcoholism and severe child maltreatment. *American Journal of Orthopsychiatry, 56,* 481-485.

Finkelhor, D. (1988). *Stopping family violence: Research priorities for the coming decade.* Newbury Park, CA: Sage.

Flanzer, J. P. (1990). Alcohol and family violence: Then to now—who owns the problem. *Journal of Chemical Dependency Treatment, 3,* 61-79.

Fullilove, M. T., Fullilove, R. E., Smith, M., & Winkler, K. (1993). Violence, trauma, and posttraumatic stress disorder among women drug users. *Journal of Traumatic Stress, 6,* 553-563.

Funkhouser, J. (1991). *The role of communications in prevention.* Washington, DC: National Institute of Drug Abuse (Monograph Series).

Gaines, J., & Kandal, S. R. (1992). Counseling issues related to maternal substance abuse and subsequent sudden infant death syndrome in offspring. *Clinical Social Work Journal, 20,* 169-177.

Gondolf, E. W. (1995). Alcohol abuse, wife assault, and power needs. *Journal of Substance Abuse Treatment.*

Gondolf, E. W., & Foster, R. A. (1991). Wife assault among VA alcohol rehabilitation patients. *Hospital and Community Psychiatry, 42,* 74-79.

Hamberger, K. L., & Hastings, J. E. (1994). Personality correlates of men who batter and nonviolent men. *Journal of Family Violence, 6,* 131-145.

Hampton, R. L., & Coner-Edwards, A. F. (1993). Physical and sexual violence in marriage. In R. L. Hampton, T. P. Gullotta, G. R. Adams, E. H. Potter, & R. P. Weissberg (Eds.), *Family violence: Prevention and treatment* (pp. 113-141). Newbury Park, CA: Sage.

Hampton, R. L., & Newberger, E. H. (1985). Child abuse incidence and reporting by hospitals: The significance of severity, class, and race. *American Journal of Public Health, 75,* 56-60.

Hawk-Norton, M. (1994). How social policies make matters worse: The case of maternal substance abuse. *Journal of Drug Issues, 24,* 517-526.

Hegar, R. L., Zuravin, S. J., & Orme, J. G. (1994). Factors predicting severity of physical child abuse injury: A review of the literature. *Journal of Interpersonal Violence, 9,* 170-183.

Higgins, P. G., Clough-Hendel, D., & Wallerstedt, C. (1995). Self-esteem of pregnant substance abusers. *Maternal Child Nursing Journal, 23,* 75-81.

Hillbrand, M., Foster, H. G., & Hirt, M. (1991). Alcohol abuse, violence, and neurological impairment. *Journal of Interpersonal Violence, 6,* 411-422.

Hilliard, F. (1995). *Women and substance abuse: Understanding the problem.* Racine: Wisconsin Association of Alcohol and Other Drug Abuse.

Holtz, H., & Furniss, K. (1993). The health care providers role in domestic violence. *Trends in Health Care, Law, & Ethic, 8,* 48-57.

Johnson, R. J., & Montgomery, M. (1989). Children at multiple risk: Treatment and prevention. *Journal of Chemical Dependency Treatment, 3,* 145-163.

Kagle, J. K. (1987). Women who drink: Changing images, changing realities. *Journal of Social Work Education, 23,* 21-28.

Kantor, G. K., & Straus, M. A. (1987). The drunken bum theory of wife beating. *Social Problems, 27,* 214-230.

Kantor, G. K., & Straus, M. A. (1989). Substance abuse as a precipitant of wife abuse victimizations. *American Journal of Drug and Alcohol Abuse, 15,* 173-189.

Kaplan-Sanoff, M., & Leib, S. A. (1995). Model intervention programs for mothers and children impacted by substance abuse. *School Psychology Review, 24,* 186-199.

Keller, E. L. (1996). Invisible victims: Battered women in psychiatric and medical emergency rooms. *Bulletin of the Menniger Clinic, 60,* 1-21.

Kerr, P. M. (1992, October). Domestic violence and substance abuse: How can we integrate. *Coalition Reporter: New Jersey Coalition for Battered Women,* pp. 33-34.

Lemle, R., & Mishkind, M. A. (1989). Alcohol and masculinity. *Journal of Substance Abuse Treatment, 6,* 213-222.

Leonard, K., & Jacob, T. (1988). Alcohol, alcoholism, and family violence. In V. B. Van Hasselt (Ed.), *Handbook of family violence.* New York: Plenum.

Leonard, L. E., & Blane, H. T. (1992). Alcohol and marital aggression in a national sample of young men. *Journal of Interpersonal Violence, 7,* 19-30.

Leukefeld, C. G., & Tims, F. M. (1993). Treatment of cocaine abuse and dependence: Directions and recommendations. In *Cocaine treatment: Research and clinical perspectives* (Research Monograph 135). Washington, DC: National Institute on Drug Abuse.

Levy, A. J., & Brekke, J. S. (1990). Spouse battering and chemical dependency: Dynamics, treatment, and service delivery. *Journal of Chemical Dependency Treatment, 3,* 81-97.

MacMurray, V. (1979). The effect and nature of alcohol and abuse in cases of child neglect. *Victimology, 4,* 29-45.

Manzano, T. A. (1990). *The Tulsa model: Integrating family violence and alcohol/drug treatment for abusive males.* Austin: University of Texas Press.

Marcenko, M. O., & Spence, M. (1995). Psychosocial correlates of child out of home living arrangements among at risk pregnant women. *Families in Society, 76,* 369-375.

Marcenko, M. O., Spence, M., & Rohweder, C. (1994). Psychosocial characteristics of pregnant women with and without a history of substance abuse. *Social Work, 22,* 17-22.

Mariano, C. (1989). The case for interdisciplinary collaboration. *Nursing Outlook, 37,* 285-299.

Martin, S. E. (1992). The epidemiology of alcohol-related interpersonal violence. *Alcohol Health and Research World, 22,* 230-236.

McCance-Katz, E. F. (1991). The consequences of maternal substance abuse for the child exposed in utero. *Psychosomatics, 32,* 268-274.

McClelland, D., Davis, W., Kalin, R., & Warner, E. (1972). *The drinking man.* New York: Free Press.

McGaha, J. E., & Leoni, E. L. (1995). Family violence, abuse, and related family issues of incarcerated delinquents with alcoholic parents compared to those with nonalcoholic parents. *Adolescence, 30,* 473-482.

Melvin, S. Y. (1995). Domestic violence: The physician's role. *Hospital Practice, 30,* 45-52.

Merrick, J. C. (1993). Maternal substance abuse during pregnancy: Policy implications in the United States. *Journal of Legal Medicine, 14,* 57-71.

Miczek, K. A., DeBold, J. F., Haney, M., Tidey, J., Vivian, J., & Weerts, E. M. (1994). Alcohol, drugs of abuse, and violence. In A. J. Reiss & J. A. Roth (Eds.), *Understanding and preventing violence* (Vol. 3, pp. 377-570). Washington, DC: National Academy Press.

Mignon, S. I. (1994, March). *Substance abuse and domestic violence: What is the real connection.* Paper presented at the annual meeting of the Academy of Criminal Justice Services, Chicago, IL.

Miller, B. A., & Downs, W. R. (1993). The impact of family violence on the use of alcohol by women. *Alcohol Health and Research World, 17,* 137-143.

Miller, B. A., Downs, W., & Gondoli, M. G. (1990). Alcoholic women as victims of spousal violence. *Brown University Digest of Addiction Theory and Application, 9,* 2-3.

Milner, J. S., & Chilamkurti, C. (1991). Physical child abuse perpetrator characteristics: A review of the literature. *Journal of Interpersonal Violence, 6,* 345-366.

Minnesota Coalition for Battered Women. (1992). *Safety first: Battered women surviving violence when alcohol and drugs are involved.* Duluth: Minnesota Program Development, Inc.

Murphy, C. M., & O'Farrell, T. J. (1994). Factors associated with marital aggression in male alcoholics. *Journal of Family Psychology, 8,* 321-355.

National Coalition Against Domestic Violence. (1996). *Fact sheet on domestic violence.* Washington, DC: Author.

National Institute on Drug Abuse. (1993). *Second National Conference on Drug Abuse Research & Practice: An alliance for the 21st Century.* Washington, DC: Author.

Neff, J. A., Holamon, B., & Schluter, T. D. (1995). Spousal violence among Anglos, blacks, and Mexican Americans: The role of demographic variables, psychosocial predictors, and alcohol consumption. *Journal of Family Violence, 10,* 1-21.

Paymar, M., & Pence, E. (1993). *Working with men who batter: The Duluth model.* New York: Springer.

Pelletier, D., & Coutu, S. (1992). Substance abuse and family violence in adolescents. *Canada's Mental Health, 40,* 6-12.

Pollack, V., Briere, J., Schneider, L., Knop, J., Menick, S., & Goodwin, D. W. (1990). Childhood antecedents of antisocial behavior: Parental alcoholism and physical abusiveness. *American Journal of Psychiatry, 147,* 1290-1293.

Rainbolt, B., & Greene, M. (1990). *Behind the veil of silence: Family violence and alcohol abuse.* Hazelden, MN.

Roberts, A. R. (1988). Substance abuse among men who batter their mates: The dangerous mix. *Journal of Substance Abuse Treatment, 5,* 83-87.

Rynerson, B. C., & Fishel, A. H. (1993). Domestic violence prevention training: Participant characteristics and treatment outcomes. *Journal of Family Violence, 8,* 253-260.

Schiff, M., & Cavaiola, A. A. (1993). Child abuse, adolescent substance abuse, and "deadly violence." *Journal of Adolescent Chemical Dependency, 2,* 131-141.

Schwartz, I. (1989). Alcohol and family violence. *Journal of the American Medical Association, 262,* 351.

Skrip, C., & Kunzman, K. (1991). *Women with secrets: Dealing with domestic abuse and childhood sexual abuse in treatment.* Hazelden, MN.

Slade, M., Daniels, J., & Heisler, C. J. (1991). Application of forensic toxicology to the problem of domestic violence. *Journal of Forensic Sciences, 36,* 708-713.

Somers, M., Love, R., Evans-Schaeffer, H., & Soucar, E. (1994). Domestic violence prevention training: Participant characteristics and treatment outcomes. *Journal of Family Violence, 9,* 383-388.

Sorensen, E., Goldman, J., Ward, M., & Albanese, I. (1995). Judicial decision making in contested custody cases: The influence of reported child abuse, spouse abuse, and parental substance abuse. *Child Abuse & Neglect, 19,* 251-260.

Steinbock, M. R. (1995). Homeless female-headed families: Relationships at risk. *Marriage and Family Review, 20,* 143-159.

Stith, S. M., Crossman, R. K., & Bischof, G. P. (1991). Alcoholism and marital violence: A comparative study of men in alcohol treatment programs and batterer treatment programs. *Alcoholism Treatment Quarterly, 8,* 3-20.

Straus, M. A. (1991). Physical violence in American families: Incidence, rates, causes, and trends. In D. Knudsen & J. Miller (Eds.), *Abused and battered* (pp. 17-33). New York: Aldine de Gruyter.

Straus, M. A., & Gelles, R. (Eds.). (1990). *Physical violence in American families: Risk factors and adaptations in 8,145 families.* New Brunswick, NJ: Transaction

Straus, M. A., Gelles, R. J., & Steinmetz, S. K. (1980). *Behind closed doors: Violence in the American family.* Garden City, NY: Anchor/Doubleday.

Thomann, N. (1992, June). *Substance abuse and minority women.* Paper presented at the Minority Women's Health Issue Forum, Denver, CO.

Tims, F. M., & Leukefeld, C. G. (1993). Treatment of cocaine abusers: Issues and perspectives. *Cocaine treatment: Research and clinical perspectives* (Research Monograph 135). Washington, DC: National Institute on Drug Abuse.

Tolman, R. M., & Bennett, L. W. (1990). A review of quantitative research on men who batter. *Journal of Interpersonal Violence, 5,* 87-118.

Tracy, E. M. (1994). Maternal substance abuse: Protecting the child, preserving the family. *Issues in Substance Abuse, 39,* 534-540.

VanBremen, J. R., & Chasnoff, I. J. (1994). Policy issues for integrating parenting interventions and addiction treatment for women. *Topics in Early Childhood Special Education, 14,* 254-274.

Vanfossen, B. E., & Bonham, G. S. (1992). *Evaluation of substance abuse assessment* (Report No. 3). Center for Suburban and Regional Studies, Towson State University, Maryland.

Warner, J. E., & Hansen, D. J. (1994). The identification and reporting of physical abuse by physicians: A review and implications for research. *Child Abuse & Neglect, 18,* 11-25.

Wekerle, C., & Wolfe, D. A. (1993). Prevention of child physical abuse and neglect: Promising new directions. *Clinical Psychology Review, 13,* 501-540.

Wheat, F. I., & Connors, J. J. (1991). *Families with supported investigations: Prevalence of substance abuse and domestic violence.* Massachusetts: Department of Social Services, Office for Professional Services.

Wilsnack, S. (1984). Drinking, sexuality, and sexual dysfunction in women. In S. Wilsnack (Ed.), *Alcohol problems in women* (pp. 51-75). New York: Guilford.

Wolfe, D. A., Reppucci-Dickson, N., & Hart, S. (1995). Child abuse prevention: Knowledge and priorities. *Journal of Clinical Child Psychology, 24,* 5-22.

Woodall-Jones, B. (1994, July). *Psychological abuse: Another form of violence against women.* Paper presented at the annual meeting of the National Black Nurses' Association, Inc., Atlanta, GA.

Woodhouse, L. D. (1992). Women with jagged edges: Voices from a culture of substance abuse. *Qualitative Health Research 2,* 262-281.

Zubretsky, T. M., & Digirolamo, K. M. (1994). Adult domestic violence: The alcohol connection. *Violence Update, 4,* 8-11.

• *CHAPTER 12* •

The Prediction, Assessment, and Treatment of Family Violence

GARY M. BLAU
DORIAN LONG

Every 5 to 10 seconds, there is an episode of family violence in the United States (Chez, 1988; Monahan, 1996; Stark & Flitcraft, 1987). An angry husband smacks his wife across the face, a frustrated stepfather throws his 6-year-old son through a wall, a betrayed woman stabs her boyfriend in front of her three children. Family members are often the target of each other's violence. Nearly 20% of all murders involve family members as victim and perpetrator, almost 33% of all female homicide victims are killed by their husbands or boyfriends, and 27% of all violence against women is caused by intimates (U.S. Department of Justice, 1994). Straus and Gelles (1986) estimate that more than 2 million women living in couples are abused each year in the United States, and the National Center on Child Abuse and Neglect (1988) has published data indicating that there are more than 1 million reports of child abuse or neglect every year. What is disconcerting, however, is that family violence statistics are thought to grossly underestimate actual incidents (Emery, 1989).

Accurate statistics of violent incidences in families are difficult to obtain, for, as Emery (1989) points out, there are no consistent definitions of what constitutes family violence. Rather, each author may have a different perception of violent behavior (see Arias, Samios, & O'Leary, 1987; Berk, Berk, Loseke, & Rauma, 1983; Craft & Staudt, 1991; Gonzalez-Ramos & Goldstein, 1989; Jaffe, Wolfe, Wilson, & Zak,

1986; Muram, Miller, & Cutler, 1992). Definitions of family violence are further complicated by political, legal, and cultural orientations. For example, some authors posit that family violence must be defined within the sexist organization of the society (Bograd, 1988). Other authors write that family violence must be defined within the context of cultural norms (Hampton, 1987; Sigler, 1989). Still other authors argue that family violence definitions must take into account the legal statutes that govern domestic behavior (Stark & Flitcraft, 1988).

A broad approach to the term considers *violence* to be "behavior that involves the direct use of physical aggression against other household members which is against their will and detrimental to their growth potential" (Lystad, 1986, p. xii). Blau and Campbell (1991) suggest that violent behavior can be described as a continuum ranging from acts of omission (e.g., failure to protect a child from witnessing violence) to acts of verbal commission (e.g., demeaning, threatening, intimidating) to acts of physical commission (e.g., physical altercations, sexual victimization). The specific behaviors must first be identified so that the relationship of the behavior to societal standards may be assessed. Using this concept as a foundation, this chapter seeks to provide an overview of current prediction, assessment, and treatment issues for physically aggressive families. The first section discusses issues related to predicting violence. The second section addresses the assessment process, and the third section reviews current treatment approaches.

Prediction of Family Violence

Predicting violence and predicting violence in the family is perhaps the most controversial topic for mental health professionals (Poythress, 1992). Yet, not only does the criminal justice system rely on predictions of potential dangerousness as part of judicial decision making, mental health professionals have a mandated duty to warn third parties of potential client violence (*Tarasoff v. Regents of the University of California,* 1976), and all states have mandated child abuse reporting laws. Unfortunately, despite the reliance on predictions of future violence and the requirement that mental health professionals protect individuals and family members from potential client violence, there are no national standards to guide judgments about predicting dangerousness (Borum, 1996).

The first difficulty in trying to predict violence is related to base rates. *Base rate* is the term used to describe the prevalence for a specific type of behavior within a particular population over a particular period of time (e.g., suicide, aggression). Although base rates for violent behaviors are higher than previously believed, such behaviors are not common in the general population. It is therefore important to identify risk factors that give rise to violent behaviors. Monahan and Steadman (1994) and Mossman (1994) have identified a variety of risk factors for violent behaviors, including individual (e.g., perceived stress), historical (e.g., past episodes of violence), clinical (e.g., mental illness), and contextual (e.g., social support) variables. Measuring these variables can provide a more systematic attempt to predict violent behaviors (Schopp, 1996).

The Family Violence Prevention Fund (located at 383 Rhode Island Street, Suite 304, San Francisco, CA 94103-5133) and the Center for the Prevention of Sexual and Domestic Violence (located at 936 North 34th Street, Suite 200, Seattle, WA 98103) have also identified a set of risk factors that correspond to increased probability of family violence. These risk factors include threats or fantasies of homicide or suicide, depression, access to weapons, obsessions about a partner or family member, pet abuse, propensity toward rage reactions, and consumption of drugs or alcohol.

Only recently has behavioral science begun to develop standardized tools to predict violence (Borum, 1996). Historically, mental health professionals have relied on clinical judgment. Borum (1996) writes that the first such attempt to standardize and predict violence can be found in the Dangerous Behavior Rating Scheme.

The Dangerous Behavior Rating Scheme represented a significant advance in the standardized prediction of dangerousness (Borum, 1996). Based on Megargee's (1976) conceptualization of predicting dangerousness, this semistructured instrument included items relating to anger, rage, tolerance, and guilt. Interestingly, although the items appeared clinically relevant as measures of dangerousness to self or others, empirical review has not been promising. There have been difficulties with interrater reliability and predictive validity. In a longitudinal study, for example, the Dangerous Behavior Rating Scheme had only a .16 correlation with violence after 1 year (Menzies, Webster, McMain, Staley, & Scaglione, 1994). Despite this lack of empirical support, the importance of the rating scheme as an initial attempt to systematically evaluate the potential for dangerousness should not be undervalued.

Webster, Harris, Rice, Cormier, and Quinsey (1994) developed an instrument for assessing dangerousness that used both clinical and statistical approaches. Named the Violence Prediction Scheme, this instrument combined the 12-item Violence Risk Assessment Guide (Harris, Rice, & Quinsey, 1993) with a 10-item clinical tool. The clinical component included factors such as history, self-presentation, adjustment, symptoms, and treatment progress. Information about the Violence Prediction Scheme can be obtained from the University of Toronto, Centre of Criminology (905-978-7124).

Kropp, Hart, Webster, and Eaves (1994) have developed a 20-item clinical checklist of factors related to spousal assault called the Spousal Assault Risk Assessment Guide. Used primarily as a clinical guide for assessing the risk of violence in men arrested for spousal assault, the guide has four main sections, criminal history, psychosocial adjustment, spousal assault history, and current offense factors. Initial interrater reliability data are good, and high risk scores have been linked with reoffending behavior. Interested readers can contact the British Columbia Institute of Family Violence in Vancouver, British Columbia (604-669-7055) for more information.

More specific to predicting risk in families, many authors have described strategies to standardize risk assessment tools (Doueck, English, DePanfilis, & Moote, 1993; McDonald & Marks, 1991). More recently, due to the link between substance abuse and violence against children (Blau, Whewell, Gullotta, & Bloom, 1994), the need to develop instruments that predict risk in families affected by substance abuse has been identified. Olsen, Allen, and Azzi-Lessing (1996) present such an instrument. The Risk Inventory for Substance Abuse-Affected Families contains eight scales that include parental commitment to recovery, patterns of substance use, effect of parental substance abuse on their ability to care for child(ren), parental well-being, and neighborhood safety. Test-retest, interrater, and internal consistency reliability data have yielded positive results. Test-retest correlations ranged from .71 to .98, interrater reliability correlations ranged from .55 to .91, and internal consistency correlations ranged from .55 to .85 (Olsen et al., 1996). Further work will be needed to determine if this instrument has predictive validity.

Assessment of Family Violence

Because decisions regarding the occurrence of violence within a family have substantial impact on children and their families, it is crucial that the development and use of assessment procedures serve as a means of facilitating treatment planning and monitoring client progress. There are two distinct types of assessment: investigative assessment and interventive assessment (Goldstein & Gonzalez-Ramos, 1989). Mouzakitis (1985) writes that an investigative assessment, often conducted by protective service or police personnel, must ascertain the severity and nature of the violent behavior. In doing so, investigative personnel must make a determination regarding the continued risk to individuals within the home and the necessity for legal/court involvement (see Stein, Chapter 4, this volume). Specifically, Mouzakitis (1985) writes that investigative personnel must be able to evaluate whether the perpetrators are capable of controlling their hostile and aggressive impulses, whether they recognize that their behavior is abusive or problematic, whether they demonstrate cooperation, and whether there is continued risk for additional violence. The investigative assessment is further encumbered by the crisis nature of the situation. The individuals are not participating on a voluntary basis, the circumstances may be potentially life threatening, and any diagnostic procedures may be viewed as intrusive.

Interventive assessment (also called continuous assessment) typically occurs after the crisis situation has stabilized (Goldstein & Gonzalez-Ramos, 1989). Asen, George, Piper, and Stevens (1988) and Belsky (1980) offer research that supports the use of an ecological approach to evaluation. Such an approach involves gathering data regarding the functioning of children, adults, and families, as well as gaining an understanding of the impact of the social environment on these individuals and families. Individual assessments may be conducted to determine a person's physical, intellectual, emotional, developmental, and social status. The family system may be evaluated to gain an understanding of communication patterns, roles and structure, child-rearing practices, social integration, and resources (e.g., housing, financial). The assessment of the family must be made within its social and environmental context to address the family's stressors and support network.

In most cases, the assessment process is conducted by professionals, each of whom has his or her own worldview (Sarason, 1981). Thus, it is not surprising that family violence assessment is criticized as subjective. Interpretations, predictions, and decisions that rely on techniques such as interviewing and projective testing could therefore be biased by the investigator's perceptions of violence.

Standardized measurements have been developed in an effort to decrease such bias. These instruments seek to improve the validity of data collection procedures and to provide a strategy for evaluating prevention and intervention strategies. Standardized assessment methods include self-report inventories, behavioral rating scales, structured interviews, and observational coding systems. These instruments may be used at multiple levels: individual, family, and environment. At the individual level, the association between violence and such factors as self-esteem, coping styles, depression, interpersonal relationships, and parenting skills are measured (Belsky, 1980; see also Milner & Crouch, Chapter 2, this volume). For example, in her study of the relationship between child abuse and neglect and maternal depression, Zuravin (1984) found that mothers who were moderately or severely depressed were over 180% more likely to abuse their children than nondepressed mothers.

Individual inventories to assess such factors as depression, anxiety, self-esteem, and stress include the Beck Depression Inventory (Beck & Beamesderfer, 1974), the Children's Depression Inventory (Saylor, Finch, Spirito, & Bennett, 1984), the Revised Children's Manifest Anxiety Inventory (Reynolds & Richmond, 1978), and the Coopersmith Self-Esteem Inventory (Coopersmith, 1981).

For issues of parental violence, a more specific individual assessment is the Parenting Stress Index (Abidin, 1983). The Parenting Stress Index provides an assessment of parental frustration and self-esteem (Abidin, 1983). Using a 5-point Likert scale, a parent indicates his or her level of agreement with 101 items, from *strongly agree* to *strongly disagree.* Subscales include measures of parent depression or unhappiness, parent attachment, restrictions imposed by the parental role, and a parent's sense of competence. Test-retest reliability correlations between .69 and .91 have been demonstrated depending on the length of time that has elapsed between test administrations (Grotevant & Carlson, 1989). Grotevant and Carlson (1989) also report that numerous studies have demonstrated the Parenting Stress Index's content, construct, and criterion-related validity. For example, Mash, Johnson, and Krovitz (1983) found that the index successfully discriminated between samples of physically abusive and nonabusive mothers.

For abusive mothers, the Maternal Esteem Scale has been used to provide specific information about an individual's feelings regarding her parental role (Koeske & Koeske, 1990). On this scale, a respondent rates herself as a mother on 14 trait adjectives, using a 5-point Likert scale. A response of 5 to such traits as sympathetic, moody, or ambitious represents the mother's perception of the trait as *always or almost always true,* whereas a response of 1 indicates that a respondent believes the trait to be *never or almost never true.* High scores are interpreted as reflecting a positive sense of self-esteem as a mother. Low maternal self-esteem may be a contributor to violence against children.

Standardized assessment instruments have also been developed to evaluate family interaction and relationships. Family measures can provide specific descriptions of dysfunctional processes (e.g., marital discord, reciprocal cycles of aversive behavior, reinforcement of inappropriate behavior, ineffective use of appropriate consequences). Researchers have found that abusive families display distorted patterns of parent-child interactions, as well as dysfunctional marital relationships (see Milner & Crouch, Chapter 2, this volume). Examples of instruments include the Parent-Child Behavioral Coding System (Forehand & McMahon, 1981), the Dyadic Adjustment Scale (Spanier & Filsinger, 1983), the Family Adaptability and Cohesion Evaluation Scale (Olson, 1986), the Index of Marital Satisfaction (Hudson, 1982), the Index of Spouse Abuse (Hudson & McIntosh, 1981), and the Adult-Adolescent Parenting Inventory (Bavolek, 1984).

One widely used self-report inventory is the Adult-Adolescent Parenting Inventory (Bavolek, 1984). The inventory consists of 32 statements reflecting perception of the parent's role and the child's role within the family. A parent is instructed to circle his or her level of agreement with each statement on a 5-point Likert scale ranging from *strongly agree* to *strongly disagree.* A respondent can also mark *uncertain.*

An analysis of responses yields constructs of parenting attitudes, including inappropriate expectations, empathy, corporal punishment, and role reversal. Scores, which have been standardized for white, black, Hispanic, and Asian parents, develop a profile that Grotevant and Carlson (1989) describe as having discriminant validity based on the instrument's ability to distinguish between abusive and nonabusive populations. Studies of internal reliability are in the adequate range (coefficients from .70 to .86) (Bavolek, 1984; Grotevant & Carlson, 1989). Responses on the Adult-Adolescent Parenting Inventory, as with all self-report measures, may be susceptible to a social desirability effect and may therefore measure cognitive awareness of culturally determined expectancies rather than actual parental behavior.

Environmental measures take into account such factors as life stress and social support. Howing, Wodarski, Guadin, and Kurtz (1989), for example, write that social isolation is one of the most powerful factors distinguishing maltreating from nonmaltreating families. Straus, Gelles, and Steinmetz (1988) write that personal life stress (e.g., loss of job, death of a family member) and lack of effective social support tend to increase the likelihood of violence and child abuse. Examples of environmental measures can be found in the Family Inventory of Life Events and Changes (McCubbin & Patterson, 1983) and the Social Support Behaviors Scale (Vaux, Riedell, & Stewart, 1987).

The Social Support Behaviors Scale is a 45-item self-report inventory designed to measure five areas of support: emotional support, socializing, practical assistance, financial assistance, and advice/guidance. Respondents record the likelihood of receiving support on a 5-point scale (from *no one would do this* to *most family members/friends would certainly do this*). Another instrument that assesses the social support of a family is the Inventory of Socially Supportive Behaviors (Barrera, Sandler, & Ramsay, 1981). A 40-item self-report measure, the inventory provides an understanding of the frequency and source of an individual's available support. Respondents indicate, on a 5-point scale ranging from *not at all* to *about every day,* the frequency with which support was obtained from other people. Individuals who are identified as sources of support may be used as resources for the family during the treatment process.

Several measures have been developed that attempt to account for all levels of assessment. These ecological-type assessment devices include the Child Abuse Potential Survey (Milner, Gold, Ayoub, & Jacewitz, 1984), the Family Risk Scales (Magura, Moses, & Jones, 1987), and the Child Well-Being Scales (Magura & Moses, 1986).

The ultimate goal of all assessment strategies, whether individual or family, subjective or objective, is to assist practitioners and researchers in screening, treatment planning, monitoring client change, and program evaluation. Of particular importance to clinical practitioners is the use of these devices in the development of treatment interventions.

Family Violence Interventions

Interventions for violent families include the provision of shelters or safe houses, the removal of the perpetrator, and the placement of endangered children (Jennings, 1990). Therapeutic interventions are often employed as part of a rehabilitative process. Clinical interventions for violent families include treatment for abusive parents, therapy for victims, family therapy, and community-based therapy. For a comprehensive evaluation of treatment approaches specific to the battering male, the reader is directed to Chapter 9 by Bennett and Williams in this volume.

Treatment for Abusive Parents

There are numerous strategies for working with violent parents. Research suggests that behavior therapy is particularly effective (Bornstein & Kazdin, 1985; Crimmins, Bradlyn, St. Lawrence, & Kelly, 1984; Howing et al., 1989; Trickett & Kuczynski, 1986; Wolfe et al., 1982). Behavioral methods are based on the assumption that violent behavior is learned through socialization. For example, a parent may be "rewarded" for spanking a child by the cessation of the unwanted behavior. Behavioral treatment involves teaching new behavioral responses. A parent is taught to chart a child's behavior, to reward positive behaviors, and to practice nonviolent discipline procedures such as time-out, response cost, and withdrawing privileges. Behavioral strategies such as role-playing, modeling, and rehearsal may be employed (Bornstein & Kazdin, 1985). Behavioral techniques have been shown, by some studies, to increase knowledge of appropriate parenting and to reduce violent behaviors (Wolfe & Sandler, 1981). These strategies, however, have been criticized for failing to address the cognitions of abusive individuals (Gambrill, 1983).

The importance of modifying the cognitions of abusive parents has received considerable attention (Morton, Twentyman, & Azar, 1988). Berkowitz (1983), for example, argues that aggressive behavior occurs when an organism perceives a stimulus to be aversive, a theory referred to as *aversively stimulated aggression* (Emery, 1989). When a negative perception is coupled with a history of reinforcement for violent behavior, aggressive behavior has a higher probability of occurrence (Vasta, 1982). This conceptualization suggests interventions using cognitive-behavioral strategies. Aversive stimuli may result from unrealistic parental expectations or the misattribution of negative intent to a child's behavior. For example, a young woman in therapy with one of the authors insisted that her 8-month-old child was violent, when, in fact, the infant was simply thrashing his arms in excitement. This young woman also stated that her baby, who was developmentally unprepared to walk, would be able to walk "if he weren't so lazy."

In an attempt to modify the negative cognitions of abusive parents, Whiteman, Fanshel, and Grundy (1987) used a cognitive-behavioral intervention. Participants were taught to reduce their feelings of anger and aversive arousal by attributing a less negative meaning to a potentially provoking situation. Participants were also taught to evaluate alternative response options. Results of this six-session intervention were quite good, and the authors concluded that this methodology could greatly enhance clinical interventions for violent families (Whiteman et al., 1987).

Unfortunately, despite the numerous studies supporting the effectiveness of behavioral and cognitive-behavioral interventions, these approaches are criticized for failing to account for the complexity of violent behavior (Jennings, 1990). Although observable expressions of violence may be eliminated in the short term, it is unlikely that the elimination of violent behavior will be maintained. Jennings (1990) states that a short-term approach will only reach the "tip of the iceberg" (p. 50) and is simply unrealistic. In addition, if a perpetrator is assessed to have sociopathic or antisocial tendencies, treatment will most likely have no effect (see Bennett & Williams, Chapter 9, in this volume).

As an alternative to short-term individual therapy, Jennings (1990) calls for a lifelong approach. Long-term monitoring and support (similar to the methods used in substance abuse recovery) are favored over brief involvement. Unfortunately, there are few long-term supportive programs and even fewer evaluation studies (Wesch & Lutzker, 1991). Abusers often drop out of treatment after a period of abstinence or when legal proceedings have concluded. In addition, long-term approaches tend to be insight oriented, and this method has been criticized because many perpetrators do not have the verbal capacity, cognitive ability, or financial resources to benefit from this strategy (Howing et al., 1989).

More recent clinical interventions with abusive parents are based on a developmental model (Gondolf, 1987). For example, Kohlberg's (1981) conceptualization of the stages of moral reasoning and action can be incorporated into the therapy. Kohlberg characterized moral thought as developing at three levels, each having two stages. In Level 1 (preconventional), moral behavior is a response to perceived threat of external consequences. In Level 2 (conventional), moral behavior is motivated by expectation or duty, and in Level 3 (postconventional), moral behavior is dictated by values and ethical principles. Gondolf and Hanneken (1987) describe abusers as being unconcerned about anyone but themselves and only concerned about their own outcome (e.g., incarceration). This ideology corresponds to the most primitive level of Kohlberg's theory. The goal of therapy, therefore, is for the abuser to develop a higher level of moral functioning. Gondolf (1987) states that clinicians must first respond to the abuser's denial and egocentrism. The abuser often feels justified for using violence and is totally preoccupied with his or her own needs and wants. At this stage, it is important to identify parameters of acceptable behavior and to delineate the rewards and consequences of specific behaviors. External constraints may be the only motivating factor for abusers in this state, and therapeutic confrontation may be necessary for the abuser to acknowledge the dysfunctional nature of the violent behavior. For example, Wolfe, Aragona, Kaufman, and Sandler (1980) and Irueste-Montes and Montes (1988) report that court orders may be needed to facilitate treatment participation. Protective service leverage also may be necessary to engage families in treatment.

Once the abuser has recognized that his or her behavior has caused severe harm to him- or herself and others, the next stage requires self-control, introspection, and relationship building (Gondolf, 1987). This corresponds to Level 2 of Kohlberg's theory, in which behavior is performed out of conformity. The abuser becomes aware of other people's feelings and explores his or her own past as a means of understanding the root of the violent behavior. This insight becomes the foundation for the development of empathy.

In the final stage of treatment based on Kohlberg's developmental formulation, the abuser is encouraged to analyze violent behavior in terms of societal and cultural influences. This is thought to facilitate the development of Level 3 thought and action in which behavior is performed out of a sense of principle. Gondolf (1987) states that guiding abusers into community service or social action helps reinforce and maintain their attempts to change.

Despite evidence recognizing the importance of individual interventions for abusive parents, many authors (Feazell, Myers, & Deschner, 1984; Howing et al., 1989; Jennings, 1987; Rosenbaum, 1986; Steinfeld, 1989; Taubman, 1986) write that individual treatment is not sufficient to produce behavioral change and prevent future episodes of violence. For example, in a study of 19 federally funded demonstration projects, Daro (1988) concluded that individual therapy was less effective in reducing the propensity toward violence than other treatment modalities. Thus, at the very least, individual interventions should be augmented by alternative approaches. One of the most popular alternatives to individual therapy is group work.

Group Therapy for Abusive Parents. Groups are believed to provide a powerful impetus for change by incorporating peer feedback and allowing for the validation of feelings (Cohn & Daro, 1987). Howing et al. (1989) write that groups allow for the mutual sharing of coping strategies and serve to reduce the social isolation experienced by many abusers. A variety of groups have been developed to treat and prevent violent behavior in families (Gondolf, 1987). For abusive parents, parent training programs are often employed. The basic tenet of these programs is that abusive parents have unrealistic expectations of their children, lack sufficient child management skills, and lack basic knowledge about interaction and communication.

Parent groups are typically time limited and didactic, and information is presented on child development, behavior management techniques (e.g., contingency contracting), stress reduction procedures, and family interaction patterns. Psychoeducational groups average between 6 and 12 sessions and usually last for a period of less than 3 months (Jennings, 1987). Using a problem-solving and discussion format, parents (or other adult perpetrators) are encouraged to develop alternatives to violent behaviors and are taught about the cycle of violence (Dodge, Bates, & Pettit, 1990), which is the typical pattern of abusive behavior in families. In the first phase, there is increased tension and anger. In the second phase, emotions erupt into violent actions such as threatening, hitting, slapping, choking, throwing, and sexual assault. The third (and final) phase, referred to as the calm phase, is marked by apologies and promises. The abuser may blame the violence on external factors (e.g., alcohol) and reassure the victim that it "won't happen again." Unfortunately, not only does the violence typically happen again, but the length of time spent in Phase 3 will decrease as the violence is repeated (Stark & Flitcraft, 1987).

Many psychoeducational programs have reported positive outcomes. Increases in knowledge and skill, as well as reductions in the overall propensity toward violence, have been demonstrated (Cohn & Daro, 1987). Cohn and Daro (1987) report that adults who received educational group counseling were more likely to demonstrate progress in treatment than adults who did not receive these services. Most effectiveness studies, however, fail to assess the long-term impact of programs.

This is unfortunate, because evidence suggests that abusive parents do not transfer their learning to home situations (Goldstein, Keller, & Erne, 1985).

Self-help groups have been found to be a successful adjunct in family violence treatment (Howing et al., 1989). The most widely known self-help group is Parents Anonymous. With more that 1,500 chapters nationwide, Parents Anonymous provides peer support for abusive parents through regular meetings and the use of a mentoring or sponsorship model. In this model, the individuals who have become successful in controlling their violence become the support system for individuals who continue to struggle with the propensity toward violence. Although volunteer and professional sponsors are often difficult to obtain, the use of this strategy as a component in service delivery has been found to reduce overall recidivism rates in participants (Cohn & Daro, 1987). This model also has been applauded because it recognizes that perpetrators of violence need long-term assistance and support to remain in control of their behaviors (Jennings, 1990).

Anger control groups have become an increasingly popular strategy in treating violent offenders. Many of these groups are based on cognitive-behavioral principles, although there is often an educational component. Edelson (1984) describes a program for battering males in which participants are taught to reduce violent behavior by learning to cope more effectively with anger. Initially, each group member is taught to become self-observant. The idea is for the participant to identify the physical, behavioral, and cognitive cues that are associated with feelings of anger. Participants are often asked to keep a diary or "anger log" to describe any anger-provoking situation, complete with a description of the thoughts and feelings associated with the incident and the recording of any coping strategy that led to the successful avoidance of violence. To facilitate successful coping, anger control groups often try to restructure irrational thoughts or faulty belief systems. For example, an individual who believes he or she must have control over everything needs to modify this belief to avoid unnecessary conflicts over such issues as child rearing and finances. Anger control groups also attempt to increase alternative responses to anger-producing situations. For example, conflict resolution skills and self-relaxation techniques may be taught as a more appropriate response to anger. Edleson (1984) and Deschner and McNeil (1986) have demonstrated that improving the ability to control anger significantly increases the possibility that conflicts can be resolved nonviolently.

Therapy for Victims

The needs and functioning of victims are also important when developing interventions for violent families. Individual and group treatment approaches have been used. Although insight-oriented therapies have been attempted with battered women, most theorists and practitioners advocate a cognitive approach to treatment (Cox & Stoltenberg, 1991). Insight approaches are based on pathology (e.g., inadequate personality), whereas cognitive approaches tend to focus on skill development. If the battered woman lacks the necessary skills to extricate herself from an abusive situation, she must be taught to identify alternative strategies. For victimized women, Stark and Flitcraft (1988) write that autonomy and empowerment are the most important therapeutic goals. The idea is to restore personal power so that the battered woman will be capable of acting in her own best interest. Many authors contend that victims of violence develop feelings of helplessness, which, in turn, undermine self-esteem and the ability to seek help (Hilberman, 1980; Stark & Flitcraft, 1988). The battered woman may feel trapped and subordinate; she may experience agitation, anxiety, and depression; and she may not have the resources or support to prevent future episodes of violence. This treatment must engender support and advocacy and facilitate the identification of alternatives and options.

A child's trauma is experienced in accordance with his or her developmental level. A child may feel intense rage, fear, and guilt and may exhibit withdrawn, aggressive, or defiant behaviors. A child may also develop interpersonal difficulties (e.g., poor attachment) and view him- or herself as bad or worthless. These feelings may be exacerbated if the child must also experience multiple placements or rejections.

Howing et al. (1989) state that individual therapy for abused children is often the preferred intervention. The use of behavior therapy has received the most empirical support (Burgess, Anderson, Schellenbach, & Conger, 1981). For example, the behavioral technique of contingency contracting has been shown to effectively increase the prosocial behavior of abused children (Howing et al., 1989). In addition to exhibiting negative observable behaviors, however, the abused child often internalizes the abuse and needs to communicate the trauma as a means of reworking, piecemeal, what was experienced as overwhelming (Mann & McDermott, 1983). This may be best communicated through play.

Play is a child's most natural form of communication, and a skilled therapist can facilitate an abused child's symbolic expression of feelings and fantasies in a safe manner. Mann and McDermott (1983) describe a four-phase framework for treating abused children. In Phase 1, the goal is to establish rapport and learn how to play. In this stage, the therapist seeks to establish trust and to understand the metaphor of the youngster's play. In Phase 2, the child explores the trauma through the process of disclosure. Whereas some children may directly verbalize their experiences, others may communicate through art, story, or puppets. Mann and McDermott (1983) refer to this process as "regression and abreaction" (p. 293). This process involves the weakening of emotional tensions through reliving (via thoughts, feelings, actions, or imagination) the circumstances of the conflict. As the child makes statements and develops play themes reflecting abuse, the therapist provides a corrective emotional experience and assists the child in establishing more functional coping mechanisms.

In Phase 3 of therapy, which Mann and McDermott (1983) call the testing of real relationships and the development of impulse control and self-esteem, the abused child is aided in developing empathy and is helped to identify his or her own strengths. Phase 4 involves the process of termination. The therapist must slowly discontinue therapy, with respect for the child's feeling of rejection and abandonment. Although historically supported (Bixler, 1976; Ginott, 1976), there has been very little research on the effectiveness of play therapy with abused children. Green (1978) and Crenshaw, Rudy, Treimer, and Zingaro (1986), however, have found that play therapy improves the overall functioning of abused children.

Group Therapy for Victims. For victims, participation in group therapy has been widely supported in both the clinical and research communities (Daro, 1988). In his seminal work, Yalom (1975) contends that involvement in groups is "curative" (p. 60), especially when compared with other forms of intervention. To demonstrate this, Yalom, based on input from professionals, developed a list of potential curative factors (e.g., having people listen, finding out that other people have similar problems). Using a Q-sort procedure, Yalom then asked for prior group participants to rank the relative importance of these curative factors. In sum, group involvement was deemed effective because it allowed participants to receive modeling and feedback from other group members who had similar experiences and needs. Groups were thought to help members gain insight, develop support, and increase hope. Thus, as

Daro (1988) states, groups can often be a potent strategy when helping children and adults cope with their victimization.

Although long-term, analytically oriented therapy groups have been used with victimized populations, cognitive and behavioral strategies are more common (Blau & Campbell, 1990). Cox and Stoltenberg (1991) provide a good example of a group treatment program. These researchers, using a control group design, investigated the use of group procedures for battered women who had voluntarily sought protective shelter from their abusive situations. Women were assigned to either the experimental or control group based on the time of year they sought services. Women in the experimental condition received a group treatment program consisting of five modules: the cognitive module, the self-assertiveness and communications skills module, the problem-solving module, the vocational counseling module, and the body awareness module. The treatment program consisted of 12 hours of training (three times a week for 2 weeks) as well as weekly individual counseling sessions. This investigation found that women in the experimental conditions demonstrated significant pre-post improvement on measures of affect (anxiety, depression, and hostility), assertiveness, and self-esteem. A major limitation of this study, however, is that there was no longer-term follow-up. Thus, it is unknown whether the skills learned during group participation helped to prevent future episodes of victimization.

Perhaps the most recent advance for the treatment of victimized women is the use of mentoring or mutual-aid groups. Mentoring groups have assisted with the improvement of academic skills (peer tutoring) and the prevention of drug and alcohol abuse (peer counseling) (Danish, 1991). For victimized women, the first step in developing a mentoring program is to train a group of peers to become advocates for women who are in abusive relationships. A professional facilitator is typically necessary and can provide technical and clinical assistance. Training for peer advocates includes education on such topics as the cycle of violence and the battering syndrome as well as instruction in listening skills and ways to access resources. The peer advocates have often experienced their own victimization but have demonstrated some form of successful coping, thus becoming role models. The role of the peer advocate/mentor is to provide information and support to decrease the risk of family violence, reduce stress factors, enhance self-esteem and self-sufficiency, and increase the appropriate use of community resources.

Group therapy has also been used to treat victimized children. Behavioral methods have received the most empirical support. For example, social skills groups have been shown to help maltreated children overcome social deficits and improve peer relationships (Fantuzzo et al., 1988). These groups target specific social behaviors (e.g., making eye contact) and develop reward systems to increase identified behaviors. This technique may be particularly useful with younger, withdrawn children (Steward, Farquhar, Dicharry, Glick, & Martin, 1986). As in adult groups, the ability to share information about traumatic experiences also has been deemed a curative factor in children's groups.

Family Therapy

Interventions may be designed to involve, in varying degrees, both the victim and the abuser. One such intervention is a model for family therapy with abusive families described by Bowen (1976). The underlying concept is that family patterns, such as the intergenerational transmission of violent behaviors, must be understood and altered to prevent future episodes of violence. Although there is very little research on the effectiveness of this technique, many professionals now recognize family violence as a family systems problem (Bolton & Bolton, 1987). Problems in family structure, boundaries, and communication are all factors that give rise to the potential for violence. Therapeutic interventions include reorganizing the loyalties between generations, developing self-family differentiation, exploring family projection schemes, and improving communication and listening skills. Daro (1988) concluded that family therapy is particularly useful for neglectful families. Benefits also have been demonstrated, however, for physically abusive families. Assisting families in restructuring their interactions and relationships can facilitate improved functioning and reduce the chance for violence (Woods, 1988). One technique that has been proposed is the transgenerational themes strategy (Anderson, 1984). By this method, family members trace their family history back several generations to understand how the family of origin has affected current functioning. Once this understanding is established, the clinician can help the family alter maladaptive patterns through the development of new family themes.

Family therapy has received much criticism for not taking into account the potential for retraumatization of victims (Mann & McDermott, 1983). In fact, inappropriately forcing victims to attend therapy with their abusers may create significant anxiety, fear, and guilt (Sigler, 1989). For example, an abusive, self-absorbed parent may be unconcerned if he appears threatening or intimidating in front of his victimized child. Howing et al. (1989) state, however, that family therapy can be particularly valuable in the later stages of treatment. Once the abused victim and other family members have progressed in individual and group therapy, family therapy can facilitate additional change, for example, by allowing confrontations and the expression of feelings. Clinicians must use caution, however, to ensure that this treatment approach respects the needs of all participants.

Community-Based Interventions

Perhaps the most recent advance in service delivery for violent families is the use of community-based interventions. The most common of these interventions is family support in the home (Barth, 1990; Roberts, Wasik, Castro, & Ramey, 1991). Although providing therapy in a family's home is not a new idea (tracing its history to the early roots of social work), the incorporation of this model is often seen as innovative (Woods, 1988). Home-based services combine the provision of concrete services, such as responding to a family's basic needs for food, clothing, medical services, and transportation, with other services, such as respite care and legal assistance (Roberts & Wasik, 1990; Zigler & Black, 1989). The belief is that providing service in a family's home will allow for more accurate assessment, provide the opportunity to model behaviors in the environment in which they will be adopted, and increase a family's feelings of empowerment by developing resources (Nelson, 1990). This, in turn, may serve to improve family functioning and reduce the probability of future violence (Halpern, 1986).

Home-based services, such as parent aide programs, may be provided by volunteers or paraprofessionals. Parent aide programs have become widespread in North America. In fact, the U.S. Department of Health, Education, and Welfare produced a manual on the subject in the late 1970s (Gifford, Kaplan, & Salus, 1979). Parent aides may visit a home for 2 to 4 hours per week and are trained to provide emotional support for the abusive family, teach parenting skills, and assist in securing appropriate concrete resources such as medical care, food stamps, or Aid to Families with Dependent Children (AFDC), now known as Temporary Assistance to Needy Families. Parent aides may also help with concrete tasks such as improving nutritional habits and home cleanliness (Lines, 1987).

In a 5-year study of the effectiveness of parent aide programs, Lines (1987) compared a group of abusive mothers who received parent aide services with a group who did not: 36 clients received the services, and the average rate of the monthly contact was 22 hours. Lines (1987) reports that the parent aide program was highly successful. Reabuse rates were less than 3% for program participants (1 in 36) compared with an average rate of 8% in the comparison group. Positive effects were also found in that the abusive mothers viewed their child or children more favorably, were able to identify appropriate resources, and felt more confident in their ability to cope with future crises. Parent aide programs have also been found to be cost-effective (Daro, 1988; Miller, Fein, Howe, Gaudio, & Bishop, 1985). Halpern (1984) and Haynes, Cutler, Gray, and Kempe (1984), however, reported no differences in the outcome when clients of a parent aide program were compared with a control group. In addition, Barth (1991), in his experimental evaluation of in-home child abuse prevention services, reported that the efficacy of paraprofessionals is unclear. Therefore, it is recommended that parent aides not be used in isolation but, instead, as part of a comprehensive treatment approach (Barth, 1991; Hornick & Clarke, 1986).

The need for home-based therapeutic services has also been advanced (Eyberse, Maffuid, & Blau, 1996; Nelson, Landsman, & Deutelbaum, 1990; Woods, 1988). Being in the home, the clinician may gain a more complete understanding of a client's unique situation. The clinician can observe the physical characteristics of a family's home (e.g., cleanliness, furnishings, space), the dynamics of interaction patterns (e.g., family seating arrangement, behavioral roles), and a host of other factors such as emotional status, medical needs, and available resources and supports. Woods (1988) writes that a home-based therapist also sends a message to the family that the therapist is willing to reach out, thus facilitating the establishment of rapport. This may be particularly advantageous when a therapist's culture, ethnicity, or financial status differs from those of the client (Gray & Nybell, 1990).

Many authors currently are advocating for more in-home service, particularly for abusive families (Eyberse et al., 1996; Montalvo, 1986; Sefarbi, 1986; Simon, 1986; Woods, 1988). Home-based models are thought to enhance the probability of a successful outcome. It is rare, however, for a clinical treatment plan to include a strategy for any extended in-home service. Rather, home-based clinical interventions tend to be short-term and crisis-oriented (Wesch & Lutzker, 1991).

Family preservation is the term ascribed to in-home interventions for families who are at imminent risk of having a child or children removed from the home due to abuse or neglect (Maluccio, 1991). Although there are several theoretical models for family preservation service (Barth, 1990), the basic program includes a crisis orientation, a focus on the family, the use of home-based services delivery, strict time limits (usually between 4 and 12 weeks), concrete objectives, intensive involvement (often as much a 20 to 25 hours per week), an emphasis on education and skill building, coordination, networking, and 24-hour accessibility (Maluccio, 1991). In an outcome study of family preservation programs, Pecora, Fraser, Haapala, and Bartlome (1987) evaluated the percentage of children who were able to remain safely in their home environment for a year following the initial referral to the preservation program. The results were astonishing. Almost 93% of the at-risk children receiving family preservation service remained with their families. Unfortunately, the results have been severely criticized. First, there has yet to be a systematic evaluation of a family preservation program that uses a randomly assigned control group. In addition, problems with outcome measures have been raised. For example, defining success as a child remaining with his or her family does not reflect the possibility that a foster placement may actually be in the child's best interest. Finally, program services (e.g., intake criteria, theoretical foundation) vary, and this has reduced the generalizabilty of results (Whittaker, Kinney, Tracy, & Booth, 1990). Despite these criticisms, however, this model is currently enjoying widespread support among professionals who treat abusive families, and some families may prefer in-home treatment to that of an office or clinic setting.

Comprehensive Service Delivery

The most common criticism leveled against any clinical intervention for violent families is the lack of service integration (Emery, 1989; Helfer, 1991; Howing et al., 1989; Wesch & Lutzker, 1991). Indeed, studies of particular treatment modalities (e.g., groups for battered wives, anger control groups, parent aides) often cite the need to involve the abusive family's total ecological system in treatment planning. The complexity of violent behavior and its association with poverty, drug and alcohol use, societal standards, poor medical condition, and mental illness, clearly suggest that single programs will likely fail to produce long-lasting change. Therefore a new focus is being directed to treatment models that offer comprehensive services.

One of these models is described by Wesch and Lutzker (1991). In a 5-year evaluation of Project 12-Ways, an ecobehavioral approach is used in which participants can receive parent-child training, basic skill training, social support, health maintenance and nutrition, home safety, problem-solving training, stress reduction counseling, money and time management training, job finding, self-control training, and alcohol counseling. Referrals to the program come directly from the state protective service department, and all families were identified as having problems with abuse or neglect. Although several methodological problems were noted in the study (e.g., use of recidivism rates as a measure of program success, lack of measures on factors associated with family violence), it was concluded that families served by Project 12-Ways had lower rates of child abuse and neglect and lower incidences of child placements than families who did not receive the services. Such results indicate that providing a range of services may be necessary to increase positive outcomes for violent families.

Blau and Campbell (1991) state that treatment for violent families should be developed as a continuum of service approaches. One end of the continuum is traditional outpatient therapy, followed by intensive outpatient therapy, short-term home-based services, and longer-term home-based services. Blau and Brumer (1996) argue that service delivery must be organized into comprehensive systems of care that can coordinate treatment and develop service plans that are based on the unique needs of each child and family. Such comprehensive systems of care greatly enhance the possibility of eliminating violence and improving family functioning.

Conclusion

Despite some reports of success, there is a lack of methodologically sound evaluation of issues related to family violence. Research must continue to address the relationship between risk factors and violent behaviors and how successful outcomes relate to such factors as the type and degree of abuse, specific treatment components, and the setting and timing of clinical interventions. The literature in this area has blossomed in the past decade, however, and a variety of longitudinal projects are currently being evaluated. In addition, current research has led to several conclusions. One is that treatment cannot be isolated. The use of a single approach or intervention does not produce significant behavioral change (Daro, 1988). Therefore, the current trend toward comprehensive service delivery is warranted. Perpetrators and victims of family violence must be able to access a continuum of interventions to appropriately meet their needs and improve functioning (Blau & Campbell, 1991). This also reduces the burden on individual clinicians and service providers. Professionals may become overwhelmed by the intensity of violent families, and the incorporation of a service network allows for peer consultation.

Another conclusion is that short-term models may not be expected to have long-term impact. Families may require ongoing therapeutic assistance to remain violence free. Helfer (1991), in his article on the potential status of domestic violence in the year 2007, writes that professionals should endeavor to develop eight standardized therapeutic interventions that would readily be available and ongoing. The first intervention consists of services to meet the family's basic needs. Helfer (1991) refers to these as logistical improvement services, which include helping families with food, shelter, heat, electricity, and transportation. The second intervention involves health care and the procurement of medical service. The third intervention is to create social and personal support services. These include such services as phones, parent aides, or big brothers. Fourth, families should have access to support groups (e.g., Parents Anonymous). Fifth, family-oriented counseling should be available. For example, parent groups and anger control groups would be standard components in service delivery. Sixth, Helfer (1991) believes that skills training programs must be included. For example, interpersonal, educational, and career development activities should be incorporated into treatment plans. Seventh, one-on-one therapy would be available when necessary; and eighth, training programs and support would be offered to community professionals (e.g., foster parents, teachers) who would work with violent families.

In addition to therapeutic interventions, there must be a comprehensive service delivery network to facilitate assessment, prevention, and training activities. There must also be a national commitment to address the societal problems that give rise to violent behavior. These mechanisms may improve service delivery activity, continue to develop and implement successful programs, and reduce the incidence and prevalence of family violence.

References

Abidin, R. R. (1983). *Parenting stress index manual.* Charlottesville, NC: Pediatric Psychology Press.

Anderson, L. (1984). A systems theory model for foster home studies. *Child Welfare, 61*(1), 37-47.

Arias, I., Samios, M., & O'Leary, K. D. (1987). Prevalence and correlates of physical aggression during courtship. *Journal of Interpersonal Violence, 2,* 82-90.

Asen, K., George, E., Piper, R., & Stevens, A. (1988). A systems approach to child abuse: Management and treatment issues. *Child Abuse & Neglect, 12,* 45-57.

Barrera, M., Jr., Sandler, I. N., & Ramsay, T. B. (1981). Preliminary development of a scale of social support: Studies on college students. *American Journal of Community Psychology, 9,* 435-447.

Barth, R. P. (1990). Theories guiding home-based intensive family preservation services. In J. K. Whittaker, J. Kinney, E. M. Tracy, & C. Booth (Eds.), *Reaching high-risk families: Intensive family preservation in human services.* New York: Aldine.

Barth, R. P. (1991). An experimental evaluation of in-home child abuse prevention services. *Child Abuse & Neglect, 15,* 363-375.

Bavolek, S. J. (1984). *Handbook for the adult-adolescent parenting inventory.* Schamburg, IL: Family Development Associates.

Beck, A. T., & Beamesderfer, A. (1974). Assessment of depression: The Depression Inventory. In P. Pichot (Ed.), *Psychological measurements in psychopharmacology: Modern problems in pharmacopsychiatry* (Vol. 7). Paris: Karger, Basel.

Belsky, J. (1980). Child maltreatment: An ecological integration. *American Psychologist, 35,* 320-335.

Berk, R. A., Berk, S. F., Loseke, D. R., & Rauma, D. (1983). Mutual combat and other family violence myths. In D. Finkelhor, R. Gelles, G. Hotaling, & M. Straus (Eds.), *The dark side of families: Current family violence research.* Beverly Hills, CA: Sage.

Berkowitz, L. (1983). Aversively stimulated aggression: Some parallels and differences in research with animals and humans. *American Psychologist, 38,* 1135-1144.

Bixler, R. H. (1976). Limits of therapy. In C. E. Schaefer (Ed.), *Therapeutic use of child's play.* New York: Jason Aronson.

Blau, G. M., & Brumer, D. (1996). Comments on adolescent behavior problems: Developing coordinated systems of care. In G. M. Blau & T. P. Gullotta (Eds.), *Adolescent dysfunctional behavior: Causes, intervention, and prevention.* Newbury Park, CA: Sage.

Blau, G. M., & Campbell, D. R. (1990, October). *Family violence: Theory, treatment, and research.* Workshop presented at the annual convention of the Connecticut Psychological Association, Stamford, CT.

Blau, G. M., & Campbell, D. R. (1991, April). *Clinical interventions in the treatment of children who observe violence: Family assessment and clinical issues.* Workshop presented at the Connecticut Association of Mental Health Clinics for Children Conference, Hartford, CT.

Blau, G. M., Whewell, M., Gullotta, T. P., & Bloom, M. (1994). The prevention and treatment of child abuse in households of substance abusers: A research demonstration progress report. *Child Welfare, 73*(1), 83-94.

Bograd, M. (1988). Feminist perspective on wife abuse: An introduction. In K. Yllö & M. Bograd (Eds.), *Feminist perspectives on wife abuse.* Newbury Park, CA: Sage.

Bolton, F. G., & Bolton, S. R. (1987). *Working with violent families: A guide for clinical and legal practitioners.* Newbury Park, CA: Sage.

Bornstein, P. H., & Kazdin, A. E. (1985). *Handbook of clinical behavior therapy with children.* Homewood, IL: Dorsey.

Borum, R. (1996). Improving the clinical practice of violence risk assessment. *American Psychologist, 51*(9), 945-956.

Bowen, M. (1976). Use of family therapy in clinical practice. *Comprehensive Psychiatry, 7,* 345-374.

Burgess, R. L., Anderson, E. A., Schellenbach, C. J., & Conger, R. D. (1981). A social interactional approach to the study of abusive families. *Advances in Family Interventions: Assessment and Theory, 2,* 1-46.

Chez, R. A. (1988). Women battering. *American Journal of Obstetrics and Gynecology, 158*(1), 1-4.

Cohn, A. H., & Daro, D. (1987). Is the treatment too late? What ten years of evaluative research tells us. *Child Abuse & Neglect, 11,* 433-442.

Coopersmith, S. (1981). *Coopersmith Inventory.* Palo Alto, CA: Consulting Psychologists Press.

Cox, J. W., & Stoltenberg, C. D. (1991). Evaluation of the treatment program for battered wives. *Journal of Family Violence, 6*(4), 395-413.

Craft, J. C., & Staudt, M. M. (1991) Reporting and founding of child neglect in urban and rural communities. *Child Welfare, 70*(3), 359-370.

Crenshaw, D. A., Rudy, C., Treimer, D., & Zingaro, J. (1986). Psychotherapy with abused children: Breaking the silent bond. *Residential Group Care and Treatment, 3*(4), *25-38.*

Crimmins, D. B., Bradlyn, A. S., St. Lawrence, J. S., & Kelly, J. A. (1984). A training technique for improving the parent-child interaction skills of an abusive neglectful mother. *Child Abuse & Neglect, 8,* 533-539.

Danish, S. J. (1991, June). *Go for the goal: A school-based prevention program.* Institute presented at the Biennial Hartman Conference on Children and their Families, New London, CT.

Daro, D. (1988). *Confronting child abuse: Research for effective program design.* New York: Free Press.

Deschner, J. P., & McNeil, J. S. (1986). Results of anger control training for battering couples. *Journal of Family Violence, 1*(2), 111-120.

Dodge, K. A., Bates, J. E., & Pettit, G. S. (1990). Mechanisms in the cycle of violence. *Science, 250,* 1678-1683.

Doueck, H. J., English, D. J., DePanfilis, D., & Moote, G. T. (1993). Decision making in child protective services: A comparison of selected risk assessment systems. *Child Welfare, 72,* 441-452.

Edleson, J. L. (1984, May-June). Working with men who batter. *Social Work,* pp. 237-241.

Emery, R. (1989). Family violence. *American Psychologist, 44*(2), 321-328.

Eyberse, W., Maffuid, J., & Blau, G. M. (1996). New directions for service delivery: Home-based services. In G. M. Blau & T. P. Gullotta (Eds.), *Adolescent dysfunctional behavior: Causes, intervention and prevention.* Thousand Oaks, CA: Sage.

Fantuzzo, J. W., Jurecic, L., Stovall, A., Hightower, A. D., Goins, C., & Schachtel, D. (1988). Effects of adult and peer social initiations on the social behavior of withdrawn, maltreated preschool children. *Journal of Consulting and Clinical Psychology, 56*(1), 34-39.

Feazell, C., Myers, R., & Deschner, J. (1984). Services for men who batter: Implications for programs and policies. *Family Relations, 33,* 217-223.

Forehand, R. L., & McMahon, R. J. (1981). *Helping the noncompliant child: A clinician's guide to parent training.* New York: Guilford.

Gambrill, E. D. (1983). Behavioral interventions with child abuse and neglect. *Progress in Behavior Modification, 15,* 1-56.

Gifford, C. D., Kaplan, F. B., & Salus, M. K. (1979). *Parent aides in child abuse and neglect programs* (No. 79-30200). Washington, DC: U.S. Department of Health, Education, and Welfare, National Center on Child Abuse and Neglect.

Ginott, H. G. (1976). Therapeutic intervention in child treatment. In C. E. Schaefer (Ed.), *Therapeutic use of child's play.* New York: Jason Aronson.

Goldstein, A. P., Keller, H., & Erne, D. (1985). *Changing the abusive parent.* Champaign, IL: Research.

Goldstein, E. G., & Gonzalez-Ramos, G. (1989). Toward an integrative clinical practice perspective. In S. M. Ehrenkrantz, E. G. Goldstein, L. Goodman, & J. Seinfeld (Eds.), *Clinical social work with maltreated children and their families: An introduction to practice.* New York: New York University Press.

Gondolf, E. W. (1987). Changing men who batter: A developmental model for integrated interventions. *Journal of Family Violence, 2,* 335-349.

Gondolf, E. W., & Hanneken, J. (1987). The gender warrior: Reformed batterers on abuse, treatment, and change. *Journal of Family Violence, 2,* 177-191.

Gonzalez-Ramos, G., & Goldstein, E. G. (1989). Child maltreatment: An overview. In S. M. Ehrenkrantz, E. G. Goldstein, L. Goodman, & J. Seinfeld (Eds.), *Clinical social work with maltreated children and their families: An introduction to practice.* New York: New York University Press.

Gray, S. S., & Nybell, L. M. (1990). Issues in African American family preservation. *Child Welfare, 69*(6), 513-523.

Green, A. H. (1978). Psychopathology of abused children. *Journal of the American Academy of Child Psychiatry, 17,* 92-103.

Grotevant, H. D., & Carlson, C. I. (1989). *Family assessment: A guide to methods and measures.* New York: Guilford.

Halpern, R. (1984). Lack of effects for home-based early intervention? Some possible explanations. *American Journal of Orthopsychiatry, 54,* 33-42.

Halpern, R. (1986). Home-based early intervention: Dimensions of current practice. *Child Welfare, 63,* 387-398.

Hampton, R. C. (1987). *Violence in the black family: Correlates and consequences.* Lexington, MA: Lexington Books.

Harris, G. T., Rice, M. E., & Quinsey, V. L. (1993). Violent recidivism of mentally disordered offenders: The development of a statistical prediction instrument. *Criminal Justice and Behavior, 20,* 315-335.

Haynes, C. F., Cutler, C., Gray, J., & Kempe, R. S. (1984). Hospitalized cases of nonorganic failure to thrive: The scope of the problem and short-term lay health visitor intervention. *Child Abuse & Neglect, 8,* 229-242.

Helfer, R. E. (1991). Child abuse and neglect: Assessment, treatment, and prevention, October 21, 2007. *Child Abuse & Neglect, 15,* 5-15.

Hilberman, E. (1980). Overview: The "wife-beater's wife" reconsidered. *American Journal of Psychiatry, 137,* 1336-1347.

Hornick, J. P., & Clarke, M. E. (1986). A cost/effectiveness evaluation of lay therapy treatment for child abusing and high risk parents. *Child Abuse & Neglect, 8,* 309-318.

Howing, P. T., Wodarski, J. S., Guadin, J. M., & Kurtz, P. D. (1989, July). Effective interventions to ameliorate the incidence of child maltreatment: The empirical base. *Social Work,* pp. 330-338.

Hudson, W. W. (1982). *The clinical measurement package: A field manual.* Chicago: Dorsey.

Hudson, W. W., & McIntosh, S. R. (1981). The assessment of spouse abuse: Two quantifiable dimensions. *Journal of Marriage and the Family, 43,* 873-888.

Irueste-Montes, A. M., & Montes, F. (1988). Court-ordered vs. voluntary treatment of abusive and neglectful parents. *Child Abuse & Neglect, 10,* 309-318.

Jaffe, P., Wolfe, D., Wilson, S., & Zak, L. (1986). Similarities in behavioral and social maladjustment among child victims and witnesses to family violence. *American Journal of Orthopsychiatry, 56*(1), 142-146.

Jennings, J. (1987). History and issues in the treatment of battering men: A case for unstructured group therapy. *Journal of Family Violence, 2,* 193-213.

Jennings, J. (1990). Preventing relapse versus "stopping" domestic violence: Do we expect too much too soon from battering men? *Journal of Family Violence, 5*(1), 43-60.

Koeske, G. F., & Koeske, R. D. (1990). The buffering effect of social support on parental stress. *American Journal of Orthopsychiatry, 60*(3), 440-459.

Kohlberg, L. (1981). *The philosophy of moral development.* San Francisco: Harper & Row.

Kropp, P. R., Hart, S. D., Webster, C. D., & Eaves, D. (1994). *Manual for the Spousal Assault Risk Assessment Guide.* Vancouver: The British Columbia Institute on Family Violence.

Lines, D. R. (1987). The effectiveness of parent aide in the tertiary prevention of child abuse in South Australia. *Child Abuse & Neglect, 11,* 507-512.

Lystad, M. (1986). *Violence in the home: Interdisciplinary perspectives.* New York: Brunner/Mazel.

Magura, S., & Moses, B. S. (1986). *Outcome measures for child welfare services: Theory and applications.* Washington, DC: Child Welfare League of America.

Magura, S., Moses, B. S., & Jones, M. A. (1987). Assessing risk and measuring change in families: The Family Risk Scales. In S. Magura & B. S. Moses (Eds.), *Outcome measures for child welfare services: Theory and applications.* Washington, DC: Child Welfare League of America.

Maluccio, A. N. (1991). Family preservation: An overview. In A. L. Sallee & J. C. Lloyd (Eds.), *Family preservation.* Riverdale, IL: National Association for Family Based Services.

Mann, E., & McDermott, J. F., Jr. (1983). Play therapy for victims of child abuse and neglect. In C. F. Schaefer & K. J. O'Connor (Eds.), *Handbook of play therapy.* New York: John Wiley.

Mash, E. J., Johnson, C., & Krovitz, K. (1983). A comparison of the mother-child interactions of physically abused and nonabused children during play and task situations. *Journal of Clinical Child Psychology, 12,* 337-346.

McCubbin, H. I., & Patterson, J. M. (1983). Stress: The family inventory of life events and changes. In E. E. Filsinger (Ed.), *Marriage and family assessment: A sourcebook for family therapy.* Beverly Hills, CA: Sage.

McDonald, T., & Marks, J. (1991). A review of risk factors assessed in child protective services. *Social Service Review, 65,* 113-132.

Megargee, E. J. (1976). The prediction of dangerous behavior. *Criminal Justice and Behavior, 3,* 3-22.

Menzies, R., Webster, C. D., McMain, S., Staley, S., & Scaglione, R. (1994). The dimensions of dangerousness revisited. *Law and Human Behavior, 18,* 1-28.

Miller, K., Fein, E., Howe, G. W., Gaudio, C. P., & Bishop, G. V. (1985). A parent aide program: Record keeping, outcomes, and costs. *Child Welfare, 44,* 407-419.

Milner, J. S., Gold, R. G., Ayoub, C., & Jacewitz, M. M. (1984). Predictive validity of the Child Abuse Potential Inventory. *Journal of Consulting and Clinical Psychology, 52,* 879-884.

Monahan, J. (1996). Violence prediction: The last 20 years and the next 20 years. *Criminal Justice and Behavior, 23,* 107-120.

Monahan, J., & Steadman, H. J. (Eds.). (1994). *Violence and mental disorders: Developments in risk assessment.* Chicago: University of Chicago Press.

Montalvo, B. (1986, January-February). Lessons from the past. *Family Therapy Networker,* p. 39.

Morton, T. L., Twentyman, C. T., & Azar, S. T. (1988). Cognitive-behavioral assessment and treatment of child abuse. In N. Epstein, S. E. Schlesinger, & W. Dryden (Eds.), *Cognitive-behavioral therapy with families.* New York: Brunner/Mazel.

Mossman, D. (1994). Assessing predictions of violence: Being accurate about accuracy. *Journal of Consulting and Clinical Psychology, 62,* 783-792.

Mouzakitis, C. (1985). Intake-investigative assessment. In C. Mouzakitis & R. Varghese (Eds.), *Social work treatment with abused and neglected children.* Springfield, IL: Charles C Thomas.

Muram, D., Miller, K., & Cutler, A. (1992). Sexual assault of the elderly victim. *Journal of Interpersonal Violence, 7*(1), 70-76.

National Center on Child Abuse and Neglect. (1988). *Study of national incidence and prevalence of child abuse and neglect: 1988* (Contract 105-85-1702). Washington, DC: U.S. Department of Health and Human Services.

Nelson, K. (1990, Fall). How do we know that family-based services are effective? *Prevention Report,* pp. 1-3.

Nelson, K., Landsman, M. J., & Deutelbaum, W. (1990). Three models of family-centered placement prevention sources. *Child Welfare, 69,* 3-21.

Olsen, L. J., Allen, D., & Azzi-Lessing, L. (1996). Assessing risk in families affected by substance abuse. *Child Abuse & Neglect, 20*(9), 833-842.

Olson, D. H. (1986). Circumflex model seven: Validation Studies and FACES III. *Family Process, 25,* 337-351.

Pecora, P. J., Fraser, M. W., Haapala, J. D., & Bartlome, J. A. (1987). *Defining family preservation services: Three intensive home-based treatment programs.* Salt Lake City: University of Utah, School of Social Work, Social Research Institute.

Poythress, N. G. (1992). Expert testimony of violence and dangerousness: Roles for mental health professionals. *Forensic Reports, 1*(5), 135-150.

Reynolds, C., & Richmond, B. (1978). What I think and feel: A revised measure of children's manifest anxiety. *Journal of Abnormal Child Psychology, 6,* 271-280.

Roberts, R. N., & Wasik, B. H. (1990). Home visiting programs for families with children birth to three: Results of a national survey. *Journal of Early Intervention, 14,* 274-284.

Roberts, R. N., Wasik, B. H., Castro, G., & Ramey, C. T. (1991). Family support in the home: Programs, policy, social change. *American Psychologist, 46*(2), 121-137.

Rosenbaum, A. (1986). Group treatment of battering men: Process and outcome. *Psychotherapy, 23,* 607-612.

Sarason, S. B. (1981). *Psychology misdirected.* New York: Free Press.

Saylor, C., Finch, A., Spirito, A., & Bennett, B. (1984). Children's Depression Inventory: A systematic evaluation of psychometric properties. *Journal of Consulting and Clinical Psychology, 52,* 955-967.

Schopp, R. F. (1996). Community risk assessment: Accuracy, efficacy and responsibility. *American Psychologist, 51,* 939-944.

Sefarbi, R. (1986). To reclaim a legacy: Social rehabilitation. *Child and Adolescent Social Work Journal, 3,* 38-49.

Sigler, R. T. (1989). *Domestic violence in context: An assessment of community attitudes.* Lexington, MA: Lexington.

Simon, R. (1986, January-February). Across the great divide. *Family Therapy Networker,* p. 26.

Spanier, G. B., & Filsinger, E. E. (1983). The dyadic adjustment scale. In E. Filsinger (Ed.), *Marriage and family assessment: A sourcebook for family therapy.* Beverly Hills, CA: Sage.

Stark, E., & Flitcraft, A. (1987). Violence among intimates: An epidemiological review. In V. B. Van Hasselt, R. L. Morrison, A. S. Bellack, & M. Hersen (Eds.), *Handbook of family violence.* New York: Plenum.

Stark, E., & Flitcraft, A. (1988). Personal power and institutional victimization: Treating the dual trauma of woman battering. In F. M. Ochberg (Ed.), *Post traumatic therapy.* New York: Brunner/Mazel.

Steinfeld, G. (1989). Spouse abuse: An integrative-interactional model. *Journal of Family Violence, 4,* 1-23.

Steward, M., Farquhar, L. C., Dicharry, D. C., Glick, D. R., & Martin, P. W. (1986). Group therapy: A treatment of choice for young victims of child abuse. *International Group of Psychotherapy, 36,* 261-277.

Straus, M. A., & Gelles, R. J. (1986). Societal change and change in family violence from 1975 to 1985 as revealed through national surveys. *Journal of Marriage and the Family, 48,* 465-480.

Straus, M. A., Gelles, R. J., & Steinmetz, S. K. (1988). Beyond the bravado: Sex roles and the exploitative male. *Social Work, 31,* 12-18.

Tarasoff v. Regents of the University of California, 131 Cal. Rptr. 14, 555 P.2d 334 (1976).

Taubman, S. (1986). Beyond the bravado: Sex roles and the exploitative male. *Social Work, 31,* 12-18.

Trickett, P. K., & Kuczynski, L. (1986). Children's misbehaviors and parental discipline strategies in abusive and nonabusive families. *Developmental Psychology, 22,* 115-123.

U.S. Department of Justice. (1994). Domestic violence between intimates. In *Selected findings* (NLJ 149259, pp. 1-9). Washington DC: Bureau of Justice Statistics.

Vasta, R. (1982). Physical child abuse: A dual-component analysis. *Developmental Review, 2,* 125-149.

Vaux, A., Riedell, S., & Stewart, D. (1987). Modes of social support: The Social Support Behaviors (SS-B) Scale. *American Journal of Community Psychology, 15,* 209-237.

Webster, C. D., Harris, G. T., Rice, M. E., Cormier, C., & Quinsey, V. L. (1994). *The Violence Prediction Scheme: Assessing dangerousness in high risk men.* Toronto, Ontario, Canada: Centre of Criminology, University of Toronto.

Wesch, D., & Lutzker, J. R. (1991). A comprehensive 5-year evaluation of Project 12 Ways: An ecobehavioral program for treating and preventing child abuse and neglect. *Journal of Family Violence, 6*(1), 17-35.

Whiteman, M., Fanshel, D., & Grundy, J. F. (1987, November-December). Cognitive-behavioral interventions aimed at anger of parent at risk of child abuse. *Social Work,* pp. 469-474.

Whittaker, J. K., Kinney, J., Tracy, E. M., & Booth, C. (1990). *Reaching high risk families: Intensive family preservation in human services.* New York: Aldine.

Wolfe, D. A., Aragona, J., Kaufman, K., & Sandler, J. (1980). The importance of adjudication in the treatment of child abusers: Some preliminary findings. *Child Abuse & Neglect, 4,* 127-135.

Wolfe, D. A., & Sandler, J. (1981). Training abusive parents in effective child management. *Behavior Modification, 5*(3), 320-335.

Wolfe, D. A., St. Lawrence, J., Graves, K., Brehony, K., Bradlyn, D., & Kelly, J. A. (1982). Intensive behavioral parent training for a child abusive mother. *Behavior Therapy, 13,* 438-451.

Woods, L. J. (1988, May-June). Home-based family therapy. *Social Work,* 211-214.

Yalom, J. D. (1975). *The theory and practice of group psychotherapy.* New York: Basic Books.

Zigler, E., & Black, K. B. (1989). America's family support movement: Strengths and limitations. *American Journal of Orthopsychiatry, 59,* 6-19.

Zuravin, S. J. (1984). *Child abuse, child neglect, and maternal depression: Is there a connection?* Unpublished manuscript.

Index

About the Contributors

Jo-Ellen Asbury, Ph.D., is Associate Professor and Head of the Department of Psychology at Bethany College. A social-personality psychologist by training (University of Pittsburgh), her teaching interests include courses on race, gender, and the history of psychology. Her research focuses primarily on African Americans who have experienced domestic violence but also includes qualitative methodologies.

H. David Banks, Ph.D., is Adjunct Professor at Trinity College and the University of Maryland. He teaches health education at Trinity and human sexuality at the University of Maryland. He also serves as the director of research and evaluation at Volunteers of America's national office in Alexandria, Virginia. He earned his Ph.D. in human development from the University of Maryland, and he holds master's degrees in social work and public health from the University of Texas at Austin and the University of North Carolina at Chapel Hill respectively.

Larry W. Bennett, Ph.D., is currently Assistant Professor, Jane Addams College of Social Work, University of Illinois at Chicago. Prior to joining that faculty, he was a member of the faculty at Carthage College in Kenosha, Wisconsin, and worked for 15 years in Illinois mental health and family service agencies. He cofounded the Turning Point Men's Program in Woodstock, Illinois, in 1985. His research and publications focus on the relationship between substance abuse and domestic violence, the structure and effectiveness of community-based batterers intervention programs, and the link between various forms of men's violence, such as sexual harassment, dating violence, and adult partner abuse.

Gary M. Blau (Ph.D., Clinical Psychology) is currently the Bureau Chief, Office of Quality Management for the Connecticut Department of Children and Families. He also holds a clinical faculty appointment at the Yale Child Study Center. In his capacity as Bureau Chief, he provides leadership and oversight to Connecticut's service delivery system for children and adolescents. He is an active member of the National Association of State Mental Health Program Director's Division of Children, Youth, and Families, and he has been a member of that group's Executive Committee. He currently serves as the chairperson (July 1998–July 2000).

Michele Cascardi, Ph.D., is co-founder of the Dating Violence Prevention Project, Inc., in Philadelphia. Its mission is to develop, evaluate, and disseminate school- and community-based programs to prevent adolescent dating violence. She is also a project director, at Women Against Abuse, of a community-based initiative to prevent teen dating violence among urban adolescents. Other interests include the longitudinal study of depression and post-traumatic stress disorder in battered women and their treatment.

Julie L. Crouch, Ph.D., is a research associate at the Medical University of South Carolina and is the coordinator of child and family services with the National Crime Victim Research and Treatment Center, a specialty clinic that serves victims of crime and other traumatic events. Her research interests include the study of victim effects associated with child physical and sexual abuse and the description of factors that might buffer the effects of child maltreatment.

Howard Dubowitz is Associate Professor of Pediatrics at the University of Maryland School of Medicine, where he directs the Child Protection Program. He is involved in clinical work, research, teaching, and child advocacy. His clinical work includes interdisciplinary consultation on cases of suspected abuse and neglect, and he is also active in general pediatrics. His current research activities are in the study of child neglect—its antecedents and outcomes—and in the area of preventing neglect. He chairs the Committee on Child Maltreatment of the American Academy of Pediatrics, Maryland Chapter.

Richard J. Gelles is the Joanne and Raymond Welsh Chair of Child Welfare and Family Violence, School of Social Work, University of Pennsylvania. He is the author or coauthor of 23 books and more than 100 articles and chapters on family violence. He received his A.B. degree from Bates College (1968), an M.A. in sociology from the University of Rochester (1971), and a Ph.D. in Sociology at the University of New Hampshire (1973). He edited the journal *Teaching Sociology* from 1973 to 1981 and received the American Sociological Association, Section on

Undergraduate Education, Outstanding Contributions to Teaching Award in 1979.

Linner Ward Griffin is Associate Professor and the Associate Dean for Graduate Studies in the School of Social Work and Criminal Justice Studies at East Carolina University (ECU) in Greenville, North Carolina. In addition, she serves as the associate director for educational programs of the ECU Center on Aging. She has an extensive background in social work practice with individuals and families in geriatric, health, and mental health settings. Her academic research has yielded numerous publications in the areas of elder abuse/elder maltreatment, adult protective services, and organ transplantation.

Robert L. Hampton received his A.B. degree from Princeton University and his M.A. and Ph.D. from the University of Michigan. He is Associate Provost for Academic Affairs, Dean for Undergraduate Studies, and Professor of Family Studies and Sociology at the University of Maryland, College Park. He is a Gimbel Mentoring Scholar. He has published extensively in the field of family violence. He is one of the founders of the Institute on Domestic Violence in the African American Community. His research interests include interspousal violence, family abuse, male violence, community violence, stress and social support, and institutional responses to violence.

Brenda Jones Harden is Assistant Professor in the Institute for Child Study/Department of Human Development at the University of Maryland, College Park. She has worked in the child welfare field since 1978 as a clinician, program planner, and administrator. She is currently conducting research on children exposed to community violence, maltreated and foster children, and children exposed to substances in utero. As part of each of these research initiatives, she has implemented and evaluated programs to address the needs of these populations of children and their families.

Donna Harrington, Ph.D., is Developmental Psychologist and Assistant Professor at the University of Maryland School of Social Work, where she teaches courses in research, statistics, and human behavior. Her research interests are in the areas of child maltreatment and developmental outcomes for children in high risk environments.

Pamela Jenkins is Associate Professor of Sociology and Director of Grants and Development for the Women's Center at the University of

New Orleans. She has combined an active research agenda with social action in her community. Her research interests include a long-term study of incarcerated battered women, class issues in shelter life, and the links between domestic and community violence. In New Orleans, she is working on building coalitions among academics, activists, and service providers who define child and family safety from a community-based framework.

Sally A. Koblinsky is Professor and Chair of the Department of Family Studies at the University of Maryland, College Park. She is the author or co-author of more than 50 articles and chapters that focus on parenting and child development issues, including community violence, homeless families, adolescent pregnancy prevention, and school-age child care. She has received funding from the federal government and private foundations for more than 25 community-based research and intervention projects involving at-risk families. She is currently co-director of a U.S. Department of Education grant examining the role of families and Head Start in promoting positive developmental outcomes for preschoolers in violent neighborhoods.

Dorian Long is a psychiatric social worker at the Connecticut Department of Children and Families. In this position, she assists the director of mental health in the development of plans to meet the mental health needs of Connecticut's children, provides case consultation and assessment, and serves as a resource regarding the Connecticut Access Medicaid Managed Care program. Following her undergraduate training at Saint Joseph College, West Hartford, she earned her M.S.W. at Fordham University, New York. Her interests include family-centered practice, child welfare, family violence, and health care access.

Joel S. Milner, Ph.D., is Professor of Psychology, Distinguished Research Professor, and Director of the Center for the Study of Family Violence and Sexual Assault at Northern Illinois University. He has received funding for family violence and sexual assault research from federal agencies such as the National Institute of Mental Health, National Center on Child Abuse and Neglect, and the Department of Defense. He is the author or coauthor of more than 130 book chapters and articles, most of which are in the area of family violence. His current research interests include the description and prediction of intrafamilial child sexual abuse and the testing of a social information-processing model of child physical abuse.

Christopher M. Murphy is Associate Professor of Psychology at the University of Maryland, Baltimore County, and batterers' services coordinator at the Domestic Violence Center of Howard County, Maryland. His current research is on the efficacy of psychosocial interventions for domestic abusers, domestic violence among alcoholics, and the development of aggression in dating relationships.

Suzanne M. Randolph is Associate Professor of Family Studies at the University of Maryland, College Park. She earned her B.S. in psychology from Howard University in Washington, D.C., and her M.S. and Ph.D. in developmental psychology from the University of Michigan at Ann Arbor. She is principal investigator for a Head Start community violence prevention study funded by the U.S. Department of Education, National Institute of Early Childhood Learning and Development; and co-principal investigator for a study of ecological correlates of development in African American children in poverty funded by the U.S. Department of Health and Human Services.

Theodore J. Stein, Ph.D., J.D., received his doctoral degree from the University of California at Berkeley and his law degree from Albany Law School. He is Professor of Social Welfare at the School of Social Welfare, State University of New York at Albany. He has published books and articles on a number of topics relating to child welfare, including permanency planning, decision making, and the law.

Maria Vandergriff-Avery is a doctoral student in family studies at the University of Maryland, College Park. She earned her master's degree in family studies from the University of Tennessee, Knoxville. Her research interests include marital power, domestic violence, and gender role issues.

Oliver J. Williams, Ph.D., is currently Associate Professor of Social Work, University of Minnesota. Prior to joining the faculty at Minnesota, he was on the faculties of Illinois State University and West Virginia University. He has been a practitioner in the field of domestic violence for over 20 years, including work with child welfare, delinquency, and battered women's agencies. He has created and conducted counseling groups for partner abuse treatment programs. As an academic, his research and publications have centered on creating effective service delivery strategies that will reduce the violent behavior of African American men who batter.